Foodservice Profitability
A Control Approach

SECOND EDITION

Edward E. Sanders
Timothy H. Hill

Prentice
Hall

Upper Saddle River, New Jersey 07458

Library of Congress Cataloging-in-Publication Data

Sanders, Edward E.
   Foodservice profitability : a control approach / Edward E. Sanders, Timothy H. Hill.—
2nd ed.
     p. cm.
   Includes index.
   ISBN 0-13-032182-6
   1. Food service—Cost control.   I. Hill, Timothy H.   II. Title.
TX911.3.C65 S26 2001
647.95'068'1—dc21

         00-042800

Publisher: Dave Garza
Production Editor: Linda Zuk
Production Liaison: Barbara Marttine Cappuccio
**Director of Manufacturing
  and Production:** Bruce Johnson
Managing Editor: Mary Carnis
Manufacturing Buyer: Ed O'Dougherty
Art Director: Marianne Frasco
Cover Design Coordinator: Miguel Ortiz
Cover Design: Joe Sengotta
Cover Illustration: Andrew Bylo, SIS/Images.com
Marketing Manager: Ryan DeGrote
Editorial Assistant: Susan Kegler
Composition: WordCrafters Editorial Services, Inc.
Printing and Binding: Courier Westford

Prentice-Hall International (UK) Limited, *London*
Prentice-Hall of Australia Pty. Limited, *Sydney*
Prentice-Hall Canada Inc., *Toronto*
Prentice-Hall Hispanoamericana, S.A., *Mexico*
Prentice-Hall of India Private Limited, *New Delhi*
Prentice-Hall of Japan, Inc., *Tokyo*
Prentice-Hall Singapore Pte. Ltd.
Editora Prentice-Hall do Brasil, Ltda., *Rio de Janeiro*

10 9 8 7 6 5 4 3 2 1
ISBN 0-13-032182-6

Contents

List of Tables

Foreword

This book, *Foodservice Profitability: A Control Approach*, is the most comprehensive and best illustrated text on managing a foodservice operation available anywhere in the world. Designed for operations of all sizes and in any segment of foodservices, it serves as an "operations manual" with a constant focus on the bottom-line profit or budgetary goals. An easy-to-read, no-nonsense writing style allows one to get to the information desired almost immediately. Its practical, "hands-on" approach ensures its immediate application to any and all types of foodservice operations. The forms, used for illustrative purposes, can be reproduced and implemented on the spot. In an era of increasing competition within the industry, and with consumers demanding increased value for their money, disciplined and efficient cost control and timely information on which to base management decisions are essential for success. This book is the guide to how to maximize revenues, control expenses, and optimize your financial objectives. It can prove to be your most valuable asset. Use it wisely—and often.

William P. Fisher, Ph.D.
President & CEO, American Hotel & Motel Association
Former President & CEO, National Restaurant Association

Perspective

A primary function that will affect the level of success of any foodservice operation is management's ability to control costs. We believe that to talk in generalities about systems without at least presenting the components of a system would be a disservice to the reader. Therefore, this book will often refer to forms that have been developed to illustrate a control principle, strategy, or tactic. We are not suggesting that the way that these forms illustrate control methods is universally applicable; however, if exemplary systems or forms are not used to teach principles, the reader will not be able to understand the concepts being taught. The reader must exercise judgment in the use and design of control systems and reporting forms, so that what is used provides the necessary information for making correct or better decisions.

The book will demonstrate how to arrive at the right financial numbers and percentages and what the wise manager can do to prevent problems or to correct them once they occur. Examples of forms and reports used in this text demonstrate what can be accomplished manually or with the help of a computer.

In an industry of expanding growth and opportunity, employers are increasingly seeking to recruit prospective managers whose education will allow them to quickly become involved and productive in foodservice operations. Crucial to this is an appreciation and thorough comprehension of the competitive and unpredictable climate of the industry and how internal control procedures represent management's most effective way to maximize the opportunity for and extent of success and profits.

With this in mind, this text presents very detailed technical explanations and justifications for the use of these control systems. One of the primary goals of this project from the beginning has been to create a volume that can be used both as a textbook in an academic setting and a technical guide and manual in an industry setting. Students who seriously consider and become aware of the necessity of these concepts will be in a very advantageous position when being considered for industry recruitment, and will be impressive in their positions as they implement these concerns and get results.

Edward E. Sanders
Timothy H. Hill

An Expression of
Appreciation

The authors would like to acknowledge several individuals who reviewed the manuscript during its development, and, in certain cases, faculty members within their respective departments and schools who also reviewed text materials. The evaluations and suggestions were all outstanding and have enhanced the quality of the final text.

W. Terry Umbreit, Ph.D.
Professor and Director
Hotel and Restaurant Administration
Washington State University

Ray R. Kavanaugh, Ed.D., CHA
Professor and Director
Restaurant, Hotel, Institutional, and Tourism Management
Purdue University

Steven V. Moll
Associate Professor
School of Hospitality Management
Florida International University

Nick D. Fluge, CCE
Senior Vice President, Operations
Career Education Corporation
Chief Operating Officer
Le Cordon Bleu Schools North America

H. Andy Divine, Ph.D., CHA, FMP
Professor
School of Hotel, Restaurant and Tourism Management
University of Denver

Paul D. Scoggin
Program Coordinator
Hospitality Systems Management
Chemeketa Community College

Robin Baliszewski, who recognized the need for the book; Neil Marquardt, who challenged the authors to bring forth their best; and Mary Carnis, who kept the project on schedule.

Serge D'Rovencourt, for the opportunity to talk about the state of the hospitality industry, financial controls, and a photo taking tour of the Portland Hilton.

Mark Crawford of Caffeine Machines and beverage editor for *Hospitality News* for providing the basic information to develop the espresso drink section, and Richard D. Boyd of Boyd Coffee Company for the espresso equipment demonstration and detailed discussion of coffee processing.

Gary Turner of Paychex for providing all of the tax reporting material contained in Chapter 15.

Harland L. Hill, DPA, for editorial contributions to the first chapter. In memory of Andrea Hill, who influenced her son to enter the foodservice industry.

Jay Sanders, who thoroughly reviewed, edited, and enhanced the overall presentation of the text materials. Mark Sanders, who logically questioned every principle that was expressed. Dad appreciated the help.

Lori Smith, Earlene Naylor, and Brenda Carlos of the *Hospitality News Group,* who faithfully jumped in whenever the project needed their technical assistance, advice, or opinions.

Linda Zuk, who supervised editorial/production and interior design with a "trust me" spirit that resulted in a book that exceeded the authors' expectations in every detail of professionalism.

Finally, many thanks to Nick Drossos, executive chef, restaurant general manager, restaurant owner, mentor, and loyal friend to Ed Sanders, who took a personal interest in his career as a young restaurant manager and rigorously taught him the skills that he had learned over a successful 40-year career in the foodservice industry.

 ## Personal Note

The authors wish to express heartfelt appreciation for the support of their families during a three-year writing process: our wives, Linda A. Sanders and Judith D. Hill, and of course our children.

 ## Acknowledgment

Food and Beverage Operation: Cost Control and Systems Management, Second Edition (Prentice Hall, 1989) by Charles Levinson has been referenced in Chapters 1, 3, 5, 10, 11, 12, and 13.

Organization of Text

This textbook is written so that the chapters flow in a logical sequence that builds a cumulative understanding of foodservice cost controls. The chapters are also self-contained, so that the reader can go directly to any chapter for specific information. The text is thus very versatile, and it can be used as a guide for thorough, overall comprehension of managing cost controls as well as an easily referenced manual for specific industry concerns.

Chapter 1, "The Control Process," provides a general explanation of the control process, the operating environment of a foodservice operation, functions that generally occur, and cost relationships among the menu, the level of service, labor, and technology. The aspects of the internal and external environments that influence how management and employees perform their duties are introduced. The evaluation of controls, the value of information, and the type of information that is available to manage a foodservice establishment is also discussed.

Chapter 2, "Food Cost/Food Cost Percentage," includes more detailed purposes and functions of cost control. The examples and explanations provide comprehensive applications to every type of foodservice operation.

Chapter 3, "Inventory Management," covers the process of keeping enough inventory to meet customers' needs without investing more money than is necessary. How to properly account for, store, and assess the value of inventory is discussed. Inventory turnover rate is demonstrated as a method for tracking the use of inventory.

Chapter 4, "Requisitions and Transfers," discusses the documents used to order food and nonfood items and track the movement of products from one department or unit to another. Their specific uses and applications are shown by examples in the accountability cycle.

Chapter 5, "Purchasing Functions," describes proper ordering in anticipation of usage, establishing par amounts where applicable, and effectively using bid sheets to get the best prices on the products being purchased.

Chapter 6, "Receiving Merchandise and Processing Invoices," covers the knowledge and accountability required to document the receiving process, and to record the invoices for tracking and timely payment.

Chapter 7, "Quality Standards, Specifications, Yield Analysis, and Plate Cost," discusses the relationships of these concepts as they are specifically defined for a foodservice operation. Standardized recipes and product specifications begin the menu costing process.

Chapter 8, "Food Production Control," covers identifying the quantities to produce in order to meet customers' needs, then informing the cooks how much to prepare, and finally monitoring the presentation to ensure proper portioning.

Chapter 9, "Menu Sales Analysis," describes the process of comparing the amount of each menu item sold in relation to all menu items sold. Menu items are categorized by profitability and popularity, and subsequent decisions are made.

Chapter 10, "Beverage Cost/Beverage Cost Percentage," discusses all the ingredient costs for preparing alcoholic beverages. The principles of control for menu development, purchasing and receiving, tracking product movement, producing, and serving are similar to those for foodservice operations.

Chapter 11, "Bar and Inventory Control," covers efficient receiving, storage, and usage, beginning with the liquor storeroom inventory and ending with customer pouring and cash accountability. Also, the application of automated bar systems is considered.

Chapter 12, "Beverage Production Control and Service," starts with standardized recipes and management decisions regarding pouring and other procedures. Employee theft can be prevented by using systems that account for the number of drinks sold and properly managing inventory. Complying with state laws and posting house policies that both employees and patrons can read and understand is also essential.

Chapter 13, "Controlling Payroll Costs and the Cost of Employee Turnover," discusses a primary concern of foodservice owners and managers, beginning with payroll cost, which may be controlled by establishing budgets, using work schedules, and monitoring actual costs. The process can be accomplished either manually or electronically. Employee turnover is discussed, along with reasons and solutions.

Chapter 14, "Measuring Staff Performance and Productivity," describes methods of examining the quantity, efficiency, and quality of work, as well as dependability and responsibility of employees. Sales per hour; covers per hour; person hours; mishaps per hour; and shift, month, and annual production charts are discussed.

Chapter 15, "Control Practices Applied to Human Resources Issues, Wage Laws, and Working Conditions," discusses the critical factors that affect sexual harassment prevention and compliance with the Americans with Disabilities Act, the Equal Employment Opportunity Act, the Family and Medical Leave Act, the Immigration Reform and Control Act, and the Occupational Safety Health Act. The importance of identifying hazardous chemicals with Material Safety Data Sheets is discussed, as is the Tax Equity and Fiscal Responsibility Act (TEFRA) and the Tip Reporting Alternative Commitment (TRAC) for tax reporting. General working conditions, employment of minors, and workers' compensation insurance are also addressed.

Chapter 16, "Monitoring the Sales Process," explains how to monitor sales by cash, check, and credit/debit cards, along with proper control of customer guest checks, either manually or electronically. Accounting for accuracy, theft prevention, measuring productivity, sales tracking, inventory control, and waste prevention are also discussed.

Chapter 17, "Pricing and Sales Forecasts," discusses two basic methods: the food (or beverage) cost percentage method and the contribution method.

Identifying competing foodservice operations, their pricing, and their menu item sales forecasting are explained.

Chapter 18, "Select Topics: Self-Inspections, Customer Feedback, Nonfood Inventories, and Espresso Drinks," discusses topics that all too often do not get the necessary attention. Self-checks are important for proper completion of tasks according to set standards. Evaluations by customers from comment cards, shopper reports, and focus groups provide helpful information. Nonfood inventories, including paper goods, china and flatware, and equipment, also need to be considered. Espresso drinks, which include caffe lattes, cappuccinos, and mochas, continue to grow in popularity and are explained with a cost analysis for each drink.

About the Authors

Edward E. Sanders
Editor in Chief
Hospitality News Group

Ed is the founder and editor in chief of the *Hospitality News Group*, which publishes regional foodservice industry newspapers. He is a Certified Food Executive and a Certified Purchasing Manager; his professional career has included being chief operating officer for a regional chain of restaurants, an associate professor of business, and procurement director of a large-volume foodservice operation. He has a master of science degree in international management from the American Graduate School of International Management and a doctor of business administration degree in management and organization. He was the co-founder and director of industry relations for the Hotel, Restaurant and Resort Management Program at Southern Oregon University. He is also co-author of *Catering Solutions: For the Culinary Student, Foodservice Operator, and Caterer* (Prentice Hall, 2000).

Timothy H. Hill
Associate Professor of Business
Central Oregon Community College

Tim is a certified Foodservice Management Professional with experience in managing restaurants and lodging operations, and has owned two restaurants. He earned his Ph.D. from Washington State University. He founded the Hotel Management program at Brigham Young University–Hawaii Campus and the Hospitality, Tourism, and Recreation Management program at Central Oregon Community College. He also was a partner in founding the Cascade Culinary Institute at Central Oregon Community College. Futher, he has been a consultant in customer service and human resource management for resorts, hotel chains, independent restaurants, and lodging operations.

1

The Control Process

Learning Objectives

After reading this chapter and completing the discussion questions and exercises, you should be able to:

1. Define *control.*
2. List and describe the two different types of environments that influence how managers and employees do their jobs in foodservice operations.
3. Relate the functions that occur in the front of the house of a foodservice operation.
4. Relate the functions that occur in the back of the house of a foodservice operation.
5. Identify the purposes of control systems.
6. Recognize that the types of control systems used in food and beverage operations will differ according to the type, size, and concept of the facility.
7. Describe the process of management control.
8. Relate what influences the development of a menu.
9. Identify and describe the relationship between the level of service and the dollar amount spent on labor.
10. Discuss what a reliable measure is as it pertains to management control.
11. Describe the two approaches to evaluation.
12. Understand the role of information in managing a foodservice operation.
13. Demonstrate an understanding of the impact of technology upon the costs of operating a foodservice establishment.
14. Name the different types of information documents used in foodservice operations.
15. Understand how to achieve foodservice operating goals in the most efficient manner.

About the Control Process

The control process affects every part of the foodservice operation. To understand the control process involves understanding internal and external operating environments, the need for control processes and procedures, the purpose of controls, the basic control process, the control process applied to costs and technology, the reliability and validity of control measures, the evaluation of management controls, the value of information, and types of information.

The control process within a foodservice operation sets forth efficient control techniques designed to maximize food and beverage sales, control expenses, manage employees, and maximize profits. This first chapter will overview and describe the principles and techniques of using information to operate foodservice operations effectively and profitably. A general understanding of the control process and the internal and external operating environments is needed in order to understand the setting in which foodservice operations take place. Subsequent chapters will elaborate, clarify, and show the practical importance of many of the concepts introduced here. Also, the importance of an adequate **information system** to support the operational and management control function will be outlined, and various types of information will be introduced regarding the operation of a foodservice facility of any type, size, and concept.

To **control** means to exercise authority over, restrain, regulate, verify, or check some function. It implies a method, device, or system that accomplishes one or more of these purposes. In the foodservice industry, the term **cost control** has come to mean control over all items of income, expenses, and the flow of products and services, which are both internal and external to a foodservice operation.

Every foodservice operation, regardless of its size, type, or method of service, must have some system of cost control. A system is a collection of things that work together to create a specified outcome.

Foodservice Environments

All businesses operate within an **internal environment** and an **external environment**. The internal environment consists of functions carried on within the organization to achieve organizational objectives. Three functional areas constitute the internal environment and directly influence how managers and employees perform their duties. These areas include front-of-the-house functions, back-of-the-house functions, and management functions.

Factors in the external environment also influence how managers and employees perform their duties. Some external environment factors are government regulations, local market conditions, labor-force demographics, national economic conditions, supplier relations, new technology, and media.

The manager of a foodservice operation must recognize that these two environments exist and that the controls described later in this book are designed to help the foodservice operation succeed within these environments. Figure 1-1 shows these two environments and their relationship to each other. A brief overview of these two environments may be helpful.

Information System
A method of processing information used for management purposes and functions.

Control
A means of exercising authority over, restraining, regulating, verifying, or checking some function.

Cost control
The process of regulating, checking, and exercising authority over income, expenses, and the flow of products and services internal or external to a foodservice operation.

Internal environment
Involves the front-of-the house functions, back-of-the-house functions, and management functions.

External environment
Includes factors such as government regulations, local market conditions, labor-force demographics, national economic conditions, supplier relations, new technology, and media.

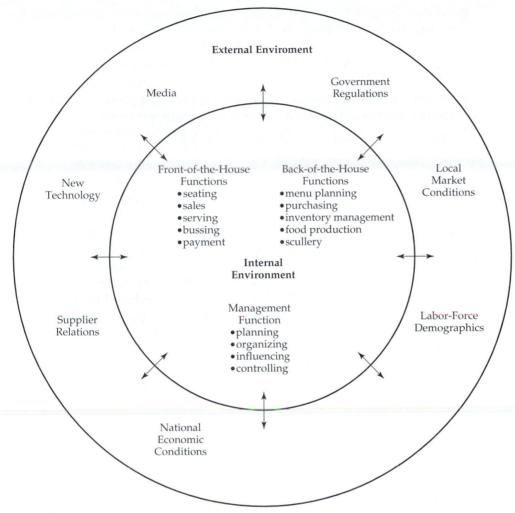

FIGURE 1-1
Relationship of Internal and External Environments

THE INTERNAL ENVIRONMENT

Within the internal environment, five basic functions occur in the **front of the house.** These functions occur in different ways depending upon the type of customer and **foodservice concept.** They are:

- *Seating.* This refers to managing customer flow through the foodservice facility, regardless of whether it is a fine-dining restaurant, family restaurant, or fast-food takeout operation. A facility layout and design that allows for ease in service and customer movement consistent with the foodservice concept is critical.

- *Sales.* Customers order food and beverage items. The selection of these items may occur in a variety of ways, ranging from a hand-held printed menu to a lighted menu board behind a takeout counter.

- *Serving.* This is the delivery of food and beverage items to the customer, with all related foodservice needs being fulfilled. Specifically, the food and beverage items are served at the proper temperature with appropriate condiments and other accompaniments.

Front of the house
The guest contact areas of a foodservice operation.

Foodservice concept
May range from a family restaurant to fine dining, cafeteria dining, or fast food, with each of these types of operations having different types of food, service, and ambience to offer the customer.

- *Bussing.* Simply noted, all the dishes, glasses, and flatware required for service are removed from the tables when not needed. In fast-food operations, customers may clear their own tables and bussing may just mean keeping the establishment free of soiled paper and wiping off tables and chairs as needed.

- *Payment.* Collecting payment from the customer can be accomplished by the waitstaff, fast-food counter person, or cashier.

Back of the house
Non–customer contact areas of the foodservice operation.

The five basic functions in the **back of the house** will also vary according to the type of customer and foodservice concept. The functions are as follows:

- *Menu planning.* Deciding the food items to be offered to customers and making subsequent changes.

- *Purchasing.* Ordering and obtaining the food, beverage, and nonfood items needed to supply the foodservice operation.

- *Inventory management.* Receiving what has been purchased, placing it in the appropriate areas of the storeroom, and managing the use of these items for food production and to maintain the foodservice facility.

- *Food production.* The actual preparation of the food to be served to customers.

- *Scullery.* The maintenance of all food preparation utensils, cooking pots and pans, china, glasses, flatware, and other items used to prepare and serve the food. Maintenance includes washing, sanitizing, storing, and keeping enough items in inventory for the foodservice operation to succeed in serving the customer.

Management function
Planning, organizing, influencing, and controlling activities.

The **management functions** enable the front- and back-of-the-house functions to operate successfully. The management functions include planning, organizing, influencing, and controlling all the internal functions as well as assessing the external factors to determine their impact on internal operations.

- *Planning.* This is the key activity. Operational success is rare unless planning is done adequately. It starts with the owner/manager's basic assumption that customers targeted in a population area will, over an extended period of time, repetitively purchase an adequate number of specified menu items delivered via a particular foodservice concept within a price range that will generate a satisfactory level of profit. Within the constraints of the menu, price range, and foodservice concept, the manager must develop a plan to create sufficient product demand as well as to ensure the necessary production to meet that demand, thus attaining the organization's profit goal. In general, the plan must:

  1. Specify the physical facility and equipment needed.
  2. Assign the responsibilities and duties associated with each of the aforementioned internal functions to positions, and specify the relationships between positions, thus defining the organization structure.

3. Define the **operational procedures** necessary within and between functions, including the accompanying information flow as well as detailed methods for the performance of each function.

4. Specify the necessary personnel, in numbers and qualifications, including recruitment and training plans.

5. Set forth a **financial plan** for the start-up and ongoing operation, including projected **cash flow,** to ensure that funds are available to meet obligations on a timely basis.

6. Identify the **management controls** needed to ensure that production and financial goals are met, and plan for their implementation.

■ *Organizing and influencing.* This effort is directed toward putting the plan into action. It consists of obtaining the necessary financing, acquiring facilities, purchasing and installing equipment, hiring and training personnel, directing personnel, providing for the flow of information, and, in general, exerting the influence necessary to meet the goals of the organization. This is accomplished through a strong **organizational culture,** whereby employees know how to perform and what is expected of them.

■ *Controlling.* When operations are ongoing, management must determine, either directly through observation or indirectly through previously designed management control reports, whether the organization is achieving expected progress toward its goals. If this is not the case, and corrective action is required so that the operation is again moving toward its goals, such action must be taken through planned interventions. This evaluation and intervention may lead to improving of operational procedures, eliminating nonfunctional procedures, and changing or eliminating goals.

A detailed discussion of all these functions is beyond the scope of this book. The focus of this book is, however, to delve more deeply into the controlling functions as they are applied to all areas of the foodservice operation.

THE EXTERNAL ENVIRONMENT

The foodservice operation interacts with its external environment. Factors related to the external environment are:

■ *Government regulations.* Federal, state, and local governments require compliance with a variety of licensing, inspection, and reporting requirements in a timely manner. This can be time-consuming for the foodservice manager. Another related activity may involve establishing contacts with local, state, and national professional associations as well as political action groups, which may have an influence over the development of regulations and reporting requirements.

■ *Local market conditions.* Keeping informed of changes in local market conditions is essential. This might include street improvements, competitors' efforts to attract and keep business, changes in traffic patterns, and competition starting up or discontinuing business.

Operational procedures
The methods by which management requires certain processes to be completed.

Financial plan
The plan for how money will be spent in an operation.

Cash flow
A description of how cash is used in a foodservice operation.

Management controls
Methods of comparing and exercising authority over a foodservice operation's performance to attain established operating goals.

Organizational culture
The shared values, beliefs, attitudes, and norms that help to direct employee behavior by creating a sense of purpose.

FIGURE 1-2
*Flash*Bake Oven The revolutionary *Flash*Bake oven uses quartz halogen lamps to cook foods from the inside out and from the outside in simultaneously. Using a combination of intense visible light and infrared energy, foods are cooked to perfection and in a flash. The oven cooks everything from appetizers and chicken breasts to pizzas and fresh fish. *Courtesy of Vulcan–Hart Company.*

- *Labor-force demographics.* Recruiting and hiring practices are influenced by local labor-market conditions. While there is little a foodservice manager can do to determine labor-force demographics, certain control techniques can be used to hire qualified people.

- *National economic conditions.* National economic conditions affect everyone. Managers must watch changes to predict their impact on internal operations as well as on the external environment. Activities related to this include reading foodservice trade publications; being involved with local, state, and national restaurant and other professional associations; and keeping informed on the local economic conditions that could have a direct impact upon business.

- *Supplier relations.* While purchasing is considered part of the internal environment, it also involves interacting with the external environment. Suppliers are a major source of information for developing menus and monitoring the marketing environment. Suppliers sponsor food and equipment shows to provide the opportunity for foodservice managers to sample new food and beverage products and advancements in foodservice equipment.

- *New technology.* New developments in kitchen equipment are more energy-efficient, cost-effective, and labor-saving (for an example, see Figure 1-2). Also, information system software and hardware exemplify how new technology continues to advance foodservice operations.

- *Media.* Television, radio, and newspapers not only provide information regarding external factors, but they are also an excellent resource for reaching the target population that the foodservice manager desires to serve through promotional advertising.

The Need for Control Processes and Procedures

In the early days of foodservice operations, the types of controls needed and the records maintained were relatively simple. The cash went into the cash box (register) and daily expenses were taken care of by a transfer of cash out of the cash register. Envelopes may have been used for weekly and monthly expenses, as money was reserved for payroll, rent, utilities, and so on. At the end of the week or month, whatever was left over was the profit.

In today's business environment, with various taxes, business and license fees, credit cards, accounts payable schedules, payroll taxes, pension plans, vacation plans, health plans, and innumerable other items, individual entrepreneurs, as well as corporations of all sizes, need more detailed information. Complex situations require sophisticated systems. Often, foodservice operations are run by absentee management or community public-service agencies, such as health care providers and schools. Additional controls and reports are therefore necessary. While some health care providers and schools may operate on a not-for-profit basis, they must avoid losses and have information available so that they can keep supervising entities informed and comply with various local, state, and federal laws.

Regardless of whether there is a profit or not, federal, state, and local governments require monthly, quarterly, and yearly reports concerning the financial status of businesses. At the same time, businesses have become agents of the government—collecting taxes on sales, withholding payroll taxes from employees, and paying these sums to the government according to a structured time schedule.

In less complicated times, the decision to purchase equipment or to construct a building might have been based exclusively on the production needs of the organization. Today, however, this decision may be influenced by the type of business ownership; the depreciation allowed by the government; a variety of local, state, or federal regulations; leasing options versus ownership; and the obsolescence of the equipment, building, or location.

Working and ownership arrangements have changed markedly over the years. The sales volume and size of a food and beverage operation may reach millions of dollars; the operation may employ a large number of people who must be controlled by a system that will assure management that all income is being received and that all products are either sold or properly utilized. A business may own one or more establishments, yet the owner may not necessarily be personally involved in supervising day-to-day operations. When this is the case, authority must be delegated to other responsible people. In turn, systems must be devised to determine who bears the responsibility if deviations from owner/manager expectations occur.

Employers and employees have a vital interest in ensuring that control systems are reliable and effective. Managers use control systems to help pinpoint responsibility for inefficiencies, errors, and fraud. Employees should be aware that control systems can protect them and reward them for good performance. If an employee is doing an outstanding job, management should be able to detect this and reward or possibly advance the employee. If theft occurs, innocent employees have a substantial interest in the control system.

An efficient system will be able to identify the source of the theft, both deterring such occurrences and avoiding damage to employee morale through unsubstantiated suspicion.

The Purpose of Controls

The primary responsibility for safeguarding the **assets** of foodservice establishments and preventing and detecting inefficiencies, errors, and fraud rests upon management. Thus, controls for the foodservice industry are designed for three primary purposes:

1. To determine the efficiency of the operation.

2. To prevent fraud or theft by employees or guests. Unlike in the retail industry, however, practically all thefts in foodservice organizations are committed by the employees, not the customers.

3. To ensure that the operation functions in a manner that complies with the goals of management; specifically, to determine that what occurs in the foodservice operation is what management planned to occur in food preparation and service to customers.

Whatever the type of food served, the particular function of the foodservice operation, the method of service, and the type of ownership and organization structure, the control system should cover every facet of the operation. The primary objective of a control system may differ for various types of foodservice operations. For a restaurant operator, the first concern is to increase profits. For a school foodservice director or other not-for-profit operator, it may be to lower operating costs. Each must approach his or her task with a control system tailored to the needs of the organization. The types of systems used in food and beverage operations will differ. What may be effective in one organization may be utterly useless in another.

The Basic Control Procedure

Managers control the various aspects of the foodservice operation. Simply expressed, the manager knows that something should be done in a specific way, observes whether what is actually occurring is what should be occurring, and corrects the situation as needed. See Figure 1-3 for an illustration of how this process works. Management control consists of the following set of procedures:

1. *Setting standards.* Management sets a **standard,** based upon specific **criteria,** to be achieved or maintained for a specified condition with or without tolerances for deviation from that standard.

2. *Measuring performance.* An ongoing or periodic measurement of the condition for which the standard is set occurs, using the same measures that defined the standard.

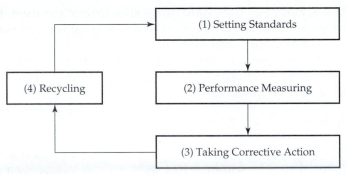

FIGURE 1-3
Management Control Process

3. *Taking corrective action.* A specific planned intervention is triggered whenever the ongoing or periodic measurement of the standard-related condition falls above or below the standard or its specified tolerances, if any.

4. *Recycling through the process.* Failing to achieve the standard may result in lowering or abandoning the standard or the criteria used to set the standard. It may require replanning operational procedures to attain the unmet standard. If the standard was easily attained, the standard may need to be raised to a higher level, and replanning may be necessary to achieve the higher standard. Careful observations throughout normal business operations may also suggest better procedural methods and evaluation techniques so that the standard is accurately measured.

A thermostat is a good metaphor to illustrate the nature of a control. Suppose the manager, based on management criteria, decides the air in the restaurant should be maintained at 70°F and sets the thermostat accordingly. A measuring device (a column of mercury) constantly measures the temperature. When the temperature falls below 70°F, the heating unit to which the thermostat is attached is automatically triggered to send heat to the area. When the desired temperature is reached, an automatic message is sent to the heating unit, shutting it off. In actual practice, the control unit may delay sending signals to the heating unit until the temperature reaches a full degree or more above or below 70°F. A two-degree tolerance prevents the heating unit from turning off and on continually, as this could be annoying to patrons and cause excessive equipment wear.

In this example, the manager set a standard, 70°F, for the temperature of the restaurant. A standard usually reflects a subgoal or subobjective related to attaining an overall goal or a higher subobjective. For example, the manager's overall goal is to make a profit from the restaurant. In order to do so, the manager must keep the restaurant full of paying customers. To accomplish that, the temperature level must satisfy the comfort level of the patrons. Thus, one of the criteria for setting the standard is the temperature comfort level of the patrons.

More than one criterion is likely to be operative in setting a standard. In the interest of making a profit, the manager undoubtedly used cost as a second criterion by selecting the lowest temperature that will achieve the first criterion. Thus, the standard was set at 70°F, not 72°F. Many criteria may be used in setting a single standard, and many standards are normally involved in a single business. Notice that the standard in this example is stated not as "a comfortable temperature" but in measurable terms, that is, 70° F. No margin should be left for interpretation of the standard. An effective standard should have the same meaning to all concerned. It should be set forth in measurable terms whenever possible.

The Control Process Applied to Costs

Before we narrow the focus to more specific concepts concerning controls, an introduction to costs of some of the aforementioned functions and their relationships is in order. Therefore, a brief consideration of the costs related to the menu, service and labor, and new technology follows.

THE MENU

The menu is determined by the type of customer market that is targeted. Specifically, with each type of market, a foodservice manager must determine the best type of menu suitable for the needs of that market. In designing a given menu, the manager must consider not only information on the market itself (age, gender, economic and employment conditions, frequency of eating out, and so on), but also the skill levels of the employees, the availability of products, and innumerable other factors that will affect the overall salability and profitability of the menu.

The type of menu to be offered and the pricing structure are determined by management. However, with menus that change frequently, the function of menu planning is often the duty of a chef or a dietician (in school or health care foodservice).

Menu planning is among the more complex tasks of foodservice management. This is due to the large number of variables that directly affect the cost of food and beverages and the difficulty in assigning a value to each variable. Monitoring the menu should be an ongoing process from the time of implementation. Changes in customer preferences and in the cost of food and beverage purchases may require changes in menu offerings and pricing.

The amount of money spent to purchase food and beverages is dependent upon the menu. The menu is a detailed list of the food and beverages that is presented to the customer on a menu board (sign) on a wall, or on a hand-held document. Management's decisions about menu content are the most important decisions made in a foodservice operation. They determine or influence:

- The amount of money necessary to set up and maintain the operation.
- The targeted customer population to be served.
- The level of service to be offered.
- The type of equipment and facilities needed.
- The skill level needed in the kitchen and serving areas.
- The production ingredients to be ordered and stored.

- The nonfood items used in serving, such as china, flatware, paper products, and so on.
- The number and complexity of management controls.
- The operational and management information required.

Obviously, there are different cost implications for a menu of 15 items offered by a walk-up espresso bar than for a menu of 75 items offered by a fine-dining operation.

SERVICE AND LABOR

The amount of money spent on labor is referred to as the **labor cost.** Labor cost is largely dependent upon the level of service rendered by the cooking and serving staff.

The more complicated the menu, the greater the skill needed by those preparing the food items. Thus, a more complicated menu requires higher labor costs to prepare the menu items. The inverse relationship is also true; the less complicated the menu, the less it costs to prepare menu items.

The relationship is the same regarding service. Generally, a limited-service foodservice establishment requires less skilled and therefore less expensive labor. As staff services are reduced, customer self-service usually increases. Consequently, labor costs are reduced. Customer self-service increases when customers elect to dine from a salad bar, carry their own trays in a cafeteria or a fast-food establishment, or serve themselves in a buffet setting. In the latter, management loses control of portion size. The trade-off is reduced waitstaff costs for potentially increased food costs, unless control of portions is maintained.

Conversely, full service requires additional skill and often increased numbers of those rendering the skill. This means labor costs will be higher. A full-service operation requires waitstaff to secure the order, deliver all food and beverages to the customer, and present the guest check.

NEW TECHNOLOGY

New technology affects costs and operating efficiencies. For example, in a full-service setting, the customer's order is taken by a waitperson and transmitted either verbally or by a handwritten guest check to the kitchen staff. The costs of time elapsed and staff time depend upon the distances between the serving and preparation areas. With the advent of new technology, waitstaff in some operations no longer use guest checks as a way to send orders to the kitchen but rather use a hand-held touchscreen terminal or a fixed-position terminal with a touchscreen (see Figure 1-4). Service and communications are improved using this new technology between waitstaff and kitchen staff, thereby reducing costs.

Likewise, technology has created silent vibrating pocket pagers that notify waitstaff that orders are ready (see Figure 1-5). As a result, they do not need to check the kitchen regarding the readiness of their orders. The time saved by the waitstaff enables them to serve the food faster, as well as serving a greater number of tables, increasing **table turnover.** Thus, not only is there greater productivity, but also the waitstaff have the potential to increase their personal earnings by receiving greater numbers of tips (see Figure 1-7).

Labor cost
The amount of money spent on labor.

Table turnover
The number of times a table is used during the hours that the foodservice operation is open for business.

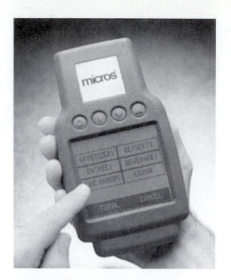

FIGURE 1-4
Hand-Held Touchscreen Terminal
Courtesy of Micros.

New technology is also elbowing its way into production via new automated kitchen equipment and more sophisticated information systems. These new developments enable rapid and frequent changes of menus by changing recipes stored in **databases.** Similarly, other technologies are causing changes in purchasing, inventory control, sales, and payment functions. A seamless integrated information system using a point-of-sale terminal can trace the impact of activities that produce **data** using an in-store network (see Figure 1-6). For example, the effect of a single sales order on inventory, purchasing, production, labor costs, and so on can be recorded, summarized, and, when desired, presented to management at any terminal throughout the foodservice operation.

Database
A collection of information that has been identified and arranged so that it can be retrieved from a computer.

Data
Factual information.

FIGURE 1-5
Silent Vibrating Pocket Pager This pager by Signologies has a full one-mile range, automatically repages servers, and pages the manager with tardy server ID numbers. It saves time by digitally displaying which servers have been paged and immediately notifies the entire staff of sold-out items.

FIGURE 1-6
Point-of-Sale Terminal   The point-of-sale terminal combines point-of-sale information with management control functions. *Courtesy of Micros.*

The new technology is here, and more is coming (see, for example, Figure 1-7). Each has its costs and its savings. Each possesses potential for changes in organization, procedures, and management, which translates into a more efficient foodservice operation through improved methods and new habits.

Reliability of Management Control Measures

For management controls to be effective, they must be exact, reliable, and standard-related measures. They must also provide information that will trigger action or inaction as prescribed by a standard when certain conditions are met or not met. A *reliable measure* is one that will give the same results when applied repeatedly to the same value of a condition. In the restaurant heating example, the thermostat is a reliable measure of temperature. In the business world, measures rely largely on symbols such as words or numbers for com-

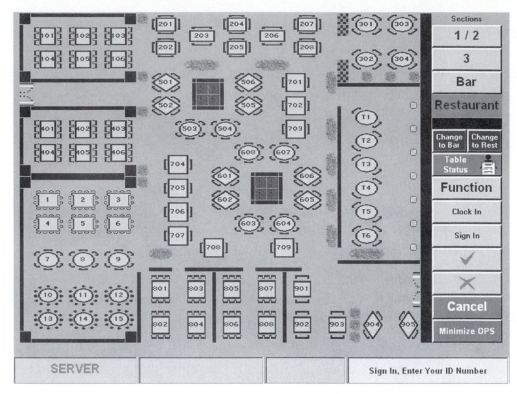

FIGURE 1-7
Table Service Management   Touch-screen flow management system designed to maximize a restaurant's customer service efficiency. This system reduces customer wait times by shortening the time a table remains empty between departing and arriving customers. *Courtesy of Micros.*

munication. If standards and their related measures are vague or ambiguous, they are subject to misinterpretation by employees. Employee interpretation is variable because different meanings have often been attached to the same symbols by people with different experiences. For example, "Maintain a seven-day supply of peaches" is a poor standard. Both "seven-day supply" and "peaches" are subject to interpretation. A better standard would be: "Maintain a supply of 24 cans of Elberta peaches, #10 can size, sliced (300–350 count), light syrup."

Except where machines may be in use, triggered actions or inactions are not automatic. Foodservice managers rely largely on employee responses. Clear and exact statements of criteria for action or inaction will help to limit possible human misinterpretation.

Evaluation of Management Controls

Evaluation
The process of comparing performance data to established standards.

After management control standards have been established and related performance data have been gathered, it is necessary to determine the results. This process is called **evaluation.** There are two approaches to evaluation: process evaluation and impact evaluation.

PROCESS EVALUATION

Process evaluation involves determining whether the standard set forth by management actually was implemented properly by staff. Such evaluation was not appropriate in the heating example because temperature was controlled automatically by the thermostat. If the thermostat failed, uncomfortable occupants would make it known.

Processes dependent upon human action are not as reliable as an electronic thermostat. Management must take steps to determine whether the standard is properly implemented. Depending upon the standard, this determination may require different approaches. One may be a simple management observation; another may be a complete inventory of supplies to determine whether ordering standards are being observed. Still another approach may employ sampling—that is, systematically observing a small number of actions from which to draw a conclusion about the degree of compliance of all similar actions with that standard. This approach employs statistical treatment of data to infer the degree of compliance. The approach to process evaluation will depend largely on the specification of the standard; no overall technique can be set forth. To be able to evaluate the importance of a standard, it is necessary to know the degree to which it was followed.

Process evaluation
A determination of whether the operational procedures were properly used by staff.

IMPACT EVALUATION

Assuming that a standard was implemented as designed, it then becomes necessary to ask the question, "So what?" What difference did the standard make in attaining overall management goals? Methods employed to answer this question are called **impact evaluation.** Did the standard negatively or positively influence achievement of management goals? In the heating example, were the occupants comfortable at 70°F, or were they prompted to consider leaving or not returning because they were too cold? On the other hand, would they have been comfortable at 68°F, allowing the heating expense to be reduced in the winter? After experiencing operations using the standard and gathering pertinent data, management may leave the standard the same or adjust it in accordance with findings relative to the standard's effect on the desired results. The data needed to make the impact evaluation may be produced routinely in daily operations or may be gathered independently.

Impact evaluation
A determination of whether the achievement of the standard negatively or positively affected the foodservice operation.

An example of impact evaluation in the foodservice industry is as follows: Suppose management establishes a production standard of 20 servings of shrimp with curried pasta for each evening of the week. Daily counts of shrimp with curried pasta sold ranged from 8 to 13 servings, with all but three days being between 10 and 11 servings. Analysis of the production standard reveals that it is wasteful. Management elects to revise the production standard temporarily and prepare only 11 servings of shrimp with curried pasta instead of 20 servings.

Management may be puzzled by the drop in consumption of shrimp with curried pasta because the 20-serving daily production standard was based upon previous sales experience. Therefore, management decides to do a process evaluation of the preparation of shrimp with curried pasta to determine whether the product is being prepared properly.

Taste, appearance, and amount of food presented were the three criteria used in developing the management controls for the preparation of shrimp with curried pasta. The main portion of the meal consists of three items served on the same plate. To control the taste, management has prescribed a specific recipe for each item. To control the appearance, the color of vegetable, garnish used, and serving arrangement have been specified. The amount of vegetables is controlled by designating the size of the serving. Taste samplings may verify that the taste either is the same or is not. If it is not the same, management next determines whether prescribed recipes are being faithfully followed. Observation of dished-up plates should provide feedback on appearance and serving size. If shrimp with curried pasta is being prepared according to control standards, the change to 11 servings appears justified until sales increase.

On the other hand, if preparation standards are being violated, such as if a new cook is using his or her own recipe, the violations must be eliminated. Note that in this case, the standard of taste was not measurable, but a different approach (recipe) was used to control it. Also, note the interrelationship between process and impact evaluations. If the process evaluation cannot confirm that management standards were followed, then the process evaluation cannot be used as a valid method of measuring deviations from management standards.

The Value of Information

In every business, an underlying information system supports its operation and management. The information may be verbal, written, electronic, or a combination of these. The quality of the system will vary depending upon the skill of its designer and the resources available to implement it. Ideally, the information system will support the business operation with timely, accurate data to help it operate efficiently. Much of the necessary information will be generated as transactions occur during the course of business operation. Some management information, such as local market conditions, will originate outside the confines of the business—in the external environment.

In the foodservice industry, the operational information system should serve each of the functions and factors described in the external and internal environments. In addition, information available to managers must provide the basis for setting goals, planning strategies, implementing procedures, and evaluating results. This should include all the information required for implementing management controls, setting standards, determining progress toward those standards, and evaluating a standard's impact upon goal achievement.

Although all foodservice managers must determine the information required to operate their establishment and the format in which they wish to receive it, a number of forms have been included in the following chapters to suggest the data needed to support specific management controls. Whether the data should be presented manually or electronically is a decision best left to those implementing an information system designed for a specific foodservice operation. When presented, these forms accomplish the immediate objective of demonstrating efficient food, beverage, and labor cost control techniques. Some specific types of information relevant to a foodservice operation are menu information, food cost information, beverage cost information, labor cost information, and sales cost information.

MENU INFORMATION

The menu provides the customer with essential information for making a choice. It is designed to reflect the foodservice concept. Chosen by the manager or owner, this concept depends upon the type of service and food to be offered. For illustrative and example purposes, it is assumed that a foodservice concept has already been chosen for control techniques being discussed in the following chapters. Examples of concepts are:

- All-you-can-eat buffet
- Upscale hamburgers
- Seafood restaurant
- Fifties diner
- College dorm foodservice
- Health-care foodservice
- School foodservice

- Mexican theme restaurant
- Continental fine dining
- Old-fashioned pizza parlor
- Japanese restaurant
- Italian theme restaurant
- Soup and delicatessen
- Steak house

There are literally hundreds of concepts. Each type of concept conjures up a mental picture of a specific foodservice establishment.

FOOD COST INFORMATION

The menu determines the ingredients needed to produce meals. **Food ingredients** consist of all food product items used to produce meals. The information needed to control food purchasing, storage, and preparation costs may be presented manually or electronically. Traditionally, it has been presented on such forms as the following:

Food ingredients
All food product items used to produce meals.

- Food cost reports
- Standardized recipes
- Bid sheets
- Invoice payment schedules
- Requisitions and transfers
- Other inventory reports
- Plate cost charts
- Food production charts
- Food cost percentage reports

- Menu analysis charts
- Recipe cost charts
- Order sheets
- Inventory forms
- Service system charts
- Yield charts
- Portion control charts
- Food mishap reports

All of the information that these forms collect can be used as needed for successfully managing a foodservice operation.

BEVERAGE COST INFORMATION

As with food costs, beverage costs must be controlled. Many of the techniques used for controlling beverage costs are the same as for controlling food costs.

Techniques for ordering, payment, transferring, and requisitioning are the same as for food. Data unique to beverage control are collected by using the following forms:

- Beverage cost reports
- Beverage recipes
- Bar and inventory control reports
- Liquor storeroom inventory reports
- Sample house policy

- Beverage cost percentage reports
- Pour cost charts
- Alcohol use reports
- Beverage mishap reports

LABOR COST INFORMATION

Besides the ingredients, all foodservice establishments must use labor and facilities to accomplish their service goals. Labor and productivity information can be collected and evaluated using the following:

- Labor cost forms
- Job descriptions
- Kitchen production charts
- Daily work sheets
- Payroll cost estimates
- Time cards
- Human resources audits
- Workers' compensation reports
- Safety and sanitation reports

- Labor cost percentage reports
- Performance standards
- Waitstaff production charts
- Work schedules
- Payroll cost reports
- Tip reporting forms
- I-9 forms
- OSHA report forms
- Productivity charts

The result of faithfully using these types of forms is that they will assist in operating efficiently, within projected costs, and within the law.

SALES COST INFORMATION

Sales information is related to the sale and service of menu items to customers. It is also related to collecting money and measuring how satisfied customers are with their experience. Information is collected and monitored using:

- Guest checks
- Cashier's reports
- Customer count and table turnover reports
- Customer satisfaction standards

- Guest check daily reports
- Waitstaff sales reports
- Daily, monthly, and annual reports
- Work flow charts

The presented lists of forms in each category are not to be considered all-inclusive, but cover most of the situations a foodservice manager may encounter.

The purpose of this chapter has been to explain the general nature of controls as they are related to food and beverage operations. How to apply the basic control procedure in a variety of operational situations is covered in the following chapters of this book.

SUMMARY

1. Foodservice profitability requires the manager to have a general understanding of the control process and operating environment of a foodservice operation, functions that generally occur in a foodservice operation, and cost relationships between the menu, level of service, labor, and technology.

2. Cost control is the process of regulating, checking, and exercising authority over income, expenses, and the flow of products and services internal and external to a foodservice operation.

3. All businesses operate within two environments: internal and external. The internal environment consists of functions carried on within the organization to achieve organizational objectives. Aspects of the internal environment that influence how management and employees perform their duties are front-of-the-house, back-of-the-house, and management functions.

4. Five functions occur in the front of the house: seating, sales, serving, bussing, and payment.

5. Five functions occur in the back of the house: menu planning, purchasing, inventory management, food production, and scullery. These functions will vary according to the foodservice concept and type of customer targeted.

6. The four functions of management are planning, organizing, influencing, and controlling.

7. Factors in the external environment also influence how managers and employees perform their duties. Some external environment factors are government regulations, local market conditions, supplier relations, new technology, and media.

8. The purpose of controls is to determine the efficiency of the operation, prevent theft, and ensure that the operation functions according to the goals of management.

9. The basic control procedure consists of setting standards according to criteria, measuring performance against the standard, taking corrective action, and recycling through the process.

10. The control process is applied to costs associated with the menu, service and labor, and new technology.

11. Control measures must be reliable and valid.

12. After management control standards have been established and related performance data gathered, it is necessary to determine the results. This process is called evaluation. The two evaluation approaches are process evaluation and impact evaluation.

13. Proper use of information is vital to the success of a foodservice operation. The foodservice manager should know the value of collecting needed information and be able to analyze the information so that it assists in achieving the organization's goals.

14. The types of control systems used in food and beverage operations will differ. What may be effective in one organization will be utterly useless in another.

KEY CONCEPTS

Assets

Back of the house

Cash flow

Control

Cost Control

Criteria

Database

Data

External environment

Evaluation

Financial plan

Foodservice concept

Food ingredients

Front of the house

Impact evaluation

Internal environment

Labor cost

Management controls

Management functions

Operational procedures

Organizational culture

Process evaluation

Standards

Table turnover

DISCUSSION QUESTIONS AND EXERCISES

1. Present examples of an internal environment situation and an external environment situation to the class.

2. What are the functions that occur in the front of the house?

3. What are the functions that occur in the back of the house?

4. What are the four functions of management?

5. Why is it important to understand the factors related to the external environment of a foodservice operation?

6. Give an example that demonstrates what influences the development of a menu plan.

7. Visit a fast-food foodservice operation. Note how technology is being used to cook and serve food to customers. Write a brief paper on what you have discovered.

8. Define *control.*

9. List and describe the procedures of management control. How do you think these procedures could be used in a foodservice operation?

10. A chef uses a recipe from the standardized recipe file to prepare black bean salsa. Another chef prepares the same item using a personal recipe. If you are a manager of this foodservice operation and wanted to evaluate the quality of the black bean salsa, what is the criterion for measuring the flavor of this item? What problem do you have?

11. What is the problem with the following standard statement? "Maintain a supply of spaghetti."

12. What are the two different kinds of evaluations?

13. In the statement, "All hamburgers are to be cooked to an internal temperature of 155°F," what type of evaluation will take place?

14. What role does information play in a profitable foodservice operation?

15. List six different kinds of foodservice concepts.

16. List six different types of documents related to food cost information.

17. List six different types of documents related to beverage cost information.

18. List six different types of documents related to labor cost information.

19. List four different types of documents related to sales cost information.

20. What interest do employees have in ensuring that there are adequate control systems?

21. Why has there been a need for more sophisticated control systems?

22. Why is it necessary to assign responsibility in control systems?

2

Food Cost/
Food Cost Percentage

Learning Objectives

After reading this chapter and completing the discussion questions and exercises, you should be able to:

1. Describe how food cost is determined.

2. Understand that costs are similar within categories of foodservice operations such as fine dining, fast food (quick serve), family restaurant, buffet, cafeteria, school foodservice, health care foodservice, or special-event catering.

3. Illustrate the inverse relationship between food costs and labor costs.

4. Recognize that food cost reporting will be conducted at different time intervals according to the policy of a company's management.

5. Explain why reducing food product quality or cutting portion sizes as a short-term plan for combating increasing costs could result in loss of customer loyalty.

6. Complete a food cost report.

7. Calculate a food cost percentage.

8. Explain the results that can be generated from an integrated computer system.

9. Complete a department food cost report.

About Food Cost

Among the very first things with which a foodservice manager will be confronted is managing food cost. To be successful at the task, the foodservice manager must fully understand all the areas within the foodservice operation that can increase or decrease food cost.

Simply stated, **food cost** is the actual cost of purchasing the raw food products and related ingredients. These costs are measured and expressed in terms of a percentage, which is referred to as the **food cost percentage.** This chapter will explain how the foodservice manager actually calculates a food cost percentage.

The task is not at all difficult once the dollar amounts are gathered from cost reports. Then, with the help of a basic calculator, the foodservice manager calculates the percentages. A more advanced foodservice operation will use a computer to complete the task in a very fast and efficient manner. The foodservice manager must still comprehend the information fed into the computer; thus he or she needs to understand the factors influencing food cost. As the foodservice manager becomes skilled and proficient at the task of managing food cost, this task will become part of the daily routine of managing a foodservice operation.

A foodservice manager may be asked the question, "What should the food cost be for this or that type of foodservice operation?" As the foodservice manager acquires a few years of successful management experience, coupled with a basic understanding of food cost, the question will be easy to answer.

Often, when the owner or senior management feels the food cost is too high, a new foodservice manager will be given the assignment of doing something about it. When this occurs, it represents an excellent opportunity for the new foodservice manager to demonstrate the skills and capabilities that can set forth a very promising career.

Introduction to Food Cost

Food cost is the total dollar amount spent on food in a foodservice operation. When foodservice managers talk about food cost, they are usually referring to the cost as a percentage. For instance, a manager may state, "Food cost was 32 percent last month." Understanding food cost goes beyond calculating a simple percentage. A foodservice manager who effectively manages food cost also understands how to manage **inventory** by using **inventory sheets, inventory turnover** reports, **requisitions,** and **transfers,** as well as properly receiving merchandise and processing **invoices.**

Foodservice managers choose the food cost percentage they wish to have as an operating goal. This decision also involves setting quality standards and portion sizes. The food cost percentage should be controlled with only a small degree of fluctuation. Food cost can be maintained through the effective use of information and control reports prepared on a regular and scheduled basis.

This does not mean that costs cannot at any time be improved, perhaps through a more efficient preparation method or improved buying practices. Management should be continuouslly aware of all factors that could decrease the costs of the foodservice operation.

At the heart of earning a profit or meeting a budget in a foodservice operation is the ability of the foodservice manager to control food cost. A key tool for controlling food cost is to use a **food cost report.** This report is a valuable tool for understanding how to manage food cost.

■ ■ ■ ■ ■

Table 2-1 Typical Food Cost Percentages

	LOW	MEDIUM	HIGH
Family Restaurant	27%	30%	36%
Fine Dining	25%	27%	38%
Fast Food (Quick Serve)	28%	31%	39%
Cafeteria	33%	36%	37%
Buffet	35%	40%	46%

Understanding Food Cost

Many philosophies may be expressed by different foodservice managers as to what a normal food cost or food cost percentage should be for the typical foodservice operation. What the cost should be really depends upon the type of foodservice operation. Foodservice operations generally fall into one of the following categories:

Family restaurant

Fine dining

Fast food (quick serve)

Cafeteria

Buffet

Within each of these categories, different types of foods are served (such as ethnic foods, steak dinners, and so on). Each may have a different type of theme (such as an Old West saloon, French bistro, or American diner). Also, there are different service styles ranging from formal fine dining to a walk-up snack bar. Each category, type, and style has a food cost percentage range that is normal for that particular type of operation. Typical food cost percentages by category are listed in Table 2-1.

As a general guideline, if a foodservice operation runs a high food cost percentage, the labor cost percentage should be lower. Such is the case with fast-food restaurants that hire people with limited skills at minimal pay to prepare inexpensively priced items. Generally, this type of operation experiences high-volume sales. Thus, food items are typically prepared from frozen, ready-to-go products.

An opposite situation is that of a fine-dining restaurant. These operations employ skilled chefs and a professional waitstaff serving higher-priced food. The menu items are typically prepared from scratch, as opposed to being purchased, prepared, or frozen and quickly assembled. As a result, the food cost will be lower and the labor cost higher in a full-service operation than in a limited-service operation. Each category, fine dining to fast food, maintains a cost that is typical for its own function.

The purpose of food cost control is to be able to offer complete foodservice at the lowest possible cost. This is done in a way that is consistent with the stated policy of the foodservice operation regarding the quality and the specific **portions** (also known as standard portion sizes) that are to be served. Management has the full responsibility of accounting accurately for all food

Portion
The specific quantity of an item of food.

items purchased and sold in the foodservice operation. Accurate records must be maintained in the form of reports, and the responsibility for these is properly delegated to people in production and supervision. If no appropriate form exists, one should be created to meet the specific needs of the foodservice operation. Also, many standard computer software programs allow foodservice managers the freedom of creating a variety of reports that will fit their needs.

The typically small owner-operated restaurants will find it difficult to produce reports. Often they depend on a bookkeeper or accountant to provide report information at the end of the month. They have inadequate management control procedures. This is financially dangerous for any type of foodservice operation. A small-restaurant operator needs to use the most effective type of controls possible. These controls must be fully integrated into the foodservice operation. The reason is obvious. Better-informed managers are better equipped to make the necessary decisions that will maintain profitability and competitiveness.

The Food Cost Report

The only way to accurately identify the cost of food sold and the food cost percentage is to prepare a food cost report. The food cost report indicates the actual cost percentage of food used for all food sales for any given period of time. There are many different opinions as to how often a food cost report should be prepared. Some managers believe that tabulating once a month is adequate. Others feel that once every two weeks is sufficient. Still others insist that any longer than a week is far too risky. A foodservice manager who uses a computerized system can generate a daily food cost report.

Preparing a food cost report on a weekly basis provides for tight control of costs. This frequency allows comfortable control and leaves less room for any big surprises. Doing a weekly report allows management adequate time to react intelligently to fluctuating food costs.

Increasing or fluctuating food costs can usually be attributed to one or more of the following circumstances:

Supplier
Business that sells food and nonfood items to foodservice operations.

1. *Product cost increases.* **Suppliers** may increase prices due to shifts in market conditions. This means that total costs of food preparation will also increase.

2. *New employees not properly trained.* Employees may not:
   - Put the proper amount of food (too much or too little) on the plate being served to the customer
   - Store items in the proper place
   - Know what to do with leftovers (the food not sold at the end of the day)

   All these actions lead to higher costs.

3. *Theft of products or cash from sales.* Foodservice operations are always vulnerable to theft by employees, unscrupulous delivery people, and sometimes even customers.

4. *Product spoilage or waste.* If any food items spoil or are not fresh due to improper handling or incorrect product rotation, they cannot be served to the customer. Some food items are only partially used, then thrown away. All of these things add to the cost of food.

5. *Owner/manager on vacation or on sick leave.* The owner/manager usually is the person supervising the operation to ensure that people are trained, that theft does not occur, and that portions are what they should be. If the owner/manager is not present in the operation, this function goes unattended, which means that costs could increase.

6. *Mathematical mistakes or incorrect counts on inventory.* Arithmetic errors may dramatically increase or decrease the reported cost.

7. *Products issued without requisitions or transfers.* This means that items are taken from inventory or the kitchen without being recorded as being taken. The food cost report would then indicate that there is more in inventory than really exists.

8. *Forgetting to record invoices on the **invoice payment schedule.*** This means that there is less food recorded as being purchased than was actually purchased.

9. *Employee meal credit, promotional/free meals, or steward sales not being properly recorded.* All these items cost money. If they are not recorded, the food cost report will not indicate all the food costs of the operation.

10. ***Menu mix*** *out of balance.* The menu mix is the number of each menu item sold in relationship to the other items sold. If recipes are followed and suppliers' prices are constant, each menu item has a fixed cost for its ingredients. Some menu items cost more than other items. If more of the expensive menu items are sold, the food cost would increase more than was expected.

Both short-term and long-term solutions can be found during difficult times of rising product costs. Among the worst possible short-term decisions that can be made is to cut the food product quality, reduce the portion sizes, and increase prices simultaneously. Restaurant managers who do this find that they lose sales to competitors. The first thing that management should do is closely examine and evaluate the effectiveness of existing food cost controls. The controls should reflect thorough and tight handling of products from the initial point of purchase to the final resulting sale. When costs continue to rise, menu prices have to be gradually increased over a scheduled period of time.

HOW TO CONSTRUCT A FOOD COST REPORT

The food cost report is a tool used to track costs. It can be used to discover why food costs fluctuate. An example of a food cost report is shown in Table 2-2. This form demonstrates the basic method of identifying the cost of food sold as well as the food cost percentage for a one-week period. The food cost report begins with the **opening inventory,** which is the previous week's **closing inventory.**

Every closing inventory becomes the opening inventory for the following period. To further see how inventory is treated, refer to Chapter 3. The total food purchases are taken from the invoice payment schedule (see

Invoice payment schedule
A form used to document all purchases during a given period of time and to ensure that suppliers are paid in a timely fashion.

Menu mix
The number of each menu item sold in relationship to the other items sold.

Opening inventory
A physical count of the inventory at the beginning of an accounting period. An accounting period may be one week, two weeks, one month, and so on.

Closing inventory
A physical count of the inventory at the ending of an accounting period.

Period Ending __1/17/XX__

DEBITS

Opening Inventory (1/10/XX)	$ 9,871.15
Total Food Purchases	+ 6,758.25
Debit Total	16,629.40 (A)

CREDITS

Closing Inventory (1/17/XX)	$ 10,001.95
Employee Meal Credit	+ 614.00
Promotional/Free Meals	+ 20.00
Steward Sales	+ 115.00
Credit Total	10,750.95 (B)

COST OF FOOD SOLD . . . . $ 5,878.45   (C)
(a – b = c)

TOTAL FOOD SALES $15,945.90

COST OF FOOD SOLD
$5,878.45

(divide) ÷   =

FOOD COST PERCENTAGE
.369 × 100 = 36.9 %

TOTAL FOOD SALES
$15,945.90

Prepared by _____Clerical_____   Date ___1/20/XX___

Debit is an accounting term used to indicate an inflow into an account. In this example, opening inventory and total food purchases are inflows into the food cost.

Credits are outflows from the food cost account. In this example, closing inventory, employee meal credit, promotional/free meals, and steward sales are outflow food costs.

Chapter 6) and must be added to the *opening inventory*. Careful attention must be given to the invoice payment schedule. All the products that have been used in production and counted as inventory should be listed on the schedule. Products that have not been used or counted as inventory should not be listed but will be listed on the following period's payment schedule.

The credits include the closing inventory, **employee meal credit, promotional/free meals,** and **steward sales.** The closing inventory is the dollar value of the inventory taken the last day of the period. An employee meal credit is the amount charged for employee meals. It is usually taken from the payroll register, which identifies the days of the week and number of hours worked by each employee, along with the amount charged per day for each employee meal. Promotional/free meals are those meals given away by the owner/manager for entertainment of friends or professional associates, to accommodate a disgruntled customer, or as a promotional gift certificate. Steward sales represent food sold to an employee, manager, or owner at cost. The cost of food sold is calculated by subtracting the credit total (B) from the debit total (A).

The **total food sales** is the sum total of all food sales for the period, which has typically been recorded on a **daily sales report** (see Table 16-3). The total food sales are then recorded on the food cost report. Finally, the food cost percentage is determined by dividing the cost of food sold by the total food sales and multiplying by 100.

When food cost percentages are calculated with the aid of an **integrated computer system,** the program will often allow for a detailed breakout of specific food cost percentages by different departments. In an integrated computer system, the software and hardware are combined so that an accounting program will include traditional account reports, point-of-sale information, and various types of managerial accounting reports using one or more computer terminals. The percentages reported depend upon the foodservice operation's menu and needs. The list could include meats, poultry, seafood, bakery, dairy, produce, and groceries, as well as nonfood items such as paper products, cleaning supplies, pest control services, building maintenance, taxes and insurance, utilities, advertising and promotion, and administrative expenses. All of these and more, if applicable, are calculated as percentages in relationship to total sales.

This information helps to establish budgeted amounts to spend in relationship to actual or projected net food sales. Often a foodservice manager will decide the food cost dollar amount in relationship to a percentage of total sales, such as 30 percent. This budgeted percentage is then converted into the food cost dollar amount. For example, if the restaurant expects $100,000 in sales for the next month, the food cost budget would be 30 percent of $100,000 ($100,000 × .30) or $30,000.

The Department Food Cost Report

The **department food cost report** does the very same thing as the food cost report. The only difference is that it focuses upon a specific department within a foodservice operation, if more than one exists. The goal is to arrive at an accurate cost of food sold and the food cost percentage for the department.

Employee meal credit
The amount charged for employee meals.

Promotional/free meals
Meals given away by the owner/manager for entertainment of friends or professional associates, to accommodate a disgruntled customer, or as a promotional gift certificate.

Steward sales
Food sold to an employee, manager, or owner at cost.

Total food sales
The sum total of all food sales for the period.

Daily sales report
The form used to record food sales.

Integrated computer system A combination of software and hardware that is combined so that a variety of reports may be generated such as traditional account reports, point-of-sale information, and various types of managerial accounting reports using one or more terminals.

Department food cost report A form used to calculate department food cost percentage.

Table 2-3   Department Food Cost Report

Department __Bagel Shop__   Period Ending __1/17/XX__

DEBITS

Opening Inventory (1/10/XX)	$ 1,235.10
Total Food Requisitions:	
Storeroom	+ 1,918.15
Production Kitchen	+ 2,101.00
Transfers In	+ 78.95
Debit Total	5,333.20 (A)

CREDITS

Closing Inventory (1/17/XX)	$ 1,195.25
Employee Meal Credit	+ 343.00
Promotional/Free Meals	+ 8.00
Transfers Out	+ 33.50
Credit Total	1,579.75 (B)

COST OF FOOD SOLD . . . . $ 3,753.45   (C)
(a – b = c)

TOTAL FOOD SALES $10,958.35

COST OF FOOD SOLD
$3,753.45

(divide) ÷   =

FOOD COST PERCENTAGE
.343 × 100 = 34.3 %

TOTAL FOOD SALES
$10,958.35

Prepared by _____Clerical_____   Date __1/20/XX__

The importance of departmentalizing is to be able to determine the actual costs for each department. This allows the manager maximum financial control for each department. It removes the possibility of a problem going undetected in a department. Refer to the example in Table 2-3.

Normal food costs can be identified within each department, such as those that may exist within a large hotel. Examples are 25 to 38 percent for a fine-dining restaurant, 25 to 32 percent for a catering department, and 29 to 36 percent for a quick-service food cart.

HOW TO CONSTRUCT A DEPARTMENT FOOD COST REPORT

The department food cost report calls for much of the same information as the food cost report. Instead of purchases being taken from the invoice payment schedule, purchases will be represented by food requisitions from the storeroom, production kitchen, and transfers in.

Requisitions are purchase orders in which foodservice personnel obtain products from designated storage facilities within the business establishment (refer to Chapter 4). A transfer is a document that tracks the movement of products in or out of a department to and from another department (again, refer to Chapter 4). For example, if the formal dining room in a large hotel closes at 9:00 P.M., it can transfer the leftover french rolls to the adjacent family restaurant to be used later that evening. The family restaurant, in turn, can transfer any remaining pies and cakes upon closing to 24-hour room service or a quick-service food cart located in the hotel. In this way, transfers in and out of departments are being documented, and food quality and freshness are being maintained.

SUMMARY

1. Food cost is the dollar amount spent on food that is used in the production of menu items. When this dollar amount is compared as a ratio to sales, a food cost percentage is determined.

2. Food cost percentages vary according to type of menu and service.

3. If the total foodservice operation contains several outlets, such as a formal dining room, family restaurant, fast-food takeout bar, and so on, then each department's food cost should be determined.

4. Increasing or fluctuating food costs can usually be attributed to product cost increases, poorly trained employees, theft, spoilage, waste, incorrect portion sizes, lack of supervision, mathematical errors, or poor accounting practices.

5. The form used to summarize data related to food cost is generally referred to as a food cost report. Data on this form include opening inventory, total food purchases, closing inventory, employee meal credit, promotional/free meals, steward sales, cost of food sold, total food sales, and the food cost percentage.

6. If a department food cost report is used, data include opening inventory, total food requisitions (storeroom, production kitchen, transfers in), closing inventory, employee meal credit, promotional/free meals, transfers out, cost of food sold, total food sales, and food cost percentage.

KEY CONCEPTS

Closing inventory

Daily sales report

Department food cost report

Employee meal credit

Food cost

Food cost percentage

Food cost report

Integrated computer system

Inventory

Inventory sheet

Inventory turnover

Invoice

Invoice payment schedule

Menu mix

Opening inventory

Portion

Promotional free meals

Requisition

Steward sales

Suppliers

Total food sales

Transfer

DISCUSSION QUESTIONS AND EXERCISES

1. Explain the following statement: "At the heart of earning a profit in a foodservice operation is the ability of the manager to control food cost."

2. What do managers take into consideration when deciding what food cost percentage they should use for their operations?

3. In Table 2-1, what type of restaurant seems to have the lowest food cost? The highest food cost?

4. What is the purpose of food cost control?

5. What is a food cost report?

6. How often should a food cost report be completed?

7. What are the possible actions that a foodservice manager can take when product costs unexpectedly and rapidly increase?

8. The dining room of a large restaurant operation closes at 10:00 P.M. and its lounge closes at 2:00 A.M. State laws mandate that lounge operations must offer hot food items, so the restaurant cooks up a batch of chicken just before closing time. The cooked chicken is then taken to the lounge where it is kept in a warmer. The restaurant uses a department food cost report. The restaurant also uses a transfer form to track the transactions between the dining room and the lounge. At the end of the month the food cost seems high in the dining room. What could be the problem?

9. Given the following information, fill out a food cost report (see Appendix A for a blank form). Physical inventory taken on 2/21/xx was valued at $2,475; physical inventory taken on 2/28/xx was $2,895. Total food purchases, taken from invoices, were $7,060; steward sales were $125.35; employee meal credit during the period was $745.25; promotional/free meals were $325.00; and sales for the period were $15,540.

10. Given the following information, complete a department food cost report for a sandwich shop–deli (see Appendix A for a blank form). Physical inventory taken on 3/31/xx was valued at $1,275; physical

inventory taken on 4/7/xx was $1,985. Total food requisitions were as follows: storeroom, $2,345; production kitchen, $2,285; and transfers in were $695.00. Also, transfers out were $435.35; employee meal credit, $600.55; promotional/free meals, $175.00; and sales for the period were $10,255.

3

Inventory Management

■ ■ ■ ■ ■ ■ ■ ■ ■ ■ ■ ■ ■ ■

Learning Objectives

After reading this chapter and completing the discussion questions and exercises, you should be able to:

1. Defend the argument that inventory should be taken on the same day of the week and at the same time of the accounting period.

2. Discuss how to keep storage areas organized.

3. Understand the concepts of inventory rotation, especially FIFO.

4. Identify the components of an inventory item description.

5. Describe how inventory should be taken for efficiency, speed, convenience, and accuracy.

6. Calculate inventory extensions, allowing for large price fluctuations that may occur within certain commodities, such as meat products.

7. Describe perpetual inventory.

8. Describe how to calculate an inventory turnover rate.

9. Discuss why, if food cost percentages are significantly higher than they should be, the inventory turnover may be too low.

10. Explain why inventory should be large enough to avoid running out of products, yet small enough to be properly rotated.

11. Understand that inventory turnover rates depend upon the type of foodservice operation and its location.

About Inventory Management

Success in managing a foodservice inventory, small or large, is essentially a matter of how well the foodservice manager comprehends the importance of the dollar investment in the inventory. The investment can range from a few hundred dollars for a small quickservice operation to tens of thousands of dollars for a large foodservice operation.

The financial investment in both food and nonfood items represents the goods that will be processed and sold at a profit. If the goods are wasted, mismanaged, stolen, or allowed to spoil, the profit potential will shrink. If the profit shrinks too much, the foodservice operation's future may be threatened.

Good inventory management is at the beginning of the foodservice manager's quest to control and manage food cost. This chapter will clearly demonstrate efficient ways to accomplish the goal of effective inventory management.

Inventory Storage

Inventory storage
Storage may be for a matter of hours or for several months, depending upon the characteristics of the products.

Every piece of merchandise must be placed somewhere and kept for a period of time. The orderly placement of merchandise is essential so that it can be easily found, retrieved, and issued. In some cases the storage period may be only for a matter of hours. In other cases it may be several months. The period of time and conditions for the storage of the product are governed by the characteristics of the product itself.

Perishable goods
Food items that will spoil in a short period of time if not stored properly.

Dry goods
Food items packed in cans, bags, plastic, and so on, that can be stored at room temperature.

Paper goods
Items such as napkins, cups, lids, straws, film wrap, and toilet tissue.

Par amount
A predetermined level or number of an item kept in inventory.

Collectively, all items used (**perishable goods, dry goods,** beverages, **paper goods,** and so on) in the production of the menu are referred to as *inventory.* Dairy, meat, and other perishable products are more difficult to control. It is recommended that the storage of perishable merchandise be centralized—that is, that all merchandise of the same type be stored in one location. Often this is not feasible, since several departments may need the same item.

For example, each foodservice location in a large sports arena may need fresh milk, with each location requiring a specific minimum stock. Occasionally, one location may suddenly find itself with a surplus of milk or another may find itself short. The recommended procedure is to maintain a minimum **par amount** (see Chapters 4 and 5) at each location and to store the major supply in one central location. The products issued from this central location are tracked by the use of requisitions or transfers, and are accounted for in the same manner as issues from the storeroom.

The purpose of properly managing dry goods is the same as for perishable goods. The basic difference is that dry goods usually are not as expensive as perishable goods and by their nature are easier to store and monitor. Even so, foodservice managers must carefully rotate dry-goods inventories and manage their use.

Introduction to Inventory Management

Inventory management
The process of keeping enough physical inventory on hand so that customers' needs are met without spending more than necessary.

Physical inventory
The actual amount of inventory that has been physically counted and physically exists in storage.

Accounting period
A standardized time period (day, week, month, and so on) between the tabulation of accounting records.

Inventory management is the process of keeping enough physical inventory on hand so that customers' needs are met without spending more than necessary. Inventory management also involves controlling the inventory so that it does not sell out and is stored properly in designated locations.

Inventory management starts with taking **physical inventory** at the close of an **accounting period.** An accounting period can be one day, one week, one month, three months, and so on. Taking inventory means an actual hands-on count of every item stored in the foodservice operation. Taking physical inventory can be a fairly easy task to complete. The task, to be accurate, should follow an established procedure. After physical inventory is taken, the dollar value of the inventory must be established. This information is used to calculate inventory cost for an accounting period.

Determining physical inventory and calculating its value at the close of an accounting period is referred to as a **periodic inventory system.** This is different from a **perpetual inventory system,** described later in the chapter. The distinction between a periodic inventory system and a perpetual inventory system is that a periodic system calculates the value of inventory at the end of an accounting period and a perpetual system calculates the value of inventory each time an item is either used or added to inventory.

The rest of this chapter deals with managing food inventory. Alcoholic beverage inventory and inventory management systems used in a bar or lounge are covered in Chapter 11.

Periodic inventory system
A way of tracking inventory at the end of an accounting period.

Perpetual inventory system   A continuous way of tracking inventory.

When to Take Inventory

Inventory should be taken during a practical time. Many foodservice managers will take inventory when the foodservice operation is closed. This may be either in the late evening or in the early morning. While that certainly is a good time, it may not be the most practical. Taking inventory after the foodservice operation closes may require paying overtime wages and inconveniencing employees. Also, it is impossible for a 24-hours-a-day operation to close just to take inventory. Therefore, many managers prefer to take inventory during slow periods of the business day. Slow periods often are times such as between 9:00 and 11:00 A.M. or between 1:30 and 4:30 P.M. This is the only alternative for the 7-days-a-week, 24-hours-a-day operations.

When inventory is taken during the business day, it is important to remember three critical points:

1. Establish a consistent day and time that the inventory is to be taken within the accounting period. For example, inventory is taken every Friday at 10:00 A.M. if done weekly. Doing this will ensure consistent reporting of calculated food cost percentages. It creates a standard period of time so that inventory information can be accurately measured and compared. If a manager decides to take inventory on another day, or perhaps on the same day but at 3:00 P.M. instead of at 10:00 A.M., the inventory amount reported would not be standardized. There would be additional sales and perhaps additional products to consider. Doing this would make the inventory information not exactly comparable with that of the previous week (period), resulting in fluctuating food cost percentages. Consistent information must be used to properly analyze what is going on in the foodservice operation.

2. Do not schedule or accept deliveries during the time that the inventory is being taken.

3. Inventory the food in actual production. An accurate dollar amount must be assigned to the food that is being prepared in the kitchen,

FIGURE 3-1
Storeroom Shelves   Products in this storeroom are categorized and alphabetized.

food that is being held in refrigerated reach-in boxes, and food on the steam table. Other difficult items to count, such as spices, must also be assigned a fixed dollar amount. For example, all opened spices may have cost $72.00 unopened. The manager may assume that all of the spice containers will average being half full. Thus, an average of $36.50 will be assigned as the dollar value of all opened spices. This dollar amount will be used until the manager believes that significant price increases have occurred or until the number of spices being used has changed.

How to Take Inventory

Before taking inventory, storage areas should be organized according to the type of products to be stored. This means that canned and dry goods are kept in one area; produce, dairy, and other perishables are kept in refrigerated reach-ins and/or walk-ins; and frozen items are kept in the freezer. In each area, the manager should categorize and alphabetize products as much as possible. Also, if possible, label each shelf under the item so that items cannot be easily misplaced. Every storage area, if more than one is used, should be organized. For example, a coffee shop may keep its inventory separate from the **storeroom** within a large hotel or resort property. Refer to Figure 3-1 for a picture of a storeroom showing how shelves should be organized.

Another important part of managing inventory is to rotate stock. As items are added to inventory, the items already in stock should be used before the newer items. This process is referred to as **FIFO**, an acronym for *first in, first out*.

Storeroom
An area where quantities of food and nonfood items are kept.

FIFO
An acronym standing for *first in, first out*, a process of rotating inventory so that the first items purchased are the first items used in the kitchen.

Inventory should be taken by two people. One person conducts the hands-on count and calls out the quantity and product name. The other person writes the quantity numbers on the inventory sheet or enters counts into a hand-held computer device designed for inventory management. This procedure maximizes efficiency, speed, convenience, and accuracy.

The process of taking inventory follows the format of the inventory sheet shown in Table 3-1. The products on the inventory sheets should be listed as the products appear on the shelves. Figure 3-2 shows a computer-generated inventory sheet; Figure 3-3, a computer-generated category summary sheet.

ITEM DESCRIPTION

The inventory sheet demonstrates how to categorize and alphabetize products. The item description is in the first column of the inventory sheet, showing the categories of juices, fruits, and vegetables, with the items alphabetized within each category. If the same item appears in different unit sizes, or at a significantly different price, it should be listed and counted separately. An example is tomato juice, which is shown in two different can sizes. A few blank lines should be left between product categories to allow adequate space to write in any price or unit size difference as well as new products that may be added.

UNIT

The Unit column is used to list the sizes of the individual items. The example units are for various can sizes. Units may be in pounds, cans, or any other unit of measurement.

QUANTITY

The Quantity column lists the physical count of items that make up the inventory. Occasionally, unit size and quantity may be confused. For example, flour is usually listed by pounds instead of bags. The person counting may say "four," meaning four 25-pound bags of flour, instead of "one hundred," the number of pounds of flour. The inventory would be short by 96 pounds.

PRICE

The Price column shows the individual price of each unit. To calculate the price per unit, it is essential to know the price of the items according to how they were purchased. For example, a 25-pound bag of cake flour may cost $6.90. The unit price could be listed as the cost of one pound of cake flour, or it may be listed as the cost of one 25-pound bag of cake flour. It is important to list the unit consistently by the pound or by the bag. If the unit chosen is by the pound, then the total price of the bag, $6.90, would be divided by the number of pounds in the bag, 25. Thus, $6.90 divided by 25 would be $.276 per pound. Another example could be fruit cocktail. The unit size may be #10 cans. Assume a case of fruit cocktail costs $26.46. Usually fruit cocktail is packed six #10 cans to the case. Thus, if the unit is one can, then the $26.46 is divided by 6, resulting in a unit price of $4.41 per can.

Table 3-1 Inventory Sheet

Date	1/17/XX	Page	1 of 12
Time	10:00 A.M.	Department	Storeroom
Taken by	Storeroom Manager	Location	Shelves (Canned Goods)
(and)	Assistant	Priced by	Storeroom Manager
Approved by	Owner/Manager	Extended by	Clerical

ITEM DESCRIPTION	UNIT	QUANTITY	PRICE		EXTENSION	
JUICES:						
Apple	46 oz	8	1	49	11	92
Grape	64 oz	9	3	18	28	62
Grapefruit	46 oz	14	1	17	16	38
Grapefruit - Pink	46 oz	16	1	22	19	52
Pineapple	46 oz	12	1	17	14	04
Tomato	46 oz	15		96	14	40
Tomato	5.5 oz	21		27	5	67
V-8	5.5 oz	19		27	5	13
FRUITS:						
Fruit Cocktail	#10	13	4	41	57	33
Peaches-Halves	#10	7	3	98	27	86
Peaches-Sliced	#10	15	3	86	57	90
Pears-Halves	#10	6	3	87	23	22
VEGETABLES:						
Beets-Shoestring	#10	6	3	05	18	30
Beets-Sliced	#10	9	2	62	23	58
PAGE TOTAL					$ 323	87

```
                      Physical Inventory Worksheet
                        Foodservice Profitability

Inventory Item                  Quantity        Cost per Unit          Extension
Fruits
fruit cocktail                    13         $4.41/#10  cans            $57.33
peaches- halves                    7         $3.98/#10  cans            $27.86
peaches - sliced                  15         $3.86/#10  cans            $57.90
pears - halves                     6         $3.87/#10  cans            $23.22

Juices
juice, apple                       8         $1.49/46 oz ca            $11.92
juice, grape                       9         $3.18/64 fl oz            $28.62
juice, grapefruit                 14         $1.17/46 oz ca            $16.38
juice, grapefruit pink            16         $1.22/46 oz ca            $19.52
juice, pineapple                  12         $1.17/46 oz ca            $14.04
juice, tomato                     15         $0.96/46 oz ca            $14.40
juice, tomato 5.5 oz              21         $0.27/5.5 fl o            $5.67
juice, V8                         19         $0.27/5.5 fl o            $5.13

Vegetables
beets - shoestring                 6         $3.05/#10  cans            $18.30
beets - sliced                     9         $2.62/#10  cans            $23.58
```

FIGURE 3-2
Computer-Generated Inventory Sheet

At this point, it is important to recognize that not all purchases are made at the same price. Prices for certain commodities can fluctuate, even within a given week. For example:

Ground beef, **NAMP** #136 (North American Meat Processors Association, specification number 136) may have a Monday delivery price of $1.89 per pound for 50 pounds and a Wednesday delivery price of $2.29 per pound for 125 pounds. The difference is a $.40-per-pound increase in price. The $2.29-per-pound price would be listed on the inventory sheet as being the most current cost. If the inventory was taken on Friday and the physical count on hand was 65 pounds, then using $2.29 would provide the accurate price. If for some reason only a small portion of the ground beef was actually used and the inventory reflected 160 pounds on hand, the ground beef should then be listed twice at the two separate prices, as follows: 35 pounds at $1.89, 125 pounds at $2.29. This provides for complete accuracy in identifying the actual cost of products. However, if the price difference between Monday and Wednesday was only three cents, using the higher price would be acceptable.

NAMP
The North American Meat Processors Association has an established set of industry standards/specifications for meat ordering and purchasing.

```
                      Physical Inventory Worksheet
                        Foodservice Profitability

Inventory Item                  Quantity        Cost per Unit          Extension

Fruits subtotal ...............................................        $166.31
Juices subtotal ...............................................        $115.68
Vegetables subtotal ...........................................        $ 41.88

Grand total ...................................................        $323.87
```

FIGURE 3-3
Computer-Generated Inventory Category Summary Sheet

A small degree of accuracy is lost, but this may be fine, as the increase was so minor.

Extreme caution is emphasized so as not to become too liberal in taking shortcuts. Good judgment coupled with inventory-taking experience will allow the process to become automatic.

EXTENSION

Extension
The dollar value of inventory, determined by multiplying the price by the quantity.

An **extension** is calculated by multiplying the unit price by the quantity. The unit price is the cost of each unit. The quantity, as mentioned before, is the physical count. Multiplying these two figures equals the extension dollar amount. This shows the total amount of money in inventory for that particular item.

After each inventory item extension has been calculated, the extensions should be added. The total is the dollar value of all inventory. This dollar amount is used to calculate food cost and food cost percentages. Upon completion of the inventory, it is important to check for mathematical accuracy. The most common errors occur in calculating extensions.

Book Value versus Actual Value

Book value
The value of the inventory calculated from invoices minus what was used during the accounting period.

A method for double-checking the value of inventory is to compare the **book value** of the inventory with the actual physical count value. The book value is the value of the inventory calculated from invoices minus what was used during the accounting period. Computers have made the calculation of book value fairly easy to accomplish. A comparison between book value and physical count value should be made, and the total amounts for both should be close. The book value typically is larger because the amount on the books usually does not account for some of the small losses due to human error and losses during the processing of food products as a result of shrinkage. Book value is determined as follows:

Opening inventory (closing inventory for previous accounting period)		$4,230.00
Purchases	+	3,780.00
Subtotal		8,010.00
Requisitions	−	4,125.00
Book value (closing inventory for current period)		$3,885.00
Actual physical inventory value	−	3,862.15
Difference (variance)		$ 22.85

When a wider than acceptable difference occurs between book value and physical inventory value, it can usually be attributed to one or more of the following factors:

1. Mathematical mistakes or incorrect counts.
2. Large cost/price fluctuations.
3. Products issued without requisitions (further discussed in Chapter 4).
4. Theft.

■ ■ ■ ■ ■

Table 3-2   Spoilage Report

Spoilage Report		
Department __Kitchen__	Date __4/21/XX__	
	Prepared by __Storeroom Manager__	
QUANTITY/ITEM DESCRIPTION	**PRICE**	**EXPLANATION**
¼ box lemons	$ 6.50	Moldy - obtain credit
TOTAL	$6.50	

5. Products that spoiled and were tossed out without the dollar amounts being recorded.

REGARDING THEFT

Most foods do not have high values in relationship to weight or volume, with the exception of meats and some seafoods. Few people will bother to steal low-dollar-value items, since the risk of being caught far outweighs the value of the product. Of the several thousand items kept in stock in many restaurants, only about 10 percent of them have high dollar values. Management's efforts to secure items from theft or pilferage should concentrate primarily on these items.

This does not mean that normal security should be ignored. But just as with liquors, special locked areas should be assigned to key items, with a limited number of personnel allowed access to these areas. Since most of the items of high dollar value require similar types of storage conditions (refrigerated or frozen) or perhaps occupy limited space (as with jars of caviar), it becomes fairly simple to give priority ratings to these types of merchandise and to set up accurate control systems to account for all items. A separate freezer with locks and limited access should be maintained for high-value foods (meats and seafoods), while one with unlimited access is acceptable for low-value items, such as frozen french fries or vegetables.

REGARDING SPOILAGE

Foodservice managers should keep spoilage to a minimum by the proper rotation of goods, but natural spoilage and shrinkage does occur. The simplest method to document spoilage is to report an item spoiled or damaged on a separate **spoilage report** (see Table 3-2). The manager should closely watch this figure to ensure that no excessive amounts of spoilage occur. Note that this form may generate a request for credit forwarded to the appropriate supplier.

Spoilage report
Report that documents spoiled or damaged items.

Perpetual Inventory System

A perpetual inventory system constantly informs the foodservice manager of the current situation of any products kept in inventory. It is a continuous way of tracking inventory. If the manager wants to know how much apple juice is on hand at any given time, he/she looks at the perpetual inventory chart (see Table 3-3).

A **bin card** may also be used. A bin card is a smaller version of a perpetual inventory chart. Due to the difficulty and cost of managing a perpetual inventory system, its use is somewhat limited to foodservice operations that have installed computer equipment and software to manage the system.

There are two primary purposes for using a perpetual inventory system. First, it ensures that enough inventory is available to prepare menu items at all times. Second, it allows the manager to constantly be aware of the status and value of every inventory item.

Most perpetual inventory systems are really modifications of calculating the book value of inventory. To ensure that the perpetual system is working, an actual inventory should be taken periodically. That way the manager can be assured that the perpetual system is accurate.

HOW A PERPETUAL INVENTORY SYSTEM WORKS

Each item in inventory has a perpetual inventory chart. Every addition to the existing inventory through purchases is recorded, and, in turn, every item requisitioned for use is subtracted from the chart. Although this system represents extreme control and accuracy, it requires dedication and the ability to record and recalculate every time a transaction occurs.

This task may be made easier by using scanning devices. Scanning devices usually look like a pistol that is connected by a cord to a computerlike calculator (as seen in grocery stores). All the operator has to do is point the device at the Uniform Product Code (UPC) symbol on the side of the package and pull the trigger (some units do not use a trigger). The UPC symbol is a series of lines of various widths that represent a number associated with the product. As the scanner reads the UPC number, the price value and the product identification is recorded. The person using the device then enters on the keypad the number of units on hand. This information is recorded on a tape or disk. The information on the tape or disk is then entered into the computer using specially designed application software. The computer compiles the extensions and generates the needed reports. This system is used by several large foodservice chains and by some large foodservice distributors, but only within product categories to which the system can be applied.

Keeping the Right Inventory in the Right Place

Regardless of whether a periodic or perpetual inventory system is used, the department and location should be listed on the inventory sheet for ease and convenience in taking the inventory. If there are several departments, the

■ ■ ■ ■ ■

Table 3-3   Perpetual Inventory Chart

Location:	Bagel Shop						

Item: Apple Juice	Unit: 46 oz.						

DATE	BEGINNING	ADDITIONS	DELETIONS	ENDING	UNIT PRICE	EXTENSION	INITIAL
1/10/XX	9	0	2	7	$ 1.49	$10.43	sm
1/11/XX	7	0	2	5	1.49	7.45	sm
1/12/XX	5	0	2	3	1.49	4.47	sm
1/13/XX	3	0	2	1	1.49	1.49	sm
1/14/XX	1	12	1	12	1.49	17.88	sm
1/15/XX	12	0	1	11	1.49	16.39	sm
1/16/XX	11	0	1	10	1.49	14.90	sm
1/17/XX	10	0	2	8	1.49	11.92	sm

different inventories could be color coded—for example, white paper for the storeroom, blue paper for the bagel shop, and yellow for the dining room. Color coding would make the different inventories easily identifiable.

The original copy of the completed inventory should be sent to the manager's office as a permanent record. A duplicate copy could be used in the storeroom for reference in preparation for the next period's inventory as well as in the pricing of requisitions.

Inventory Turnover

Unlike inventories for other types of industries, the size of inventories that are maintained in foodservice operations relate not only to keeping up the quality of the inventory (avoiding spoilage, ensuring freshness, and so on), but also to the amounts required to be in process to meet the level of usage (sales). Ideally, inventories should be reduced to a controlled minimum, since an inventory ties up capital.

Inventories allow for the fact that some time is needed to process goods (cooking, preparation, and so on) and that there will be a period of time between delivery and sale. With highly perishable goods, this period is kept to a minimum. Deliveries of this type of merchandise are more frequent, and are often made daily. In some cases, the size of the storeroom facilities dictates that increased delivery frequency be maintained. In other cases, a larger storeroom combined with the nonperishability of the product permits larger inventories to be stocked.

Inventory turnover rate The number of times that the total inventory is used during a given accounting period.

The appropriate **inventory turnover rate** is directly related to product usage. Some inventory products will be used more and others less. An inventory should be large enough to avoid running out of products during peak business times, yet small enough to be properly rotated. Rotating the inventory means that the products on the inventory shelves should be used within 1 to 28 days for most items.

Stockouts A term indicating that there is no more of a particular item in stock.

A well-planned inventory balance is critical in order to avoid frequent small-quantity buying or **stockouts.** Small-quantity buying can result in higher unit costs for products as well as additional labor and processing expenses. It can also become stressful and difficult to have to make special trips to a wholesale grocer to pick up the out-of-inventory items. In contrast, too large of an inventory may result in unnecessary product spoilage or deterioration, as well as too much money tied up in inventory.

HOW TO CALCULATE INVENTORY TURNOVER RATE

An inventory turnover rate can be calculated as follows:

$$\frac{\text{Cost of food sold}}{\text{Average inventory cost}} = \text{Inventory turnover rate}$$

Average inventory cost The beginning and ending inventory added together and divided by two.

The cost of food sold can be taken from the food cost report. The **average inventory cost** is determined by adding the opening and closing inventory for the period and dividing the total by two.

The cost of food sold divided by the average inventory cost equals the inventory turnover rate. Using average inventory helps minimize the impact of low and high inventory counts over the period of time being analyzed. The following is an example of how to calculate inventory turnover.

Suppose the food cost report for the first week of May indicates a closing inventory of $10,000. This means that the opening inventory for the second week of May is also $10,000. The food cost report for the end of the one-week period indicates a closing inventory of $12,000. The actual amount spent on food for the period (cost of food sold), was $11,500. The average inventory for the period is the sum of the opening and closing inventories divided by two. This is calculated as follows: Opening inventory ($10,000) plus closing inventory ($12,000) equals $22,000. $22,000 is then divided by 2, resulting in an average inventory of $11,000 ($22,000 ÷ 2 = $11,000).

Using these numbers, the average inventory turnover is calculated as follows:

$$\frac{\$11,500 \text{ (Cost of food sold)}}{\$11,000 \text{ (Average inventory cost)}} = 1.04 \text{ (Inventory turnover rate)}$$

The number 1.04 means that the entire inventory turned over one time during the accounting period. Most of the time the inventory turnover figure is actually reported in decimals such as 1.04. The precision of the number may not be that important. If a figure of 1.04 is calculated, it can be rounded down to 1. If the figure is 1.83, it can be rounded up to 2. This depends upon the degree of emphasis that the foodservice manager places upon decimal reporting.

HOW TO USE INVENTORY TURNOVER INFORMATION

A careful foodservice manager wants to keep inventory turnover from being too high or too low. To do so, he or she must strike a balance between product stockouts and increased food costs. If the operation receives deliveries frequently, does not have any outages, and is hitting its target food cost percentage, then the inventory turnover is probably acceptable; there is a balance between how much food needs to be prepared and the amount of food kept in inventory.

If the foodservice operation is constantly running out of products, however, the result will be unhappy customers and a stressed service staff. The inventory turnover rate may be as high as 7, with frequent shortages. If this happens, the amount of food needed for preparation and what is kept in inventory is out of balance. The inventory should be examined and perhaps increased to a point where shortages and/or stockouts no longer occur.

If the inventory turnover has slowed to .5 and the cost of goods sold went up, it is possible that the cost of managing inventory has gone up. Some of the costs of managing inventory could be spoilage, deterioration, and products becoming dehydrated in the freezer.

As a general rule, the value of the total food inventory should equal about 1½ times the weekly consumption of food. If an establishment consumes (at cost) $10,000 worth of food per week, the average inventory should be $15,000. This allows for safety factors to preclude stockouts and helps to reduce the amount of time spent ordering and processing deliveries. This equals an inventory turnover of about 35 times per year.

If inventories are larger than this (except in unusual cases where the establishment is located in a remote area and deliveries are made infrequently), the result will often be excess losses due to spoilage, excess capital tied up in inventory, and perhaps waste due to carelessness if controls have not been established.

If inventories are too small, extra time must be spent ordering, stockouts will occur, goods may be improperly processed, and extra labor will be required to ensure that food is processed in a timely fashion.

For different product lines, the following inventory amounts are recommended:

Bakery, produce, meat, fish, poultry, dairy products	2-day supply
Frozen products	1-week supply
Canned or dry goods	1½- to 2-week supply
Other nonperishable low-value items, paper goods	2- to 4-week supply

SUMMARY

1. Inventory management is the process of keeping enough inventory on hand so that customers' needs are met without spending more than necessary. The foodservice manager must properly account for inventory, store inventory, and assess the value of inventory.

2. When inventory appears to be misvalued, it is usually due to mathematical mistakes, large cost/price fluctuations, products issued without requisitions, theft, and/or products that spoiled and were tossed out without the dollar amounts being recorded.

3. A tool for tracking the use of inventory is the inventory turnover rate. This is the number of times that the inventory is completely used during the accounting period. The rate is dependent upon the type of foodservice operation. A rate that is too low means that food may be spoiling; a rate that is too high may result in product stockouts during peak business hours.

KEY CONCEPTS

Accounting period	NAMP
Average inventory cost	Paper goods
Bin card	Par amount
Book value	Periodic inventory system
Dry goods	Perishable goods
Extension	Perpetual inventory system
FIFO	Physical inventory
Inventory management	Spoilage report
Inventory storage	Stockout
Inventory turnover rate	Storeroom

DISCUSSION QUESTIONS AND EXERCISES

1. What are the possible problems that might occur in calculating the value of inventory if it is not taken on the same day of the week and at the same time of the accounting period?

2. What are the three critical points to remember when inventory is taken during the business day?

3. Describe how inventory should be physically counted.

4. What information should be present on an inventory sheet?

5. Determine the book value difference if an operation has an opening inventory of $3,500, purchases during the period of $3,000, requisitions of $3,400, and actual physical inventory value of $3,050.

6. Describe the advantages and problems of using a perpetual inventory system.

7. How does a perpetual inventory system work?

8. If the foodservice operation is not running out of food and the food cost percentage is on target, what is occurring?

9. What is the acceptable number of days that inventory should be held?

10. Why will the turnover rate be low if an operation maintains too high an inventory?

11. Explain how average inventory cost is calculated.

12. If the opening inventory is $3,000, the closing inventory is $7,000, and the cost of food sold is $27,000, what is the turnover rate?

13. Arrange with a foodservice manager in your community to help count a physical inventory.

14. Calculate the extensions for the inventory listed on the sample inventory sheet that follows.

15. Discuss the ideal size of inventory that should be maintained. Explain why.

16. Set up a control system for low-value and high-value merchandise.

Inventory

Date	1/17/XX	Page	1 of 12
Time	10:00 A.M.	Department	Storeroom
Taken by	Storeroom Manager	Location	Shelves (Canned Goods)
(and)	Assistant	Priced by	Storeroom Manager
Approved by	Owner/Manager	Extended by	Clerical

ITEM DESCRIPTION	UNIT	QUANTITY	PRICE		EXTENSION	
JUICES:						
Apple	46 oz	10	1	49		
Grape	64 oz	19	3	18		
Grapefruit	46 oz	12	1	17		
Grapefruit - Pink	46 oz	14	1	22		
Pineapple	46 oz	21	1	17		
Tomato	46 oz	13		96		
Tomato	5.5 oz	20		27		
V-8	5.5 oz	18		27		
FRUITS:						
Fruit Cocktail	#10	12	4	41		
Peaches-Halves	#10	8	3	98		
Peaches-Sliced	#10	11	3	86		
Pears-Halves	#10	3	3	87		
VEGETABLES:						
Beets-Shoestring	#10	5	3	05		
Beets-Sliced	#10	8	2	62		
PAGE TOTAL				$		

4

Requisitions and Transfers

■　　　■　　　■　　　■　　　■　　　■　　　■　　　■　　　■　　　■ 　　■　　■　　■

Learning Objectives

After reading this chapter and completing the discussion questions and exercises, you should be able to:

1. Decide how a requisition should be used if the foodservice operation has several departments within one property (such as a large hotel or resort, sports arena, or health care center) or is a unit in a chain that is part of a central storage distribution center.

2. Understand and describe how a par amount requisition system should be used if the foodservice unit has a high-volume business.

3. Comprehend how a requisition system keeps the foodservice operation from having stockouts during peak business times.

4. Recognize that accurately completed transfers are used similarly to requisitions.

5. Describe the use of a transfer to keep track of the movement of products from one department or unit to another within a foodservice operation.

About Requisitions

Requisitions are a simple way of preparing a grocery list, much like the person who is sent to the supermarket with a list of items to purchase for dinner. If the person going to the market is buying items for two different people, then two lists are needed, along with two receipts and separate cash envelopes to keep the change separate.

A requisition system accomplishes the same goal and is best suited for large foodservice operations with more than one department (for example, a hotel that has a dining room with a separate coffee shop). The function of the system is to separate the food and nonfood items used by each department, so that the costs can be assigned and identified within each category and department (see Figure 4-1).

FIGURE 4-1
Requisition Process

1. A requisition is prepared by the department needing products

2. The requisition is sent to the storeroom

3. Food items are put on a service cart and sent to the requisitioning department

4. The department receives the products

It is necessary to identify the costs directly associated with each department so that a food cost report can be prepared for each one. A dining room will generally offer different menu items at typically higher prices than a coffee shop. The hours of operation may be different. Also, different cooks and managers may be involved. All of these factors and more will result in different food costs.

When the food cost for each department falls within an acceptable range that allows for the anticipated profit, the foodservice operation is running smoothly. If the food cost is not within the acceptable range, management should quickly determine the cause. This chapter will discuss the use of requisitions designed to meet the specific needs of any type of foodservice operation.

Requisition Defined

Requisition
A written order to obtain products from the shelves of the storeroom, the walk-in refrigerator, or the freezer.

A **requisition** is a written order to obtain products from the shelves of the storeroom, the walk-in refrigerator, or the freezer. A requisitioning system controls and tracks the movement and use of all products within a foodservice operation. Requisitions are typically used in large-volume foodservice operations with units that are part of hotels, resorts, health care providers, large country clubs, and other organizations with multiple foodservice locations. These operations have multiple departments, such as a bagel shop, dining room, catering service, snack bar, and so on. Basically, requisitions are in-house documents used to track the use of raw food products and nonfood products.

The manner in which requisitions are used depends upon the size of the operation. In smaller foodservice operations, requisitions are usually completed by the executive chef or kitchen manager and turned in to the manager or owner. In larger foodservice operations, requisitions may be filled out by **line cooks, sous chefs,** or **executive chefs** and turned in to a storeroom manager. The storeroom manager is in charge of all stores, both food and nonfood, and will issue the items to the requesting department.

PAR AMOUNT REQUISITION

A requisition can be prepared in two basic formats. The first is called a **par amount requisition.** The par amount requisition is a preprinted requisition sheet with par amounts (a predetermined level or numbers of an item kept in inventory) assigned to each inventory item in regular use. This can easily be done when dealing with a department such as a snack bar with a fixed, limited menu, or a unit within a department that uses a fixed amount of products, such as a coffee shop that repeatedly uses juices, postmix (a method of dispensing carbonated beverages), and pies. (See Table 4-1.)

The par amount requisition is a list of all the products that the department uses, which are listed under "Item Description." It also lists the unit size when applicable. A par amount is established on the basis of usage and in anticipation of sales. However, it is important to note that if there is a large banquet or a special event in the community, sales will be higher than normal, so the par amounts will have to be temporarily increased.

If the par amount is maintained, there should always be an adequate amount of products available. The manager must keep in mind that the par amount must be continually adjusted as sales increase or decrease. Also, the manager should make adjustments for certain days of the week that may be busier than others. The par amount requisition can be one page or several pages in length. It can also be used in conjunction with **blank requisitions.**

The uniqueness of the par amount requisition is that it reduces the risk of omitting items used during the peak periods such as breakfast, lunch, or dinner. By avoiding shortages or stockouts during the rush hours, the employees will experience less stress and customer satisfaction is further assured.

The par amount requisition example in Table 4-1 shows some stock items that a coffee shop would typically replenish daily at 10:00 A.M., a slow period following breakfast and before lunch. As shown in the example, juices are to be restocked after the morning breakfast rush. The juice will thus be in place and properly chilled for the next morning. Postmix and fresh pies will be in place for lunch and dinner business. This will keep up a balance of product quality, freshness, and ready availability. The best time to prepare the requisition is during the slow periods. Typically, slow times to conveniently restock are between 10:00 and 11:00 A.M. and 2:00 to 4:00 P.M. Foodservice managers should use whatever time best suits the foodservice operation.

The on-hand amount on the par amount requisition is the physical count of the item kept in the appropriate storage area. To determine the order, subtract the on-hand number from the par. The (unit cost) price for each item is

Line cook
A station cook is responsible for preparing the bulk of the food served to guests.

Sous chef
Answers to the executive chef and is second in command, may schedule line cooks and help them as necessary.

Executive chef
Responsible for all kitchen operations.

Par amount requisition
A preprinted requisition sheet with par amounts assigned to each inventory item in regular use.

Blank requisition
A blank form that is filled in with the items that are needed.

Table 4-1 Par Amount Requisition

Date	1/13/XX	Requisition Number	524
Time	10:00 A.M.	Department	Coffee Shop
Prepared by	Coffee Shop Manager	Priced by	Storeroom Manager
Delivered by	Busperson	Extended by	Clerical
Received by	Coffee Shop Manager	Approved by	Owner/Manager

ITEM DESCRIPTION	PAR	ON HAND	ORDER	PRICE		EXTENSION	
JUICES:							
Apple (46 oz)	2	2	0	1	49	-	--
Grapefruit (46 oz)	3	½	2	1	17	2	34
Pineapple (46 oz)	2	1½	0	1	17	-	--
Tomato (46 oz)	3	1	2		96	1	92
V-8 (5.5 oz)	6	2	4		27	1	08
POST-MIX:							
Cola (box)	2	½	2	33	00	66	00
Diet Cola (box)	1	⅔	0	33	00	--	--
Root Beer (box)	1	¼	1	33	00	33	00
Lemon-Lime (box)	1	⅓	1	33	00	33	00
PIES:							
Apple (10 in)	2	0	2	3	60	7	20
Blueberry (10 in)	1	0	1	4	85	4	85
Cherry (10 in)	3	0	3	5	05	15	15
Chocolate (10 in)	1	0	1	4	25	4	25
Lemon (10 in)	2	0	2	4	25	8	50
Boston Creme (9 in)	1	0	1	5	25	5	25
TOTAL						$ 182	54

Original Copy: To remain in the storeroom.
Duplicate Copy: To be returned to the issuing department.

Transfer-Out Department   ⟶   Transfer-In Department
(Example: Dining Room)   (Example: Coffee Shop)

FIGURE 4-2
Transfer Process

taken directly from the most recent invoice, so current pricing is always maintained. Extensions are calculated by multiplying the price by the order.

BLANK REQUISITION

The second requisition format is a blank requisition. The only difference between a par amount requisition and a blank requisition is that the blank one does not have the product items and par amounts preprinted on the form. The manager must fill in the requisition with the items needed, each time they are needed. The blank requisition is used for items that are not needed on a daily basis. An example of a blank requisition is shown in Table 4-2.

Requisitions may be printed with sequential numbers in the same manner as personal checks. The requisition resembles a check written to the storeroom for products. The sequential numbering system allows the manager to track requisitions and how they are used, making it easy to account for every requisition should the potential exist for mishandling or misuse. If a mistake is ever made, as with a bank check, the requisition can be voided, the error recorded, and the next number used. If the potential for mishandling does not exist, preprinted numbers are not necessary. Finally, all requisitions should identify by name the person preparing, delivering, and receiving the products. This will tighten the physical control when theft or sloppy order filling may be a problem.

W hen to Use Transfers

The purpose of a **transfer** is to document the movement of products from one department or unit to another (see Figure 4-2). The difference between a requisition and a transfer is that a requisition is used to document and obtain products from storage areas, while transfers keep track of products that have already been accounted for by a requisition.

A transfer provides a record that accurately tracks costs. For example, an initial cost occurs when the foodservice operation purchases products. The products are then requisitioned from the storeroom to be used in the dining room. After the products are in the dining room, they may be moved to the coffee shop, which is a different department. To track the cost of the product from the dining room department to the coffee shop department, a transfer document like the one in Table 4-3 is used. Generally, transfers should be used in the following situations.

1. *Between departments within the same operation.* For example, when a hospital coffee shop closes at 2:00 A.M., any leftover products such as the dinner special, soup, salad mix, and so on from dinner in the coffee shop could be moved to the hospital employee cafeteria.

Transfer
A document that tracks the movement of products from one department or unit to another to provide an accurate record of costs.

Table 4-2   Blank Requisition

Date 1/13/XX		Requisition Number 357	
Time 6:15 A.M.		Department Kitchen	
Prepared by Chef		Priced by Storeroom Manager	
Delivered by Busperson		Extended by Clerical	
Received by Chef		Approved by Owner/Manager	

ITEM DESCRIPTION	UNIT	QUANTITY	PRICE		EXTENSION	
Lettuce	case	1	11	50	11	50
Tomatoes	box	½	14	75	7	38
Poultry Seasoning	12 oz	1	5	50	5	50
Ground Oregano	15 oz	1	5	53	5	53
Paprika	18 oz	1	4	25	4	25
TOTAL					$34	16

Original Copy: To remain in the storeroom.
Duplicate Copy: To be returned to the issuing department.

Transfers are typically used in hotels, hospitals, schools, country clubs, resorts, chain restaurants, and any type of foodservice operation with multiple departments. Another example is the use of a transfer to track the movement of products from a bar to a kitchen when wine is needed for cooking.

2. *Between units within the same geographic area.* One unit may have a shortage, so it obtains a transfer of items from another nearby unit (for example, a transfer of products between elementary school kitchens when one has a larger or different kind of storage capacity than the other). One school may keep meat in a freezer and another school may have the facilities only to cook it. A transfer would be used to track the movement and cost of the meat from school A to school B. Basically, school A is selling meat to school B. Another example occurs when there are multiple units of a chain. When one unit runs out of product, it obtains what it needs from the other unit by using a transfer.

An established method of handling transfers ensures that all operating areas of a foodservice operation have sufficient products. An effective method may also play a significant role in maintaining product quality and freshness, especially with such items as bakery products. As shown in Table 4-3, if a dining room closes at 9:00 P.M. and an adjoining coffee shop is open until 12:00 A.M., then the pies and cakes can easily be transferred with the opportunity of being sold later that evening.

HOW TO USE A TRANSFER

A transfer is very similar to a requisition, as shown in Table 4-3. The original copy of a transfer should remain with the issuing department and the duplicate copy should be sent to the receiving department. At the close of each shift, each department or unit should turn in copies of all transfers to a designated manager or the accounting office.

In Table 4-3, the dining room manager in a hotel has decided to transfer some pies to the coffee shop. The manager has listed the pies on a transfer in the same manner as on a requisition. The manager keeps one copy of the transfer for the dining room records and the second copy is sent to the coffee shop with the pies. The actual delivery of the pies may be done by a busperson or cook. The original transfer would be included with other papers from the shift, such as charge vouchers, checks, and so on, and given to the manager or the accounting office.

ELECTRONIC REQUISITIONS AND TRANSFERS

The decision to use computers to track requisitions and transfers depends on the foodservice operation's need for immediate access to information and the volume of business. Requisitions and transfers are generally done manually and processed according to specific needs and within established time frames.

Requisitions and transfers may be electronically controlled in a variety of ways. One of the easiest to use is a system of **terminals** at strategic locations. Terminals would be placed in the kitchen, storage area, cook's station,

Terminal
A device that displays information and is used to enter and receive information.

Table 4-3 Transfer

Transfer from	Dining Room		to	Coffee Shop	

Date	1/14/XX	Transfer Number	271
Time	9:15 P.M.	Priced by	Dining Room Manager
Prepared by	Dining Room Manager	Extended by	Clerical
Delivered by	Busperson	Approved by	Owner/Manager
Received by	Coffee Shop Manager		

ITEM DESCRIPTION	UNIT	QUANTITY	PRICE		EXTENSION	
Lemon Pie	10 inch	1	4	25	4	25
Cherry Pie	10 inch	½	5	05	2	53
Pumpkin Cheesecake	16/slice	3 slices	11	78	2	22
TOTAL					$9	00

Original Copy: To remain with the issuing department.
Duplicate Copy: To be sent to the receiving department.

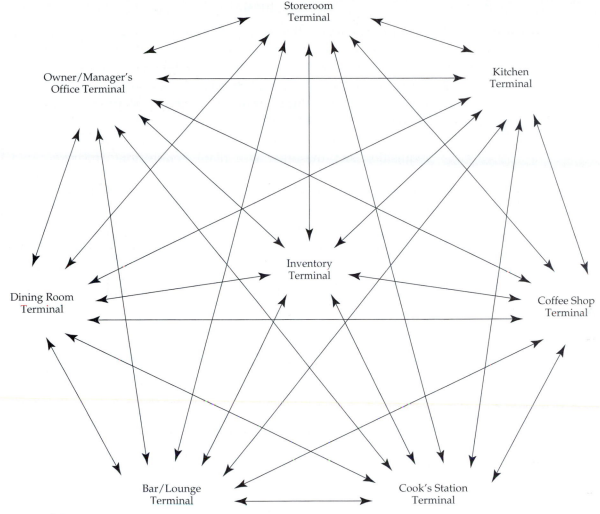

FIGURE 4-3
Requisitions and Transfers Using Computers

dining room, coffee shop, bar or lounge, and any other area or unit that may use a requisition or transfer. In addition, the various terminals would be connected to each other to form a **network**. In a network, the software and hardware used allows all the terminals to communicate with each other.

When a cook needs to take items out of one of the storage areas, he or she records the transaction using the appropriate terminal. When the cook uses the terminal, the requisition or similar form appears on the screen. The description of the item and required information entered. The items and employees involved have identification numbers that are entered to assign accountability to the appropriate person.

The benefit of using computers is that once the identification of the item and the number of units being requested are entered, the computer does the rest of the work. The price and extension are automatically entered and calculated by the computer, and the item is subtracted from inventory. Figure 4–3 illustrates how an electronic requisition and transfer system might interact in a fine-dining restaurant.

Network
A collection of personal computers or terminals that are linked together via lines and software.

SUMMARY

1. Requisitions are written orders, similar to shopping lists, that are primarily used by kitchen personnel to order food and nonfood products from the storeroom to prepare menu items.

2. Requisitions are typically used in large-volume foodservice operations that have multiple locations at the same property, such as hotels, resorts, health-care centers, and so on.

3. There are two types of requisitions. One is a preprinted par amount requisition and the other is a blank requisition. The preprinted forms are convenient for foodservice operations with fixed menu items that are assigned par amounts in anticipation of sales. Blank forms are used for items that typically are not used on a daily basis or with any established frequency.

4. A transfer is a form used to track the movement of products from one department or unit to another.

5. The difference between a requisition and a transfer is that a requisition is used to document and obtain products from a storeroom, while a transfer keeps track of products that have already been accounted for by requisitions.

6. The requisition and transfer process can be simplified by using a computer network. As the required data are entered into a computer, the stock is immediately deleted from the storeroom inventory and added to the inventory of the requesting department.

7. Managers use requisitions and transfers to track inventory and to better control the amount of inventory required to operate their foodservice operation.

KEY CONCEPTS

Blank requisition

Executive chef

Line cooks

Network

Par amount requisition

Requisition

Sous chef

Terminal

Transfer

DISCUSSION QUESTIONS AND EXERCISES

1. Describe how a requisition should be used if a foodservice operation has many departments within one property, such as a large hotel or resort, or is one unit of a chain that operates a central storeroom distribution center.

2. Describe the difference between using a par amount requisition system and a blank requisition system. When should each be used and how should each be used?

3. Describe how to use a transfer to keep track of the movement of products from one department or unit to another within a foodservice operation. Use a diagram if it is helpful.

4. How could a computer network in a foodservice operation be used to facilitate using both requisitions and transfers?

5. Assume that you are the coffee shop manager of a large hotel and on 1/10/XX at 9:15 P.M. you need the items listed below from the storeroom. You go to the storeroom manager to obtain these items. The storeroom manager reaches below the counter and pulls out a requisition numbered 547.

Three lemon pies, 10 inch, $ 4.25 ea.

One poultry seasoning, 12 oz, $ 5.50 ea.

One ground oregano, 15 oz, $ 5.96 ea.

Ten pounds of ground beef, $1.98/lb.

Complete a blank requisition using this information (see Appendix A for a blank form).

6. Assume that you are the coffee shop manager in a hospital. The hospital operates four types of foodservice operations: one for the patients, an executive dining room for senior managers and doctors, a coffee shop on the main level for visitors, and a cafeteria for employees. At closing time, you notice that you have the following items still available: half of a prime rib (8 pounds—cooked cost is $5.70 per pound); three fresh strawberry pies (invoice cost is $5.50 each); and sixteen baked potatoes (cost is .30 each). The cafeteria stays open all night and is usually very busy. Complete a transfer (see Appendix A for a blank form) to move these items from the coffee shop to the cafeteria. The transfer number is 271, the date is 1/4/XX, and this transfer was performed at 9 P.M.

7. What is the major advantage of being able to transfer products to other units?

5

Purchasing Functions

■ ■ ■ ■ ■ ■ ■ ■ ■ ■ ■ ■ ■ ■

Learning Objectives

After reading this chapter and completing the discussion questions and exercises, you should be able to:

1. Determine what to purchase in meeting the needs of a foodservice operation.
2. Understand how to develop good relationships with suppliers.
3. Make certain that the price paid is competitive by requesting price quotations from two or three suppliers.

About Purchasing

For some foodservice operations, the primary role of the **buyer** is to ensure that the operation has all the food, beverage, and nonfood items required. This role, however, is only part of the function of the buyer. The buyer may be the unit manager, owner, or purchasing agent. The responsibility of buying depends upon the organizational size and sales volume of the foodservice operation.

As technology continues to improve and the selection of products increases in quality as well as variety, the buyer is faced with the difficult task of determining which products should actually be used in an operation. The buyer's decisions are based on the varying degrees of quality, the needs of the operation, and the **true cost** of the products.

In earlier days, the buyer (the steward, dietician, food and beverage manager, or owner) had little choice when buying products. For example, if french fries were on the menu, the buyer had to purchase fresh whole potatoes, limiting the purchase to a specific variety. Today, however, he or she may purchase fresh whole potatoes already partially cooked, potatoes that are fully cooked, french fries that merely require reheating, or perhaps an instant potato mixture. The buyer's decision is based upon a number of factors, such as the quality of the final product, skill level of the employees, cost of the product, overall cost of production (including such factors as space allocation,

Buyer
The person who purchases food, beverage, and nonfood items.

True cost
The cost of an item after preparation.

Prime cost
The cost of the food plus the cost of the labor needed to produce the product.

Quality
Measured by specific characteristics, attributes, and standards.

equipment required, building costs, and labor costs), and of course, customer acceptance.

Every day the average foodservice establishment uses hundreds of products. The buyer must make decisions relating to each of the products, based on obtaining the best-quality product for a specific purpose and obtaining it at the lowest possible price.

The lowest price, however, can be a misleading term. In the case of the french fries, even if all of the different products eventually are of equal quality when placed in front of the customer, it is obvious that with some of them additional processing is required. This processing requires a certain amount of labor and creates labor costs as well as some other incidental costs related to preparation and cooking equipment.

In contrast, the chef is responsible not only for producing quality food, but also for keeping the costs of labor to a minimum. If partially or even fully prepared foods are purchased, the labor costs for preparation will be kept low but the cost of buying the food will most likely be higher. Therefore, the chef's objectives and the buyer's objectives may be in conflict.

Most foodservice managers today are more concerned with **prime cost**. Prime cost is the cost of the food product plus the labor cost to produce the product. In the case of french fries that are fully cooked and need only to be reheated, there is little labor cost, but the food cost would most likely be the highest. With the purchase of fresh, raw, unpeeled potatoes, the food cost would most likely be the lowest but preparation costs would be high.

Food and beverage managers or buyers are responsible for determining the lowest prime cost. They must make alterations to purchasing policies or products in conjunction with the chef and others responsible for the actual preparation of the menu items.

Quality can be widely interpreted. Quality for one type of foodservice operation may be completely different from that in another. The quality of a hamburger for a fast-food restaurant featuring 99-cent hamburgers will obviously differ from the quality of a $3.95 hamburger in a family restaurant.

The determination of quality may also differ from one operation to another or from one guest to another. For example, a quality pie crust with lard used as the shortening agent may be unacceptable to individuals who dislike the distinctive taste imparted by this product. Or perhaps the taste of aged meat is unfamiliar to certain customers but desired by others. Despite the fact that quality meat has an extensive fat covering, marbling may be considered unacceptable in certain areas of the country. The quality of service in a family restaurant also differs from the quality of service set forth in a fine-dining restaurant. Each, however, may be the most appropriate for the respective establishments, and proper procedure according to the standards established by management.

Just as quality differs from operation to operation, it may also change within an operation. In discussing quality, the standard varies with the purpose for which the product is used as well as with the type of operation. Given this, the role of a buyer is to purchase the best quality for a specific product purpose at the lowest possible price.

In order to accomplish this objective, the buyer must be aware of all factors influencing the quality of the product outside the foodservice operation. The buyer must also be alert to the conditions within the operation that will alter or influence the quality of the end product to be served. It would be foolish for a buyer to purchase a whole side of beef if no one in the operation has the required skills to cut and trim it into the correct cuts of meat. Nor should the buyer purchase unpeeled potatoes if the necessary in-house equipment for the operation (a potato peeler) is either inoperable or nonexistent.

Conditions in the general economic community that appear to have no direct bearing upon a foodservice operation may greatly affect the products that are available for use. The buyer who is unaware of weather conditions in various parts of the country may suddenly find that the cost of produce has unexpectedly either risen or fallen due to a change in harvest conditions. A sudden freeze in the producing areas may cause the price of lettuce and other similar products to double within just a few days. The corn or grain harvest one year might affect the cost of beef the next year as feed costs change. The effect of governmental policies on price supports and other farm policies is a crucial factor in the overall costs of goods purchased. In addition, transportation expenses are an integral part of the overall costs of raw products. A strike by transportation workers may cause a shortage or a complete absence of products from the market. The devaluation of the dollar causes a price increase for all imported products. The alert buyer may be able to stock up on some items just prior to price increases.

Efficient buyers must get their information from many sources. They must not become so preoccupied with the internal needs of their own organizations that they ignore some of the basic tools necessary to perform their tasks. They should be able to use trade publications, product web sites, government agricultural bulletins, stock market reports, commodity bulletins, wholesale daily reports, and food supplier and equipment web sites in order to be aware of price changes.

Information regarding new products, price changes, and special sales from each individual supplier should be shared with the buyer by the salesperson of each supplying company. Too often the salesperson becomes merely an order taker, either because of a lack of foresight or due to the attitude of buyers who clearly demonstrate that they merely wish to place orders. This lack of interest by both parties often creates undue costs for the operation, as opportunities for discount buying or special purchases are overlooked. This does not mean that buyers need to devote a great deal of time to every salesperson who comes, but they should indicate a willingness to listen and be receptive to new ideas and be interested in information on sales or other important changes.

In the course of doing business with the various salespeople, buyers will develop an awareness as to which salespeople do indeed pass on information and which ones are merely trying to sell or take orders. Good salespeople will be aware of the needs of the foodservice operation to which they are selling. They may have a number of products on sale during a week, but refrain from mentioning them because they realize that those products do not fit the needs of that particular foodservice operation. They save the buyer's time as well as their own and, in turn, earn the respect and appreciation of the buyer. When a product may be useful, buyers will listen more closely, since they know the information is important to their operation.

Correct ordering begins with a thorough understanding of inventory management. The concept is fairly simple: Don't run out of goods and don't have too much on hand.

When the foodservice operation is out of a product, the result is often a loss in potential profit, because a customer may order either something of lesser value or nothing from the menu. A case in point occurs when a customer orders a New York steak dinner with a piece of apple pie for dessert, only to have the waitress say, "Sorry, we are out of New York steaks this evening and we just served our last piece of apple pie." The customer may decide to go to another restaurant or perhaps may just order a dinner salad with the thought of never returning to the restaurant again.

The selection of suppliers is based upon good business principles. Suppliers selected are dependable, have competitive prices with fresh products, have on-time deliveries (that include all the products ordered), and have prompt service when situations require it.

Determining What to Order

Ordering
The process of obtaining products for use by a foodservice operation.

Supplier
A company that sells products to foodservice businesses.

Ordering involves two steps. The first is to determine which food, beverage, and nonfood items need to be ordered and in what quantities. The second is deciding with which **suppliers** to place the order. Ordering is part of the process of managing inventory. It is the first step in the process, which ends with the production of finished menu items. Orders are based upon current inventory and the food needed to satisfy the expected demands for menu items within a certain time frame.

One key in determining what to order is knowing how much of any given item should be on hand in inventory. It is recommended that a par amount be established for all merchandise purchased. To review, a par amount is the minimum amount of a given item needed on hand in anticipation of demand. The idea is not to have too much or too little of any item in inventory. Par amounts are used for several logical reasons. A par amount level:

- Reduces the possibility of spoilage through good inventory rotation.
- Eliminates the need for greater storage space and facilities.
- Reduces the temptation of theft.
- Reduces the dollar investment in inventory.
- Provides an adequate supply of food items to meet the expected product demand.

Assume that a foodservice operation uses sliced cling peaches for preparing salads. The specification is a #10 can, sliced (300 to 350 count per can), light syrup. Every day at least three cans are used and some days up to five cans may be used. To be certain that there are enough peaches on hand, the foodservice unit should have at least six cans in inventory at all times. So the *per day* par amount is six #10 cans. The par amount level for between deliveries depends on how often deliveries take place. If deliveries occur twice a week, then the par amount that needs to be on the shelf is the number of days between deliveries multiplied by the maximum number of items used. In this example it would be calculated as follows:

Maximum number of items used per day	6 #10 cans
× Number of days between deliveries	×3.5
Inventory par amount	21 #10 cans

A par amount of 21 cans means that the foodservice operation should have a minimum of 21 #10 cans of sliced peaches on the shelf on the day after delivery. Since #10 cans of peaches are packed six to a case, the par amount may be adjusted to accommodate how the product is packed. So instead of 21 cans as par amount, 24 cans would be used because there are six #10 cans to the case (6 × 4 = 24).

Determining how many cases of peaches to order at any given time will depend upon the number of cans currently on the shelf. If there are only four cans on the shelf and delivery is expected the following afternoon, the amount of peaches to be ordered would be determined as follows:

Par amount of #10 cans of peaches needed	24
Number of #10 cans of peaches on hand	− 4
Total number of #10 cans of peaches to be ordered	20

In this example, since there are six cans per case, 20 cans divided by 6 cans equals 3.33 cases. The foodservice unit should order four cases.

Of course, this is all based upon the ease of availability. At certain times, a product is not readily available or will be increasing in price. This is when advance buying may become the most economical decision. Buying enough when products are available and when significant price increases are expected will save money and ensure that supplies remain in stock.

The process of determining a par amount is used for every item kept in inventory. Par amounts are essential information for ordering. After par amounts have been calculated, the first step in determining what to order has been accomplished. The second step is completing an order sheet.

ow to Order Using an Order Sheet

The **order sheet** represents a systematic approach to controlling what to buy from specific suppliers (see Table 5-1). An order sheet may be set up to accommodate ordering on a daily, semiweekly, weekly, semi-monthly, or monthly basis. The order sheet starts with the name of the supplier. It also asks for an item description and unit of order. The remaining boxes in the form show the manner of establishing par amounts and determining the amount to be ordered.

The first column, Item Description, should include the name of the product to be ordered, an identifiable variety, brand name, grade, and identification number or some other description of the product in terms of standard and quality.

The next column, Unit, is used to indicate the unit of the item being ordered. The unit represents how items are packaged for delivery. In the example, lettuce is delivered by the case.

After the unit column, the next 14 columns alternate identifying the day and order. In the Day column, indicated by the day of the week, a par amount,

Order sheet
A form that identifies each item used in inventory to calculate the amount of product to order.

Table 5-1   Order Sheet

Supplier ___Town Produce___   Date ___1/17/XX___

Item Description	Unit	Mon	Order	Tue	Order	Wed	Order	Thu	Order	Fri	Order	Sat	Order	Sun	Order
Lettuce, Iceberg	case	par / on hand		3 / 1/2	3					6					

hereafter referred to as *par*, is recorded in the upper left corner of the box. Par is established on the basis of anticipated sales for each day. The *on-hand* amount is the actual product amount in inventory and is written in the lower right corner of the box. The difference between what is written in the upper left corner and the lower right corner is the amount to be ordered. This figure is recorded in the adjacent Order column to the right of the Day column.

For example, the par for lettuce, written in the upper left corner, is three cases. This represents the par amount needed for a scheduled Tuesday delivery. The actual amount of lettuce on hand is ½ case, recorded in the lower right corner. The order amount is the difference between three cases and ½ case of lettuce, which is 2½, rounded to three cases. Three cases of lettuce need to be ordered. This amount is to be written in the Order column. An order for a Tuesday delivery would normally be prepared late in the day or at the close of business on Monday and telephoned, faxed, or e-mailed to the supplier for next-day delivery. Suppliers may start processing orders as early as 1:00 A.M. for early-morning deliveries.

This system exercises tight control of inventory, ensuring proper rotation and reducing the possibility of spoilage as the older items are used first. It is ideally used for produce, dairy, and bakery products. As a rule, these items are supplied on a contract basis as opposed to a daily or weekly bid.

Purchasing What Is Needed from Suppliers

After the buyer calculates how much product to order, he or she should place the order. The order will be placed by telephone, fax, **online**, or, in some cases, directly with the supplier's representative. Supplier representatives generally visit foodservice operations at least once a week. Effort should be given to developing a working relationship with representatives and suppliers. Developing a professional relationship is to the advantage of the foodservice manager. Occasionally, emergencies occur that require an early-morning or weekend delivery. Based upon a sound relationship, a supplier usually responds in order to accommodate a good account.

It is also important to remember that the supplier's main goal is to make a sale at the highest possible price while at the same time remaining competitive. Suppliers strive to build a relationship with their customers by being competitive and providing good service. They realize that foodservice managers want to buy at the lowest possible price, receive all the items that were ordered, and receive the items at a time when they are able to manage the products' arrival.

With the supplier's and foodservice manager's goals in mind, the following criteria should be used for deciding which suppliers to use:

1. Select suppliers who enjoy a reputation of dependability. This means that suppliers deliver ordered products courteously and on time, minimize **back orders,** and make no unauthorized substitutions. If a substitution is to be made, a sales representative should have the courtesy to call to reach an agreement for substituting another product before delivery.

Online ordering The process of ordering from suppliers or supplier brokers through the World Wide Web.

Back order Occurs when a supplier is out of the product and is waiting for shipment from the manufacturer.

2. Select suppliers who are competitive and offer prices similar to those of their competition.

3. Select suppliers who provide service. This means suppliers who provide information on products that enhance the foodservice operation's ability to compete for customers. Some suppliers provide information on pricing and help with menu ideas.

The third step after filling out an order sheet is to establish the days and times for deliveries. For example, groceries may be delivered Monday and Friday between 1 and 3 P.M. Produce and dairy products may be delivered Tuesday and Friday between 6 and 8 A.M. Bakery items might be delivered on Monday, Wednesday, Thursday, and Friday between 6 and 7 A.M. Items such as meat, fish, and poultry may be delivered on a regular schedule or according to the needs of the foodservice operation.

Getting the Best Price

Foodservice operations in large metropolitan areas have many suppliers from which to choose. As might be expected, operators located in small cities and towns have fewer suppliers from which to select their products. The environment's competitiveness depends upon the number of suppliers in relationship to the number of foodservice operations in a trading area. In most cities and towns there is quite a bit of competition. Therefore, when a foodservice operation requests price quotations from competing suppliers, it is assured of getting the best possible price within the community.

Bid sheet
A form that itemizes each product to be ordered and is used to compare prices between different suppliers.

The basic considerations of negotiation are price, service, delivery schedule, and terms. A **bid sheet** (see Table 5-2) is an effective tool for determining the best price. The bid sheet represents the most efficient way to document and compare price quotations. To determine the best price, the buyer must initially request price quotations. In most cases, suppliers will usually provide a computer printout (see Figure 5-1), a printed price sheet, or a verbal quote to the buyer of products and prices. Usually this information is available on a weekly basis. Upon receiving it, the buyer should write the information provided by the sales representative on a bid sheet.

When a supplier provides a printout, it can be used as a resource for completing a bid sheet as long as it contains the following information:

1. A list of each item needed.

2. Unit size as purchased.

3. Quantity to be ordered.

Bid sheets can also be used with suppliers interested in submitting bids who do not provide scheduled computer printouts. The smaller suppliers will quote prices through the salesperson calling upon the foodservice operation. Nearly always, the salesperson carries a current price book and in some cases a notebook (laptop computer). The prices can then be entered on the bid sheet. To save time, managers should prepare bid sheets that list the most common items they purchase on a regular basis. The buyer will be able to intelligently compare prices on an item-by-item basis with each supplier.

Table 5-2 Bid Sheet

			Date 12/19/XX	
ITEM DESCRIPTION	QUANTITY UNIT		SUPPLIER'S NAME	
		METRO SUPPLY	ALL STAR SERVICE	TRI–STATE WHOLESALE
Cereal, Cheerios, General Mills 14–15 oz	cs	70.00	65.00	67.50
Total				

◆ *ChefTec Software*

Bids

Foodservice Profitability

All Stocked Items

Inventory Item	Vendor	Date	Valid For	Cost	Quantity
cereal, Cheerios	All Star Service	6/7/00	days	$65.00	1 case
	Metro Supply	6/7/00	days	$70.00	1 case
cereal, Raisin Bran Kellogg	All Star Service	6/7/00	days	$53.90	1 case
	Metro Supply	6/7/00	days	$54.00	1 case
	Tri-State Wholesale	6/7/00	days	$55.00	1 case
chili powder	All Star Service	6/7/00	days	$4.75	20 oz
	Metro Supply	6/7/00	days	$4.45	20 oz
flour	All Star Service	6/7/00	days	$12.75	1 750ml
	Metro Supply	6/7/00	days	$12.50	1 750ml
fruit punch, Welchade	All Star Service	6/7/00	days	$15.80	1 12/46 oz
	Metro Supply	6/7/00	days	$16.50	1 12/46 oz
gelatin, cherry jello	All Star Service	6/7/00	days	$25.10	1 case
	Metro Supply	6/7/00	days	$26.10	1 case
juice, apple	All Star Service	6/7/00	days	$18.45	1 12/46 oz
	Metro Supply	6/7/00	days	$18.00	1 12/46 oz
juice, grapefruit	All Star Service	6/7/00	days	$14.75	1 12/46 oz
	Metro Supply	6/7/00	days	$14.25	1 12/46 oz
juice, tomato	All Star Service	6/7/00	days	$11.80	1 12/46 oz
	Metro Supply	6/7/00	days	$11.75	1 12/46 oz
juice, tomato 5.5 oz	All Star Service	6/7/00	days	$13.25	1 48/5.5 oz
	Metro Supply	6/7/00	days	$12.80	1 48/5.5 oz
lemon drink, Welchade	All Star Service	6/7/00	days	$16.22	1 12/46 oz
	Metro Supply	6/7/00	days	$16.00	1 12/46 oz

FIGURE 5-1
Computer-Generated Detailed Bids Report

The next step would be to circle the best price on each item. This should be followed by totaling each Supplier column. Buying the best-priced items from all three suppliers is appropriate if the quantities are large enough to meet each supplier's minimum delivery dollar amount. While being dependent on just one supplier may be risky, a manager may pick the one supplier with the overall best prices. Requesting weekly bids can be time-consuming. Also, the increased complexity of scheduling and working with several suppliers may be impractical.

Many successful foodservice operators request quarterly or annual supplier bids. This can save time and money and build excellent supplier relationships. Bid sheets must also be compared to invoices at the time of delivery to verify that the price quoted was the price charged.

Most independent foodservice operations and many individual units of chains order directly from sales representatives or by phone from the bid sheets. However, schools, health care centers, hotel chains, and restaurant chains may use a **purchase order** (see Table 5-3). The purchase order is num-

Purchase order
A numbered form that identifies the quantity ordered and lists a complete description of what is being ordered, along with the price, unit cost, extension, and total.

■ ■ ■ ■ ■
Table 5-3 Purchase Order

Name	Foodservice Chain		
Address	1000 Main Street	PURCHASE ORDER NUMBER	1054
	American City		

Tel 000.000.0000	Fax 000.000.0000	Authorized by _Manager_	Date Issued January 20, xxxx
		Signature	

SUPPLIER

ABC Supply
Company Name

123 Broadway
Street Address

American City
City, State, Zip Code

000.000.0000   000.000.0000
Telephone   *Fax*

Fred Sample
Contact Name

Required Deliver Date   February 8, xxxx

Terms   Attach invoice to delivery slip;

payment net 30 days from delivery date

Freight Charges   ☐ Collect (Amount) $ _____
☐ FOB   ☒ Pre-paid

Special Instructions   Deliver before 10:00 A.M.

QUANTITY	UNIT	ITEM DESCRIPTION	UNIT COST		EXTENSION	
2	4 Ft	Steel Storage Cabinets with key lock doors;	285	00	570	00
		Catalog #3030				
				TOTAL $	570	00

Copies to: Supplier, Purchasing, Receiving, Accounts Payable

bered, identifies the quantity ordered, and lists a complete description of what is being ordered along with the unit cost, extension, and total. A purchase order is very similar to an **invoice,** except that an invoice is what the supplier uses to document what was delivered and received by the foodservice operation. These will differ only when the supplier fails to deliver all the items on the purchase order.

Emerging trends that will dramatically streamline the purchasing process are using the Internet to order directly from suppliers and using supplier-provided software to place orders—the objective being to make the process more timely and efficient for the foodservice operation and the supplier. This reduces the amount of labor and creates a better linkage with suppliers to improve response time and decrease the cost of transactions, thus reducing the cost of inventory management.

SUMMARY

1. Ensuring that the foodservice operation does not run out of products used to produce meals is the goal of proper ordering.

2. Ordering involves determining which items and in what amounts need to be ordered from designated suppliers.

3. Determining what and how much to order is directly related to effective inventory management. This involves determining how much product to always have on hand so that the foodservice operation does not run out of needed products. This is accomplished by calculating par amounts for every item in the inventory. These par amounts are then used as part of an order sheet to track the availability and need of products.

4. When products are depleted to a predetermined level, more are ordered. The amount ordered is determined by using the order sheet.

5. Selecting and actually ordering the needed products is the next step. This is done by carefully selecting suppliers that are dependable, competitively priced, and provide needed services.

6. To get the best price, the foodservice manager should use a bid sheet. The bid sheet is a form used to list products needed by the foodservice operation.

7. Suppliers submit their prices, which are then listed by the manager in columns next to each other on the bid sheet. The manager then designates the supplier with the best prices for each product. Individual items may be ordered from different suppliers, or the supplier that provides the best overall prices may get the entire account.

8. Purchase orders are typically used by large foodservice operations with purchasing departments.

9. A purchase order is a form that identifies the quantity ordered and lists a complete description of what is being ordered along with the unit cost, extension, and total.

KEY CONCEPTS

Back order

Bid sheet

Buyer

Invoice

Ordering

Order sheet

Prime cost

Purchase order

Quality

Supplier

True cost

DISCUSSION QUESTIONS AND EXERCISES

1. Write a description of the steps involved in ordering.

2. How would you ensure that the price you are receiving is competitive? Explain in detail.

3. How would you select suppliers?

4. Using the order sheet that follows, complete the order column so that par amounts are attained.

5. Referring to the bid sheet that follows, which supplier would you use if you were to buy from only one? If you decided to buy from more than one, from which supplier would you buy each item?

6. Why is purchasing food today more complex than it was 25 or 30 years ago?

7. What are the basic objectives in ordering and purchasing food?

8. Discuss the timing of ordering in relationship to deliveries and give an example.

Supplier ___Town Produce___ Date ___1/17/XX___

Item Description	Unit	Mon	Order	Tue	Order	Wed	Order	Thu	Order	Fri	Order	Sat	Order	Sun	Order
Lettuce, Iceberg	case	5 / 2				6 / 1				15 / 2					
Apples (80 ct)	box	2 / 1/2				1 / 0				4 / 1					
Mushrooms	box	1 / 1				1 / 1				3 / 0					
Potatoes, U.S. #1	100 lb bag	3 / 1				3 / 1/2				8 / 0					

BID SHEET

Date 12/19/XX

ITEM DESCRIPTION		QUANTITY UNIT	SUPPLIER'S NAME		
			METRO SUPPLY	ALL STAR SERVICE	TRI–STATE WHOLESALE
Drink, Frt. Punch, Welchade	24-11.5 oz	cs	$ 8.70	$ 8.65	$ 8.25
Drink, Lemon, Welchade	24-11.5 oz	cs	8.70	8.60	8.35
Cereal, Cheerios, General Mills	14-15 oz	cs	70.00	65.00	67.50
Cereal, Raisin Bran, Kellogg	12-20 oz	cs	53.90	52.80	50.25
Gellatin, Cherry, Jello	12-24 oz	cs	24.10	23.80	23.90
Flour, All-Purpose, Fisher	1-25 lb	bag	6.10	5.80	6.10
Flour, Cake/Pastry, Fisher	1-50 lb	bag	13.80	13.25	13.55
Seasoning Salt, Lawrys	4–5 lb	cs	49.00	42.50	48.00
Gravy Mix Country, Le Gout	24-7 oz	cs	36.25	38.00	35.00
Pie, Apple Unbaked, Rich's	6-10 in.	cs	17.75	18.74	18.50
Cup, Foam 4 oz, Handi-kup	25-40 ct	cs	12.75	13.00	12.25
Total					

6

Receiving Merchandise and Processing Invoices

■ ■ ■ ■ ■ ■ ■ ■ ■ ■ ■ ■ ■ ■

L earning Objectives

After reading this chapter and completing the discussion questions and exercises, you should be able to:

1. Determine whether deliveries from the supplier match what was ordered.

2. Identify the product quality and grade compared to what was ordered.

3. Compare all invoices against what was actually ordered and delivered.

4. Use scales so that all items sold by weight, such as meat, can be placed on a scale and the weight compared to the total weight of those items on an invoice (allowing for packing materials).

5. Demonstrate an understanding that all products should be immediately moved into storage upon having been checked in.

6. Describe why it is important that weight scales, a small hand-held calculator, order sheets, purchase orders, bid sheets, and a stamp used to mark the back of invoices should be easily accessible to the person who receives merchandise.

7. Recalculate invoices that accompany products delivered to the foodservice establishment to check for accuracy.

8. Monitor invoices by using an invoice payment schedule.

A bout Receiving Merchandise and Processing Invoices

The person assigned to receive the food, beverage, and nonfood products that have been ordered should be both knowledgeable and experienced. Being able to recognize that the quality of the goods delivered is consistent with what was ordered is essential. For example, it would be extremely awkward and difficult to have someone receiving, inspecting, and checking in fresh and frozen meat products who had little knowledge of fat content, marbling, color, and so on. While most suppliers try their best to deliver the exact products that have been ordered, errors do occur. The importance of a thorough and complete receiving procedure conducted by a professional and knowledgeable person becomes apparent.

This skill is acquired through training and experience, particularly with meat, poultry, and seafood items. Also needed is knowledge of proper handling and storage of food items. This chapter details receiving procedures along with invoice processing and payment, a critical function to sound inventory management. In addition, the prompt and efficient manner in which a foodservice operation receives merchandise and pays the bills will further establish strong relationships with suppliers.

Receiving Merchandise—Step One

Receiving person
The person responsible for accepting products from suppliers.

Orders are initially placed for products in anticipation of usage, as explained in Chapter 5. As the products are delivered, a designated **receiving person** should be responsible for receiving the products. The key to ensuring proper receipt of products is to have a person:

- with enough knowledge to be able to identify the product quality and grade

- who is able to read the number of units and price and then compare this information to what was ordered

- who has access to the order sheets, purchase orders, and bid sheets, and has these documents with him or her as the merchandise is received

- who understands how to use a hand-held calculator and weight scales

If several different people are receiving merchandise and they are not properly trained, the result can be loss of control over inventory. Unauthorized substitutions, receipt of poor-quality merchandise, incorrect weights, and other problems are more likely to occur. Proper receiving of high-cost items such as meat, fish, and poultry is particularly important.

The designated receiving person should ensure that accurate weights and amounts are present. Checking weights is time-consuming. An easy way to check weights for most foodservice operations is to put all items sold by weight on the scale (see Figure 6-1). After all items are put on the scale, compare the total weight of all items as reported by the scale to the total weight as reported by the **invoice.** Of course, a small discrepancy for packing materials should be allowed. If the discrepancy is reasonable, the order should be accepted. If the weight seems high or low, each individual item should be weighed.

Invoice
A form that accompanies the products that are delivered and provides an itemized list of what was delivered. It also serves as a bill for payment.

The receiving person should compare the items that are physically present to what is on the invoice and also to what was ordered. If a different

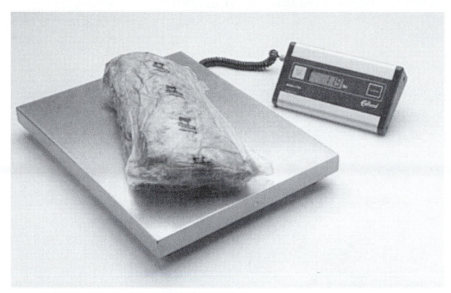

FIGURE 6-1
Product Being Weighed In. *Courtesy of Edlund Company, Inc.*

amount appears on the invoice than was actually delivered, a correction should immediately be made. The correction is handled by the delivery person by crossing off the incorrect amount, writing in the correct amount, and initialing the change. Some suppliers prefer the delivery person to issue a credit memo for the difference instead of making any changes on the original invoice. Both procedures are acceptable and commonly used.

There are always two copies of an invoice: the original and the duplicate. Once the invoice is signed by the person receiving the merchandise, the original goes back to the delivery person and the duplicate remains with the receiving person.

The same method is followed when incorrect products are substituted, incorrect merchandise is included, or merchandise is missing from the order but listed on the invoice. Incorrect product substitutes and products not ordered must immediately be rejected and sent back.

Receiving Merchandise—Step Two

The next step is to document the receiving process. By documenting the process, the receiving person accepts responsibility for the order received. The receiving person should stamp the back of the invoice with a rubber stamp that includes the information shown in Figure 6-2.

After the blanks have been filled in, the receiving person delivers the invoices to the manager on duty, accountant, bookkeeper, accounts payable person, or other designated person responsible for paying the invoice. By using this stamp, the receiver and the person doing the price/extension check are made accountable for their work.

Date Received	_____ (actual date) _____
Received by	_____ (signature or initials) _____
Prices/Extensions Verified and Corrected by	_____ (an assigned clerical function to verify prices and recalculate the invoice for accuracy) _____
Payment Approval	_____ (owner, manager, or accounts payable person) _____

FIGURE 6-2
Using a Receiving Stamp

 rocessing Invoices

Processing invoices, from the time that products are delivered to final payments, can be a simple and efficient task when a basic procedure is established and followed. The procedure should ensure that a product ordered at a designated price and quantity is actually what was delivered to the foodservice operation.

The receiving function ensures and verifies that all the products that were ordered have been received. Controls must be set up to ensure that the quality is the same as what was ordered and that there have not been any substitutions, changes, or deterioration in the products. Several people may be responsible for paying the invoice, such as the bookkeeper, accounts payable person, controller, office manager, or owner. Whoever is responsible for paying the bills should establish an **invoice payment schedule**. An invoice payment schedule is a form used to ensure that suppliers are paid in a timely fashion.

The simplest way to pay invoices is to list them on an invoice payment schedule. This is a formal way of documenting all purchases during a given period of time. The invoices are grouped by company and are listed in chronological order. They are then put in alphabetical order and recorded on the invoice payment schedule, as shown in Table 6-1.

The payment schedule is determined by the terms of agreement initially set forth by each supplier. Their terms may range from requiring payment upon receipt to payment being due within 10 to 30 days from the date of the invoice. Discounts of 2 percent are occasionally available when payment is made within 10 days. Checks are issued as needed, such as every Friday for the 10-day accounts and on the 15th and 25th of the month for the 30-day accounts.

The invoice payment schedules can be separated by categories (see Figure 6-3). Nonfood categories would be items such as cleaning and maintenance supplies, pest control services, paper supplies, utilities, and so on. This makes cost analysis and percentage calculations an easy task. A quick reference to the invoice payment schedules can determine the total costs in each category for a given period.

The invoice payment schedule in Table 6-1 is organized according to payment periods. Most payment periods are monthly or semimonthly. The

Invoice payment schedule A form used to document all purchases during a given period of time and to ensure that suppliers are paid in a timely fashion.

■ ■ ■ ■ ■

Table 6-1 Invoice Payment Schedule

Period Ending __1/17/XX_____ Page __1__ of __4_____

Prepared by __Clerical_____ Invoices Certified Correct By

Date __1/20/XX_____ _____Owner/Manager_____

DATE	INVOICE NO.	SUPPLIER	AMOUNT		TOTAL AMOUNT	
1/13	02786	Old Town Bakery	96	76		
1/15	02842	Old Town Bakery	71	54		
1/16	02911	Old Town Bakery	76	87		
1/17	02939	Old Town Bakery	121	37	366	54
1/16	191183	Regional Seafood	363	48	363	48
1/13	4284	Tri-County Meats	676	90		
1/16	5601	Tri-County Meats	897	53	1,574	43
1/10	11877	Metro Supply	2,409	75		
1/13	13956	Metro Supply	1,932	51	4,342	26
1/13	0987	Valley Dairy	101	40		
1/15	1119	Valley Dairy	87	35		
1/17	1178	Valley Dairy	124	52	313	27
PAGE TOTAL					$6,959	98

ChefTec Software

Detailed Purchases

Foodservice Profitability

Categories All categories
Start Date 6/1/00
End Date 6/30/00
Select By Stocked, Raw Inventory, No Change, Increases, Decreases

Vendor All Vendors

Item	Date	Vendor	Invoice	Quantity	Units	Cost	Cost/Unit	Flag	% Change
beef round steak	6/13/00	Tri-County Meats	4284	112	lb	$358.45	$3.20/lb		
beef, ground 90% lean	6/1/00	Tri-County Meats	4124	5	lb	$12.25	$2.45/lb		
beets - shoe string	6/19/00	Metro Supply	145687	1	6/#10	$18.30	$18.30/6/#10		
beets - sliced	6/19/00	Metro Supply	145687	1	6/#10	$15.76	$15.76/6/#10		
brandy	6/8/00	Barney's Foods	11325	750	ml	$3.87	$0.01/ml		
butter	6/15/00	Valley Dairy	1119	5	lb	$6.40	$1.28/lb		
carrot	6/7/00	Barney's Foods	11312	5	lb	$2.45	$0.49/lb		
celery	6/7/00	Barney's Foods	11312	5	lb	$1.45	$0.29/lb		
cheese, American	6/17/00	Valley Dairy	1258	40	lb	$80.95	$2.02/lb		
cheese, American	6/15/00	Valley Dairy	1119	40	lb	$80.95	$2.02/lb		
cheese, brie	6/17/00	Valley Dairy	1258	10	lb	$43.57	$4.36/lb		-12.9%
cheese, brie	6/13/00	Valley Dairy	1093	10	lb	$50.00	$5.00/lb		
cheese, cheddar	6/13/00	Valley Dairy	1093	25	lb	$51.40	$2.06/lb		
chili powder	6/1/00	Barney's Foods	11211	20	oz	$4.40	$0.22/oz		
cream, heavy	6/1/00	Valley Dairy	822	1	qt	$2.75	$2.75/qt		
fish veloute	6/1/00	Barney's Foods	11211	1	gal	$11.25	$11.25/gal		
flour	6/15/00	Barney's Foods	11427	50	lb	$7.70	$0.15/lb		
fruit cocktail	6/19/00	Metro Supply	145687	1	6/#10	$26.46	$26.46/6/#10		
garlic	6/1/00	Barney's Foods	11211	1	bulb	$1.41	$1.41/bulb		
garlic salt	6/1/00	Barney's Foods	11211	1	lb	$1.60	$1.60/lb		
hamburger bun	6/30/00	Old Town Bakery	03221	15	package	$20.80	$1.39/package		
hot dog	6/1/00	Barney's Foods	11211	1	lb	$1.92	$1.92/lb		
hot dog bun	6/15/00	Old Town Bakery	02842	113	package	$71.54	$0.63/package		
hot dog bun	6/13/00	Old Town Bakery	02786	160	package	$96.76	$0.60/package		4.7%
juice, V8	6/19/00	Metro Supply	145687	1	48/5.5 oz	$12.96	$12.96/48/5.5 oz		
juice, Welches grape	6/19/00	Metro Supply	145687	1	12/64 oz	$38.16	$38.16/12/64 oz		
juice, apple	6/19/00	Metro Supply	145687	1	12/46 oz	$17.88	$17.88/12/46 oz		
juice, grapefruit	6/19/00	Metro Supply	145687	1	12/46 oz	$14.04	$14.04/12/46 oz		
juice, grapefruit pink	6/19/00	Metro Supply	145687	1	12/46 oz	$14.64	$14.64/12/46 oz		
juice, pineapple	6/19/00	Metro Supply	145687	1	12/46 oz	$14.04	$14.04/12/46 oz		
juice, tomato	6/19/00	Metro Supply	145687	1	12/46 oz	$11.52	$11.52/12/46 oz		
juice, tomato 5.5 oz	6/19/00	Metro Supply	145687	1	48/5.5 oz	$12.96	$12.96/48/5.5 oz		
ketchup	6/1/00	Barney's Foods	11211	1	case	$20.00	$20.00/case		
milk	6/15/00	Barney's Foods	11427	1	gal	$3.10	$3.10/gal		

Copyright Foodservice Profitability

Item	Date	Vendor	Invoice	Quantity	Units	Cost	Cost/Unit	Flag	% Change
mustard	6/1/00	Barney's Foods	11211	1	case	$12.00	$12.00/case		
onion	6/1/00	Barney's Foods	11211	10	lb	$5.90	$0.59/lb		
paprika	6/1/00	Barney's Foods	11211	1	lb	$3.68	$3.68/lb		
peaches - halves	6/19/00	Metro Supply	145687	1	6/#10	$23.88	$23.88/6/#10		
pears - halves	6/19/00	Metro Supply	145687	1	6/#10	$23.22	$23.22/6/#10		
pepper, ground black	6/1/00	Barney's Foods	11211	1	lb	$4.96	$4.96/lb		
pepper, red	6/1/00	Barney's Foods	11211	1	lb	$5.28	$5.28/lb		
relish	6/1/00	Barney's Foods	11211	1	case	$24.00	$24.00/case		
salt	6/1/00	Barney's Foods	11211	10	lb	$3.20	$0.32/lb		
sherry	6/1/00	Barney's Foods	11211	750	ml	$3.45	$0.00/ml		
shrimp	6/29/00	Regional Seafood	12118	94	lb	$363.48	$3.87/lb		-3.1%
shrimp	6/11/00	Regional Seafood	11211	2	lb	$7.98	$3.99/lb		
shrimp shells	6/11/00	Regional Seafood	11211	2	lb	$8.58	$4.29/lb		
sugar	6/1/00	Barney's Foods	11211	5	lb	$2.40	$0.48/lb		
thyme	6/7/00	Barney's Foods	11312	1	bunch	$0.69	$0.69/bunch		
thyme	6/7/00	Barney's Foods	11312	1	bunch	$0.69	$0.69/bunch		
tomato sauce	6/7/00	Barney's Foods	11312	1	6/#10	$21.06	$21.06/6/#10		
tomato soup	6/1/00	Barney's Foods	11211	1	case	$9.72	$9.72/case		

Total $1,655.86

FIGURE 6-3
Computer-Generated Detailed Purchases with Summary Report

```
Date: 2/12/00                        ⊹∰⊹  ChefTec Software
                          Summary of Purchases by Acct. Category
                                  Foodservice Profitability


Categories  All categories
Start Date  6/1/00
End Date    6/30/00
Select By   Stocked, Raw Inventory                        Vendor  All Vendors


        Category                    Cost            Percent

        Bakery                    $189.10             11.4
        Cheese                    $306.87             18.5
        Dairy                      $12.25              .7
        Dry Good                  $106.26             6.4
        Fish                       $19.83             1.2
        Fruits                     $73.56             4.4
        Grocery                   $191.32            11.6
        Meat                      $372.62            22.5
        Produce                    $12.59              .8
        Seafood                   $371.46            22.4
        No Category                 $0.00             0.0


               Total           $1,655.86
```

FIGURE **6-3**
Computer-Generated Detailed Purchases with Summary Report *Continued*

schedule is in chronological order, the invoice numbers are listed in ascending order with the amounts, and the invoices are grouped together in alphabetical order by supplier. This is done so that only one check per supplier will be issued. This saves time and money. Figure 6-3 is an example of computer-generated detailed purchases with summary report.

Electronic Processing of Invoices

User-friendly software allows foodservice personnel, presumably the manager or buyer, to enter each item listed on the invoice. Each item then is added to an electronic inventory form. The result is that the manager knows how much inventory is present. As the inventory is used, requisitions and transfers are electronically processed. An inventory balance is available every day.

As invoices are electronically processed, the program generates invoice payment schedules at the same time. The invoice payment schedules may be organized by type of supplier or by type of inventory item. On the days that checks are to be sent, the computer program can be instructed to total the amounts owed to suppliers, take discounts when applicable, and actually print the checks to the suppliers. In one entry step, all the financial and accounting information needed to track and pay for inventory is processed. Figure 6-4 illustrates the electronic flow of information.

SUMMARY

1. Receiving merchandise is a two-step process.

2. In the first step, products are received by a person who knows how to identify product quality and grade, is able to compare the invoices

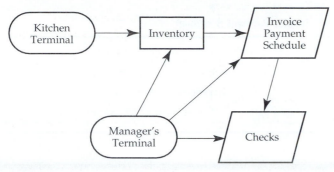

FIGURE 6-4
Flow of Information for Processing Invoices Using Computers

with the order sheets to verify that the proper products were ordered, and has the capability to use weight scales and a hand-held calculator.

3. The second step is documenting the receiving process.

4. Documentation involves verifying that the amount spent was the amount the manager budgeted to spend.

5. If there were errors on the invoice, or if the products delivered were not what was ordered, corrections must be made by the delivery person and receiving person.

6. If the supplier has made unauthorized substitutions, adjustments may need to be made to the delivery as well as to the invoice.

7. Invoices are recorded on an invoice payment schedule. This schedule helps to track whether invoices have been paid and discounts have been taken. It also aids the clerical staff in paying the invoices in a timely manner.

KEY CONCEPTS

Invoice
Invoice payment schedule
Receiving person

DISCUSSION QUESTIONS AND EXERCISES

1. What is the principle of receiving?

2. Describe the purpose of an invoice.

3. What should a receiving person know in order to perform effectively?

4. Describe the proper method of receiving products.

5. What happens to the invoice after it has been reviewed by the receiving person?

6. What is an invoice payment schedule and how is it used by the foodservice manager?

7. Describe the invoice tracking process.

8. What errors do you see in the following invoice payment schedule?

Invoice Payment Schedule

Period Ending	1/17/XX		Page	1	of	4	
Prepared by	Clerical		Invoices Certified Correct by				
Date	1/20/XX			Owner/Manager			

DATE	INVOICE NO.	SUPPLIER	AMOUNT		TOTAL AMOUNT	
1/13		Old Town Bakery	$ 96	76	$ 96	67
1/16	191183	Regional Seafood	363	48	363	48
1/13	4284	Tri-County Meats	676	90		
1/13	13956		2,409	75		
1/10	11877	United Wholesale	1,932	51	4,342	26
1/13	0987	Valley Dairy	101	40		
1/09	11119	United Wholesale	87	35	188	75
PAGE TOTAL					$4991	16

7

Quality Standards, Specifications, Yield Analysis, and Plate Cost

Learning Objectives

After reading this chapter and completing the discussion questions and exercises, you should be able to:

1. Identify the quality of food that will be consistent with the foodservice concept.

2. Write specifications for the food items that make up the menu for the foodservice operation.

3. Create or obtain recipes that will become preparation standards.

4. Complete a recipe cost chart for each recipe.

5. Do a yield analysis on food items in which quantity and quality may change during production.

6. Do a yield analysis on items that are sold in specific and unspecific counts.

7. Identify the cost of every plate of food served.

8. Continually review food costs in order to maintain financial balance and control.

About Quality Food Standards

The goal of a foodservice operation is to satisfy customers by meeting or exceeding their expectations. Basic expectations are: timely service, cleanliness, and good-quality food. Good food, to most people, means serving hot food hot and cold food cold. It also means offering the food quality expected, given the type of physical surroundings and the price charged. The art of managing a foodservice operation is to determine customer expectations and coordinate staff activities to satisfy those expectations. The proper use of information derived from experience in operating the foodservice operation will help the manager consistently deliver food that meets customer expectations. This same information may be used to identify quality, determine ingredient specifications, develop standardized recipes, keep track of costs, and develop service standards.

The **plate cost** represents the total cost of the food that is actually served to the customer on the plate. This includes all the ingredients that go into preparing the final food product.

Certain food products need to be measured with consideration of their final **yield,** or the net usable product. This is the case with most raw meat, which will have some shrinkage from cooking, along with fat and bones that may have to be removed. The remaining meat goes on the plate to be served to the customer. With foods characterized by shrinking, it is critical to maintain yield standards. If the yield falls below desired standards, such as raw meat that may be of lesser quality, profit will drop because there is less product to sell. Also, if the quality decreases, the customer may be disappointed enough to complain or simply not return again.

Food products, by their very nature, will have varying degrees of quality and yield. They are also subject to price fluctuations, as market conditions may dictate an increase or decrease in prices. Hence, it is extremely important to develop and maintain **quality standards** and specifications for standardized recipes that should be consistently followed. The latter will ensure that food preparation will always remain the same, leaving little room for error or possible disappointment of customers.

This chapter explains the importance of identifying quality standards and specifications, continually reviewing food product yields, and keeping recipe costs current, along with demonstrating the procedures to follow to maintain this delicate balance.

Plate cost
The total cost of the food served to the customer on the plate.

Yield
The net usable product.

Quality standards
Dictate the condition, measure, weight, and count or volume of products used in producing menu items.

Quality Food and Value

Quality is a perceived value. People often confuse quality with status. Thus, a fast-food hamburger chain is perceived as offering a certain level of quality and an upscale fine-dining restaurant is perceived as offering another level of food quality. In reality, both offer good-quality food. The difference is in the type of food and atmosphere. Quality in the foodservice industry should be determined according to taste, quality of ingredients, portion size, methods of preparation, and service. Low cost does not necessarily mean low quality. It usually means that the menu items will be commonly prepared in large quantities so that the cost is low and the items are sold in great numbers. With various types of foodservice operations, quality is a function of ingredient cost and cost of preparation.

Consistent taste and quality are very important in maintaining customer loyalty, goodwill, and satisfaction. Consistent taste and quality are controlled by using quality standards, which ensures that the product will always be consistently prepared and served. Quality standards define:

- the quality of food to be offered
- what ingredients are to be used

- the process of combining the ingredients (the recipe)
- the cost standards for preparing the recipe
- the method of delivering the finished product to the table and serving the guest

Determining the Quality of Food Offered

The first step in developing quality standards is to decide the type of food to be offered. This decision is connected with understanding what kind of food-service concept has been or will be chosen. For example, if the operation is designed to appeal to families with children and offers table service with a broad menu, the concept chosen will probably be that of a family restaurant, such as Denny's or IHOP (International House of Pancakes). Prices on the menu will be at a level that will appeal to family clientele.

All foodservice operations should strive to offer the highest quality menu items at a price that is appropriate for the amount of food being served. This may seem like a paradox. After all, how can high quality be associated with moderately priced foods, such as those available at a Denny's or IHOP?

The answer is that the food offered should be as high a quality as possible in relationship to the menu price of the food. To achieve high quality, food-service managers need to buy high-quality ingredients and carefully control how they are used. This is done by determining what items should be included and how each item on the menu should be prepared. It is also done through properly understanding ingredient specifications and by using standardized recipes.

Specifying Quality Ingredients

The second step in developing quality standards is to determine the ingredients for the menu items. The menu determines what ingredients are to be used.

For the foodservice manager to purchase the correct ingredients requires the use of specifications. A **specification** is a complete description of the ingredients. Specifications for ingredients usually are included in **standardized recipes** or **recipe cost charts** (both of these will be discussed later in this chapter). As you read the following, refer to Tables 7-1 and 7-2. Typically, a specification is a complete description that includes:

1. *The name of the item.* The name of an item should include all information that identifies the item to be purchased. For example, if apples are to be used, the name of the item would be Apple, Red Delicious. The type or variety is always listed (such as lettuce, romaine; onions, yellow; or cheese, mild cheddar), being as specific as possible.

2. *Quality characteristics.* Quality can be described according to the desired appearance, such as crispness, color, and age. The buyer may also want to describe quality according to standards used by the United States Department of Agriculture (USDA). Fruits, vegetables, and meats (except fish) are graded by the USDA. These standards may be obtained from regional offices of the U.S. Government Printing Office, and are available in various pamphlets and books on food purchasing.

3. *Packaging information.* This describes how the ingredients should be delivered. Food items are packaged in a variety of ways. Different packaging may affect the quality and taste of the ingredients. An example is soup, which can be purchased canned, frozen, or refrigerated.

SPECIFICATION EXAMPLES

Meat

Meat specifications are described in *The Meat Buyers Guide,* which is published by the North American Meat Processors Association (NAMP) and is generally available through most meat suppliers. This book recommends that the product be specified by NAMP item number, product name, and weight range to be purchased. For example, to order a rib roast, the foodservice manager would specify item 109: rib, roast ready, netted, range 11–13 pounds.

Suppliers may also have their own particular method of specifying meat. The following is an example of how to order sirloin steaks from Foodservice of America, a regional fullservice supplier: Top Sirloin Choice, N/R, 12/up 1/83# ave, UPC # 712AC. The codes represent a method of tracking and ordering the specified item.

Canned Fruit

Fruit may be purchased graded or ungraded by the USDA. The following is a specification for canned Elberta peaches: canned peaches, yellow, Elberta halves, U.S. Grade A, light syrup, minimum drained weight 66 ounces per #10 can, count per #10 can: 25–30, 6 cans per case, quote per case, federal inspector's certification of grade required.

Frozen Vegetables

Frozen vegetables may also be graded by the USDA. The specification for asparagus may read as follows: Asparagus, all green, spear heads and stalks 3 inches, size medium (½-inch diameter), U.S. Grade A (Fancy), product should be packed in 40-ounce cartons.

Fresh Fruit

Like other products, the type and variety are indicated along with size, grade, how they should be packed, and the degree of ripeness, when applicable. For example: fresh apples, Red Delicious, U.S. Grade A, packed 80 to the box.

FINDING INFORMATION ABOUT SPECIFICATIONS

There are several places to find out information regarding specifications. Some of the more common are:

- U.S. Department of Agriculture, Agricultural Marketing Service, for produce, milk, poultry, meat, fresh produce, and processed products. They can be reached by mail at 14 Independence Ave., S.W., Washington, D.C. 20250, by telephone at 202-720-8998, or via the Internet at **http://www.ams.usda.gov**.

- North American Meat Processors Association (NAMP), *The Guide*, 1920 Association Drive, Suite #400, Reston, VA 20191-1547. They may also be reached by phone at 703-758-1900, by fax at 703-758-8001, or via the Internet at **http://www.namp.com**.

- National Restaurant Association, The Educational Foundation, Information Service and Library, 250 South Wacker Drive, Chicago, IL. 60606. They may be reached by phone at 800-765-2122; the Educational Foundation's Internet address is **http://www.edfound.org.** The National Restaurant Association has a Web page that contains pertinent information about the foodservice industry: **http://www.restaurant.org**.

FINDING INFORMATION ABOUT INGREDIENTS

Ingredients may be purchased in numerous ways. Part of being an effective foodservice manager or buyer is to constantly learn about ingredients and how they are packaged. Three ways for learning about ingredients are from suppliers, **trade publications,** and **professional associations.**

Most suppliers are very interested in helping foodservice managers learn about their products, and generally have much of the information readily available.

Restaurants USA and *The National Culinary Review* are excellent publications for product information. These magazines are published by the National Restaurant Association and the American Culinary Federation. Among the most widely read publications is *Nation's Restaurant News*, a weekly trade journal.

Other objective information may be obtained from national associations, councils, and commissions that represent producers of products, such

Trade publications
Magazines, newspapers, and journals that are published and sold by subscription to foodservice managers.

Professional associations
Local, regional, and national associations that serve a specific professional group (such as restaurants, health care foodservice, school foodservice, and so on).

Table 7-1   Standardized Recipe

RECIPE NAME: SHRIMP BISQUE

RECIPE NO. 131

QUANTITY	INGREDIENTS	PROCEDURE
1 lb	shrimp shells	1. Sauté shrimp shells and minced onions, carrots, and celery in butter.
1 lb ea.	onions, carrots, celery	
4 oz	butter	
2 cloves	garlic	2. Add the garlic and thyme and cook for about 5 minutes.
1 bunch	thyme	
2 tbsp	paprika	3. Add the paprika and tomato sauce and cook until mixture is lightly browned.
8 oz	tomato sauce	
8 oz	brandy	4. Add the brandy and deglaze.
1.5 gal	Fish Veloute*	5. Add the Fish Veloute. Simmer for 45 minutes and strain.
1 qt	heavy cream, hot	6. Add the heavy cream
1.5 lb	shrimp, peeled and deveined	7. Dice the shrimp, sauté, and add to the soup.
6 oz	sherry	8. Add the sherry.
Dash of seasoning salt, Tabasco sauce, and Worcestershire sauce.		9. Season to taste.
*This is a white sauce made with fish, Recipe #100.		Time to Prepare: 2.00 hours. Direct Labor: .75 hours.

Recipe provided by chefs Julian Darwin, CEC, and Vern Liebelt, CEC.

as the National Meat Council or the Pear Commission. These groups offer product information and recipes that can be used in any foodservice operation. Most libraries have a directory of state and national associations and commissions.

tandardized Recipes

The third step in developing quality standards is to use standardized recipes. A standardized recipe describes (1) the recipe name and number, (2) the quantities of ingredients, (3) the ingredients, and (4) the procedure for blending and preparing the ingredients. An example of a standardized recipe for Shrimp Bisque is shown in Table 7-1.

Standardized recipes are often carried in the memory of many chefs and cooks. This practice works if only one person prepares the menu items and there is no staff turnover. If the foodservice operation requires more than one chef or cook, then it is important to use standardized recipes. The practice of using standardized recipes allows foodservice managers to deliver a consistent product to the customer.

Recipe Cost Chart

The fourth step in developing quality standards is to create a recipe cost chart for each recipe. Besides using standardized recipes, managers should have a very complete understanding of the costs of every recipe. A conversion chart (Figure 7-1) is helpful in calculating measurements. A *recipe cost chart* is a form used to calculate the cost of a specific recipe. Some foodservice operations combine standardized recipes with a Recipe Cost Chart by listing the preparation methods at the bottom of the chart. If the recipe is complex, the form will not be an adequate tool for chefs and cooks. Probably the best method is to use both a standardized recipe form, shown in Table 7-1, and a recipe cost chart, shown in Table 7-2. The recipe cost chart gives the following information:

1. The recipe number for easy filing and indexing.
2. What the recipe is used for.
3. The number of recipe cost chart pages.
4. The date when priced.
5. The yield.
6. The number of servings and the portion size.

On the recipe cost chart for Shrimp Bisque, the recipe number is 131, the recipe for Shrimp Bisque is on page number 1 of 1 page, the date priced was October 7, XXXX, the total yield is 2 gallons, usage for Shrimp Bisque is as a soup, the number of servings is 21, and the portion size is 12 ounces (1.5 cups).

To calculate the cost, each ingredient price (extension) is multiplied by the unit price. For butter, that means 4 ounces of butter times a unit price of 8 cents or .08. Unit price is calculated by dividing the quoted price, $1.28 per pound, by the number of ounces per pound, 16 ounces ($1.28 divided by 16 ounces equals .08, or 8 cents per ounce). This unit price is put in the Unit Price column. The extension is the quantity multiplied by the unit price. For butter, the extension is 4 ounces multiplied by 8 cents, which equals .32 or 32 cents (4 × .08 = .32). This process is used for all the items in the recipe cost chart.

Calculating the unit price for bulk-prepared items is a more complicated process. In the Shrimp Bisque recipe, one of the ingredients is Fish Veloute. Fish Veloute is a white sauce made with fish stock, a type of soup. The preparation of Fish Veloute is accomplished using another standardized recipe. The cost of the recipe must be included in the Shrimp Bisque. In this case, the Fish Veloute cost is $11.25 per gallon. This cost was taken from the recipe cost chart for Fish Veloute.

3 teaspoons (tsp)	=	1 tablespoon (tbsp)	1 pint	=	16 ounces
1 tablespoon	=	½ ounce	16 ounces	=	1 pound (lb)
2 tablespoons	=	1 ounce	2 pints	=	1 quart (qt)
16 tablespoons	=	1 cup	1 quart	=	¼ gallon, 32 ounces
1 cup	=	8 ounces	1 gallon	=	128 ounces
2 cups	=	1 pint	16 cups	=	1 gallon

FIGURE 7-1
Weights and Measures This chart can be referenced when converting recipe amounts.

Table 7-2   Recipe Cost Chart

Recipe Number 131	Page 1 of 1
Recipe for Shrimp Bisque	Date Priced October 7, XXXX
Total Yield 2 gallons	Number of Servings 21
Usage Soup	Portion Size 12 ounces

AMOUNT/UNIT	INGREDIENTS	UNIT PRICE	EXTENSION
1 lb	shrimp shells	$ 4.29	$ 4.29
1 lb	onions	.14	.14
1 lb	carrots	.49	.49
1 lb	celery	.29	.29
4 oz	butter	.08	.32
2 cloves	garlic	.115	.23
1 bunch	thyme	.69	.69
2 tbsp	paprika	.11	.22
8 oz	tomato sauce	.036	.29
8 oz	brandy	.115	.92
1.5 gal	Fish Veloute	11.25	16.88
1 qt	heavy cream	2.06	2.06
1.5 lb	shrimp	3.99	5.99
6 oz	sherry	.058	.35
		TOTAL COST	$ 33.16
		PORTION COST	$ 1.58

After the cost of each ingredient is determined, the extensions are added to provide a total cost. The total cost is then divided by the number of portions the recipe produces. In the Shrimp Bisque example, there are 21 portions; each portion is 12 ounces.

Every menu item should have its cost determined. To help in this process, a number of computer software programs are available to help managers and cooks determine the recipe costs.

Yield Analysis

Two methods generally used for doing a **yield analysis** are a **cooking yield chart** and directly counting usable product. Through the use of the cooking yield chart, it is possible to determine the final amount of usable product (see Table 7-3). The results of this process will also help to establish and maintain specifications and standards for buying. Once the product specifications are determined and set forth, suppliers will be able to submit prices when competitively bidding for business.

The second method is counting. Products are often sold by count; for example, Elberta peach halves, 30 to 35 count per #10 can. When products are delivered, a check is made to verify that what has been delivered is exactly what was ordered.

Yield analysis
Calculating the amount of usable food derived from raw products.

Cooking yield chart
A method for calculating the amount of usable product.

■ ■ ■ ■ ■

Table 7-3   Cooking Yield Chart

Prepared by Chef	Date 1/10/XX
ITEM DESCRIPTION: NAMP #109C, Rib Roast Ready, USDA Choice (Prime Rib) Oven Prepared	
Gross weight or volume	26 lbs
Cooking or preparation loss	− 3 lbs 8 oz
Yield after cooking	22 lbs 8 oz
ALLOWANCE FOR SERVICE LOSS:	
Trimming, slicing, and tasting	− 11 lbs
Net yield	11 lbs 8 oz
PREPARATION PROCEDURE Oven temperature 350 degrees for 3½ hours, with the bone side down. Moisture added to roasting pan.	

HOW TO USE A COOKING YIELD CHART

The cooking yield chart can be used for any food product that can be measured for a set quality standard and quantity yield. This is true both for canned goods and for meats such as beef, pork, lamb, and veal. Before the meat item is purchased already cut, the usable product was an entire animal. Figures 7-2 to 7-5 show cuts of usable meat from beef, lamb, pork, and veal.

The example in Table 7-3 demonstrates the use of a cooking yield chart with a meat product that traditionally has shrinkage, a large loss from trimming fat, and losses from the removal of bones. The cooking yield chart in Table 7-3 is being used to analyze the yield in cooking and preparing of NAMP #109C, rib roast ready, USDA Choice, 24–28 pounds. The **gross weight** is 26 pounds and the resulting **net yield** is 11 pounds, 8 ounces.

True cost would be calculated as follows:

Purchase price	$ 3.45 per lb
Quantity purchased	× 26 lbs
Total cost	$89.70

The net yield, stated earlier, is 11 pounds, 8 ounces. Converting 11 pounds 8 ounces into ounces gives 184 ounces (11 pounds × 16 = 176 ounces, plus 8 ounces = 184 ounces). To calculate the true cost, divide the cost of the meat ($89.70) by 184 ounces, which gives $.4875 per ounce ($89.70 ÷ 184 = .4875). To calculate the cost per pound, multiply $.4875 per ounce × 16 ounces = $7.80 per pound. The main point to measuring and determining net yield is to identify the true cost as served on the plate. For an 8-ounce slice of prime rib, the portion cost would be 8 ounces × $.49 per ounce = $3.92. Another way of stating it is that the **portion cost** of the prime rib for the meal is $3.92.

The cooking yield chart should be continually used for products that have the potential to vary in quality and weight. The example of the prime rib reflects a typical shrinkage and trimming loss due to traditional cooking procedures. But the loss could be greater if it is not regularly, or at least occasionally, measured. The prime rib could possibly have a higher moisture content than would normally be acceptable, resulting in a larger shrinkage. Also, a larger-than-acceptable **fat cap** (the amount of fat that is attached to one side of the rib) would increase the trimming loss.

The final cost per pound for items that vary, such as prime rib, could be significantly different. This is of particular concern when competition among meat suppliers is price motivated. Quality specifications may become sacrificed for a more competitive price. Therefore, it is possible to buy a prime rib at a cheaper price per pound but have it cost more per pound after cooking compared to a product that may cost more at the time of purchase but be cheaper on the plate (see Table 7-4).

Through the use of the cooking yield chart, quality standards can be maintained. This is particularly true when suppliers know that the foodservice operation consistently measures yields. There will be a conscious effort on the part of the suppliers to always maintain product quality and specifications.

COOKING YIELD AND CATERING

Foodservice operations that offer banquet and catering services typically have fixed banquet and catering menus with established prices. Customers who

---

Gross weight
The weight of an item before it is cooked or prepared into menu items.

Net yield
The total weight or amount of food served to the guest after preparation procedures are completed.

True cost
The cost of an item after preparation.

Portion cost
The cost of the portion of food put on the plate.

Fat cap
A layer of fat that coats one side of a prime rib that has not been oven prepared.

Table 7-4 Comparison Yield from Two Suppliers

MEAT SUPPLIER A		MEAT SUPPLIER B	
Prime rib gross weight	26 lb	Prime rib gross weight	26 lb
Price per pound	$ 3.45	Price per pound	$ 3.25
Total cost	$89.70	Total cost	$84.50
Net yield	11 lb 8 oz	Net yield	10 lb
True cost	$ 7.80/lb	True cost	$ 8.45/lb

are concerned about the prices may shop around for the best deal. The food-service manager who remains flexible can accommodate these groups. That flexibility can be established with a current knowledge of prices for all quantities served, as in the example of prime rib at 49 cents per ounce. If a group wants a prime rib dinner but has to stay within a limited budget, the portion size of the prime rib could be reduced. If the banquet menu price is for an eight-ounce portion, a change can easily be made to reduce the size to perhaps six ounces or four ounces, served au jus with a french bread underliner. This could definitely reduce the price and position the foodservice operation very competitively for banquet and catering events.

Banquet and catering events represent excellent profit opportunities because knowledge of the exact number of customers in advance eliminates guesswork, allowing production control procedures to function best.

YIELD ANALYSIS FOR CANNED PRODUCTS

Yield analysis may be used to check **net weight** and **drained weight** claims made by canneries. Net weight is the total weight of the product and the packing medium. The **packing medium** is the fluid in which the product is packed. This is usually water or a type of syrup.

The following represents how the yield of a #10 can of fruit is checked according to the traditional procedure:

1. *Note the net weight.* The net weight is the weight of all the contents of the can, and is listed on the can. All manufacturers of food products are required to list the net weight.

2. *Note the drained weight.* Drained weight is the weight of the items in the can after the medium has been poured off. Not all manufacturers list drained weight. If it is listed, then it is usually printed under the net weight.

3. *Note the product count.* The **product count** is the number or range of items in the container. The product count is usually listed on the label next to the description of the items in the can—for example, Elberta peach halves, 30–35 count per #10 can.

4. *Open the can and empty the contents.* How this is done depends upon what is in the can. If the contents of the can fill up the can, they should be poured into a bowl. Prior to pouring out the contents, the bowl should be weighed so the bowl weight can be subtracted later. After pouring the contents into the bowl, the bowl is weighed. If the

Net weight
The total weight of the product and packing medium contained in the can.

Drained weight
Only the weight of the product contained in the can.

Packing medium
The fluid or other material in which the product is packed.

Product count
The number of items or number range of items in the container.

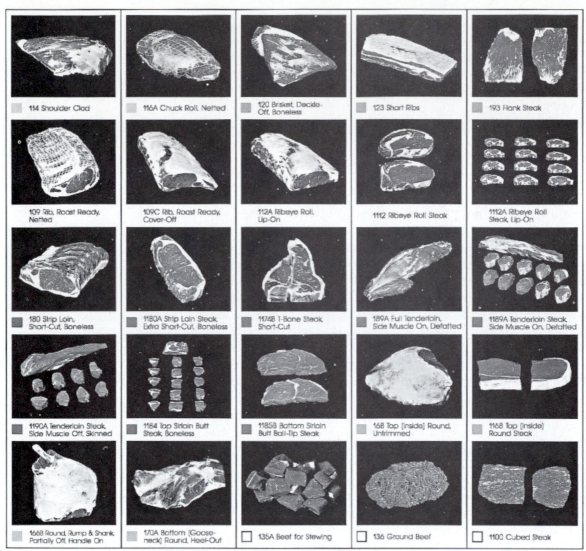

FIGURE 7-2
Purchase Specifications—Beef   *Courtesy of National Cattlemen's Beef Association.*

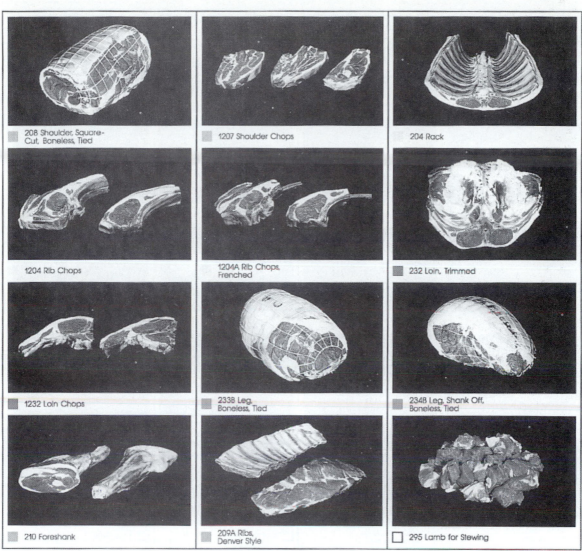

The above cuts are a partial representation of NAMP/IMPS items. For further representation and explanation of all cuts see the Meat Buyers Guide by National Association of Meat Purveyors.

Shoulder
Rack
Shank/Breast
Loin
Leg

NAMP/IMPS Number (National Association of Meat Purveyors/Institutional Meat Purchase Specifications)

National Association of Meat Purveyors
8365-B Greensboro Drive
McLean, Virginia 22102
(703) 827-5754

©1988 National Association of Meat Purveyors

National Live Stock & Meat Board
444 North Michigan Avenue
Chicago, Illinois 60611
(312) 467-5520

FIGURE 7-3
Purchase Specifications—Lamb   *Courtesy of National Cattlemen's Beef Association.*

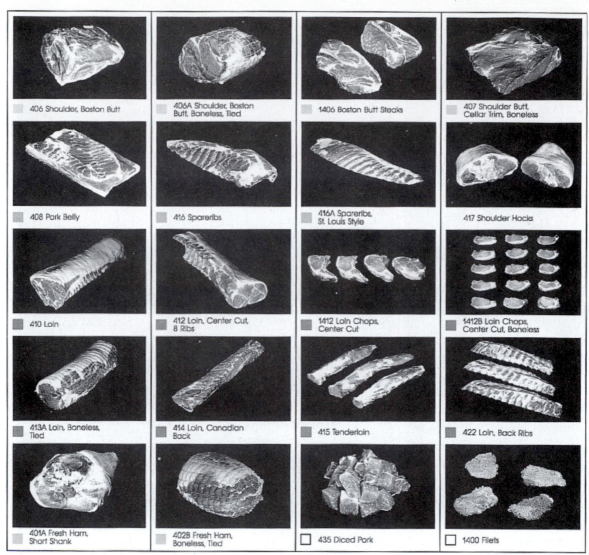

The above cuts are a partial representation of NAMP/IMPS items. For further representation and explanation of all cuts see The Meat Buyers Guide by National Association of Meat Purveyors.

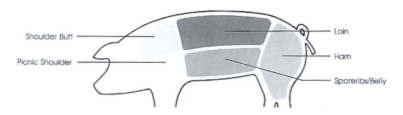

Shoulder Butt

Picnic Shoulder

Loin

Ham

Spareribs/Belly

NAMP/IMPS Number (National Association of Meat Purveyors/Institutional Meat Purchase Specifications)

National Association of Meat Purveyors
8365-B Greensboro Drive
McLean, Virginia 22102
(703) 827-5754

©1988 National Association of Meat Purveyors

National Live Stock & Meat Board
444 North Michigan Avenue
Chicago, Illinois 60611
(312) 467-5520

FIGURE 7-4
Purchase Specifications—Pork *Courtesy of National Cattlemen's Beef Association.*

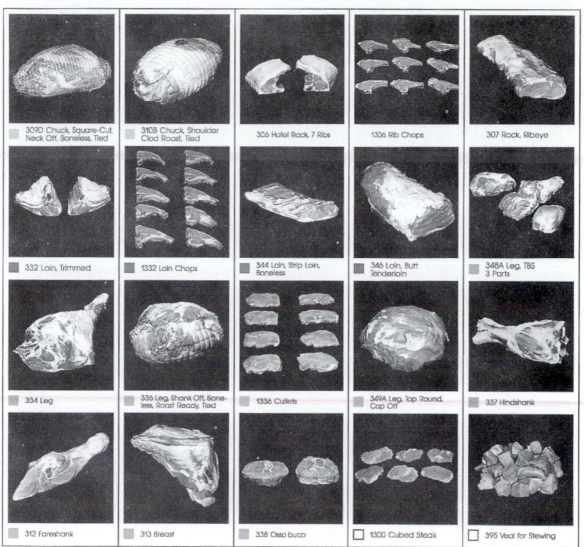

309D Chuck, Square-Cut, Neck Off, Boneless, Tied

310B Chuck, Shoulder Clod Roast, Tied

306 Hotel Rack, 7 Ribs

1306 Rib Chops

307 Rack, Ribeye

332 Loin, Trimmed

1332 Loin Chops

344 Loin, Strip Loin, Boneless

346 Loin, Butt Tenderloin

348A Leg, TBS 3 Parts

334 Leg

336 Leg, Shank Off, Boneless, Roast Ready, Tied

1336 Cutlets

349A Leg, Top Round, Cap Off

337 Hindshank

312 Foreshank

313 Breast

338 Osso buco

1300 Cubed Steak

395 Veal for Stewing

The above cuts are a partial representation of NAMP/IMPS items. For further representation and explanation of all cuts see The Meat Buyers Guide by National Association of Meat Purveyors.

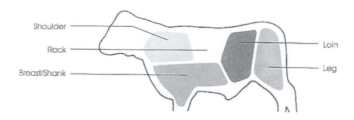

Shoulder

Rack

Breast/Shank

Loin

Leg

NAMP/IMPS Number (National Association of Meat Purveyors/Institutional Meat Purchase Specifications)

National Association of Meat Purveyors
8365-B Greensboro Drive
McLean, Virginia 22102
(703) 827-5754

©1988 National Association of Meat Purveyors

National Live Stock & Meat Board
444 North Michigan Avenue
Chicago, Illinois 60611
(312) 467-5520

FIGURE 7-5
Purchase Specifications—Veal   *Courtesy of National Cattlemen's Beef Association.*

product is packed in a medium, then two bowls will be needed, one to separate the product from the medium, and the other bowl for the product to be weighed.

5. *Compare the net weight, drained weight, or count to what is listed on the can.* If a discrepancy occurs, the chef or manager should talk to the supplier about obtaining a credit.

Regardless of how the product is packaged, a cost should be assigned to the usable food. If peach halves, 30–35 count, packed in light syrup are used and the can of peaches cost $4.36, the cost of one peach half at most is $.145 ($4.36 ÷ 30 = $.1453). If the chef wishes to make a peach and cottage cheese salad, the cost of the peach is now known.

Calculating yields for salad bars is not as difficult as it may seem. It is important to keep track of all items that are put on the salad bar. The food-service manager then calculates the cost of the items, adds the total together, and divides the total cost by the number of people who ate from the salad bar. The guest checks should indicate this. The result is the plate cost per person for eating from the salad bar. The amount that is consumed and the number of people eating from the salad bar will often vary by day of the week. Therefore, tracking usage for several consecutive days or for an accounting period will provide greater accuracy. If the foodservice operation has just begun offering a salad bar, the manager would need to estimate product usage until average use of the salad bar has been established to determine costs. An example of how this may work is illustrated in Table 7-5. According to the guest checks, 85 people ate from the salad bar. Therefore, $44.20 divided by 85 equals $.52 per serving. To calculate the yield per person of product used, divide each item by 85. For example, 5 heads of lettuce divided by 85 equals .0588 heads per person (in this case lettuce is sold by count, not weight). This same approach may be used for all items on the salad bar. Leftover amounts should be checked for quality and freshness. Reusable items should be stored until the next day.

P late Cost

The goal of managing plate costs is to control the amount spent on food that is eaten by the customer in relation to the amount paid for the food. To measure the cost of the food each customer eats, the cost of each portion or plate of food eaten should be calculated. The method of calculating costs depends upon the method of food preparation.

Most food items that appear on a plate are prepared either in batches or individually. Institutional foodservice operations (schools, health care facilities, and so on) frequently use **batch preparation** methods. Commercial foodservice operations come the closest to using **prepared-to-order** methods for each individual customer.

Batch preparation
Food prepared in large amounts and then divided into portions.

Prepared-to-order
Food prepared to each customer's order.

USING STANDARDIZED RECIPES TO DETERMINE PLATE COST

Standardized recipes are used to calculate the cost of the food used, regardless of whether a batch or prepared-to-order method of food preparation is

Table 7-5   Calculating the Cost of a Salad Bar

ITEM	COST
5 heads of lettuce, iceberg with salad mix	$ 5.35
5 lb four-bean salad	8.46
1 pint cottage cheese	1.65
5 lb elbow macaroni salad	5.40
5 lb potato salad	6.25
1 pint french dressing	2.17
1 pint blue cheese dressing	3.65
1 pint ranch dressing	3.04
1 pint italian dressing	2.70
1 lb Town House crackers	3.50
1 lb croutons	2.03
Total cost	$44.20
Number of people who ate (this number is taken from the guest checks)	85
Cost per person ($44.20 ÷ 85 = .52)	$ .52 per person

used. If a batch method is used, the total cost is divided up according to the number of portions that can be served. This is the portion cost. The individual portion costs are assembled into a menu cost. Food on prepared-to-order menus also usually uses standardized recipes.

An example of calculating the plate cost for a steak dinner comprising a steak, potato, vegetable, bread, and salad with dressing is as follows: The value of each portion is calculated by taking the total cost of the item from the invoice and dividing it by the number of items. A box of eight-ounce New York steaks (loin strip) weighs 70 pounds and contains 140 steaks. The box cost is $302.40. To calculate the cost of each steak, divide $302.40 by 140 steaks, which equals $2.18 per steak. The same process may be used for the potato (bought by the count per box), vegetable (frozen, purchased by the case, and dished up by the ounce), bread (rolls, purchased by the dozen), and salad (heads of lettuce bought by the case and cut into wedges, eight wedges to the head), and dressing (bottled, purchased by the case and served using a one-ounce ladle). The portion costs of all these ingredients is totaled to equal the plate cost.

To keep the costs current, it is critical to update the pricing on the recipe cost charts frequently due to changing supplier prices. The most recent prices are taken directly from current invoices and should always be used. Although this can be done manually, a computer application generates the fastest results. For example, if ground beef goes up 20 cents per pound and all the recipes containing ground beef are listed in the computer, a simple input of the new price would automatically adjust all the costs.

Table 7-6 shows how to cost an item that is prepared from scratch, similar to the example in Table 7-2; a computer-generated version is shown in Figure 7-6. If a scratch recipe is unique and is popular with customers, it can

Recipe Number 197	Page 1 of 1
Recipe for Chili Sauce	Date Priced 1/10/XX
Total Yield 5 gallons	Number of Servings 320
Usage To make Chili Dogs	Portion Size 2 ounce

AMOUNT/UNIT	INGREDIENTS	UNIT PRICE	EXTENSION
5 lb	ground beef	$ 1.79	$ 8.95
10 lb	chopped onions	.14	1.40
20 oz	chili powder	.22	4.40
6 oz	paprika	.23	1.38
1 oz	red pepper	.33	.33
1 oz	garlic salt	.10	.10
1 oz	black pepper	.31	.31
1½ oz	salt	.02	.03
3 46-oz cans	tomato soup	1.62	4.86
3 46-oz cans	tomato juice	.96	2.88
3 46-oz cans	water	--	--
4 oz	sugar	.03	.12
		TOTAL COST	$24.76
		PORTION COST	$ .08

Cooking Temperature Medium Heat

Cooking Time 3 Hours

Preparation Method

Thoroughly cook ground beef, then slowly add chopped onions and completely mix. Drain, then add chili powder, paprika, red pepper, garlic salt, black pepper, and salt, completely mixing with ground beef and onions. Using a 5 gallon pot, add the mix with tomato soup, tomato juice, water and sugar, thoroughly stirring. Bring to boil and continually stir to allow for thorough cooking. Simmer and serve.

Chili Sauce

Foodservice Profitability

Categories Sauce
Tools
Locations
Plate/Store

Prep

| **Yield** | 5 | gal | **Cook** 3 hours medium heat |
| **Portion** | 2 | fl oz | |

Num Portions 320

Ingredients			Cost	% of Total
5	lb	ground 90% lean beef	$12.25	41.3%
10	lb	onion	$5.90	19.9%
20	oz	chili powder	$4.40	14.8%
6	oz	paprika	$1.38	4.6%
1	oz	red pepper	$0.33	1.1%
1	oz	garlic salt	$0.10	0.3%
1	oz	ground black pepper	$0.31	1.0%
1 1/2	oz	salt	$0.03	0.1%
3	46 oz can	tomato soup	$4.86	16.4%
3	46 oz can	tomato juice	$0.00	
3	46 oz can	water	$0.00	
4	oz	sugar	$0.12	0.4%

$29.68

	Single Portion	Entire Recipe
Cost	$0.09	$29.68
Price	$0.00	$0.00
% Cost	0.0%	0.0%
Margin	($0.09)	($29.68)

FIGURE 7-6
Computer-Generated Recipe Cost Chart

become a **signature item** for the foodservice operation. A signature item is an item for which a specific foodservice operation is well known and which helps to attract customers.

The recipe cost chart in Table 7-6 covers the batch preparation of chili sauce and the prepared-to-order method of assembling the meal to serve customers (unlike Table 7-2, which only shows the costs associated with preparation and does not indicate preparation method). The recipe cost chart can be used to calculate both a batch and a portion cost. After the recipe costs are determined, the plate cost chart, as illustrated in Table 7-7, is used to calculate the cost of a meal presented to the customer. A computer-generated version is shown in Figure 7-7.

USING A PLATE COST CHART

The **plate cost chart** basically assembles all the portion costs for the meal and totals them. The form is divided into four columns: Amount/Unit, Ingredients, Unit Price, and Extension. The form allows the foodservice manager to combine the methods of calculating costs of a portion from a stan-

Signature item
An item for which a specific foodservice is well known.

Plate cost chart
Assembles all the portion costs for the meal and totals them.

■ ■ ■ ■ ■

Table 7-7   Plate Cost Chart

| | Menu Item   Chili Dog | | |
	Date Cost Calculated 1/10/XX		
AMOUNT/UNIT	**INGREDIENTS**	**UNIT PRICE**	**EXTENSION**
1	All-beef hot dog, 8 to a pound at $1.92 per pound	.24	.24
1	Hot dog bun, 8 per package at $.64 per package.	.08	.08
1	Chili Sauce, recipe #197, 2 oz ladle.	.08	.08
1	Ketchup, average cost/serving	.02	.02
1	Mustard, average cost/serving	.01	.01
1	Relish, average cost/serving	.02	.02
		TOTAL COST	0.45

ingredients; (4) the cost standards of preparing the recipe; and (5) the method of delivering the finished product to the table and serving the guest.

4. Specifications are used to obtain and use the correct ingredients. A specification includes: (1) the name of the item; (2) quality characteristics; and (3) packaging information.

5. Information about specifications may be obtained from government agencies, various trade associations, and the Educational Foundation of the National Restaurant Association.

6. The process for combining ingredients is detailed in a standardized recipe. A standardized recipe describes: (1) the recipe name and number; (2) the quantities of ingredients; (3) the ingredients; and (4) the procedure for blending and preparing the ingredients.

7. Standardized recipes are often carried in the memory of cooks and chefs. If the foodservice operation requires more than one chef or cook, standardized recipes should be used. A recipe cost chart is used to calculate the cost of a recipe.

8. A recipe cost chart looks similar to a standardized recipe.

9. To determine a recipe cost, a yield analysis must often be calculated. A yield analysis is usually calculated by one or all of the following techniques: a cooking yield chart, directly counting usable product, or calculating a cost based upon average consumption by guests.

10. Once the usable amount has been determined, a true cost is calculated by dividing the cost of the ingredient by the amount that can be used. The true cost is then posted on the recipe cost chart.

11. The costs of serving the customer are calculated using a plate cost chart. The plate cost chart basically assembles all the portion costs for the meal and totals them. The value of a plate cost chart is that it provides the foodservice manager with a complete understanding of all the costs of serving a meal to a guest. Food cost percentages can be calculated as a percentage of the price.

KEY CONCEPTS

Batch preparation
Cooking yield chart
Drained weight
Fat cap
Gross weight
Net weight
Net yield
Packing medium
Plate cost
Plate cost chart
Portion cost
Prepared-to-order

Product count
Professional associations
Quality standards
Recipe cost chart
Signature item
Specification
Standardized recipe
Trade publications
True cost
Yield
Yield analysis

DISCUSSION QUESTIONS AND EXERCISES

1. What is quality as it pertains to food served in a commercial food-service operation?

2. What do quality standards define?

3. What is a specification and what does it include?

4. Write an example of a specification.

5. List at least three sources of information regarding specifications.

6. Where can you find information about ingredients?

7. What does a standardized recipe describe?

8. Write a standardized recipe for an item that is not listed in the book and present it to the class.

9. Define the purpose of a recipe cost chart.

10. What is a yield?

11. Teach another person the principles of yield analysis and plate cost.

12. How are yield analysis and plate cost related?

13. Describe how to use a yield chart.

14. Describe how to determine a plate cost.

15. What are some typical problems associated with determining plate cost?

16. What is the net yield on an oven-prepared NAMP #109 prime rib, USDA Choice, that has a gross weight of 24 pounds, a cooking loss of 4 pounds, and a loss of 8 pounds due to trimming, slicing, and tasting? (See Appendix A for a blank Cooking Yield Chart.)

17. Recipe charts show the following portion costs for Shrimp Fettuccine: shrimp white sauce, 2 ounces, 18 cents; noodles, 5 ounces, 15 cents; peas, 2 ounces, 6 cents; bread, 1 slice, 5 cents; and dinner salad, one portion, 35 cents. Determine the plate cost using a blank Plate Cost Chart from Appendix A.

18. Draw a diagram similar to Figure 7-8 for the plate cost chart for a Chili Dog in Table 7-7.

8

Food Production Control

Learning Objectives

After reading this chapter and completing the discussion questions and exercises, you should be able to:

1. Maintain a record of how many menu items are sold by using a food sales recap report.
2. Use the information on the food sales recap report to prepare a food production report.
3. Develop plans for using leftover food to avoid waste.
4. Control the portion size of food as specified in the standardized recipe and the plate cost chart.
5. Use a portion control chart to compare how many portions should have been sold against what was actually sold.
6. Monitor how much waste occurs in the preparation and service of all food items.

About Food Production Control

The preparation of food to be sold to customers is a basic manufacturing process. A kitchen is a production plant. Raw and prepared products are ordered and received, stored and inventoried, and then assembled into products that are resold to customers. Thus, the kitchen can be viewed as the factory for the foodservice operation.

To manage a profitable kitchen, operational procedures must be in place to help direct the levels of production (how much to produce on any given day). If records are kept on the quantities of specific food items sold, production can be set in anticipation of sales.

The kitchen should always use leftover food products, along with maintaining a minimal amount of waste during the production process. Also, there should be a system to control the portion size for each food item sold. Portion sizes should be the same every time, so that every customer receives the identical amount of food and the profit margin for each item is maintained.

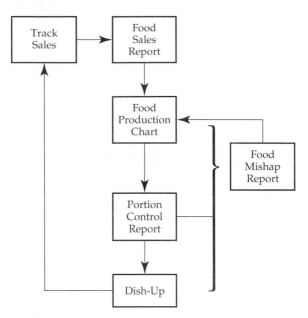

FIGURE 8-1
Food Production Control Process

This chapter demonstrates how to manage production effectively in the kitchen through the use of controls that will accurately track sales, production, and portion control. The overall process of food production control is shown in Figure 8-1.

Determining How Much to Prepare

Food production levels How much food needs to be prepared on a given day.

Food production par levels How much food must be on hand to serve the customers according to a preset food production level.

The quantity of food prepared should be determined as accurately as possible. If too little is prepared, menu items will run out, leaving customers frustrated and disappointed. If too much is prepared, the foodservice operation may increase food costs by wasting food. The first step is to track food sales. Until a foodservice manager has an understanding of how much food is sold and establishes **food production levels,** quantities must be guessed and are often inaccurate. After tracking food sales, the second step is to establish **food production par levels**. This is the amount of food that needs to be prepared for menu items each day. This is similar to maintaining inventory par levels.

Serving food according to specifications is part of food production. This means ensuring that the portions are correctly dished up. The quickest way to increase the cost of food sold is to overportion plates. Menu items are priced based upon standardized recipe costs. The costs are predicated upon portion sizes. If the size of the portion is not served, then the cost of production will either be too high or too low. Serving a portion that is larger than it should be causes the foodservice operation to lose money. Serving a portion that is smaller may cause the customer to feel cheated.

Being aware of the food that is wasted in production allows the foodservice manager to become more efficient at minimizing waste. To measure how the operation is managing its waste requires an accounting process. The accounting process requires employees to make entries on a **food mishap report,** which will be explained later in this chapter.

Food mishap report
Accounts for wasted food portions when balancing with the portion control chart.

 racking Food Sales

To establish a par level, the foodservice manager must track menu item sales or be able to determine exact pars based upon the number of customers that are served. By keeping track of the past sales of each menu item per year, month, or week, a foodservice manager can estimate customer orders. Managers keep track of sales by using a **food sales recap report** (see Table 8–1). The food sales recap report is used to record the number of menu items sold per day and the total per week.

Food sales recap report
A chart used to keep track of how many menu items were sold on specific days.

    The food sales recap report has multiple uses. The information it provides is used to develop a **food production chart** (see Table 8-2). A food production chart is used to provide guidance for cooks to forecast how much food to prepare. Also, the foodservice operation manager or kitchen manager uses the food production chart to schedule enough cooks to do the work. Other uses of the food sales recap report include determining which items to drop from the menu, which items are the most popular, whether sales promotions are working, and to track the level of business (this topic will be discussed further in Chapter 9).

Food production chart
A chart that informs cooks and chefs how much food to prepare.

    Institutional foodservice managers generally do not use a food sales recap report as the document to construct a food production chart. To determine demand, they monitor head counts. Health care and school foodservice managers, for example, usually know how many people are going to eat per meal period by counting the number of **resident heads.** This information is available from the admissions office of a health care facility, attendance office, or other office that keeps track of who is in residence. Therefore, institutional foodservice managers generally have a head count that is used to estimate the amount of food to prepare for any given day.

Resident head
A person who resides in a residential institutional environment such as a college, health care facility, penal institution, and so on.

How to Prepare a Food Production Chart

The food production chart serves as a guide. This chart tells the kitchen staff what and how much to prepare on a daily basis. By following this chart, all food production can be controlled. This reduces the possibility of overproduction or waste, as well as ensuring that enough products will be on hand and properly rotated.

    The example in Table 8-2 demonstrates the chart's function. Table 8-2 sets forth the amount of chili sauce to be prepared on Friday. The par amount of 5 gallons is established on the basis of anticipated sales. It represents the amount that should be maintained on Friday. Keep in mind that the *par* is to be adjusted as sales increase or decrease. This ensures that enough product is on hand and maintains product freshness. The chili sauce is an item used to make chili dogs, which are a weekend house special. If the chili sauce is not completely used up by Sunday, the remaining amount could be used on

Table 8-1   Food Sales Recap Report

	Department	Coffee Shop			Page	1 of 12			
	Prepared by	Clerical			Week of	1/13/XX			

MENU ITEMS	DATE: 1/13 MONDAY	14 TUESDAY	15 WEDNESDAY	16 THURSDAY	17 FRIDAY	18 SATURDAY	19 SUNDAY	TOTALS
JUICES								
Apple	31	17	21	24	29	28	19	169
Grapefruit	86	99	79	84	97	97	88	630
Orange	198	157	163	149	169	191	186	1,213
Pineapple	7	3	11	5	9	6	14	55
Tomato	40	31	28	46	39	11	47	242
Chili Dogs					54	131	97	282
Chicken Salad Sandwich	17	9	18	5	8	8	6	71
Meat Loaf Special	192							192
Weather	rain	clear	clear	cloudy	rain	rain	clear	
Other conditions			baker late		power out 15 min.			

Table 8-2 Food Production Chart

	Department	Kitchen			Page	1	of	5	
	Prepared by	Chef			Week	1/13/XX			

ITEM DESCRIPTION	Recipe Number	MONDAY	TUESDAY	WEDNESDAY	THURSDAY	FRIDAY	SATURDAY	SUNDAY
Chili Sauce	197	par / prep				5 gal / 5 gal		
Chicken Salad	255	2 lbs	2 lbs	4 lbs	2 lbs	4 lbs	2 lbs	2 lbs
Meat Loaf (Monday Special)	636	65 lbs						
Mashed Potatoes "	87	53 lbs						
Brown Gravy "	123	1 3/4 gal						
Peas (frozen) "	409	40 lbs						

Monday lunch or kept until next Friday. If a ½ gallon is left over and kept until next Friday, then 4½ gallons would be the amount prepared.

Chicken salad is an item that is made fresh daily. The par amounts have been established on the basis of anticipated sales for each day of the week. The chart indicates that two pounds are prepared daily and four pounds are prepared on Wednesday and Friday.

The meat loaf special with mashed potatoes, brown gravy, and peas is the Monday lunch and dinner special. The amount designated to prepare is the par for that day only. Any leftover amounts could go for employee lunches until the item runs out.

Food production control is easy once a production procedure is followed.

Portion Control and Presentation

After the food is prepared, the challenge is to serve the correct amount in the correct way to each customer, resident, or patient. The process is usually referred to as dishing up the food. The process of putting food on the plate is frequently called the **dish-up.** Usually food is portioned and sold according

Dish-up
The process of putting food on the plate.

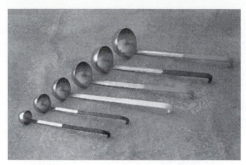

CAPACITY	COLOR
1 oz	Black
2 oz	Blue
3 oz	Ivory
4 oz	Gray
5 oz	Teal
6 oz	Orange

FIGURE 8-2
Ladle Sizes The picture shows different sizes of ladles in which the handles are color coded for ease of use. *Courtesy of the Vollrath Company.*

to weight. Therefore, scales should be handy to ensure that the portion dish-up is done properly. The following is a list of suggestions to ensure the proper dish-up:

1. If the food is in small pieces (peas, corn off the cob, and so on), use a slotted spoon or spoodle for dish-up. If it is in a liquid form (gravies and sauces, for example), use a ladle for dish-up. Figures 8-2 and 8-3 show different ladle and spoodle sizes.

2. If the food is in a semisolid form (mashed potatoes, ice cream, and so on) use a scoop for dish-up. Figure 8-4 shows different sizes of scoops.

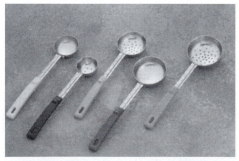

CAPACITY	COLOR
2 oz	Blue
3 oz	Ivory
4 oz	Gray
6 oz	Teal
8 oz	Orange

FIGURE 8-3
Spoodle Sizes The picture shows different sizes of spoodles in which the handles are color coded for ease of use. *Courtesy of the Vollrath Company.*

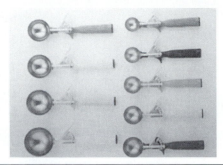

CAPACITY	MEASURE	SIZE	COLOR
5⅓ oz	⅔ cup	6	White
4 oz	½ cup	8	Gray
3¼ oz	⅓ cup	10	Ivory
2⅔ oz	5 tbsp	12	Green
2 oz	4 tbsp	16	Dark Blue
1⅝ oz	3 tbsp	20	Yellow
1⅓ oz	2⅔ tbsp	24	Red
1 oz	2 tbsp	30	Black
¾ oz	1 tbsp	40	Orchid

FIGURE 8-4
Scoop Sizes   The picture shows different sizes of scoops in which the handles are color coded for ease of use. *Courtesy of the Vollrath Company.*

3. If the item is solid, sold by the ounce, then the item will need to be cut into the portion size required. Prime rib and roasts are examples of this type of dish-up. After the item is cut, it should be weighed on a scale. Figure 8-5 shows typical portion control scales. A meat slicer may be used to regulate the size of the cut. After an initial adjustment, a meat slicer may slice cooked meat into the exact number of ounces required.

4. Purchase pre-portioned items when possible—for example, six-ounce steaks, corn on the cob, and so on.

5. Portion pies and cakes by using a pie marker prior to cutting.

Foodservice managers should regularly consult with suppliers to keep current on the newest methods of controlling the dish-up.

Tracking Portions

When menus are written and priced, a portion size for each food item must always be established, as demonstrated in the example in Table 8-3: meat loaf, 5 ounces; mashed potatoes, 4 ounces; gravy, 1 ounce; and peas, 3 ounces.

To control usage, a **portion control chart** should be prepared on a daily basis. The amounts of food left should be weighed and recorded at the close of either the shift or the day's business. The amounts sold are obtained from the food sales recap report (Table 8-1), in which the amounts have been totaled from customer guest checks, and subtracted from the total possible number, reflecting whatever difference. The total possible number is obtained by dividing the total quantity prepared by the portion size. (For example:

Portion control chart
A chart used to verify that the number of portions that should be served were actually served.

FIGURE 8-5
Portion Control Scales *Portion control scales courtesy of Pelouze.*

meat loaf, 65 pounds converted to 1,040 ounces, divided by 5 ounces (portion size) = 208 possible servings.)

The difference could be positive or negative, which will indicate over-portioning, underportioning, or possible waste (which is traced by using a food mishap report). All food products can be accurately accounted for through the consistent use of a portion control chart.

How to Prepare a Food Mishap Report

Mistakes and errors are part of doing business and are part of the food production process. Honest mistakes and errors are often made as a result of clumsiness or someone not being attentive enough to the work at hand. Whatever the circumstances, the wasted products need to be accounted for and recorded on a food mishap report (see Table 8-4).

The food mishap report serves two significant functions:

1. To account for wasted food portions when balancing with the portion control chart.
2. To identify responsibility and accountability within the production and service staff.

The food mishap report should be placed on a clipboard along with a pencil. It should be hung on a wall that is conveniently accessible to all potential users. The food mishap report in Table 8-4 reflects some typical examples of situations that often occur. The food mishap report is submitted to the man-

Table 8-3   Portion Control Chart

Department __Coffee Shop__			Page __1__ of __3__					
Day __Monday__			Final Amounts Recorded by __Cook (P.M.)__					
Date __1/13/XX__			Amounts Sold/Differences by __Clerical__					
Time __9:15 P.M.__			Approved by __Owner/Manager__					

ITEM DESCRIPTION	RECIPE NUMBER	QUANTITY PREPARED	PORTION SIZE	POSSIBLE NUMBER*	AMOUNT SOLD	DIFFERENCE*	AMOUNT LEFT	+ OR – DIFFERENCE*
Meat Loaf	636	65 lbs / 1040 ozs	5 oz	208	192	16	weight 68 ozs / 13 portions	– 3*
Mashed Potatoes	87	53 lbs / 848 ozs	4 oz	212	192	20	63 ozs / 15	– 5*
Brown Gravy	123	1¾ gal / 224 ozs	1 oz	224	192	32	31 ozs / 31	– 1*
Peas	409	40 lbs / 640 ozs	3 oz	213	192	21	42 ozs / 14	– 7*
		_____ /						NOTE: Adjust by 1, waitress dropped plate.
		Quantity Prepared ÷	Portion Size =	Possible Number*				
		_____ /		Possible Number –	Amount Sold	= Difference*		
		_____ /				Difference – Amount Left = + or – Difference*		
		_____ /						
		_____ /						
		_____ /						
		_____ /						
		_____ /						

ager along with requisitions and transfers that have been completed during the day's business.

Presentation

Presentation is the visual display of the food on the plate. Effective presentation principles are usually shown and explained in professional cookbooks. Information for controlling effective presentation falls into two categories: verbal information that tells the cooks how to prepare and present the food, and visual information that cooks can use as a model for dishing up the food. The guiding principle is that food should be presented the same way each time it is served to the customer.

Presentation is made consistent by using the following processes:

1. Follow the standardized recipe without exception. The recipe describes how the food is to be prepared and portioned.

Presentation
The visual display of the food on the plate.

■ ■ ■ ■ ■
Table 8-4   Food Mishap Report

Department	Coffee Shop			Week of	1/13/XX	

DAY	DATE	TIME	ITEM DESCRIPTION	MISHAP	NAME
Monday	1/13	7:10 A. M.	2 fried eggs	Overcooked	Carl
Tuesday	1/14	12:30 P. M.	Meat loaf special	Dropped it	Beth
Wednesday	1/15	11:05 A. M.	Boston creme pie	Fell off counter	Randy
Thursday	1/16	6:20 P. M.	New York steak	Overcooked	Greg

Report: To be sent to the office at the end of the week.

2. Take a picture of what the plate of food should look like. The picture should be posted on a picture board for the cook to see. The cook then can look at the picture and verify that the food being dished up looks exactly like the picture.

3. In fine-dining restaurants, an **expediter** will often check the food and compare the dished-up plate to a mental picture of the correct plate. In some operations, the foodservice manager plays the role of expediter.

Through the use of standardized recipes and plate pictures, the required standards can be effectively communicated to employees.

Expediter
A person who checks each order prepared by the cooks to ensure that the order has been prepared and presented correctly.

SUMMARY

1. Food production control comprises the following: (1) determining the quantities of product to produce to meet the estimated demand by customers; (2) preparing a food production chart to inform the cooking staff as to how much to produce; and (3) monitoring the presentation of the food to ensure that proper portioning (dish-up) occurs.

2. To control portioning, a portion control chart should be used to check the number of portions that actually were served against what should have been served.

3. Another control device is a food mishap report. This report is used to track food that is not served to customers.

KEY CONCEPTS

Dish-up	Food production par levels
Expediter	Food sales recap report
Food mishap report	Portion control chart
Food production chart	Presentation
Food production levels	Resident Head

DISCUSSION QUESTIONS AND EXERCISES

1. Why does it make sense to liken a kitchen to a factory?

2. Describe the food production control process.

3. What is the value of using a food sales recap report?

4. How is a food production chart prepared?

5. What is the relationship between proper dish-up and portion control?

6. How can product usage be controlled?

7. Presentation can be made consistent by using three processes. List and describe them.

8. Why is it important to require employees to use a food mishap report?

9. Describe how to complete a food mishap report.

10. Given the following information, complete a food production chart (see Appendix A for a blank form).

Chili Sauce, Recipe #225

Sunday	closing amount, 1 gallon
Monday	par is 10 gallons; closing amount, 1 gallon
Tuesday	par is 10 gallons; closing amount, 2 gallons
Wednesday	par is 12 gallons; closing amount, 3 gallons
Thursday	par is 12 gallons; closing amount, 1 gallon
Friday	par is 15 gallons; closing amount, 2 gallons
Saturday	par is 15 gallons; closing amount, 3 gallons
Sunday	par is 5 gallons; closing amount, 1 gallon

Chicken Salad, Recipe #205

Sunday	par is 5 lb; closing amount, 2 lb
Monday	par is 8 lb; closing amount, 2 lb
Tuesday	par is 8 lb; closing amount, 2 lb
Wednesday	par is 8 lb; closing amount, 1 lb
Thursday	par is 10 lb; closing amount, 3 lb
Friday	par is 12 lb; closing amount, 4 lb
Saturday	par is 12 lb; closing amount, 1 lb
Sunday	par is 5 lb; closing amount, 1 lb

11. Given the following information, complete a portion control chart for Thursday (see Appendix A for a blank form).

Chicken Salad (recipe #205)	par is 8 lb; closing amount, 2 lb; 26 portions sold, 4-ounce portion.
Mashed Potatoes (recipe #87)	par is 6 lb; closing amount, 2 lb; 24 portions sold, 3-ounce portion.
Brown Gravy (recipe #123)	par is ½ gallon; closing amount, ¼ gallon; 23 portions sold, 1-ounce portion.
Peas (recipe #409)	par is 4 lb; closing amount, 1 lb; 22 portions sold, 2-ounce portion.
Ham (recipe #422)	par is 12 lb; closing amount, 4 lb; 19 portions sold, 6-ounce portion.
Chicken Fried Steak (recipe #215)	par is 12 lb; closing amount, 1 lb; 44 portions sold, 4-ounce.
Bread Pudding (recipe #610)	par is 5 lb; closing amount, 1 lb; 23 portions sold, 4-ounce portion.

In addition, the cook dropped 8 ounces of peas on the floor.

9

Menu Sales Analysis

■ ■ ■ ■ ■ ■ ■ ■ ■ ■ ■ ■ ■

Learning Objectives

After reading this chapter and completing the discussion questions and exercises, you should be able to:

1. Tally guest checks and complete a food sales recap report.

2. Complete a menu analysis.

3. Evaluate the menu to determine which items are popular and profitable, popular and unprofitable, unpopular and profitable, and unpopular and unprofitable.

4. Determine what menu items should be deleted from the menu.

About Menu Sales Analysis

Managing a foodservice operation is much like managing any retail store that sells general merchandise along with certain specialty items. The success of the operation to a large extent depends upon management's ability to consistently provide the products that customers want at the quality and price that they expect, along with satisfying their needs and desires for new products.

To accomplish this goal, management must constantly review sales levels. This information is collected from customer guest checks as each item from the menu is totaled according to the amount sold. Therefore, foodservice managers need to identify items that are strong sellers along with items that do not sell as well.

Profitability for each menu item should also be evaluated. The popular items should be among the more profitable for the foodservice operation. The unpopular items may need to be kept on the menu if they remain profitable and generate some loyal patronage from a select group of customers, or they may need to be replaced with new items.

The constant quest of the foodservice manager is to be aware of new food products, new ways of preparing foods, and innovative food presentations. This can be a way of remaining competitive for those customers who are always looking to experience something new.

Fixed menu
A type of menu that does not change once established.

Cyclical menu
A type of menu that rotates on a regular basis so that the same menu is used periodically, such as every Monday or the first week of the month.

The decision to offer a **fixed menu,** a changing or **cyclical menu,** or a combination of fixed and cyclical menus is based primarily upon the needs of the foodservice operation's targeted market. Increasing the number of items available on a menu increases the cost of doing business, as it affects food, labor, and equipment costs.

Fixed menus normally can decrease labor costs as the employees become increasingly skilled in the tasks they perform. At the same time, the possibility of decreased food costs occurs, since the operator needs to buy only those items on the menu.

A changing menu requires additional supervision and greater skills on the part of the employees. Inventories are normally larger, but the operation can take advantage of market specials to reduce food costs. The cyclical menu offers very much the same advantages and disadvantages, but the length of the cycle may adversely affect inventories and food costs.

Finally, the combination menu is a compromise of the other types. It offers the advantages of both and also has some of the disadvantages.

The type of menu selected must be determined by the market to which a foodservice operation caters. Management should be alert to changing markets. All menus, whether fixed or cyclical, whether breakfast or dinner, whether high-priced or low-priced, must contain certain elements that will attract a loyal patronage.

This chapter will focus specifically on the methods used to analyze menu sales and profitability.

The Process of Menu Analysis

Giving the customers what they want is a constant challenge. Foodservice managers recognize that getting the customers to say, "I'll be back," happens only if they are satisfied with their experience. Institutional foodservice managers also realize that to do their jobs effectively, they must offer food that is appealing and nutritious.

The basic elements to getting customers to return are good food, efficient service, a clean environment, and a fair price. Therefore, the focus of any foodservice operation is twofold: to offer food that the customers want to eat, and to offer food that makes the operation profitable. Two tools can be used to reach these objectives: the food sales recap report and **menu analysis.** Menu analysis is depicted in Figure 9-1.

Menu analysis
A process of comparing the popularity and profit contribution of menu items.

USING A FOOD SALES RECAP REPORT

The daily sales for each item on the menu should be taken from the customer guest checks and recorded on a food sales recap report. The purpose is to be able to identify the food items that are selling well, along with those items that are not selling. This data provides information for management to review.

Knowing the exact quantities sold will help to forecast the quantities to be prepared for the food production chart (Table 8-2). Also, the figures (daily amounts sold) can be used to balance with the portion control chart (Table 8-3). Many foodservice operations have this report linked to the cash register through an integrated computer system. For example, when ringing up a

① From the guest checks

Guest Check 1012
Guest Check 1013
Guest Check 1014
. . . . . .
Guest Check 1201

② Record sales of items on the food sales recap report

Food Sales Recap Report

Department Coffee Shop
Prepared by Clerical
Page 1 of 12
Week of 1/13/XX

MENU ITEMS	DATE: 1/13 MONDAY	14 TUESDAY	15 WEDNESDAY	16 THURSDAY	17 FRIDAY	18 SATURDAY	19 SUNDAY	TOTALS
SALADS								
Chef	26	12	16	19	24	23	14	134
Cobb	16	19	19	14	17	17	18	
Chicken	58	57	63	49	69	91	86	
Oriental Stir Fry	7	3	11	5	9	6	14	
Stuffed Tomato	40	31	28	46	39	11	47	
SANDWICHES								
BLT	20	6	23	19	22	3	9	
Hamburger	105	100	125	133	156	115	95	
Cheeseburger	108	102	137	143	188	137	96	
Chicken Sal San	17	9	18	5	8	8	6	
Meat Loaf San	196							
Chili Dog					54	131	97	
Weather	rain	rain	clear	cloudy	rain	rain	clear	
Other conditions			baker late		power out			

③ Complete the menu analysis

Menu Analysis Chart

Department Coffee Shop
Prepared by Clerical
Category Sandwiches
Page 1 of 12
Week of 1/13/XX

MENU ITEM	NUMBER SOLD	PERCENT SOLD	MENU PRICE	PLATE COST	GROSS PROFIT	TOTAL GROSS PROFIT	PROFIT PERCENT
BLT	102	4.28	$3.99	$1.00	$2.99	$ 304.98	6.24
Hamburger	821	34.45	2.99	1.04	1.95	1,600.95	32.74
Cheeseburger	911	38.23	3.29	1.31	1.98	1,803.78	36.88
Chicken Sal San	71	2.98	3.99	.80	3.19	226.49	4.63
Meat Loaf San	196	8.22	4.99	2.05	2.94	576.24	11.78
Chili Dog	282	11.83	1.99	.65	1.34	377.88	7.73
Total	2,383	99.99				4,890.32	100.00

④ Compare menu items

Comparing Menu Items

POPULARITY		MENU ITEM GROSS PROFIT		TOTAL GROSS PROFIT	
Cheeseburger	38.23%	Chick Sal San	$3.19	Cheeseburger	36.88%
Hamburger	34.45	BLT	2.99	Hamburger	32.74
Chili Dog	11.83	Meat Loaf San	2.94	Meat Loaf San	11.78
Meat Loaf San	8.22	Cheeseburger	1.98	Chili Dog	7.73
BLT	4.28	Hamburger	1.95	BLT	6.24
Chick Sal San	2.98	Chili Dog	1.34	Chick Sal San	4.63

⑤ Make menu adjustments
• Raise or lower prices
• Change portion size
• Delete items
• Add items

FIGURE 9-1
Process of Menu Analysis

cheeseburger, the cashier would only have to press the cheeseburger button to ring up the price for that menu item. At that point, the computer records the item (cheeseburger) along with the price. As each item is entered into the point-of-sale terminal (cash register), the terminal records the cumulative totals of all items sold and the associated dollar amounts. If done manually, this process would require using guest checks.

At the end of the shift or business day, the amounts for all items sold are completely totaled. There are many more sophisticated computer systems available that will accommodate large menus along with more analytical approaches to reviewing menu sales.

An alternative method for tallying sales, if the operation does not have a computer software program, would be to have food sales recap reports preprinted with menu items, leaving additional space to add items (see Table 9-1). As the foodservice manager tallies the guest checks, a dot-box system or other acceptable counting method could be used for counting each menu item (see Figure 9-2A). After making the dots and boxes, a simple conversion can be made to represent the total number of each item. Figure 9-2B shows how the system works. Although labor-intensive and time-consuming when done manually, the information is critical. Another advantage of keeping a food sales recap report is that it can be used to compare current sales with past sales. Each week, the foodservice manager may take the previous year's food sales recap report and compare it to this year's food sales recap report. The differences between the years may provide information on possible trends. For example, the sales of an oriental stir fry may drop and the sales of chef salads may rise.

The food sales recap report provides the opportunity to further analyze the **menu mix.** Menu analysis is extremely important for effective menu planning. It is absolutely essential to be informed of any possible slow-moving items on the menu so that corrective action can be taken if necessary.

Menu mix
A mix of menu items that reflect varying degrees of popularity and profitability

HOW TO DO A MENU ANALYSIS

A menu analysis helps foodservice managers identify items that may not be popular or profitable. Similar menu items can be compared according to sales and **gross profit** by using a menu analysis chart (see Table 9-2). The menu analysis chart is a **spreadsheet** that lists menu items by categories (breakfast, lunch, dinner, desserts, beverages, and so on) of each item sold. Each item's popularity is shown as a percentage and each item's profitability is shown as a percentage.

Managers should keep in mind that all menu items fall into one of four categories:

Gross profit
The difference between the selling price and the cost of the menu item.

Spreadsheet
A sheet with rows and columns in which data are placed to show the numerical relationships between the items listed.

- Popular and profitable
- Popular and unprofitable
- Unpopular and profitable
- Unpopular and unprofitable

Step One—Analyzing Sales Activity

The first step in menu analysis is to record and analyze the sales activity. Table 9-2 lists sandwich item sales for the week of 1/13/XX, as taken from the

Table 9-1   Food Sales Recap Report

| Department | Coffee Shop | | Page | 1 of 12 | | | |
| Prepared by | Clerical | | Week of | 1/13/XX | | | |

MENU ITEMS	DATE: 1/13 MONDAY	14 TUESDAY	15 WEDNESDAY	16 THURSDAY	17 FRIDAY	18 SATURDAY	19 SUNDAY	TOTALS
SALADS								
Chef	26	12	16	19	24	23	14	134
Cobb	16	19	19	14	17	17	18	120
Chicken	58	57	63	49	69	91	86	473
Oriental Stir Fry	7	3	11	5	9	6	14	55
Stuffed Tomato	40	31	28	46	39	11	47	242
SANDWICHES								
BLT	20	6	23	19	22	3	9	102
Hamburger	105	100	125	133	156	115	95	829
Cheeseburger	108	102	137	143	188	137	96	911
Chicken Sal San	17	9	18	5	8	8	6	71
Meat Loaf San	196							196
Chili Dog					54	131	97	282
Weather	rain	rain	clear	cloudy	rain	rain	clear	
Other conditions			baker late		power out			

•	= 1	(dots pattern)	= 6
••	= 2	(dots pattern)	= 7
•••	= 3	(box pattern)	= 8
••••	= 4	(box with diagonal)	= 9
•••••	= 5	(box with X)	= 10

Using this system, look at how the sample Food Sales Recap Report would look before numbers were written on it. Only the first three items are used to illustrate the system.

FIGURE 9-2A
Guest Check Menu Item Tally System   Part of the task of compiling a food sales recap report is reviewing the guest checks and marking the number of each menu item sold on the report. The following system will help with this: As you note each item, mark a dot on the menu item category on the food sales recap report. Connect the dots and then put an X in the box.

food sales recap report. The first two columns (Menu Item and Number Sold) of the menu analysis chart restate information from the food sales recap report. The next column reports the percentage sold, which represents the percentage of sales each item has in relationship to total sales in that category.

Therefore, 102 BLTs were sold, out of a total of 2,383 sandwiches. The relationship of BLT sales to total sandwich sales is represented in the form of a percentage, 4.28 percent. This means that 4.28 percent of all sandwich menu items sold were BLTs. The percentage is calculated by dividing the number of BLTs sold by the total number of menu items sold and then multiplying the decimal by 100 (102 ÷ 2,383 = .0428; .0428 × 100 = 4.28%). This process is repeated for all the sandwich items on the menu.

Cheeseburgers are the most popular at 38.23%, followed by hamburgers, 34.45%; chili dogs, 11.83%; meat loaf sandwiches, 8.22%; BLTs, 4.28%; and chicken salad sandwiches, 2.98%. The meat loaf sandwich was popular for the day it was served. Cheeseburgers, hamburgers, and chili dogs could be considered popular. Chicken salad sandwiches and BLTs are obviously not as popular.

The chicken salad sandwich seems to be the least popular. It was offered every day on the menu. Management has four decision options:

1. Remove chicken salad sandwiches from the menu.
2. Adjust recipe after taste testing; a different flavor may have a positive effect.
3. Reduce or increase the price to see if demand is stimulated.
4. Do nothing; just take note of the problem.

When considering removing an item from the menu, management must also consider the overall mix of the products offered. Eating is generally considered a social experience. While many individuals eat alone, most people eat in groups of two or more, one of whom may want a slow-moving item. Thus, it may not be a bad idea to have a few slow-moving items if they help sell the more profitable, higher-selling items.

Step Two—Calculating Profitability

The second step in menu analysis is to identify the level of profitability for each menu item. Even though some items may be strong sellers, if they are

Department	Coffee Shop			Page	1	of	12	
Prepared by	Clerical			Week	1/13/XX			

MENU ITEMS	MONDAY	TUESDAY	WEDNESDAY	THURSDAY	FRIDAY	SATURDAY	SUNDAY	TOTALS
	Date: 1/13	14	15	16	17	18	19	
Salads: Chef	⊠ ⊠ ⌐·	⊠ :	⊠ ⌐·	⊠ ⊠	⊠ ⊠ ::	⊠ ⊠ :.	⊠ ::	134
Cobb	⊠ ⌐·	⊠ ⊠	⊠ ⊠	⊠ ::	⊠ ⊏	⊠ ⊏	⊠ ☐	120
Chicken	⊠ ⊠ ⊠ ⊠ ⊠ ☐	⊠ ⊠ ⊠ ⊠ ⊠ ⊏·	⊠ ⊠ ⊠ ⊠ ⊠ ⊠ ··	⊠ ⊠ ⊠ ⊠ ⊠	⊠ ⊠ ⊠ ⊠ ⊠ ⊠ ⊠	⊠ ⊠ ⊠ ⊠ ⊠ ⊠ ⊠ ⊠ ·		
Oriental Stir Fry								
Stuffed Tomato								
Sandwiches: BLT								
Hamburger								
Cheeseburger								
Chicken Sal San								
Meat Loaf Special								
Chili Dog								
Weather	rain	rain	clear	cloudy	rain	rain	clear	
Other Conditions			baker late		power out			

FIGURE 9-2B
Guest Check Menu Item Tally System *Continued.*

■ ■ ■ ■ ■

Table 9-2 Menu Analysis Chart

Department Coffee Shop   Page 1 of 12

Prepared by Clerical   Week of 1/13/XX

Category Sandwiches

MENU ITEM	NUMBER SOLD	PERCENT SOLD	MENU PRICE	PLATE COST	GROSS PROFIT	TOTAL GROSS PROFIT	PROFIT PERCENT
BLT	102	4.28%	$3.99	$1.00	$2.99	$ 304.98	6.24%
Hamburger	821	34.45	2.99	1.04	1.95	1,600.95	32.74
Cheeseburger	911	38.23	3.29	1.31	1.98	1,803.78	36.88
Chicken Sal San	71	2.98	3.99	.80	3.19	226.49	4.63
Meat Loaf San	196	8.22	4.99	2.05	2.94	576.24	11.78
Chili Dog	282	11.83	1.99	.65	1.34	377.88	7.73
Total	2,383	99.99%				$4,890.32	100.00%

■ ■ ■ ■ ■

Table 9-3   Comparing Menu Items

POPULARITY		MENU ITEM GROSS PROFIT		TOTAL GROSS PROFIT	
Cheeseburger	38.23%	Chick Sal San	$3.19	Cheeseburger	36.88%
Hamburger	34.45	BLT	2.99	Hamburger	32.74
Chili Dog	11.83	Meat Loaf San	2.94	Meat Loaf San	11.78
Meat Loaf San	8.22	Cheeseburger	1.98	Chili Dog	7.73
BLT	4.28	Hamburger	1.95	BLT	6.24
Chick Sal San	2.98	Chili Dog	1.34	Chick Sal San	4.63

losing money then the selling price should be increased or the items should be removed from the menu. Two levels of profit need to be examined: how much each menu item generates after costs, and how much total profit the item produces.

To calculate the first level of profitability, the plate cost is subtracted from the menu price. The menu price comes from the actual customer menu. The plate cost comes from the plate cost chart (Table 7-7). Gross profit is the amount the foodservice operation makes, and is calculated by subtracting the cost of the food sold from the selling price. A BLT that sells for $3.99 and has a plate cost of $1.00 generates a gross profit of $2.99 (3.99 – 1.00 = $2.99). This procedure is followed for each menu item. The items are listed from most to least profitable, as calculated by gross profit for each of the items. From the information presented in Table 9-2, the most to least profitable items are the chicken salad sandwich, BLT, meat loaf sandwich, cheeseburger, hamburger, chili dog. (See Table 9-3.)

The next level of profitability is the total gross profit. This is calculated by multiplying the amount of gross profit each item generates for the food-service operation by the number of menu items sold. As shown in Table 9-2, 102 BLTs were sold. This amount multiplied by the gross profit for BLTs, $2.99, gives the total gross profit of $304.98 (102 × $2.99). Again, this ranking process is performed for each of the menu items (see Table 9-2, Total Gross Profit column).

Often an item that does not make as much profit per unit may be the largest seller, thereby generating a sizable amount of overall profit for the foodservice operation. This is shown in Table 9-3. Listed in descending order from highest total gross profit to least total gross profit, the items are cheeseburger, hamburger, meat loaf sandwich, chili dog, BLT, and chicken salad sandwich.

Step Three—Comparing the Data

The last step in menu analysis is to compare all this information by examining the rankings of the menu items in each column. It appears that the chicken salad sandwich is not doing much for the foodservice operation even though it has the highest gross profit per unit. Some other considerations are that the BLT is also marginal and might be dropped. The meat loaf sandwich probably ought to become part of the regular daily menu. Other sandwiches could be developed and put on the menu as specials. Subsequent analyses

Monday

Daily Consolidated Revenue Center Menu Item Sales Detail
Subtotal by Family Group
MICROS Systems - Bar & Grille

From: 05/13/XXXX   To: 05/13/XXXX   Printed on May 13, XXXX - 8:34 PM

1 - Restaurant

		Sales Qty.	% of Ttl	Rtn Qty	% of Ttl	Gross Sales	% of Ttl	Item Disc	% of Total	Net Sales	% of Ttl
101002 Crab Cakes	Reg.	3	50.00%	0	0.00%	20.85	53.12%	0.00	0.00%	20.85	53.12%
101004 Fried Calamari	Reg.	2	33.33%	0	0.00%	11.90	30.32%	0.00	0.00%	11.90	30.32%
101005 Chicken Tenders	Reg.	1	16.67%	0	0.00%	6.50	16.56%	0.00	0.00%	6.50	16.56%
Total Appetizers		6	6.25%	0	0.00%	39.25	10.04%	0.00	0.00%	39.25	10.04%
101103 Onion Soup	Reg.	2	28.57%	0	0.00%	7.00	27.45%	0.00	0.00%	7.00	27.45%
101104 Clam Chowder	Reg.	2	28.57%	0	0.00%	6.50	25.49%	0.00	0.00%	6.50	25.49%
101105 Lobster Bisque	Reg.	3	42.86%	0	0.00%	12.00	47.06%	0.00	0.00%	12.00	47.06%
Total Soups		7	7.29%	0	0.00%	25.50	6.52%	0.00	0.00%	25.50	6.52%
102002 Tossed Salad	Reg.	1	16.67%	0	0.00%	3.75	12.63%	0.00	0.00%	3.75	12.63%
102003 Cobb Salad	Reg.	1	16.67%	0	0.00%	7.95	26.77%	0.00	0.00%	7.95	26.77%
102004 Spinach Salad	Reg.	4	66.67%	0	0.00%	18.00	60.61%	0.00	0.00%	18.00	60.61%
Total Salads		6	6.25%	0	0.00%	29.70	7.60%	0.00	0.00%	29.70	7.60%
103003 Cheeseburger	Reg.	1	100.00%	0	0.00%	7.95	100.00%	0.00	0.00%	7.95	100.00%
Total Burgers		1	1.04%	0	0.00%	7.95	2.03%	0.00	0.00%	7.95	2.03%
105002 Prime Rib	Reg.	2	40.00%	0	0.00%	27.90	50.96%	0.00	0.00%	27.90	50.96%
105005 Roasted Chicken	Reg.	3	60.00%	0	0.00%	26.85	49.04%	0.00	0.00%	26.85	49.04%
Total Entrees		5	5.21%	0	0.00%	54.74	14.01%	0.00	0.00%	54.75	14.01%
198002 Ice Cream	Reg.	1	25.00%	0	0.00%	3.00	20.00%	0.00	0.00%	3.00	20.00%
198004 Creme Brulee	Reg.	1	25.00%	0	0.00%	4.00	26.67%	0.00	0.00%	4.00	26.67%
198005 Tira Misu	Reg.	1	25.00%	0	0.00%	4.00	26.67%	0.00	0.00%	4.00	26.67%
198006 Bread Pudding	Reg.	1	25.00%	0	0.00%	4.00	26.67%	0.00	0.00%	4.00	26.67%
Total Desserts		4	4.17%	0	0.00%	15.00	3.84%	0.00	0.00%	15.00	3.84%
30016 Sprite	Reg	2	100.00%	0	0.00%	2.50	100.00%	0.00	0.00%	2.50	100.00%
Total Soda		2	2.08%	0	0.00%	2.50	0.64%	0.00	0.00%	2.50	0.64%
30007 Grapefruit Juice	Reg	1	50.00%	0	0.00%	1.50	50.00%	0.00	0.00%	1.50	50.00%
30008 Pineapple Juice	Reg.	1	50.00%	0	0.00%	1.50	50.00%	0.00	0.00%	1.50	50.00%
Total Juice		2	2.08%	0	0.00%	3.00	0.77%	0.00	0.00%	3.00	0.77%
30002 Coffee/Tea	Reg.	2	14.29%	0	0.00%	2.50	10.00%	0.00	0.00%	2.50	10.00%
30003 Iced Tea	Reg.	3	21.43%	0	0.00%	3.75	15.00%	0.00	0.00%	3.75	15.00%

FIGURE 9-3
Computer-Generated Food Sales Recap Report and Menu Analysis   Courtesy of Micros.

could determine if they should be permanently added to the menu if they are popular and profitable. In this way, the menu is a dynamic document, always changing to please the customer and to make the foodservice operation more profitable.

Computer-generated reports accomplish the same objectives. Figure 9-3 illustrates a system report that has generated information similar to that shown in Tables 9-1 and 9-2.

SUMMARY

1. The purpose of doing a menu analysis is to determine which menu items are popular and contribute the greatest profit for the foodservice operation. This goal is balanced against customer demands.

2. The process of doing a menu analysis involves recording sales of menu items on a food sales recap report. The information on this report is basic to menu analysis.

3. A menu analysis compares the dollar amount of each menu item sold in relationship to the dollar amount of all menu items sold in that category. It is also needed to calculate the gross profit generated by each item.

4. After the menu analysis has been completed, menu items are compared. Those that are unpopular and are not profitable should be deleted from the menu.

KEY CONCEPTS

Cyclical menu
Fixed menu
Gross profit
Menu analysis
Menu mix

DISCUSSION QUESTIONS AND EXERCISES

1. Given the following food sales recap report, complete the report and do the menu analysis (see Appendix A for a blank form).

2. What items would you change about the menu? Why? Support your decision with numbers.

3. Teach another person the basic concepts of this chapter.

Food Sales Recap Report

Department	Dining Room				Page	1 of 1		
Prepared by	Manager				Week of	1/13/XX		

MENU ITEMS	DATE: 1/13 MONDAY	14 TUESDAY	15 WEDNESDAY	16 THURSDAY	17 FRIDAY	18 SATURDAY	19 SUNDAY	TOTALS
Spaghetti	25	20	30	35	25	30	15	
Fettuccine	55	40	30	25	45	50	25	
Calzone	35	30	45	55	25	60	30	
Pasta Pesto	20	20	35	30	40	35	25	
New York Steak	10	10	20	20	25	30	15	
Skewered Shrimp	15	15	20	20	25	30	15	
Weather		rain						
Other conditions			winter festival					

Menu Prices for these items are: Spaghetti, $7.99; Fettuccine, $6.99; Calzone, $7.99; Pasta Pesto, $6.99; New York Steak, $12.99; and Skewered Shrimp, $11.99.

Plate Costs for these menu items are: Spaghetti, $1.59; Fettuccine, $1.39; Calzone, $2.39; Pasta Pesto, $1.69; New York Steak, $5.19; and Skewered Shrimp, $4.19.

10

Beverage Cost/ Beverage Cost Percentage

Learning Objectives

After reading this chapter and completing the discussion questions and exercises, you should be able to:

1. Recognize that beverage operations use principles similar to food-service operations in developing menus, using standardized recipes, and other related control forms.

2. Understand that beverage cost is the cost of goods sold in preparation of alcoholic beverages.

3. Recognize that alcoholic beverages represent a significant concentration of financial resources.

4. Recognize that the principles of controlling bar costs are similar to the principles of controlling food costs.

5. Understand the importance of paying very close attention to bar costs to ensure that revenue is received and appropriate for the operation (cash control), beverage recipes are being followed, prices are in line with costs, and suppliers are providing product at the agreed prices.

About Beverage Operations and Cost

The function of the beverage manager (like that of the food manager) is to purchase the best-quality product at the lowest price for a specific purpose. Unlike foods, however, liquors are purchased primarily by brand names, with the exception of a variety of less expensive brands that may be purchased for **well stock** or **house brands.** Well stock is the liquor that is used by the bartender whenever a customer does not specify a brand name. Refer to Figure 10-1, which shows the placement of well stock in a typical bar. The beverage operation may specify specific brands for its well stock or may identify sev-

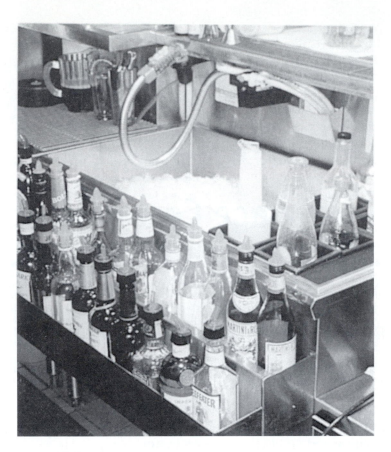

FIGURE 10-1
Well Stock   Well stock is the liquor that is conveniently located for quick service (at the speed rail), as it is the most-used liquor in any given bar.

Well stock or house brands   Liquors that are used by the bartender whenever a customer does not specify a brand name.

eral brands within various categories, such as bourbon, vodka, gin, and so on, that are acceptable. The choice would be determined by the one with the best price within each category.

In many states, the wholesale prices of alcoholic beverages are controlled, as liquor must be purchased through state-owned stores. If prices are not controlled, as in some states that have independent liquor suppliers, a common procedure is to have the suppliers submit a list of prices for each brand item. In some beverage operations, which are either large-volume or limited in the brands being offered to customers, special arrangements may be made to purchase a complete line of one brand of liquor at a certain percentage below the listed monthly price. Also, variations in price may occur because a particular brand may be listed as a special for a given period of time. In addition, certain discounts may become available should the buyer wish to purchase that product. For example, a particular brand of scotch may normally be sold for $96 per case, but if it is purchased in five-case lots, a 1 percent discount is available, and if it is purchased in ten-case lots, a 3 percent discount may be allowed. The alert buyer may be able to lower beverage costs simply by taking advantage of sale-priced brands or purchasing in liter or 1.75-liter bottles.

Many brands are assigned to only a few suppliers. In some areas of the country, only one supplier may carry a particular brand or product line. It becomes impossible for the beverage buyer to shop around to get the lowest price. Even if more than one supplier distributes the merchandise, the price is often fixed by the distiller or importer.

Obviously, when purchasing brand names, there is no major task involved in obtaining quality since all liquor of a particular brand will be of the same quality. There is normally no deterioration of quality while the liquor is in transit or storage.

Well stock—bourbon, vodka, gin, Canadian whiskey, scotch, rum, vodka, blended American liquor (sometimes called rye), and so on—can vary considerably in quality. Management should select four or five brands within each category that are deemed acceptable for the beverage operation. The buyer should then be instructed to purchase any of the selections, choosing the ones with the lowest price for that month.

Determining how large an inventory to stock and how large a selection of brands to carry are primary responsibilities of management. Decisions are based on the type of customers and the type of establishment, as well as the volume of the beverage operation. For example, a small bar that has a volume of $1,500 per week would certainly not be able to stock as many brands as one that has a volume of $15,000 per week, nor would the clientele expect the variety. The large bar would certainly be expected to stock all the major call brands (that have an asked-for name) and perhaps have a larger selection of wines, beers, and liquors.

In many states, the method of payment made by the bar operation to the supplier is governed by state law. These payments must be made within a specified period of time. Penalties are imposed should an establishment fail to pay within a specific time period. Usually, as a penalty, the supplier is required by the state to have the establishment pay for all future sales at the time of delivery. In some states, regulations require that all deliveries be on a **COD** basis.

COD
This acronym stands for cash on delivery.

In addition to supplying alcoholic beverages, every bar must have on hand all the ingredients necessary to make various drinks. The items used depend upon the system used by the bar operation. For example, sodas such as ginger ale and colas are used as a mix with alcoholic beverages. Management has the choice of using bottles, cans, or a premix or postmix non-alcoholic beverage system. In a **premix** system, a flavored soda is packaged in stainless steel tanks. In a **postmix** system, the mixer flavor comes in large syrup containers usually packaged as a bag in a box; the syrup is then mixed in a carbonator with water to produce a carbonated beverage. One of the problems with this type of system is that if the local water supply is not of high enough quality, an undesirable flavor may be imparted to the end product. This may be solved by using special filtration systems, or in some cases it may preclude the use of a postmix system. Management may decide to purchase individual bottles, cans, or tanks of premixed soda even though the cost is higher, as style of service and presentation may be of greater importance.

Premix
A method of dispensing carbonated beverages in which the carbonated water and syrup are delivered to the establishment already mixed.

Postmix
A method of dispensing soda drinks by combining the syrup and carbonated water to produce the carbonated beverage. It is ideal for high-volume usage as it provides the most economical cost.

Since the cost of **mixers** is usually low compared to the cost of alcoholic beverages, operators should attempt to use only high-quality mixers. A comparison may be made with the chef who makes excellent sauces but still utilizes the poorest-quality meat—the end product still is not very tasty.

Mixers
Items that are used to prepare or flavor alcoholic beverages (such as fruit, Bloody Mary mix, collins mix, and so on).

Juices normally are purchased in 46-ounce cans or in 5½-ounce individual serving cans. The larger cans are less expensive but may be more difficult to handle, and once opened they should be poured into bottles to maintain quality and reduce spoilage.

Bar juices and fruits may be purchased by either the bar department or the food department, which then issues them to the bar. Issues may be in bulk or as needed, depending upon the procedure of the operation. They should also be accounted for by the use of a requisition.

Some operations, particularly those that have a very limited food selection, may deal with a vendor specializing in nonalcoholic bar supplies. Others may buy fruit from a produce supplier, prepared products such as cherries and olives from a wholesale grocer, and soft drinks from a local bottling company. Each operation will base its decisions upon its particular needs, volume of sales, and internal control methods.

Many of the reports discussed in this chapter may be generated by application software, referred to hereafter as *automated systems.* Automated beverage systems will be discussed in Chapter 11.

Introduction to the Beverage Cost Control Process

An alcoholic beverage menu is the final step in the beverage cost control process. Specifications and recipes should be developed just as for food, although many recipes are universally standard. The purchase of alcoholic beverages should be based upon specifications for liquor, wine, and beer according to the needs of the beverage operation. Receiving practices and procedures are very similar to those for receiving food products. However, because of the cost involved and the accountability required, the bar manager, general manager, or owner should receive most of the alcoholic beverages. Bartenders who need to obtain beverage and supplies to stock the bar should prepare a requisition. Also, if alcoholic beverages are used in the kitchen (wine for cooking and so on), a transfer should be completed to account for items taken from the bar. A requisition should be used if the wine is to be obtained from the liquor storeroom, which should be locked and controlled by management at all times. (See Tables 4-2 and 4-3.)

Once the alcoholic beverages are in place, proper drink mix recipes must be followed to maintain a consistent beverage presentation. A beverage recipe may consist of one ounce of Jack Daniels with ice and four ounces of club soda for making a Jack Daniels bourbon and soda. The exact amount of alcoholic beverage may vary according to the specifications set forth by management. Each operation must determine its own beverage menu. An example of a beverage menu is shown in Figure 10-2.

Beverage Cost

Beverage cost
The cost of goods sold in the preparation of alcoholic beverages. This includes not only the alcohol but also the condiments and other items used in the preparation of drinks.

Pour cost or bar cost
The cost to prepare a single drink.

Beverage cost is the cost of goods sold in the preparation of alcoholic beverages. Costs include not only the cost of the alcoholic beverage but also the condiments and other items used in the preparation of drinks. The terms **pour cost** and **bar cost** are often used interchangeably with the term *beverage cost.* *Pour cost* refers to the cost of preparing a single drink, while *beverage cost* refers to the total cost of goods sold for a specific accounting period. Like food cost,

TRADITIONAL

If you thought no one could improve on these time-honored
traditions, think again. Order one and discover how history
has been rewritten the Friday's way.

FRIDAY'S MARGARITAS
Frozen or on-the-rocks, blended to perfection.

Gold–Made exclusively with Jose Cuervo Gold Tequila and triple sec.

Top Shelf–A Friday's classic featuring Jose Cuervo 1800, Cointreau and Grand Marnier.

BLOODY MARY
Vodka with Friday's special vegetable juice blend.

TEQUILA MARIA
Tequila and Friday's special vegetable juice blend.

MADRAS
Vodka with cranberry and orange juices.

SCREWDRIVER
Vodka and orange juice.

WHISKEY SOUR
Bourbon and sweet & sour.

MARTINI
Gin or vodka with dry vermouth. Chilled, straight up or on-the-rocks, served with an olive or a twist.

MANHATTAN
Bourbon and vermouth with Angostura Bitters over ice.

GIMLET
Vodka or gin and Rose's Lime Juice, garnished with a lime squeeze.

GIBSON
Vodka or gin, dry vermouth and cocktail onions.

BLACK RUSSIAN
Vodka and Kahlúa on-the-rocks.

RUSTY NAIL
Scotch and Drambuie on-the-rocks.

SEA BREEZE
Vodka, cranberry and grapefruit juices.

OLD FASHIONED
Bourbon with sweetened orange and cherry juices and a dash of Angostura Bitters.

WHITE RUSSIAN
Vodka, Kahlúa and half & half on-the-rocks.

ROB ROY
Scotch with vermouth and just a touch of orange bitters.

PLANTER'S PUNCH
Myer's Original Dark Rum, grenadine, lime and orange juices.

VODKA COLLINS
Vodka and sweet & sour topped with soda.

FIGURE 10-2
Beverage Menu   T.G.I. Friday's is a registered
trademark of T.G.I. Friday's of Minnesota, Inc.

beverage cost is used to report the total dollar amount spent. Also, like the food cost percentage, the **beverage cost percentage** is the beverage cost reported as a percentage. For instance, a manager may state, "Bar cost is 18 percent." To control beverage (bar) costs, a manager should understand how to:

- manage beverage inventory
- receive alcoholic beverages
- control **bar requisitions**
- use **bar transfers**
- maintain **pour systems**

A higher pour cost is due to serving larger drinks, charging lower prices, or not having effective cash controls. Beverage cost percentages may differ depending upon the location, type of clientele, competition, and laws affecting alcoholic beverage services.

Beverage cost percentage
Determined by dividing the cost of goods sold by the total beverage sales and multiplying by 100.

Bar requisitions and **bar transfers**   Forms used to monitor beverage inventory; they have the same appearance as food requisitions and transfers.

Pour systems
A method for controlling the quantity of alcoholic beverages used in drinks.

BEVERAGE COST PERCENTAGE GOAL

Beverage managers choose what beverage cost percentage they wish to have as an operating goal. This decision usually depends upon how the manager and/or owner wants the operation to be perceived by customers. As previously stated, beverage cost percentages may differ depending upon the location, type of clientele, competition, and laws affecting alcoholic beverage service.

A beverage cost percentage can be maintained through the use of information and control reports prepared on a regular basis. The tool for tracking beverage cost is a **beverage cost report** (see Table 10-1). By tracking the beverage cost percentage and the fluctuations that occur between accounting periods, the manager is alerted to operational corrections that need to be made.

Beverage cost report A form used to calculate beverage cost percentages.

Calculating the Beverage Cost Percentage

Calculating a beverage cost percentage is similar to calculating a food cost percentage: divide the cost by the sales. In Table 10-1, the cost of goods sold (beverage cost) is $1,481.90 for the period. This amount is divided by the total beverage sales of $7,942.25. The result, .186, is converted to a percentage of 18.6 percent (beverage cost percentage).

The total cost of goods sold is the total cost of the liquor, wine, beer, and other complements used. These figures are taken directly from a **bar and inventory control report** (discussed in Chapter 11).

Bar and inventory control report Provides a comprehensive method for tracking beverage inventory.

THE PURPOSE OF A BEVERAGE COST REPORT

The beverage cost report is prepared at the end of the accounting period. Two examples of beverage cost reports are shown in Table 10-1 and 10-2. Table 10-1 is a simple chart that shows total figures by shift and period. Table 10-2, a cost breakdown and sales analysis, goes into more detail.

Frequently, the accounting period for a bar is one week. If computerized, it can be done daily, by shift, and even hourly, depending upon the system. Experience will help management determine the type of operation checks needed. However, the accounting period should reflect the beverage cost and beverage cost percentage as well as the sales per day and sales per shift. Any fluctuations in the beverage cost percentage will immediately indicate that a problem may exist. Also, the beverage cost breakdown according to liquor, wine, and beer (as shown in Table 10-2) indicates the individual cost percentages for liquor, wine, and beer. A cash comparison, which indicates the dollar amount that should be in the cash register, is calculated by comparing sales to retail value versus quantity of liquor dispensed per shift. Calculating the sales dollars per shot is critical. Various methods exist to assist in this process and will be discussed in Chapter 11. This will show either an overage or shortage of money. Finally, the bar and inventory control report and the **liquor storeroom inventory report** (Table 11-2) will accurately account for every item of merchandise.

Liquor storeroom inventory report A form used to track the inventory of each beverage item.

Even with the use of excellent controls, there always exists the element of human error. Careless or dishonest bartenders, waitstaff, shift managers, and bookkeepers may dramatically affect the financial health of the beverage operation.

Table 10-1 Beverage Cost Report

Period Ending __1/17/XX__

Bar Location __Lounge__

DATE		DAY		SALES
January	11	Sunday	(1st shift)	$ 157.50
			(2nd shift)	278.90
	12	Monday	(1st shift)	151.85
			(2nd shift)	465.75
	13	Tuesday	(1st shift)	219.55
			(2nd shift)	603.75
	14	Wednesday	(1st shift)	208.25
			(2nd shift)	542.50
	15	Thursday	(1st shift)	294.30
			(2nd shift)	777.50
	16	Friday	(1st shift)	574.15
			(2nd shift)	1,631.65
	17	Saturday	(1st shift)	511.10
			(2nd shift)	1,525.50
		TOTAL		$7,942.25

$$\frac{\text{Cost of goods sold ($1,481.90)}}{\text{Total beverage sales ($7,942.25)}} = \text{Beverage Cost Percentage (.186} \times 100 = 18.6\%)$$

Prepared By __Clerical__

Date __1/20/xx__

Table 10-2 Beverage Cost Report with Cost Breakdown and Sales Analysis

| Bar Location | Lounge | | | | | Period Ending | 1/17/XX | |

ITEM	SUNDAY 1/11	MONDAY 1/12	TUESDAY 1/13	WEDNESDAY 1/14	THURSDAY 1/15	FRIDAY 1/16	SATURDAY 1/17	WEEK TOTAL
1ST SHIFT SALES								
Liquor	$110.50	$105.00	$169.85	$158.45	$248.15	$515.70	$457.35	$1,765.00
Wine	21.20	23.55	26.10	28.20	25.75	30.30	27.70	182.80
Beer	25.80	23.30	23.60	21.60	20.40	28.15	26.05	168.90
Shift Total	$157.50	$151.85	$219.55	$208.25	$294.30	$574.15	$511.10	$2,116.70
2ND SHIFT SALES								
Liquor	$168.85	$257.20	$332.95	$284.00	$441.65	$1,059.95	$852.70	$3,397.30
Wine	16.70	18.90	22.50	22.10	25.95	49.15	59.25	214.55
Beer	93.35	189.65	248.30	236.40	309.90	522.55	613.55	2,213.70
Shift Total	$278.90	$465.75	$603.75	$542.50	$777.50	$1,631.65	$1,525.50	$5,825.55
DAILY TOTAL	$436.40	$617.60	$823.30	$750.75	$1,071.80	$2,205.80	$2,036.60	$7,942.25

PERIOD BEVERAGE COST BREAKDOWN **SALES MANAGEMENT ANALYSIS**

ITEM	COST OF GOODS SOLD	SALES (SHIFT TOTALS)		BEVERAGE COST %		SALES	RETAIL VALUE	OVER (SHORT)
Liquor	$ 945.30	$5,162.30		18.3%		$5,162.30	$5,213.00	($50.70)
Wine	101.45	397.35		25.5		397.35	398.75	(1.40)
Beer	435.15	2,382.60		18.3		2,382.60	2,409.40	(26.80)
TOTAL	$1,481.90	$7,942.25		18.6%		$7,942.25	$8,021.15	($78.90)

| Prepared by | Clerical | | | | Date | 1/20/XX | |

Completing a Beverage Cost Report

A beverage cost report functions in much the same way as a food cost report. Its purpose is to indicate the actual cost percentage of liquor, wine, beer, and complements. Further, it shows the total amount of beverage sales for any given period of time (see Table 10-1).

Bar Location The bar location is important because a separate report must be prepared for each bar. Hotels and resorts may have several different bars. Also, some restaurant operations may have more than one bar location (such as a lounge and a service bar).

Sales By Shift, Day, and Period Sales by shift and by date and day, as well as the total sales for the period, are listed for determining trends. It is extremely important to continually analyze the sales figures. If there is an unaccountable fluctuation in the trends, a thorough investigation should be made. Even if it is determined that the controls are in good order, there is still the possibility of theft by employees.

Cost of Goods Sold The cost of goods sold is the total cost of the liquor, beer, wine, and other complements used. These figures are taken directly from the bar and inventory control report (Table 11-3).

Calculate the Beverage Cost Percentage As mentioned earlier, the beverage cost percentage is calculated by dividing the cost of goods sold by the total beverage sales and multiplying by 100.

Beverage Cost Breakdown

A beverage cost breakdown, as shown in the bottom left section of Table 10-2, separates the liquor, wine, and beer, and determines a cost percentage for each.

Total Liquor Cost/Percentage "Total liquor sales" comprises all distilled alcoholic beverages. The sale of these items is tracked by an electronic cash register, point-of-sale device, or computer. The sales may also be tracked manually by guest checks, individual waitstaff, and/or bartenders. To calculate the total liquor percentage, divide the total liquor cost (cost of goods sold) by total liquor sales. In Table 10-2, total liquor cost is $945.30 divided by total liquor sales of $5,162.30, which equals 18.3%, the liquor cost percentage.

Wine and Beer The same procedure is followed for wine and beer. Cost is divided by sales, each deriving a cost percentage. Once the desired cost percentages are achieved, they should be continually maintained. The beverage cost breakdown keeps these percentages in check, quickly reflecting any fluctuations by individual staff and shifts.

Sales Management Analysis For a dollar comparison, the actual sales according to liquor, wine, and beer as well as the total sales are listed for the period in the bottom right section of this report. The individual sales may be recorded through the use of different cash register or computer keys; for example, all liquor sales could be rung on the A key, the wine on the B key, and the beer on the C key. At the end of each shift, a register reading is taken totaling the sales for each category, as well as the total sales. The majority of cash registers automatically have this separation function, with point-of-sale systems offering very detailed information on individual product sales, inventory status, and so on.

The total retail value is taken from the bar and inventory control report (see Table 11-2). The total retail value is compared to the total sales reports to determine the actual dollar amount and whether it is over or short. In Table 10-2, liquor sales are $5,162.30. This amount is taken from the sales register. The retail sales value is taken from the bar and inventory control report. In Table 10-2 the amount is $5,213.00. The difference is $50.70. Less cash was received than product sold. Possible causes for this could be overpours, spills, improper change given, and pricing done incorrectly.

How to Use a Beverage Cost Report

The purpose of the beverage cost report is to describe the cost of goods sold over a specific accounting period. The report will identify what has occurred during the accounting period. It is an information tool that informs management of operational efficiencies. If planned costs are to be 18.5 percent and in reality, they are 18.6 percent, operations are going as planned. If costs are planned to be 18.5 percent and in reality they are 22 percent, operations are not going according to plan.

If operations are not going according to plan, management needs to identify the problem. The obvious first area to search is theft by employees. If theft does not seem feasible, other operational areas must be reviewed. These areas may involve a review to determine whether:

- beverage recipes are being followed
- prices are in-line with costs
- suppliers have raised their prices

Beverage costs need to be checked frequently, as they are crucial to making the judgment of how well the operation is doing. If employees are aware that management maintains tight control, they will be motivated to perform at their best. This does not mean that management is looking over the employees' shoulders all the time; it does mean that employees know that management is concerned about their performance.

SUMMARY

1. Beverage operations use the same principles of control as foodservice operations for menu development, purchasing and receiving, tracking the movement of products within and between departments, and producing and serving menu items. The obvious difference is in the nature of the product.

2. Comparable to food cost is beverage cost. Beverage cost is the cost of goods sold in the preparation of alcoholic beverages. This cost includes all ingredient costs for preparing alcoholic beverages.

3. The beverage cost percentage is the total cost of the beverage divided by the sales price of the beverage. When calculated on an individual basis, the cost is typically referred to as a pour cost.

4. Beverage costs are usually calculated using a beverage cost report. This report is completed for a standard accounting period. The accounting period should reflect the beverage cost and beverage cost percentage as well as the sales per day and sales per shift. Any fluctuations in beverage cost percentage will immediately indicate that a problem may exist.

5. The purpose of a beverage cost report is to describe the cost of goods sold over time. If the beverage operation is not going according to plan, the bar manager should first examine the possibility of theft, then determine whether (1) beverage recipes are being followed, (2) prices are in line with costs, or (3) suppliers have raised their prices. Successful bar managers pay close attention to the details of their operations.

KEY CONCEPTS

Bar and inventory control report
Bar cost
Bar requisition
Bar transfer
Beverage cost
Beverage cost percentage
Beverage cost report
COD

House brands
Liquor store room inventory report
Mixers
Postmix
Pour cost
Pour system
Premix
Well stock

DISCUSSION QUESTIONS AND EXERCISES

1. Define beverage cost.

2. How is a beverage cost percentage calculated?

3. Explain the purpose of a beverage cost report.

4. Where does the information come from that is used to put a beverage cost report together?

5. Why would a manager want to do a beverage cost breakdown analysis?

6. If the alcoholic beverage suppliers suddenly increase their prices, what effect would that have upon the beverage cost percentage?

7. Assume that during the past five accounting periods (each period is one week) the beverage cost percentage has increased approximately 1 percent each period. The employees have worked with the operation for over five years and are considered to be very honest (the probability that an employee or manager is stealing from the operation is very low). What could be causing the increases?

8. Given the following information, calculate the beverage cost percentage using a blank beverage cost report from Appendix A. The

first-shift sales were: Sunday, January 11, $195; Monday, January 12, $125; Tuesday, January 13, $155; Wednesday, January 14, $190; Thursday, January 15, $225; Friday, January 16, $423, and Saturday, January 17, $567; The second-shift sales were: Sunday, $495; Monday, $250; Tuesday, $310; Wednesday, $380; Thursday, $525; Friday, $1,023; and Saturday, $1,567. Invoices showed the following costs: liquor, $118; wine, $848; beer, $828.

11

Bar and Inventory Control

Learning Objectives

After reading this chapter and completing the discussion questions and exercises, you should be able to:

1. Identify the three things that must be controlled when selling alcoholic beverages.

2. Explain the general rule for establishing an inventory size.

3. Recognize that accounting for the use of alcoholic beverages is similar to accounting for food items.

4. Understand that a liquor storeroom inventory report is used to ensure proper management of inventory.

5. Explain that a bar and inventory control report is a comprehensive form used to calculate the value of inventory and estimate receipts.

About Bar and Inventory Control

Typically, the greatest concentration of dollars invested in a food and beverage inventory is associated with alcoholic beverages (beer, wine, and liquor). A single bottle of wine may cost several hundred dollars. Most of the time, the cost of a bottle of liquor or wine will range from $5.00 to $45.00.

Like food products, all alcoholic beverages must:

■ be accounted for when used

■ be inventoried

■ be constantly monitored

Controlling alcoholic beverages involves monitoring not only inventory but the flow of inventory through an operation. For an overview of how alcoholic beverages flow within a foodservice operation or bar, see Figure 11-1.

Adequate alcoholic beverage inventory systems may employ several types of controls to determine dispensing costs, record sales, and account for

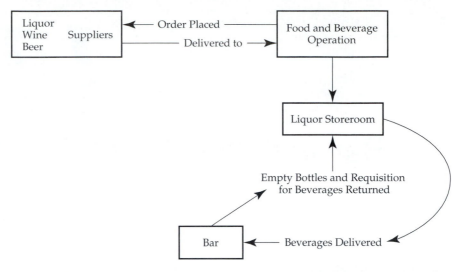

FIGURE 11-1
Flow of Alcoholic Beverages

merchandise. Systems may be used independently or combined, depending upon the needs of the operation.

Basically, there are four types of systems:

1. **Automated systems**—beverages are automatically counted as they are sold

2. Par amounts—bottle control

3. Ounce or drink control

4. Automated inventory-assist systems (such as scales with scanners)

For the vast majority of bars, the bartender is responsible for dispensing liquor, collecting payment for the liquor, and possibly even collecting payment for food sales at the bar. Therefore, in discussing beverage service and the types of inventory controls used, the methods of service and cash collection should be considered concurrently.

Although the measurement of bottle containers is in the metric system, practically every American bar and recipe book still gives measurements for individual drinks in ounces. Table 11-1 compares the two systems of measurement.

In the United States drinks are typically measured in ounces; the average drink will hold from ⅞ ounce to 1½ ounces of liquor. There are no laws requiring the beverage operator to have a standard measure, whereas in Europe the amount poured by management is generally standardized and a notice of the amount may have to be posted.

Determining Inventory Size

As a general rule, the size of the inventory should be equal to the cost of goods used during a period (typically one week). For example, if an operation had $10,000 in sales and the cost of sales was $3,000, the inventory should be

Table 11-1   Comparison of Metric and English Measure

ENGLISH		METRIC	
½ gal	64 oz	1.75 L	59.2 oz
1 qt	32 oz	1.00 L	33.8 oz
1 fifth	25.6 oz	750 mL	25.4 oz

about $3,000. At the same time, in each period the purchases should be approximately $3,000. In effect, period purchases are equal to inventory, which in turn is equal to the cost of goods sold.

Note that these are estimates, and in fact the kinds of alcoholic beverages (liquor, wine, beer) purchased and the time required for delivery also affects the size of inventory. With fine wines, it may be necessary to purchase a sufficient amount to ensure that the item can be kept on the wine list for a year or two. With liquor and beer, enough for about ten days of consumption is normally an adequate supply. For convenience, and because of some state government regulations that control payments to vendors, often only a two-week supply may be purchased at a given time.

Management must decide what brands should be carried. This decision will be influenced to a large part by the requests and tastes of guests. A club that caters to a small number of members certainly should stock the brands that the members prefer, bearing in mind how often a particular brand is requested. It would be unwise to stock a specific brand requested by only one member who orders that drink brand once a year on his or her birthday. At that rate it could take 24 years to empty one bottle. Furthermore, the selection of a particular stock to be carried will be influenced by the time of year—for example, lighter spirits, such as rum, which are consumed during the summer months. Also, any special events being scheduled, such as a fish dinner that may call for a white wine, should be taken into account. Customer preferences and space limitations should also be considered when purchasing stock.

A utomated Control Systems

Automated control systems are based on reserve (gun-type) systems similar to a soda system, individual bottle systems, or a combination of both (the gun system for house brands and an individual bottle system for call brands). Each time a drink is poured, the electronic system automatically counts what has been sold. Equally important is the fact that automated systems are designed to pour exact measured amounts. This type of system has several advantages:

- Cash accountability is maintained.
- The customer always gets the same drink.
- There is no waste from spillage.
- Underpouring or overpouring can be reduced or eliminated.

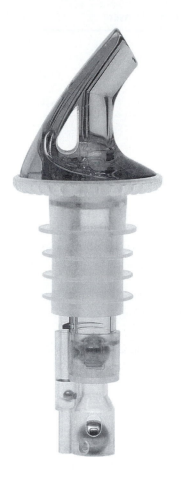

DRINKS PER BOTTLE			
Shot Size	750 ML *replaces fifth*	1 LITER *replaces quart*	1.75 LITER *replaces half gallon*
5/8 oz.	40	54	94
3/4 oz.	34	45	79
7/8 oz.	29	38	67
1 oz.	25	34	59
1 1/8 oz.	22	30	52
1 1/4 oz.	20	27	47
1 1/2 oz.	17	22	39

STANDARD MIXING RATIOS	
Glass Size	Recommended Shot Sizes
6 ounce	5/8, 3/4, 7/8 ounce
7 ounce	3/4, 7/8, 1 ounce
8 ounce	7/8, 1, 1 1/8 ounce
9 ounce	1, 1 1/8, 1 1/4 ounce
10 ounce	1 1/8, 1 1/4, 1 1/2 ounce
12 ounce	1 1/4, 1 1/2, 2 ounce
14 ounce	1 1/2, 2, 2 1/2 ounce

Shot size can vary depending on taste & volume of ice used.

FIGURE 11-2
Liquor Control Pourer   *Courtesy of Precision Pours, Inc.*

Simple systems can be used, such as a pourer attached to each bottle to control the amount poured (see Figure 11-2). Advanced electronic systems allow for separate pumps for each liquor, recording of sales on guest checks, pouring of several liquors simultaneously, and actually mixing the drinks and making cocktails. If the system is even more advanced, it will tie into a computer that provides further information for management. Some systems also control and integrate draft beer sales with liquor. Fully integrated electronic bar systems are available from a number of manufacturers. A bar of this type measures the drinks, controls the inventory, registers the amount of sales, notes who made the sales and when, and can even record them on the accounts of guests registered in a hotel.

Systems can be designed and custom tailored for the user. The dispensing system will interface with most computer and cash-control systems. Figures 11-2 through 11-8 show examples of sophisticated systems.

FIGURE 11-3
Automated Beverage System   *Courtesy of Berg Liquor Systems.*

Certain disadvantages are apparent when completely automated systems are used. A major goal of management is to please the guests' tastes. This may be difficult with some automated systems, particularly gun-type systems. Unless the right presentation is made through careful selection of the system and its installation, customer satisfaction may be adversely affected. Atmosphere and personal service may be difficult to create when customers know that their drinks are served from an electronically controlled system.

The companies marketing these systems and beverage operators who have installed them are almost unanimous in praising them. The conclusion is that the systems reduce liquor cost percentages. Part of the savings is attributable to the reduction in theft. These systems are also much more accurate in pouring exact amounts of liquor. The advantages of the system far outweigh the disadvantages, as the following summary shows:

1. Automated systems provide measured pouring, which eliminates problems of overpouring, underpouring, and spillage.

2. Customers are assured of receiving the amount they pay for and getting a consistent drink.

3. Many systems are designed to use 1.75-liter bottles, which saves the beverage operation an additional 5 to 10 percent.

4. Beverages cannot be dispensed without automatically being counted.

FIGURE 11-4
Features of an Automated System The picture illustrates how the components of an automated system are related. The point-of-sale hardware, in the upper right corner, records sales and can interface with a remote printer or PC for a full range of detailed reports such as hourly sales reports, price level changes, price/portion reports, and a variety of summary data. The system interfaces with electronic cash registers (ECRs) with pouring systems to tally sales as they occur, automatically. *Courtesy of Berg Liquor Systems.*

5. Most, though not all, systems incorporate accounting and record keeping, so that these tasks are greatly simplified.

6. In some cases, the systems are faster than manually operated ones, particularly in the making of mixed drinks or when various well liquors are poured consecutively.

7. Since all the liquor in the system is controlled by the storeroom manager, no merchandise needs to be moved. The labor cost involved with the physical moving of the merchandise and recording the issues is eliminated.

Bar and inventory control report A comprehensive method of tracking beverage inventory.

Liquor storeroom inventory report Allows the bar manager to be constantly aware of the quantity and value of the inventory.

Bottle exchange system A method of controlling inventory by exchanging an empty bottle for a full bottle.

Tracking Beverage Inventory

The **bar and inventory control report** (see Table 11-3) is one of the best ways to control alcoholic beverage inventory. This report is completed for each bar (if more than one bar exists within a given foodservice operation). The person completing the bar and inventory control report and **liquor storeroom inventory report** forms will obtain the information from requisitions. The requisition form can also be used for those who use bottle exchange systems or inventory/bin card systems.

A **bottle exchange system** is very simple and easy to use. When a bottle is emptied it is exchanged for a full bottle.

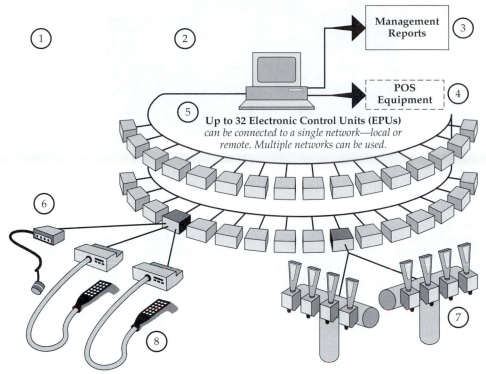

1. Laser Liquor System with Infinity
2. Infinity System Overview
3. Management Reports
4. POS Equipment
5. Up to 32 Electronic Control Units (ECUs) can be connected to a single network—local or remote. Mutiple networks can be used.
6. Up to 2 laser units and/or 1 all-bottle unit can be controlled by a single liquor ECU.
7. Up to 8 TAP1 faucets can be controlled by a single TAP1 ECU
8. Reports that can be generated are:
   Z report—display of current daily sales
   X1 system summary—display of total drinks and sales of entire system
   X2 station sales summary—report of total drinks and sales by price level and code brand
   X3 station detail—display of total drinks and sales by size, price, and code (brand) per station
   X4 hourly sales—display of hourly total drinks and sales recorded for each station in the last 48 hours
   Week ending summary—total drinks and sales by price level and code (brand) at each station over the last seven days
   Month ending summary—usage (by volume) for each code (brand) and total sales for the past 30 days
   Annual summary—usage (by volume) for each code (brand) and total sales for past year
   Revenue yield—monetary return by volume (oz or mL) for each code (brand)

FIGURE 11-5
Automated System Overview *Courtesy of Berg Liquor Systems.*

The system usually works in the following manner.

1. As a bartender empties the bottles, they are stored in a convenient location within the bar.

2. At the end of the shift, or the next morning, the empty bottles are taken to the bar manager.

3. The bar manager takes the empty bottles into the beverage store-room and replaces them with full bottles.

FIGURE 11-6
Pouring Dispenser The picture illustrates the use of pouring dispensers. Fast pouring allows the bartender to provide faster, more consistent service to customers. Other benefits include cutting drink preparation time, minimizing the loss of liquor, and better inventory control. *Courtesy of Berg Liquor Systems.*

4. The empty bottles are discarded or broken with a bottle crusher, unless such an act is unlawful. Each state has its own specific law regarding the disposal of empty liquor bottles.

The major problem with this system is that there are no records other than invoices to track the use of product. Therefore, an **inventory/bin card system** may be used to aid in this process. For each type of alcoholic beverage ordered or used, an inventory or bin card is created. Figure 11-9 is a typical example of an inventory or bin card.

Inventory or bin cards are kept with the physical inventory; when a bottle is removed from inventory, it is noted on the card. A card is kept for each type of beverage. For example, separate cards should be kept for Early Times bourbon, I.W. Harper bourbon, and so on. Historically, wine was put into bins and bin cards affixed next to the wine; thus the term *bin card* has evolved. Today, bin cards may not even be in the storage room, but kept in a file box or as part of application software. The major benefit of using a card system is that the current value of inventory is constantly known. It is a perpetual inventory system.

> **Inventory/bin card system** A method of tracking bottle exchanges using cards that are kept with the inventory.

Bar Inventory Control

Bar inventory control can be divided into two steps. First, calculate the storeroom inventory. Second, determine if the inventory has been properly used. By using a liquor storeroom inventory report (Table 11-2) and a bar and inventory control report (Table 11-3), the bar manager is able to complete these two steps, thus providing a complete system for managing alcoholic beverage inventory.

The liquor storeroom inventory report (Table 11-2) begins with the Item Description column, which lists the liquors and wines by category and in alphabetical order. For speed and convenience, the bottles should also appear on the storage shelves in the same order.

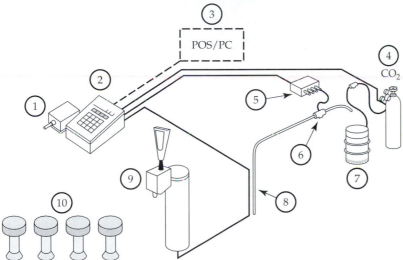

1. Power supply
3. POS/PC
5. Flow meter junction box
7. Draft supply room
9. Tap head

2. Remote console
4. Compressed air or CO_2 to console
6. Flow meter
8. Beer lines
10. Bar area

FIGURE 11-7
Draft Beer Control System   The picture shows a type of automated draft beer control system.
This particular system offers the following features:
- Optional interface to automated dispensing system and point-of-sale systems
- Designed for ease of cleaning
- Empty-keg indicator and optional shut-off
- Compact size
- Remote console
- Four portion sizes plus cancel and repeat functions
- Continual system operation
- Full range of management reports
- Dispenses wine or margaritas without modification
- Measures and dispenses by volume or time.

Courtesy of Berg Liquor Systems.

```
                    Berg All-Bottle 744 Detailed Z Report

Station      1           Date: 05/16/XX          Time: 10:57:06 PM

Z Number     5

Price Level A
                Small                Regular               Large                 Special
Code       Portions   Sales    Portions   Sales    Portions   Sales    Portions   Sales
Code 1         7      12.00        23      46.00        15      33.75        10      30.00
Code 2         3       7.50        16      36.00         8      20.00         5      15.00
Code 3         3       8.25         8      24.00         5      15.00         3       9.00
Code 4         6      12.00        10      22.50         4      10.00         6      18.00
Code 5         3       7.50         5      10.00         3       6.75         4      12.00
Code 6         2       5.50         4      10.00         5      15.00         2       6.00
Code 7         1       2.00         2       4.50         3       7.50         3       9.00

Totals        25      54.75        68     153.00        43     108.00        33      99.00

Total Sales              Price Level A           414.75

Price Level B
                Small                Regular               Large                 Special
Code       Portions   Sales    Portions   Sales    Portions   Sales    Portions   Sales
Code 1         8      14.00        25      56.00        15      33.75        13      39.00
Code 2         6      15.00        16      36.00         9      22.50         4      12.00
Code 3         5      12.25         8      24.00         7      21.00         3       9.00
Code 4         6      12.00        11      25.00         4      10.00         5      15.00
Code 5         4      10.00         6      12.00         4       9.75         4      12.00
Code 6         2       5.50         4      10.00         6      18.00         5      15.00
Code 7         3       6.00         3       6.75         5      12.50         6      18.00

Totals        34      74.75        73     169.75        50     127.50        40     120.00

Flow Meter #1 Totals     oz     132.08      Sales      46.23
Flow Meter #2 Totals     oz     257.06      Sales     128.53
Flow Meter #3 TOtals     oz     489.08      Sales     220.08

Total Sales              Price Level B           886.84

Report Total Sales       1301.59

Cumulative Sales         7883.24

Unassigned Flow Meter Sales

Price Level A
No Activity

Price Level B
Flow Meter #1 Totals     oz      32.08      Sales      11.23
Flow Meter #3 Totals     oz      48.32      Sales      21.75

Price Level C
No Activity
```

FIGURE 11-8
Detailed Z Report Using an Automated System   *Courtesy of Berg Liquor Systems.*

The unit size is listed next, followed by the opening inventory, which was the closing inventory of the previous accounting period. For Early Times bourbon, the unit size is a 750-mL bottle. The opening inventory is 87 750-mL bottles. The 750-mL bottle is one of the most popular sizes because of its ease in handling when pouring.

Next, all purchases during the period are listed (remember that purchases are taken from invoices provided by suppliers), which are added to the opening inventory to make up the totals in the Totals (A) column. Forty-eight 750-mL bottles of Early Times bourbon were purchased during the accounting period.

The columns that follow, under Requisitions by Day of Period, list the dates of the period and the number of items used per day as recorded from requisitions. For Early Times bourbon, eleven bottles were requisitioned on the eleventh; four bottles were requisitioned on the twelfth; five bottles were requisitioned on the thirteenth; seven bottles were requisitioned on the four-

Product Description Christian Bros. Chardonnay, 1 gallon

Date 1/07/XX

Prepared by Bar Manager

Cost per Case/Unit $76.80

Card Number 271

Extended by Clerical

Cost per Bottle $ 19.20

BEGINNING INVENTORY	AMOUNT USED/BOUGHT	DATE USED	BALANCE	PRICE		EXTENSION	
15	–1	1/15	14	$ 19	20	$ 268	80
14	–1	1/16	13	19	20	249	60
13	–3	1/17	10	19	20	192	00
10	+8	1/17	18	19	20	345	60

FIGURE 11-9
Inventory or Bin Card

teenth; nine bottles were requisitioned on the fifteenth; eight bottles were requisitioned on the sixteenth; and ten bottles were requisitioned on the seventeenth.

The second totals column, Totals (B), is the total number of items that have been requisitioned daily and were added together. Fifty-four bottles of Early Times bourbon were requisitioned during the week of the eleventh through the seventeenth.

The Balance A Less B column represents the difference between the Totals (A) column and the Totals (B) column. The Totals (A) entry for Early Times bourbon was 135 and the Totals (B) entry was 54; the difference is 81 $(135 - 54 = 81)$.

The Closing Inventory column should be identical to the Balance A Less B column, although a plus or minus may exist due to error, breakage, or theft. The Balance A Less B column for Early Times bourbon was 81 and the closing inventory was 81. Therefore, there is a zero in the + or – column.

Next the price (the unit cost of the merchandise, taken from invoices) multiplied by the closing inventory will determine the extension. The closing inventory for Early Times bourbon was 81; this amount multiplied by its price, $9.25, equals $749.25, the extension.

The accounting period is indicated at the top of the form. For Table 11-2, the accounting period was for the period ending January 17, XXXX.

If an exchange system or card system is used, instead of filling out a requisition, the beverage use information would be recorded directly on the bar and inventory control report.

Using a liquor storeroom inventory report allows the bar manager to be constantly aware of the quantity and value of the inventory. The dollar amount invested in inventory is typically determined by frequency and availability. The financial investment in inventory can be held to a minimum if

Table 11-2 Liquor Storeroom Inventory Report

Date 1/18/XX
Period Ending January 17, XXXX
Prepared by Clerical

Time 8:00 A.M.
Taken by Bar Manager and Assistant
Approved by Owner/Manager

ITEM DESCRIPTION	UNIT	OPENING INVENTORY	PURCHASES	TOTALS (A)	REQ 11	12	13	14	15	16	17	TOTALS (B)	BALANCE A LESS B	CLOSING INVENTORY	+ OR –	PRICE	EXTENSION
BOURBON																	
Early Times	750 mL	87	48	135	11	4	5	7	9	8	10	54	81	81	0	$ 9.25	$749.25
I.W. Harper	750 mL	63	24	87	3			2	4	2	6	17	70	70	0	11.25	787.50
Jack Daniels	750 mL	91	48	139	8	2	2	7		3	9	31	108	107	–1 (broken)	14.50	1,551.50
Jim Beam	750 mL	103	72	175	14	6	5	1	4	8	12	50	125	125	0	9.25	1,156.25
Old Crow	750 mL	48		48	2				1		4	7	41	41	0	7.95	325.95
Old Grand-Dad	750 mL	51		51		2				6	1	9	42	42	0	14.45	606.90
CANADIAN																	
Canadian Club	750 mL	49	24	73	7	1	1	1	2	8	6	26	47	47	0	13.00	611.00
Seagram's VO	750 mL	57	24	81	5	3	1	2	1	1	6	19	62	62	0	13.25	821.50
Seagrams CR	750 mL	15		15	1							1	14	14	0	20.95	293.30

Page Total $6,903.15

160

■
■ ■ ■ ■

Table 11-3 Bar and Inventory Control Report

Date 1/18/XX

Time: 9:00 A.M.

Taken by Bar Manager and Assistant

Bar Location Cedar Room

Page 1 of 7

Prepared by Clerical

Approved by Owner/Manager

ITEM NO. 1 ITEM DESCRIPTION	2 UNIT	3 OPENING INVENTORY	4 REQUISITIONS BY DAY OF PERIOD MONTH: JANUARY 11	12	13	14	15	16	17	5 TOTAL (3 + 4)	6 CLOSING INVENTORY	7 AMOUNT SOLD (5 − 6)	8 PRICE	9 COST OF GOODS SOLD (7 × 8)	10 NO. DRINKS SOLD	11 SALES PRICE	12 TOTAL RETAIL VALUE (10 × 11)	13 LIQUOR COST % (9 ÷ 12)
BOURBON																		
Early Times	750 mL	6.8	1				1		2	10.8	5.9	4.9	$ 9.25	$ 45.33	122	$2.35	$286.70	15.81%
I.W. Harper	750 mL	7.2			2	1		2		12.2	7.7	4.5	11.25	50.63	112	2.50	280.00	18.08
Jack Daniels	750 mL	9.4	3		1	1	1	1	4	20.4	8.8	11.6	14.50	168.20	290	2.85	826.50	20.35
Subtotal														$264.16			$1,393.20	18.96%
BEER																		
Heineken	btl	97	72			24		24	48	265	88	177	0.95	$168.15	177	$2.25	$398.25	42.22%
Miller	½ keg	1.5	1		1		1		1	5.5	1.3	4.2	89.20	374.64	1,848	1.65	3,049.20	12.29
Budweiser	½ keg	1.5	1		1		1		1	5.5	1.3	4.2	89.20	374.64	1,848	1.65	3,049.20	12.29
Subtotal														$917.43			$6,496.65	14.12%
WINE																		
Gallo Vin Rose	liter	3.1	1				1		2	7.1	3.9	3.2	3.60	$11.52	19	$2.15	$40.85	28.20%
Subtotal														$11.52			$40.85	28.20%
Total														$1,193.11			$7,930.70	15.04%

beverage items are conveniently available and weekly purchases and deliveries are possible. Tracking the ordering, receiving, and inventory is only the beginning of managing inventory control. Proper use of the bar and inventory control report will help the bar manager to analyze whether the inventory is being managed properly.

Bar and Inventory Control Report

The bar and inventory control report is a comprehensive method of tracking beverage inventory. The report keeps track of:

- beginning and ending inventories
- use of product by day in the period and for the entire period
- the number of drinks that should have been sold
- the retail value of those drinks
- liquor cost percentages by type of beverage

This information will help the bar manager to determine *variances*. Variances are the differences between what was actually used and what should have been used. If 108 bottles of Jack Daniels should have been used but actually 107 were used, then there is a one-bottle variance. In this case (as shown in Table 11-2) the bottle was broken and noted on the liquor storeroom inventory report. Bar managers would want to know why there is a variance, which could be due to error, breakage, or theft.

Table 11-3 displays a bar and inventory report. The report is organized by column. Refer to Table 11-3 as the following column descriptions are explained:

Column 1—Item Description Each type of beverage is listed according to category (such as bourbon, beer, or wine).

Column 2—Unit This is the size of the item described in Column 1 (such as 750-mL bottle, liter, or ½ **keg**).

Keg
An aluminum barrel used to store draft beer and ale.

Column 3—Opening Inventory At the end of each accounting period, inventory is taken and extended. This is called closing inventory. The previous accounting period's closing inventory is the current accounting period's opening inventory.

Column 4—Requisitions A requisition (see Tables 4-1 and 4-2) from the bar to the liquor storeroom should be prepared daily. This enables the bartender to maintain a par amount at the bar. As requisitions are filled and completed, they are transferred to the bar and inventory control report. This allows for the accounting of every item taken. If inventory or bin cards are used (or a similar system), then the use figures would be taken directly from the bin cards. Inventory or bin cards are kept with the physical inventory; when a bottle is removed from inventory it is noted on the card, as was previously mentioned.

Column 5—Total The total includes the opening inventory plus the requisitions by day of period (Column 3 + Column 4 = Column 5).

Column 6—Closing Inventory The closing inventory is the actual physical count of all items on hand. This is usually taken the morning after the last day of the ending period, before the bar opens. If the last day of the accounting period is a Saturday, the inventory would be taken Sunday morning before opening. Bottles that are in use are weighed and inventoried in tenth amounts. For example, a half-full bottle would be .5.

Column 7—Amount Sold This indicates the number of bottles or parts of bottles sold. The amount sold is determined by subtracting the closing inventory from the total (Column 5 – Column 6 = Column 7).

Column 8—Price This is the actual cost paid for the merchandise. The price is taken from the invoices provided by the suppliers.

Column 9—Cost of Goods Sold The cost of goods sold extension represents the price multiplied by the amount sold (Column 7 $\times$ Column 8 = Column 9).

Column 10—Number of Drinks Sold The number of drinks sold is determined by multiplying the amount sold (Column 7) by 25. The number 25 would represent 25 one-ounce drinks per 750-mL bottle of liquor. Typically a one-ounce drink is poured, but house policy may specify another size, such as $7/8$ ounce or $1\frac{1}{8}$ ounces. The main point to remember is that the total possible number of drinks per bottle or unit must be established. This total number of drinks possible assumes that all conditions are perfect and bartenders make drinks in compliance with house policy on portion amounts. Obviously, some of the portions may vary if used in cocktails (most automated systems will account for the actual portion used). On average, even allowing for cocktails, a basic number of drinks will be poured from a standard unit, such as a 750-mL bottle.

Column 11—Sales Price The sales price is the menu price, the price the customer pays. This price should be used even if the beverage is used to make a cocktail.

Column 12—Total Retail Value The total retail value is determined by multiplying the number of drinks sold by the sales price (Column 10 $\times$ Column 11 = Column 12).

Column 13—Liquor Cost Percentage The idea of calculating a percentage is to figure out the cost of the liquor, or the pour cost, in relationship to the amount of revenue taken in by liquor sales. The liquor cost percentage, also known as the pour cost percentage, is obtained by dividing the cost of goods sold by the total retail value and multiplying by 100 ([Column 9 $\div$ Column 12] $\times$ 100 = Column 13). The liquor cost percentage will fluctuate with an increase or decrease in the cost of the merchandise. The Cost of Goods Sold and Total Retail Value columns are separately totaled by category (liquor, beer, and wine) in order to provide this information for the bar cost breakdown.

Table 11-4 Nonalcoholic Bar Inventory Items

Some of the many other items that must be recorded on the inventory are as follows:

ITEM DESCRIPTION	UNIT
Cherries	gal
Olives	gal
Onions	qt
Lemons	lb
Limes	lb
Oranges	lb
Tomato juice	46 oz
Grapefruit juice	46 oz
Pineapple juice	46 oz
Orange juice	gal
Bitters	12 oz
Tabasco	12 oz
Sugar	lb
Sour mix	gal
Tonic	qt
7UP	tank/box
Coke	tank/box
Ginger ale	tank/box

The benefit of maintaining the information provided by the bar and inventory control report is that it can be used to compare what should have happened against what did happen. For example, in Table 11-3, Column 12, if the value of all drinks sold is reported as $7,930.70 and the amount reported by the cash registers is $7,928.70, there is a $2.00 difference. Usually the variances are not very large. It is up to the bar manager to determine the acceptability of the variance amounts. In this example, a drink may not have been rung up. Similarly, the liquor cost percentage should compare to the one established when pricing drinks. If the liquor cost percentage is 3 percent or more higher than what it should be, there probably is a problem. The concept of pricing to attain a certain liquor cost percentage and possible reasons for large variances will be discussed in Chapter 12.

 onalcoholic Items

All nonalcoholic items should be accounted for along with alcoholic beverages. Table 11-4 shows typical nonalcoholic items that are part of the bar inventory.

SUMMARY

1. Alcoholic beverages represent a sizable financial investment in inventory.

2. All alcoholic beverages must be accounted for when received, stored, and used.

3. Efficient alcoholic beverage inventory management occurs when proper inventory and accounting measures are practiced.

4. Central to efficient control is a system to account for storeroom inventory. A variety of inventory control systems can be used. One of the most common is a bottle exchange system. When an empty bottle is returned to inventory, a full bottle replaces it.

5. Another type of inventory control system commonly used is an inventory or bin card that must be adjusted every time a bottle is removed from inventory.

6. The liquor storeroom inventory report tracks the value of the inventory. It does this by examining the opening inventory, purchases, requisitions, ending balances, and extensions.

7. The bar and inventory control report goes further by tracking beginning and ending inventories, use of products on a daily basis, the number of drinks that should have been sold, the retail value of those drinks, and beverage cost percentages by type of beverage.

KEY CONCEPTS

Automated systems
Bar and inventory control report
Bottle exchange system
Inventory/bin card system

Keg
Liquor storeroom inventory
 report

DISCUSSION QUESTIONS AND EXERCISES

1. Teach this chapter to another person.

2. Explain the general rule for inventory size.

3. Identify the three different types of control systems.

4. Describe different types of automated control systems.

5. Explain the advantages and disadvantages of automated control systems.

6. Explain why alcoholic beverage inventory represents a sizable financial investment.

7. Explain how the bottle exchange system and the bin system work.

8. Discuss the value of using a liquor storeroom inventory report in a foodservice or lounge operation.

9. What are the benefits of using a bar and inventory control report?

10. Complete the liquor storeroom inventory report and bar and inventory control report that follow. The physical inventory (closing) taken on 1/18/XX for completing the liquor storeroom inventory was as follows: Early Times, 35 units, I.W. Harper, 70 units; Jack Daniels, 98 units; Jim Beam, 117 units; Old Crow, 51 units; Old Grand-Dad, 32 units; Canadian Club, 47 units; Seagram's VO, 73 units; and Seagram's CR, 23 units.

Liquor Storeroom Inventory Report

Date 1/18/XX   Time 8:00 A.M.

Period Ending January 17, XXXX   Taken by Bar Manager and Assistant

Prepared by Clerical   Approved by Owner/Manager

ITEM DESCRIPTION	UNIT	OPENING INVENTORY	PURCHASES	TOTALS (A)	REQUISITIONS BY DAY OF PERIOD — MONTH: JANUARY							TOTALS (B)	BALANCE A LESS B	CLOSING INVENTORY	+ OR −	PRICE	EXTENSION
					11	12	13	14	15	16	17						
BOURBONS																	
Early Times	750 mL	67	48		11	4	10	15	10	10	20					$ 9.25	
I.W. Harper	750 mL	73	24		3		2	4	2		6					11.25	
Jack Daniels	750 mL	81	48		8	2	2			3	9					14.50	
Jim Beam	750 mL	95	72		14	6	5	1	4	8	12					9.25	
Old Crow	750 mL	58			2				1		4					7.95	
Old Grand-Dad	750 mL	41				2				6	1					14.45	
CANADIAN																	
Canadian Club	750 mL	49	24		7	1	1	2		8	6					13.00	
Seagram's VO	750 mL	67	24		5	3	1	2	1	1	6					13.25	
Seagram's CR	750 mL	25				1										20.95	

Page Total

Bar and Inventory Control Report

Date 1/18/XX
Time 9:00 A.M.
Taken by Bar Manager and Assistant

Bar Location Cedar Room
Page 1 of 7
Prepared by Clerical
Approved by Owner/Manager

ITEM NO. 1	2	3	4 REQUISITIONS BY DAY OF PERIOD MONTH: JANUARY							5	6	7	8	9	10	11	12	13
ITEM DESCRIPTION	UNIT	OPENING INVENTORY	11	12	13	14	15	16	17	TOTAL (3 + 4)	CLOSING INVENTORY	AMOUNT SOLD (5 − 6)	PRICE	COST OF GOODS SOLD (7 × 8)	NO. OF DRINKS SOLD	SALES PRICE	TOTAL RETAIL VALUE (10 × 11)	LIQUOR COST % (9 ÷ 12)
BOURBON																		
Early Times	750 mL	13.6	2				2		4		11.8		$ 9.25		224	$2.35		
I.W. Harper	750 mL	14.4			4	2		4			15.4		11.25		224	2.50		
Jack Daniels	750 mL	18.8	6	2	2		2	2	8		17.6		14.50		580	2.85		
BEER																		
Heineken	btl	194	144			48		48	96		176		0.95		354	$2.25		
Miller	½ keg	3.0	2		2		2		2		2.6		89.20		3,696	1.65		
Budweiser	½ keg	3.0	2		2			2	2		2.6		89.20		3,696	1.65		
WINE																		
Gallo Vin Rose	liter	6.2	2				2		4		7.8		3.60		38	$2.15		
Total																		

12

Beverage Production Control and Service

■　　　■　　　■　　　■　　　■　　　■　　　■　　　■　　　■　　　■　　　　　　■　　　■　　　■

Learning Objectives

After reading this chapter and completing the discussion questions and exercises, you should be able to:

1. Use standardized recipes for alcoholic beverages.
2. Establish a method for controlling how much alcoholic beverage is poured into a glass.
3. Calculate a pour cost for each alcoholic beverage recipe.
4. Reconcile sales by comparing what was sold according to the cash register reading with what was sold according to guest checks.
5. Identify several ways management could steal from a bar operation.
6. Identify the six most popular ways employees could steal from a bar operation or from customers that patronize a bar operation.
7. Recognize that state laws are becoming stricter and, in many states, may require those who serve alcoholic beverages to complete an alcohol server education course.
8. Understand the value of posting house policies that both employees and patrons can read and understand.
9. Understand why a log sheet should be kept as a protection against lawsuits.
10. Comprehend the responsibility needed to ensure that employees serving alcoholic beverages are trained to recognize and deal with intoxicated patrons.

About Beverage Production, Control, and Service

Beverage production and inventory control are very similar to food production control. The primary difference is that beverages are always in standard-sized bottles and containers.

Standard recipes for each drink must be established and uniformly followed in the same manner in which food recipes are followed. If the beverage operation does not have standardized recipes, bartenders will prepare drinks according to their own preferences or the way they were previously trained.

Management's responsibility is to create a system that promotes honesty and accuracy in accounting for sales dollars and correct product usage, always keeping in mind the temptations associated with preparing alcoholic beverages.

The final responsibility of management is to promote responsible alcoholic beverage service. Increasingly, beverage operations are being held responsible for ensuring that the customer does not drink too much. The financial consequences of serving too many alcoholic beverages to a customer may be devastating to the beverage operator, server, and customer.

Introduction to Beverage Service

Front bar
Located in a public area of the restaurant.

Service bar
Typically located in or next to the kitchen for waitstaff to pick up beverages with meals.

Special-function bar
A portable bar used in a room for private parties, catered events, and group functions.

Lounge or **bar**
A separate room that is expressly designed for serving alcoholic beverages.

Alcohol service usually occurs in four different places or settings. The first is a **front bar.** The front bar is located in a public area of the restaurant in full view of the dining room area. The second is a **service bar.** A service bar is often in or next to the kitchen. It is not in a public area of the restaurant and is used by waitstaff to serve beverages with meals. The third is a **special-function bar.** A special-function bar, as the phrase indicates, is a bar set up for functions. It is portable and is used for private parties, catered events, and group functions. The fourth is a **lounge** or **bar.** The lounge or bar is part of the foodservice operation and is located in a separate room that is expressly designed for serving alcoholic beverages. It may also serve as a service bar for a nearby dining room. Each type of bar has its own par amount and is subject to the inventory management procedures described in Chapter 11.

Beverage Production Control

Free pouring
A pouring method in which the bartender estimates how much beverage is being poured from a bottle into the customer's glass.

Controlling the production of alcoholic beverages is primarily done by consistently pouring the correct amount into a glass. Bartenders who believe they should be able to customize drinks according to customer taste are not consistently pouring the same amount of alcoholic beverage for the same type of drink. When bartenders do this, it becomes difficult to price drinks and to control costs. The primary way of controlling pour costs is to ensure that the bartender is using a standardized recipe. A popular source for standardized recipes is *The Bartender's Companion* (Plotkin, P. S. D. Publishing Inc., 1997). After determining the recipes to use, the bar manager should use one of the following four methods to ensure that drink ingredients are properly poured.

Free pouring occurs when a bartender pours the alcoholic beverage straight from the bottle, estimating how much liquid has left the bottle. The bartender estimates how much beverage is coming out of the bottle as he or she prepares drinks to customer orders.

Measured pour occurs when the bartender uses a measuring glass that is marked. Most alcoholic beverages are measured by the 7/8 ounce, 1 ounce, or 1 1/8 ounce. The bartender pours the alcoholic beverage into the measure glass (jigger or shot glass), then pours the alcohol into the serving glass. These measure glasses are marked so the bartender may pour to the line that represents a certain amount of liquor.

Bottle control systems involve using devices to control the amount of beverage poured from a bottle. This is done by using a type of pouring cap that is placed in the bottle top to release a set measurement when poured (see Figure 11-2). This gives the effect of free pouring but with a control.

Pour guns are hand-held devices used to control pouring. The nonalcoholic type is a pour gun used for club soda, seltzer, ginger ale, coke, and so on. The amount poured is estimated by the bartender. A variety of commercial systems are also available for controlling how much alcohol is poured (see Figure 11-6). The pour gun has a series of buttons on the back of the handle indicating the type of alcoholic beverage to be dispensed. For example, if the bartender presses the appropriate button for gin, a prescribed amount of gin comes out. As mentioned in Chapter 11, automated pouring devices have been developed so that all a bartender needs to do is to press the button and out comes the mixed drink.

Historically, the free pour method has been preferred by both the bartender and the customer. Some customers believe they actually get more alcoholic beverage when a free pour is used, as the bartender displays the personal touch of pouring and/or mixing the drink. It represents a nostalgic way of preparing alcoholic drinks. Customer attitudes are changing as the demand for consistent quantities of liquor being served every time becomes more prevalent.

Mixed drinks use a combination of an alcoholic beverage and water or some other nonalcoholic ingredient, such as club soda, ginger ale, etc. **Cocktails** use a combination of two or more alcoholic beverages, sometimes referred to as a blended drink. Beers and ales are served by the bottle or drawn from a keg and served by the glass or pitcher. Wines are served by the glass from a bottle or carafe. **Aperitifs** and **cordials** are types of mixed drinks, served from the bottle or used in recipes of multiple alcoholic beverages. **Neat** drinks are alcoholic beverages poured from the bottle into a glass and consumed—no ice, water, or other additions.

Another method to control how much alcoholic beverage is served is the size of the serving glass. A six-ounce wine glass can be used to serve four ounces of wine. A small stein controls how much beer can be poured into it. A large glass for large drinks and a small glass for small drinks is the general concept. Figures 12-1 and 12-2 show the different types and sizes of glasses.

Pour Cost

The cost of each drink is referred to as the **pour cost.** The pour cost is directly tied to the recipe used. As in plate cost for a meal, each individual ingredient has a cost. The total cost of all the ingredients used in a drink served is the pour cost. See Table 12-1 for an example of determining a pour cost.

Measured pour
A pouring method in which the bartender pours the beverage into a glass that has been marked, indicating how much beverage is to be poured into the customer's glass.

Bottle control systems
Involve using devices to control the amount of beverage poured from a bottle.

Pour guns
Hand-held devices used to pour both nonalcoholic and alcoholic beverages.

Mixed drink
A combination of liquor and water or some other nonalcoholic ingredient.

Cocktail
A combination of two or more liquors.

Aperitifs and cordials
Types of mixed drinks, served from the bottle.

Neat
Describes liquor poured from the bottle into a glass and consumed—no ice, water, or other additions.

Pour cost
The cost of the drink.

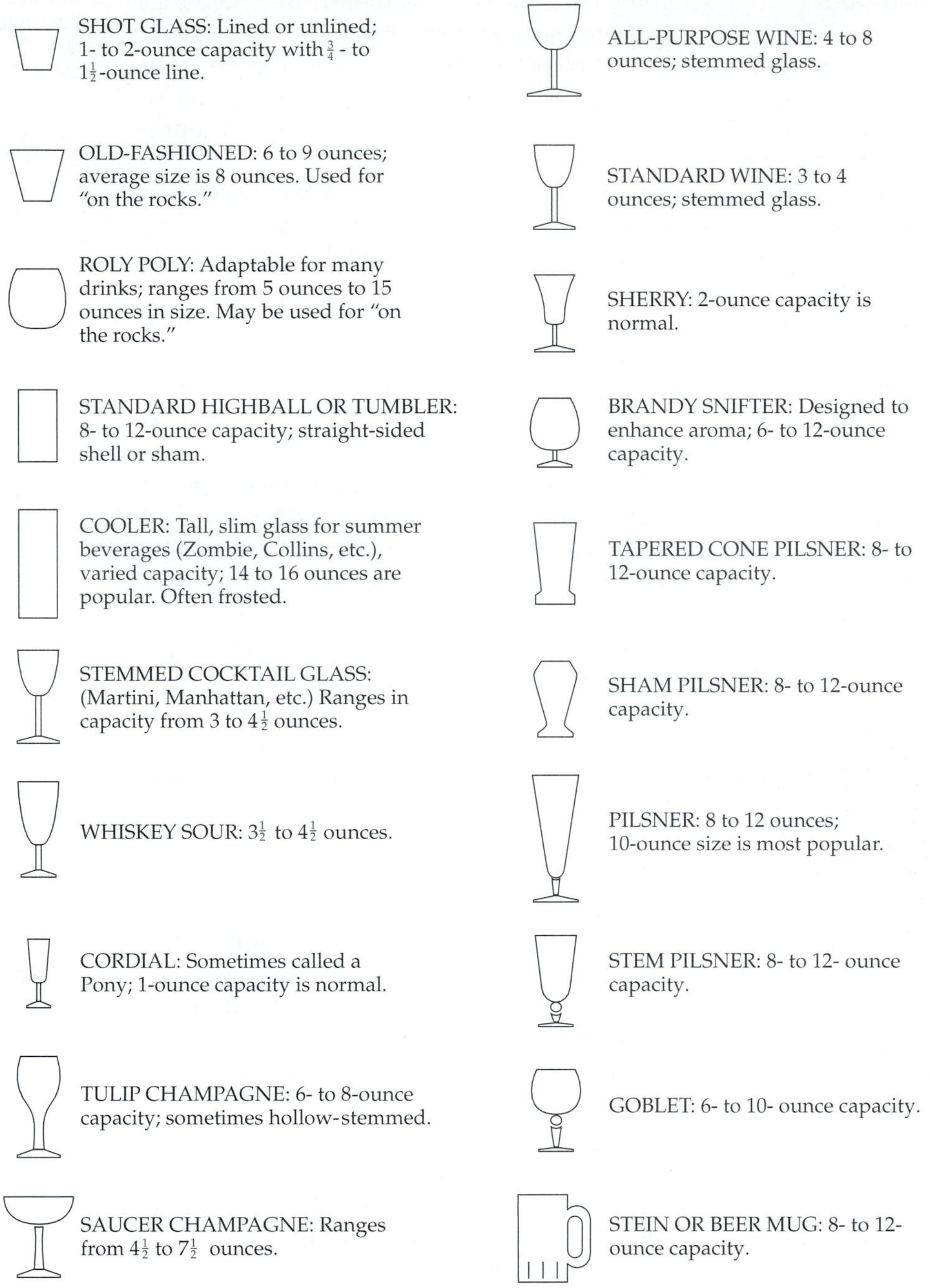

SHOT GLASS: Lined or unlined; 1- to 2-ounce capacity with $\frac{3}{4}$- to $1\frac{1}{2}$-ounce line.

ALL-PURPOSE WINE: 4 to 8 ounces; stemmed glass.

OLD-FASHIONED: 6 to 9 ounces; average size is 8 ounces. Used for "on the rocks."

STANDARD WINE: 3 to 4 ounces; stemmed glass.

ROLY POLY: Adaptable for many drinks; ranges from 5 ounces to 15 ounces in size. May be used for "on the rocks."

SHERRY: 2-ounce capacity is normal.

STANDARD HIGHBALL OR TUMBLER: 8- to 12-ounce capacity; straight-sided shell or sham.

BRANDY SNIFTER: Designed to enhance aroma; 6- to 12-ounce capacity.

COOLER: Tall, slim glass for summer beverages (Zombie, Collins, etc.), varied capacity; 14 to 16 ounces are popular. Often frosted.

TAPERED CONE PILSNER: 8- to 12-ounce capacity.

STEMMED COCKTAIL GLASS: (Martini, Manhattan, etc.) Ranges in capacity from 3 to $4\frac{1}{2}$ ounces.

SHAM PILSNER: 8- to 12-ounce capacity.

WHISKEY SOUR: $3\frac{1}{2}$ to $4\frac{1}{2}$ ounces.

PILSNER: 8 to 12 ounces; 10-ounce size is most popular.

CORDIAL: Sometimes called a Pony; 1-ounce capacity is normal.

STEM PILSNER: 8- to 12- ounce capacity.

TULIP CHAMPAGNE: 6- to 8-ounce capacity; sometimes hollow-stemmed.

GOBLET: 6- to 10- ounce capacity.

SAUCER CHAMPAGNE: Ranges from $4\frac{1}{2}$ to $7\frac{1}{2}$ ounces.

STEIN OR BEER MUG: 8- to 12- ounce capacity.

FIGURE 12-1
Different Types and Sizes of Glasses

First, establish the gross costs of the items included in the recipe. In Table 12-1, the recipe for a Pink Lady, the gin is actually Gilbey's Gin, sold in 750-mL bottles. The unit price (one bottle) is $8.95. The cost per ounce is 35.2 cents. Since the recipe calls for one ounce, the cost is 35.2 cents.

The same process is used for calculating the cost of the grenadine and half-and-half cream. A cost per ounce is determined. The cost per ounce is then multiplied by the recipe amount to give the cost. The grenadine per-ounce cost is 47.2 cents. The cost for the recipe is determined by multiplying

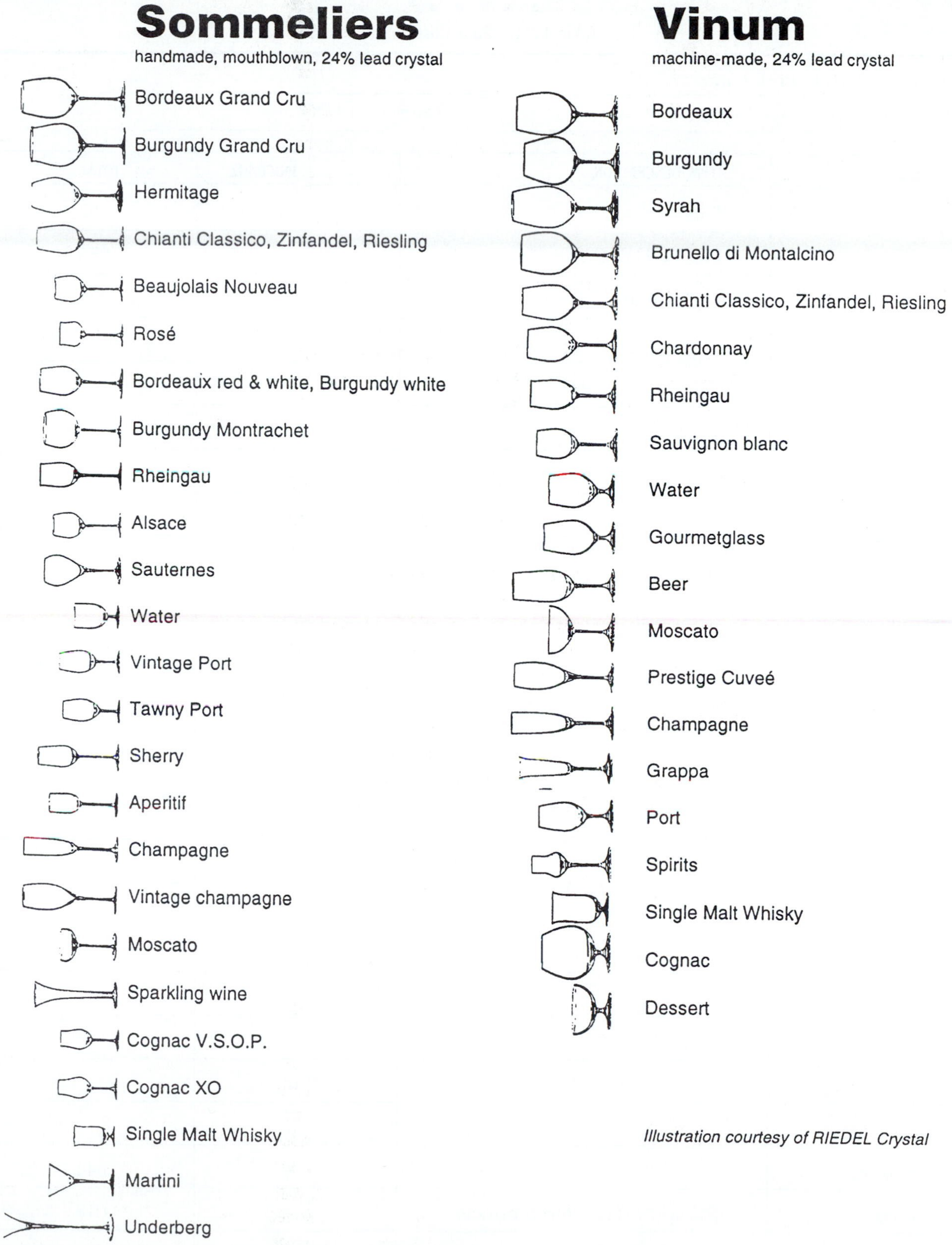

Sommeliers

handmade, mouthblown, 24% lead crystal

- Bordeaux Grand Cru
- Burgundy Grand Cru
- Hermitage
- Chianti Classico, Zinfandel, Riesling
- Beaujolais Nouveau
- Rosé
- Bordeaux red & white, Burgundy white
- Burgundy Montrachet
- Rheingau
- Alsace
- Sauternes
- Water
- Vintage Port
- Tawny Port
- Sherry
- Aperitif
- Champagne
- Vintage champagne
- Moscato
- Sparkling wine
- Cognac V.S.O.P.
- Cognac XO
- Single Malt Whisky
- Martini
- Underberg

Vinum

machine-made, 24% lead crystal

- Bordeaux
- Burgundy
- Syrah
- Brunello di Montalcino
- Chianti Classico, Zinfandel, Riesling
- Chardonnay
- Rheingau
- Sauvignon blanc
- Water
- Gourmetglass
- Beer
- Moscato
- Prestige Cuveé
- Champagne
- Grappa
- Port
- Spirits
- Single Malt Whisky
- Cognac
- Dessert

Illustration courtesy of RIEDEL Crystal

FIGURE 12-2
Types and Sizes of Wine Glasses   *Courtesy of Riedel Crystal.*

Table 12-1   Pour Cost Chart

Name of Drink Pink Lady

Priced by Beverage Manager   Date 1/13/XX

UNIT	ITEM DESCRIPTION	PRICE/OZ	TOTAL
1 oz	Gin	.352	.352
1½ oz	Half & Half Cream	.037	.056
½ oz	Grenadine	.472	.236
Subtotal			.644
Loss	5% spirits/12% tap products		.018
TOTAL			.662

Recipe courtesy of *The Bartender's Companion: A Complete Drink Recipe Guide (3rd ed.)*, Robert Plotkin, ed., P. S. D. Publishing Inc., Tuscon, Arizona, 1997, p.104.

47.2 cents by ½ ounce, which equals 23.6 cents. The half-and-half cream cost is 3.7 cents per ounce. The recipe calls for 1.5 ounces; thus $1.5 \times 3.7 = 5.6$ cents.

The subtotal for all the ingredient costs is 64.4 cents. This does not represent all the costs, especially if a free pouring system is used. The pour cost should also allow for evaporation, overpouring, or spillage. Once an alcoholic beverage bottle is opened, there will be some loss. The guideline for this loss is 5 percent. Therefore, the gin cost multiplied by 5 percent equals 1.76 cents ($35.2 \times .05 = 1.76$). Rounding to one decimal place for cents is usually close enough, which gives 1.8 cents in this case.

Tap products are those poured from a tap, usually beers and ales. While there is not the problem of evaporation because beer is kept in a keg and the delivery system is sealed, there tends to be a loss from overpouring and spillage. Experience has shown that about 8 to 20 percent of tap products are lost. Each beverage operation should calculate its actual loss. As a guideline, allowing a 12 percent loss should be adequate.

All alcoholic beverages will evaporate to some degree. With a free pouring system, bartenders will overpour and underpour drinks. A professionally experienced bartender will pour with a high degree of accuracy on average.

Underpouring cheats the customer and overpouring cheats the beverage operation. Also, there will be some spillage. As a general rule, three to four drinks out of 100 will be spilled by a bartender or waitperson. To allow for these operational errors, as previously mentioned, 5 percent of the cost should be added to the ingredient costs.

In Table 12-1, the alcoholic beverage used was gin. Gin is a distilled spirit. Distilled spirits and wines usually incur a 5 percent loss due to evaporation, over- and underpours, and spillage. The loss should be calculated only for the alcoholic ingredient cost.

Reconciling Sales

Reconciling sales is comparing what the cash register indicates was sold to what was actually sold. To do a reconciliation, a system must be in place. Probably the simplest system is similar to the one suggested for a foodservice operation. Thus, no drinks are prepared unless a guest check has been written and handed to the bartender. Even the bartender must prepare a guest check if he or she serves drinks at the bar. Electronic or computer systems do this automatically.

Every drink is also issued a cash register receipt. The receipt is placed on the table or bar with the drink. This allows a simple visual check. Usually, by issuing receipts, the manager may be able to quickly look over the room or at a table and know that a customer has paid.

By using guest checks and receipts for drinks, the totals on the guest checks can be compared to the cash register totals. The totals on the guest checks should be the same as those on the cash register. This system protects against most cash shortage problems.

Probably the best protection for the operation and the customer is an attentive manager and an appropriate electronic cash register and/or point-

Reconciling sales
The process of comparing cash register sales with what was actually sold.

of-sale liquor control system. An attentive manager watches to ensure that systems are being used and policies are being followed. In addition, an attentive manager will be able to see if theft collusion between a waitperson and bartender is occurring (see "Avoiding Theft By Nonmanagement Employees" later in this chapter for further explanation). Also, effective inventory controls and watching the pour cost and beverage costs will ensure a properly operated beverage service.

Avoiding Theft by Management and Bookkeeping Staff

Any foodservice operation that serves alcoholic beverages risks theft. Also, practically any control mechanism that is put into place to prevent theft is vulnerable to being breached. However, an operation should protect itself to the maximum against theft and make theft efforts easier to catch. Some of the more common methods of theft used by management or bookkeepers are discussed here.

UNAUTHORIZED CONSUMPTION

The downfall of many managers has been a cavalier attitude about drinking on the job or just before or after work. Some states prohibit managers, including owners, from consuming alcoholic beverages while at work. A recommended rule is that all employees, including managers, may not drink on the job. Occasionally customers will want management to drink with them. This is not a good idea. In fact, it is not a good idea to give any drinks away, even as a promotion. Giving out free alcoholic beverages is suggestive of irresponsible beverage service. The establishment may be open to lawsuits if free drinks are given to customers.

KICKBACKS

Suppliers may offer money to managers to sell their products, rather than offering legitimate discounts for volume purchases. A manager may also be offered a bribe to carry a line of products. While the bribe is not necessarily stealing from the operation, the practice usually leads to overpricing and other costs to cover the bribe. Besides, this type of collusion is against the law.

BOOKKEEPING

Bookkeepers may steal by not making deposits or by reporting cash short. Also, they may pay fictitious bills to themselves.

INVENTORY

Some employees may deliberately underreport items in inventory and then steal the item.

Proper attention from management, correct completion of inventory, and constant watching of what is going on in the operation should minimize opportunities for managers and bookkeepers to steal. Nearly all thefts will eventually be discovered if a proper inventory system, cash system, and other controls are being used.

voiding Theft by Nonmanagement Employees

The temptation to cheat the bar operation or customers when serving alcoholic beverages exists for some employees. Some of the more common methods of dishonesty are mentioned here.

PLAYING WITH THE CASH REGISTER

Following is a list of ways that employees may tamper with the sales process:

- The employee doesn't ring up the sale and keeps the cash, or **underrings** the sale and keeps the difference.
- Bartenders serve and collect for sales between shift changes.
- Waitstaff reuse guest checks and register receipts to order drinks that have not really been ordered, pocketing the cash from the sale of the drink to the customer.
- An employee performs an incorrect **overring** or void and keeps the money.

Underring
Occurs when the cashier enters an amount into a cash register or point-of-sale terminal that is less than the price of the item being recorded.

Overring
Occurs when the cashier enters an amount into a cash register or point-of-sale terminal that is higher than the price of the item being recorded.

PHONY WALKOUT

A waitperson claims a phony customer walkout after the customer has paid and keeps the money. If an operation allows a customer to run up a tab, the amount taken by the waitperson or bartender could be sizable.

PHANTOM BOTTLE

A bartender brings in his or her own bottle of liquor onto the shift and pockets the cash from its sale. A way to guard against this is to have a policy that prohibits employees from bringing in any large purses, jackets, or bags to the bar. Also, the manager should frequently review and analyze the sales figures on the beverage cost report (Tables 10-1 and 10-2). If sales appear to fluctuate during a bartender's days off (in other words, if more sales occur in those days), the potential for a phantom bottle problem exits. A change in the bartender's shift schedule may reflect further sales fluctuations. Therefore, identifying sales trends is important.

SHORT POUR

Less than the recipe amount of alcoholic beverages is used to serve drinks. The difference between the amount that should have been sold and the amount that was sold is kept by the bartender. This method can also be used when a bartender and waitperson collude in selling the difference amount and equally pocketing the cash.

OVERCHARGING CUSTOMERS

The customer is deliberately charged more than the menu price. The difference between the menu price and the amount collected is kept by the employee. Another way to do this is to have a customer sign a credit card voucher in advance and then overcharge for drinks or charge for drinks not served.

DILUTING

Water is substituted for liquor and then used to mix drinks. The liquor poured off is also sold and the employee keeps the money for the drinks.

THEFT

Employees take bottles of liquor, beer, or wine from storage areas.

Every operation needs to institute controls to prevent these practices. All of these practices are difficult to trace. A sound beverage service system will help to prevent theft from the operation and the customer.

Discouraging and preventing theft can be accomplished by controlling pouring techniques, creating an order system that documents drink orders, and maintaining tight controls over inventory. While free pouring may be the most impressive and desirable method of making drinks according to many bartenders, pouring a consistently sized shot requires much practice. Using a shot glass helps to limit overpours; however, it still is easy to abuse. Automatic drink dispensers give management the greatest control. Although automated dispensing systems represent a significant investment, they typically pay for themselves in a short period of time.

A variety of systems are available to help track drink orders and preparation. The basic principle behind all of these systems is to separate the ordering and preparation of drinks so that a double check system is in place. All orders should be submitted on guest checks or front-of-the-house electronic systems that report orders of drinks to the bartender. This creates evidence of an order and helps management to track problems that may occur, although drinks ordered by customers at the bar directly from the bartender are the most difficult to track.

Open container laws
State laws restricting the transfer of open alcoholic beverages in an automobile.

Alcoholic service training
Certain states require those who serve alcoholic beverages to complete an approved training program.

Third-party liability
A state law that makes those who serve alcoholic beverages liable for serving alcoholic drinks to people who are considered legally drunk.

License requirements
State laws that require foodservice and beverage operations to acquire a license to serve alcoholic beverages.

The Relationship between State Liquor Laws and Service

Alcohol service is highly controlled; every state has laws regulating the sale, service, and consumption of alcoholic beverages. Matters regulated by some or all states include legal drinking age (21 in all states), **open container laws,** hours of operation, required **alcoholic service training, third-party liability, license requirements,** and in some cases suggested pace of service. Many other areas are regulated depending on the political culture of the state.

Currently, many states require servers to take alcoholic service training programs. Some states have also mandated courses on how to pace service, identify an intoxicated customer, deal with an abusive drunk, and watch for fake personal identification (ID).

Social mores are changing. Responsible alcoholic beverage service is being demanded by the general public. Legally, those who serve alcoholic beverages are increasingly being held to the **prudent person rule,** which basically asks, "What would a prudent person do in this or a similar situation?" The basic answer to the question is that a prudent or responsible person would not serve alcohol to someone who is intoxicated. Nor would a prudent person allow someone who is visibly intoxicated to drive himself or herself anywhere. In some states the law is specific: do not serve visibly intoxicated customers.

Prudent person rule
A legal standard that compares what a prudent person would do in a situation to the behavior that actually occurred.

THE SEVEN MOST IMPORTANT THINGS ABOUT HAVING A LIQUOR LICENSE

1. *Selling liquor is serious business.* Alcohol is a leading cause of traffic accidents and is deemed to be a major social problem. One out of ten people has the propensity to become an alcoholic. Of those who are in accidents and have been drinking, between 40 and 60 percent became drunk in a public drinking establishment (depending upon the geographic area).

2. *Know license requirements.* Each state has different classes of licenses. Managers should know what type of license best suits their particular needs.

3. *Know license privileges.* Each state has specific regulations. It behooves the manager to know what hours of operation, seating capacity, written reports, beverage container laws, and so on apply to those who serve alcoholic beverages. The state grants the privilege to do business. Managers must prove that they are worthy of the privilege. In some states, the liquor license is considered a property right. By complying with state regulations, the manager will be able to conduct business successfully.

4. *Check the ID of anyone who looks younger than 26.* The minimum drinking age in the United States is 21. Age appearances can be deceiving. Underage people may look older than 21. As a general rule, post a sign that says, "All persons 26 and younger will be carded." The sign informs the public and makes the server or bartender's job easier.

5. *"If you are not sure, don't serve."* The general operating rule is that if you are uncertain of the age of a person, don't serve that person.

6. *In some states, if liquor is served, food must be offered.* It is a proven fact that certain foods help to absorb some of the alcohol. Therefore, some states require that food such as chicken, pizza, or sandwiches be offered.

7. *Work cooperatively with the state agency responsible for licensing.* Some states have inspections and visitors from the agency responsible for monitoring and enforcing alcoholic service laws. The manager should accompany any inspectors doing inspections. All discussions and conversations with officials should be done in a professional manner.

Management proves that it is a responsible provider of alcoholic beverages in several ways. One sign of responsibility is to have and enforce a house policy that states the house rules concerning visibly intoxicated persons. Others are posted rules, incident reports, server training, and recorded portion control liquor systems. These systems provide reports of items sold, specific quantities, dates, and times.

HOUSE POLICY

House policy
A written policy indicating how employees are to behave in given situations of alcoholic beverage service.

A **house policy** is the summation of the philosophy and attitude of management. Figure 12-3 is an example of a house policy. It is important that the house policy be written and posted in a conspicuous place. Everyone must have access to reading the house policy. This way, if the operation is ever sued, part of the defense would be that the operation made a reasonable effort to inform its employees regarding the policy of the house. A public statement also helps management to be consistent in enforcing policy.

DAILY INCIDENT LOG

Daily incident log
A form used to record incidents that occurred in serving or denying service to customers.

Possibly the best defense if ever sued as part of a third-party liability claim is to keep an accurate **daily incident log.** Many liability cases that go to court end up with witnesses providing conflicting testimony. Often it is just one person's word against another. A written record clearly documents and dates what took place and can be submitted in a court of law. A daily incident log can provide that written record.

The daily incident log is used to record a description of any episodes that occur. It also provides a place for a witness to make comments. Finally, it provides a space for all those concerned to sign. The personal signatures validate the testimony that has been offered. Table 12-2 is an example of a daily incident log. The log can effectively document irresponsible behavior and help prevent a lawsuit.

SERVER EDUCATION

Server education
An educational program for teaching servers of alcoholic beverages to control consumption by bar patrons.

Only a few states require **server education.** Although most foodservice operations offer some type of server education, the mood of the nation is that operations should take more responsibility in serving alcohol. Both the Educational Foundation of the National Restaurant Association and the National Licensed Beverage Association have developed server education programs.

As a help to operators, the checklist in Table 12-3 is provided as an example of a method of ensuring and documenting that employees have been trained properly. The table indicates the skill areas that employees should have mastered.

SUMMARY

1. Alcoholic beverages, like food menu items, are produced using standardized recipes.
2. Each alcoholic beverage ingredient is measured by the way it is poured.

TO: ALL EMPLOYEES

FROM: OWNER/MANAGER

RE: HOUSE RULES CONCERNING VISIBLY INTOXICATED PERSONS

DRINKING AND DRIVING ARE BAD MIXERS.

While we derive our livelihood from the sale of alcoholic beverages, we are concerned about the abuse of these products; patrons who drive while intoxicated are detrimental to our livelihood.

Do not serve a visibly intoxicated guest. To ensure that a guest does not leave the establishment visibly intoxicated, make a good-faith effort to remove the drink and substitute with coffee or other beverages.

The bottom line is that it is our responsibility to carefully consider our actions and judge each and every patron as to whether or not they are intoxicated. We must make this judgment whether the patron is drinking or not. Excuses such as "I am taking a cab" (whether true or not) do not relieve our responsibility.

It is my policy and the policy of this establishment to make every effort to curb service to visibly intoxicated persons. This includes regular patrons.

If you feel that someone is intoxicated and wish to stop the sale of alcoholic beverages, notify the manager on duty. You will be supported in this decision. I will never overrule decisions made by the staff.

Bartenders and floor-service personnel must be aware of the customer. They must also communicate with each other regarding possible problems or when a patron has been refused service. Chronic problems will be dealt with by refusing admittance permanently.

It is the policy of this establishment that patrons are here at our hospitality. This means that patrons shall respect the establishment and patrons shall respect all other people, including staff. We will not lose business due to a loud, unpleasant, obnoxious person! Patrons shall be cut off and asked to leave if they violate these policies.

We will not encourage excessive drinking, offer "two-fers" or other bargain rates, or permit alcohol consumption contests on our premises. When appropriate, encourage the service of a "spacer" (coffee, soft drink or other nonalcoholic beverage, or food).

At closing time, announce that it is closing time and that you will have to pick up the drinks in 30 minutes. Do not announce "last call." Put a limit of one drink per customer on any orders taken in the last 30 minutes of service.

If someone appears visibly intoxicated, try to arrange safe transportation home through his or her friends (friends don't let friends drive intoxicated) or call a taxi.

Any incident that is alcohol related or involves excessive alcohol consumption shall be recorded in our daily incident log, including a brief description and the witnesses and employees involved or present. Each employee will initial the log at the end of his or her shift regardless of whether an incident occurred.

Remember, we must recognize that taking good care of our customers and protecting them against the effects of alcohol abuse not only constitutes good business and is our legal obligation, but is also a moral imperative.

FIGURE 12-3
Example House Policy

Table 12-2   Daily Incident Log

Day   Friday _____   Date   1/18/XX _____   Shift   5:00 P.M.–2:00 A.M. _____

Who Prepared Log   Bartender _____   Manager on Duty   Manager _____

INCIDENT (DESCRIBE, PATRON'S NAME, ADDRESS, PHONE #)	TIME IT OCCURRED	NAME/PHONE # OF EMPLOYEE INVOLVED	WITNESS NAMES/ PHONE NUMBERS
Drink order refused to James J. Drunk who was acting belligerent and appeared visibly intoxicated. James J. Drunk left. Cocktail waitress tried to get cab, but person refused help and wouldn't give address or phone number.	10:30 P.M.	Cocktail Waitress 333-3333 Signed:	Bartender and Johnny Witness 444-4444 Signed:

To the best of my knowledge, the above incidents occurred as described.

Shift Servers: Witnesses:

Anna Server _____   Fred Witness _____

George Server _____   _____

_____   _____

■ ■ ■ ■ ■
Table 12-3 Alcoholic Service Training

Server Name	Ann Waitress		
Date Employed	1/7/XX	Evaluated by	Owner

OUTCOME	DATE DEMONSTRATED	NEEDS IMPROVEMENT
1. Can describe visible signs of intoxication.	1/13/XX	
2. Knows the general drink limits.	1/17/XX	
3. Demonstrates how to track the number of drinks that customers have consumed.	1/17/XX	
4. Knows not to serve more than one drink per person at a time.		1/13/XX
5. Knows the house policies on serving drinks.		1/17/XX
6. Knows how to slow service if a customer is nearing intoxication.		1/17/XX
7. Knows how to cut off service.	1/13/XX	
8. Knows the procedures for dealing with difficult customers.		1/17/XX
9. Knows to encourage customers to order food and nonalcoholic drinks.	1/13/XX	

3. There are a variety of methods used to control how alcoholic beverages are poured—from free pouring to devices that automatically pour mixed drinks.

4. To consistently serve beverages, the specific requirements and how the beverages are poured should be controlled. Likewise, it is important to calculate the pour cost of each alcoholic beverage used.

5. After beverages are sold, the revenue collected must be reconciled. Reconciling occurs when the amount sold according to the cash register reading is compared to what was sold according to guest checks. These two amounts should be the same. If they are different, the reason for the variance should be determined. The reconciliation process helps to discourage theft. This process may be done either manually or by an automated software application, whereby an automated liquor system interfaces with a point-of-sale device.

6. Efficient inventory management and service controls help to discourage theft by management and employees.

7. Theft occurs in a variety of ways. Manager theft occurs through unauthorized consumption, kickbacks, improper bookkeeping, and stealing inventory. Employee theft occurs through incorrectly ringing up drinks on the cash register, claiming phony walkouts, using phantom bottles, serving short pours, overcharging customers, diluting drinks, and outright stealing.

8. Theft may be prevented by correctly serving proper amounts of alcoholic beverages, using serving systems that account for the number of drinks sold, and properly managing inventory.

9. State laws control most aspects of alcoholic beverage service. Laws in many states require those who serve alcoholic beverages to complete an alcohol server education course.

10. Owners and managers of bar operations should use control techniques to protect themselves from lawsuits. One strategy managers may use to protect the bar operations is posting house policies that both employees and patrons can read and understand. Another technique is to require bartenders to maintain a daily incident log.

KEY CONCEPTS

Alcoholic service training
Aperitifs and cordials
Bar
Bottle control systems
Cocktail
Daily incident log
Free pouring
Front bar
House policy
License requirements
Lounge
Measured pour
Mixed drink

Neat
Open container laws
Overring
Pour cost
Pour guns
Prudent person rule
Reconciling sales
Server education
Service bar
Special-function bar
Third-party liability
Underring

DISCUSSION QUESTIONS AND EXERCISES

1. Teach the principles of this chapter to another person.

2. What are the basic problems of beverage production control?

3. What are the problems of using a free pouring system? A measured pour system? Pour guns?

4. What are the differences between mixed drinks and cocktails?

5. How can you control the cost of serving wine?

6. Describe what it means to reconcile sales.

7. Given the following beverage recipe and costs, complete a pour cost chart (see Appendix A for a blank form). Item: Long Island Iced Tea. Recipe: ½ oz gin, ½ oz vodka, ½ oz light rum, ½ oz tequila, ½ oz Triple Sec, 2 oz sweet and sour mix, 2 oz cola, and a lemon wedge. Costs are given per ounce: gin, 35.2 cents; vodka, 24.2 cents; light rum, 47.0 cents; tequila, 62.0 cents; Triple Sec, 23.4 cents; sweet and sour mix, 21.1 cents; cola, 1 cent; lemon wedge garnish, 8 cents.

8. Contact your state agency that deals with licensing issues and laws regarding alcohol beverage service and get answers to the following questions.

   a. Is there an open container law in your state?

   b. What is the blood alcohol level at which a person is considered legally drunk?

   c. What are the different types of licenses for a person who wants to serve liquor as part of a foodservice operation?

   d. Are servers required to obtain a permit to serve alcoholic beverages in your state?

   e. Are servers required to complete some type of alcoholic beverage service training in your state?

   f. Does your state have a third-party liability law?

9. Read the following scenario and then answer the related questions. The Snow Beast is a very popular restaurant and lounge located near a ski resort. It is the week after Christmas; the time is about 5:00 P.M. Four people walk into the lounge. They are boisterous and talking loudly. They seat themselves in a six-person booth. One of them waves his hand with a broad gesture, signaling the server to walk over to the table. As the server walks over, she hears various members of the party exclaim what fun they had cross-country skiing and it was too bad that they ran out of booze. The server introduces herself to the group. Everyone in the group acknowledges the server's presence. Two members of the group are slurring their words.

   a. Would you serve this group?

   b. What should the server do?

10. Explain the different ways that managers may steal from a lounge operation.

11. Explain the different ways that employees may steal from a lounge operation.

13

Controlling Payroll Costs and the Cost of Employee Turnover

. . . .

Learning Objectives

After reading this chapter and completing the discussion questions and exercises, you should be able to:

1. Understand that payroll cost is the cost of using employee labor.

2. Recognize payroll cost control as the process of managing employee efficiency, employee labor, physical facilities, the equipment interfacing with employee labor, and other resources that maximize production and efficiency.

3. Track the amount of time that an employee works by using a time sheet, a time card, or an electronic method.

4. Calculate payroll costs by determining the cost of each employee, summing the cost of all employees, and adding the indirect payroll and benefit costs.

5. Understand the significance of payroll to sales as shown by a percentage.

6. Explain how a payroll budget is used to estimate the cost of producing sales and profits.

7. Recognize that work schedules should be used to ensure that there are enough people to do the needed work and provide the desired level of customer service.

8. Use a payroll budget estimate form to ensure that the estimated schedule of employees does not exceed the budget for those employees.

9. Reduce payroll costs by using labor-saving equipment, improving kitchen layout, training staff effectively and continually, and using preprepared foods when applicable.

10. Determine the cost of employee turnover by using a turnover rate and cost chart.

11. Create and use job descriptions to hire and train people.

12. Create performance standards based upon job descriptions.

13. Evaluate employees based upon performance standards.

About Controlling Payroll Costs and the Cost of Employee Turnover

As a result of the continually rising cost of labor, increases in the minimum wage, and general improvement in working conditions throughout the entire economy, labor concerns have a dominating influence on the development of foodservice systems and the products used throughout the foodservice industry. The method or system under which the lowest combined food and labor costs can be obtained without lowering quality often dictates operating policy.

The importance of controlling payroll costs and employee turnover cannot be overemphasized, particularly in view of the fact that, as a percentage of gross sales, labor costs generally vary from about 18 percent to 38 percent, depending upon the type of foodservice operation.

The continuing trend in the use of frozen, refrigerated, and preprepared foods and the forecast for their increased usage reflects the industry's response to controlling payroll costs along with maintaining food quality standards. Improvements in food technology and advancements in labor-saving kitchen equipment are frequently introduced to the market. In real dollars, the productivity of the foodservice worker has declined in some foodservice operations that have not begun using newer methods of purchasing and preparation. This chapter specifically details methods and procedures that have proven to be effective in controlling payroll costs and the cost of employee turnover.

Introduction to Payroll Cost Control

Payroll cost control
A process of meeting cost targets by establishing a payroll budget, properly organizing the workplace, hiring correctly, reducing employee turnover, scheduling properly, and comparing actual costs to projected costs with the intent of reducing variances.

Payroll cost is the total cost of employee labor. Payroll costs are usually calculated once per accounting period. An accounting period can be monthly, biweekly, weekly, or even daily with the appropriate computer software. The payroll cost indicates the number of dollars spent in achieving the total amount of gross sales and profits for any given period of time. The payroll cost is usually prepared at the same time as the food cost. Food cost is the total dollar amount spent on food prepared in a foodservice operation, as discussed in Chapter 2. Payroll cost is as important as food cost.

Payroll cost control takes place in two stages—planning and doing. The first stage, planning, involves establishing a payroll budget, properly organizing the workplace, hiring correctly, and reducing employee turnover. The second stage, doing, consists of scheduling properly, actually incurring costs, and comparing what happened to what was planned to happen. The payroll cost control process is basically the efficient use of physical facilities, employee labor, and other resources associated with payroll to maximize productivity.

Payroll cost budgets are established by examining payroll costs in relationship to sales by an operating area or department. For example, the payroll cost of operating a French bistro that is part of a large resort would be calculated and compared to the total sales of the French bistro. It would not typically be calculated and compared to all the foodservice units that might exist at the resort. Budgets are established based upon the goals of management.

Work schedules are developed to ensure that the proper number of employees are working to meet the needs of customers. After the work schedule is developed, the estimated payroll from the schedule is compared to the payroll cost budget. If the estimate is the same or less, the schedule remains unchanged. If the estimate is higher, the schedule should be changed to meet the budget.

Payroll cost budget
A planned estimate of expenses, expressed in dollar amounts or as a percentage of sales. It is an estimate of the cost of labor needed to manage an estimated level of sales.

Work schedule
A form or template used to list the employees and the hours they work, to best use employees to accomplish the objectives of the foodservice operation.

Components of Payroll Costs

There are two components of payroll costs. One component is **salaries.** Salaries vary somewhat according to sales, but are not as flexible as **wages.** For the most part, salaries are considered to be fixed. This means that they do not change with sales. The second component of costs is wages. These costs do vary according to sales. Both salaries and wages are generally considered to be **controllable expenses.** Controllable expenses are listed as part of an **income statement.** Table 13-1 shows an example of a income statement.

An income statement lists the sources of sales and the expenses incurred to obtain the sales. In Table 13-1, the sources of sales were food sales and beverage sales. The cost of sales is the cost of producing the food and beverages served. Controllable expenses are classified as controllable because these costs tend to vary according to sales. Specifically, the percentage of salaries and wages in relation to sales will generally decrease as sales increase. Management has some degree of control over these costs. Rent, depreciation, and interest expenses generally are not considered controllable costs. These are fixed costs and do not vary according to sales. In its simplest form, the income statement formula is:

Salaries
Compensation for employees, calculated weekly, semimonthly, monthly, or annually.

Wages
Compensation for employees based upon hours worked.

Controllable expense
A type of variable expense that management has the direct responsibility to control.

Income statement
A list of sales, expenses, and profits over a period of time.

$$Sales - Expenses = Income$$

Relationship between Costs and Revenues

Both payroll cost and food cost must be controlled according to the sales volume. Foodservice operations must be profitable to remain in business, or at the minimum breakeven point if they are on a nonprofit basis. The amount of profit varies from operation to operation. The amount of the profit is directly related to the amount of the costs and sales volume. Costs are expressed in

Table 13-1   Income Statement

Period Ending ___1/31/XX___

Sales				
Food sales		$8,000		80.0%
Beverage sales	+	2,000		20.0%
Total sales	=		$10,000	100.0%
Cost of sales				
Cost of food sold		$2,300		28.8%
Cost of beverages sold	+	300		15.0%
Total cost of sales	=		$2,600	26.0%
Controllable expenses				
Salaries and wages		$2,800		28.0%
Employee benefits	+	300		3.0%
Direct operating expenses	+	350		3.5%
Marketing	+	150		1.5%
Energy and utility service	+	450		4.5%
Administrative expenses	+	250		2.5%
Repairs and maintenance	+	300		3.0%
Total controllable expenses	=	+	4,600	46.0%
Total cost of sales and controllable expenses	=	−	7,200	72.0%
Income before occupation costs, depreciation, and interest		=	$2,800	28.0%
Occupation costs				
Rent and other occupation costs		−	750	7.5%
Income before depreciation and interest		=	$2,050	20.5%
Depreciation		$ 350		
Interest	+	200		
Total depreciation and interest	=	−	550	5.5%
Net income before taxes		=	$1,500	15.0%
Income taxes		−	420	4.2%
Net income		=	$1,080	10.8%

dollars; but for the purpose of controlling them, they are also expressed in percentage form. This percentage shows the relationship between payroll costs and sales. The basic accounting method of showing the relationship between sales, costs, and profits is shown in the following simplified format.

ITEM	AMOUNT	PERCENTAGE	(HOW PERCENTAGE IS CALCULATED)
Sales	$10,000	100%	$(10,000 \div 10,000 = 1 \times 100 = 100\%)$
Costs	− 9,000	− 90%	$(9,000 \div 10,000 = .90 \times 100 = 90\%)$
Profits	$ 1,000	10%	$(1,000 \div 10,000 = .10 \times 100 = 10\%)$

See Table 13-1. The far right column shows the percentage of every item on the income statement. For sales, the percentages show the ratio of the sources of sales to total sales. In the example, 80 percent or eight of every ten dollars of sales came from food sales. Total sales is equal to 100 percent because the ratio is based upon sales. The costs, as shown in the table, are calculated in relationship to total sales.

■ ■ ■ ■ ■

Table 13-2 Typical Payroll Cost Percentages

	LOW	MEDIUM	HIGH
Family Restaurant	25%	31%	35%
Fine Dining	23%	33%	38%
Fast Food (Quick Serve)	18%	32%	37%
Cafeteria	26%	30%	35%
Buffet	20%	22%	26%

Setting a Budget

Setting the proper payroll budget is related to how a menu is priced, the type of service system used, and the level of service offered to customers. Payroll cost percentages vary according to the type of foodservice operation and volume of business (see Table 13-2).

In the income statement in Table 13-1, the payroll cost percentage is 28 percent. If this example is for a family restaurant operation, then the payroll cost is in the medium area. As a general rule, the payroll cost percentage tends to become lower as the sales volume becomes higher, as long as the increase in sales volume can be handled by the same number of employees.

Foodservice managers exercise control over an operation by limiting expenses so that costs do not exceed a predetermined level. The level of cost is usually expressed as a percentage. If payroll costs have been predetermined to be 25 percent and in reality are 30 percent, then there is a 5 percent problem. The costs need to be reduced.

Payroll Budgets

A payroll budget is a planned estimate of expenses. Usually budgets are established based upon expected sales. Management has total control over payroll budgets. A manager's success is often strongly related to his or her ability to control payroll budgets. This means that the manager must spend the correct amount of money on payroll in relationship to the sales generated by those who were paid.

A payroll estimate is a plan expressed in the form of a work schedule (see Table 13-3). From the work schedule, a payroll cost estimate is calculated by position and person. A payroll budget estimate is prepared in advance for an entire week (see Table 13-4). The budget is usually processed at the same time the work schedule is decided.

Budgets for payroll usually range from 18 to 38 percent of sales, depending on the type of foodservice operation. It is the responsibility of the foodservice manager to set the budgets. This is done by pricing meals, estimating the number of meals to be sold during specific periods of time, and calculating what the income should be for a specific period of time. More on estimating sales will be covered in Chapter 17.

Week of _____ January 13, XXXX _____				Department _____ Kitchen _____			
Date Prepared _____ 1/6/XX _____				Prepared by _____ Kitchen Manager _____			

POSITION	NAME	MONDAY	TUESDAY	WEDNESDAY	THURSDAY	FRIDAY	SATURDAY	SUNDAY
Production Cook	Joe Sample	OFF	6AM – 2PM	6AM – 2PM	6AM – 2PM	6AM – 2PM	6AM – 2PM	OFF
	(Scheduled Lunch Break) ⟶		10AM	10AM	10AM	10AM	10AM	
Production Cook	Jane Sample	6AM – 2PM	8AM – 4PM	8AM – 4PM	OFF	OFF	8AM – 4PM	6AM – 2PM
	(Scheduled Lunch Break) ⟶	10AM	1:30PM	1:30PM			1:30PM	10AM
Production Cook	Eric Sample	8AM – 4PM	OFF	(Salad Pantry) 6AM – 2PM	8AM – 4PM	8AM – 4PM	(Salad Pantry) 6AM – 2PM	OFF
	(Scheduled Lunch Break) ⟶	1:30PM		10:30AM	1:30PM	1:30PM	10:30AM	
Salad Pantry	Emily Sample	6AM – 2PM	6AM – 2PM	OFF	6AM – 2PM	6AM – 2PM	OFF	6AM – 2PM
	(Scheduled Lunch Break) ⟶	10:30AM	10:30AM		10:30AM	10:30AM		10:30AM
Dishwasher	Don Sample	8AM – NOON	8AM – NOON	OFF	OFF	8AM – NOON	8AM – 4PM	8AM – 4PM
	(Scheduled Lunch Break) ⟶						10:30AM	10:30AM
Dishwasher	Lesli Sample	NOON – 4PM	NOON – 4PM	8AM – 4PM	8AM – 4PM	NOON – 4PM	OFF	OFF
	(Scheduled Lunch Break) ⟶			10:30AM	10:30AM	10:30AM		
	(Scheduled Lunch Break) ⟶							
	(Scheduled Lunch Break) ⟶							
	(Scheduled Lunch Break) ⟶							

Once a budget is established, it may be categorized. A payroll cost of 28.5 percent may be subdivided into kitchen staff and waitstaff. Kitchen staff could be budgeted to cost 68 percent of total payroll (that is, 68 percent of the 28.5 percent), and waitstaff could be budgeted at 32 percent. This practice is fairly common in large foodservice operations. Smaller operations with fewer than fifteen employees generally do not categorize their budgets.

Developing a Work Schedule

The work schedule should represent the best effort of the foodservice manager to schedule employees in anticipation of sales. When preparing a work schedule, the manager must take many things into consideration. These include:

■ peak business periods
■ holidays

Table 13-4   Payroll Budget Estimate

Week of	January 13, XXXX		Department	Kitchen	
Date Prepared	1/6/XX		Prepared by	Kitchen Manager	

NAME	POSITION	RATE OF PAY	SCHEDULED HOURS	SCHEDULED OVERTIME	TOTAL EARNED
HOURLY EMPLOYEES					
Joe Sample	Cook	$9.50	37.5		$ 356.25
Jane Sample	Cook	8.50	37.5		318.75
Eric Sample	Cook	7.50	22.5		168.75
Eric Sample	Sal Pantry	5.50	14.5		79.75
Emily Sample	Sal Pantry	5.15	37.5		193.13
Don Sample	Dishwasher	5.15	27		139.05
Leslie Sample	Dishwasher	5.15	27		139.05
Total			203.5		$1,394.73

Allowance for Social Security, Medicare, Federal & State Unemployment Taxes:	
Total Hourly Wages $1,394.73 × Rate 1.12 =	$1,562.10

EMPLOYEE MEALS
Note: Could be added to or subtracted from the
payroll according to management's policy.

	ESTIMATED NUMBER OF MEALS	COST	
Total	24	$3.00	$ 72.00

TOTAL (Wages & Meals)	$1,634.10
Estimated Sales for Week	$9,000.00
Estimated Payroll Cost Percentage for Week	18.16%
Payroll Cost Percentage Goal	18.00%

- weather conditions
- special community events
- employee vacation times

A well-kept sales history can serve as a tremendous aid in making scheduling decisions, especially for peak sales days such as Mother's Day. The previous year's sales of that day can serve as an indication of expected sales for the current year. If sales were high, a decision to schedule additional staff would be consistent with meeting the operational requirements of those sales.

A work schedule should be prepared weekly and posted at least a week in advance. It should be posted next to the time clock or the most convenient place for all employees to read. While scheduling to meet the needs of business, it is also important to remember to maintain some degree of consistency. Radical or frequent changes in the schedule can be frustrating and upsetting and can result in the loss of good employees.

Lunch breaks should be scheduled along with the work hours for each day. The lunch break schedule must be flexible enough to accommodate business. If the foodservice operation is too busy, a break has to be postponed until a more convenient time. If this begins to happen frequently, additional scheduling adjustments should be made so as not to further frustrate employees.

One main reason employees often give for quitting a good job is frequent work schedule changes and not getting scheduled breaks. A well-planned work schedule will not eliminate job stress, but it can certainly reduce job frustration.

The main tool for planning the use of labor resources is the work schedule form. Table 13-3 is an example of such a form. The manager prepares the work schedule, taking into consideration the principles listed earlier. After the work schedule is prepared, a payroll budget estimate should also be determined (see Table 13-4). The schedule ensures that enough people will be present to do the work, while the budget ensures that those scheduled to work will not cost the operation more than can be afforded or justified.

Tables 13-3 and 13-4 show that the work is covered and within budget. Estimated sales are $9,000 for the week; the kitchen staff payroll budget is 18 percent of sales. The work schedule will cost the operation $1,634.10 for the week, including indirect costs; the payroll budget estimate is 18.16 percent. This amount is within the budget, although very closely.

In this case, management would use the budget. As the week progresses, management will need to watch for any necessary changes to the schedule to ensure that the budget is not exceeded. If sales do not materialize as estimated, management may need to change the schedule. As previously stated, this should not be done in a casual manner or employees may become frustrated and seek other employment. Maintaining payroll budgets can be difficult because foodservice industry sales are often cyclical and unpredictable.

Calculating Payroll Cost

Time cards
A method for tracking employee time worked.

Payroll cost is computed in two steps. First, the actual cost is established using **time cards** or an electronic timekeeping system. Second, the payroll

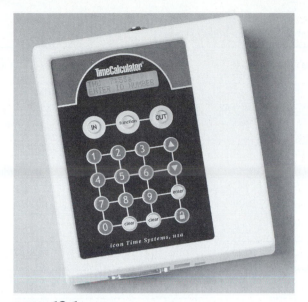

FIGURE 13-1
TimeCalculator by icon Time Systems.
The TimeCalculator automatically totals employee hours, tips, and labor costs. This information can then be output directly to a printer or personal computer. Daily and up-to-the-minute reports can be generated to aid employee scheduling and overtime tracking. The TimeCalculator may also be connected to direct cable communication or optional modem for telephone access to an accounting office or payroll service.
Courtesy of icon Time Systems.

cost percentage is determined using a **payroll cost report.** Although there are a variety of ways to calculate payroll cost, most methods may be classified into one of two categories.

- *Manual methods.* Foodservice managers may calculate their own payroll costs, use a bookkeeper or accountant, or use a combination of the two. If a manager chooses to track payroll costs, he or she may use a simple form such as a **payroll cost sheet** (see Table 13-5). If a manager uses a bookkeeper or accountant, she or he will typically use a type of mechanical time card system. The time cards are given to the bookkeeper or accountant to calculate payroll costs.

- *Electronic methods.* These include electronic time clocks, software installed in personal computers, and a time and attendance feature included in a point-of-sale system that may connect to payroll software. A vast array of hardware and software products on the market can be used to track employee work hours and calculate the payroll (see Figure 13-1).

THE MANUAL METHOD OF CALCULATING PAYROLL COSTS

Manual methods use a payroll cost sheet and/or a time clock. See Table 13-5 for an example of a payroll cost sheet that can be used by foodservice operations with limited numbers of employees. The payroll cost sheet lists all the employees: name, position, rate of pay, hours worked, overtime worked, total earned, and the total amount spent that particular day for labor.

Indirect payroll costs, including social security, Medicare taxes, federal and state unemployment taxes, and workers' compensation, are also added to

Payroll cost report
A form used to calculate payroll cost percentage and sales production per hour.

Payroll cost sheet
A form used to tabulate payroll cost for all employees.

Indirect payroll costs
Costs associated with payroll that are mandated by law, such as social security, Medicare, and federal and state unemployment taxes.

Table 13-5 Payroll Cost Sheet

NAME	POSITION	RATE OF PAY	HOURS WORKED	OVERTIME WORKED	TOTAL EARNED
Prepared by __Manager__ Day __Monday__ Date __1/13/XX__					
HOURLY EMPLOYEES					
John Cook	Cook	$9.50	8		$ 76.00
Fred Cook	Cook	8.50	8		68.00
Al Cook	Cook	7.50	6		45.00
Wonda Dishwasher	Dishwasher	5.15	4		20.60
Don Dishwasher	Dishwasher	5.15	4		20.60
Leslie Waitperson	Waitress	5.15	4		20.60
Mary Waitperson	Waitress	5.15	4		20.60
Judy Waitperson	Waitress	5.15	4		20.60
Lisa Waitperson	Waitress	5.15	4		20.60
Jack Waitperson	Waiter	5.15	4		20.60
Nick Waitperson	Waiter	5.15	4		20.60
Total			54		$353.80
Allowance for Social Security, Medicare, Federal & State Unemployment Taxes: Total Hourly Wages __$353.80__ × Rate __1.12__ =					$396.26
SALARIED EMPLOYEES					
Joe Manager	Manager				$155.00
Lynn Shift	Shift Mgr.				112.00
Dan Shift	Shift Mgr.				106.00
Total					$373.00
Allowance for Social Security, Medicare, Federal & State Unemployment Taxes: Total Salaries __$373.00__ × Rate __1.12__ =					$417.76
TOTAL (Hourly + Salaried)					$814.02

the payroll. They are calculated as a percentage of the payroll, and are a percentage dictated by law. Workers' compensation taxes vary according to the accident history of the business. These costs should be included as part of payroll costs because they are directly related to the payroll. Other benefit-associated costs are often included as part of the payroll. As shown in Table 13-1, these costs are listed on a separate expense line.

Calculating the payroll costs manually is done by multiplying the rate of pay that an employee earns by the number of hours worked. This simple task is repeated for each employee (see Table 13-5). After all wages are determined, they are added together. Indirect costs are calculated and added to the gross wages to determine the total payroll for the operation.

An easy way to calculate indirect costs is to add 1 to the indirect cost rate percentage and multiply it by the total direct costs. For example, see Table 13-5. The amount of wages (direct cost of wages) shown is $353.80. The indirect rate is 12 percent of wages for social security, Medicare, and federal and state unemployment taxes. Add the rate of 12 percent, which is equal to .12, to 1. The total is 1.12. Multiply $353.80 by 1.12 to arrive at a total of $396.26. This amount represents the payroll cost of hourly employees.

The same process is used for salaried employees. The major difference is that instead of an hourly cost, a daily cost must be established. If a person is making $32,000 a year as a salaried employee, this equals about $16.00 per hour. This hourly rate is determined by dividing the annual salary of $32,000 by 2,000 hours, which is the number of hours a typical employee works during a year: $32,000 ÷ 2,000 = $16.00. The total amount the employee earns per day is determined by multiplying the hourly rate by eight hours; $16.00× 8 = $128.00 per day. It is recognized that most salaried people work more than 40 hours per week. Even if actual hours were used to calculate daily costs, the salaried amount would be calculated by determining the total number of hours a person works per year and then multiplying by the average number of hours worked per day. The total would still be close to $128.00 per day.

The daily salaried amounts are totaled and multiplied by the indirect cost rate. In Table 13-5 the salary total amount is $373.00 and the indirect rate is 12 percent. The total is $373.00 multiplied by 1.12, which equals $417.76. Thus, the total payroll for Monday was $814.02.

The working times listed on the payroll cost sheet are typically entered by management. Time cards are used for verification of actual times worked. Much of the same information that is listed on the payroll cost sheet is also listed on the time cards (see Figure 13-2). In some very small foodservice operations, time cards are not used and an honor system may be in place. An honor system dictates that employees work the hours assigned without a time card, or they sign in and sign out on a form that is assumed to be accurate. Obviously the trust level must be high for an honor system to be used.

Time Cards

In a time card system, the employee's actual hours worked are recorded on the time card. The hours recorded on the card should correspond to the work schedule. If an electronic time clock is used, there may not be the traditional time card, but a time card will exist in the computer. The information is processed and a hard copy is printed, which accompanies employee paychecks.

```
        MULTIPLE TIMECARD REPORT *CUSTOM* TIME PERIOD FROM: 10/28/XX TO: 11/01/XX
```

2-Sayre, Grace

DATE	TIME IN	TIME OUT	LUNCH	DEPT	DEPT HRS	TIPS	STD	OT	LABOR	FLAGS
10/28/—	Mon 6:30a	Mon 1:30p		SERVERS	7.00	12.50	7.00	0.00	34.65	
10/29/—	Tue 7:00p	Tue 11:02p		HOSTESS ①	4.00		4.00	0.00	30.00	
10/30/—	Wed 6:29a	Wed 1:35p		SERVERS	7.00	15.00	7.00	0.00	34.65	
10/31/—	Thu 6:27a	Thu 1:33p		SERVERS	7.00	10.00	7.00	0.00	34.65	
11/01/—	Fri 6:25a	Fri 1:35p		SERVERS	7.00	20.00	7.00	0.00	34.65	

EMPLOYEE TOTALS: (5 DAYS WORKED)　　　　　　　　　32.00　　57.50② 32.00　 0.00　168.60③

SIGNATURE........: _____

1. Worked as a hostess at a different hourly wage rate.
2. Reported tips earned.
3. Gross wage.

FIGURE 13-2
Electronic Time Card

```
    *CUSTOM DATE RANGE* DEPARTMENT SUMMARY REPORT FOR TIME PERIOD FROM: 10/28/XX TO: 11/01/XX
```

DEPARTMENT	DEPT HRS	TIPS	ST	OT	LABOR
BUSPERSONS	38.75	0.00	38.75	0.00	191.81
CLEANUP	10.50	0.00	10.50	0.00	51.98
COOKS	61.00	0.00	61.00	0.00	655.00
HOSTESS	4.00	0.00	4.00	0.00	30.00
SERVERS	33.00	67.50	33.00	0.00	163.35

GRAND TOTALS:　　147.25　　67.50　　147.25　　0.00　1,092.14

FIGURE 13-3
Management Report

One major advantage of using an electronic time and attendance system is that employees cannot log in until their programmed time to start work. This prevents people from clocking in 10 or 15 minutes early. It also prevents employees from working other than at programmed times. Some large food-service operations have reported tens of thousands of dollars being saved by using an automated timekeeping system. If unusual situations occur, managers may always manually override the system to properly credit the employee with time worked.

Occasionally employees are requested to work longer than they were scheduled. The manager should initial the employee's time card or enter the code in the time clock (or other computer) authorizing approval. Also, the manager should write a brief note on the back of the time card explaining why the employee had to work longer.

The current time should be entered on the time card at the start and finish of every employee's shift. In addition, it should also be entered at the beginning and end of the scheduled lunch break, keeping in mind that the scheduled lunch break and the actual lunch break may be different. Requiring employees to clock in and out for fifteen-minute breaks during the shift fur-

0090-1461 JOES SAMPLE CAFE   PAYROLLS BY *PAYCHEX*   PAGE 1

HOURS AND WAGES SUMMARY

CHECK DATE	REG HRS	REG WAGES	OT HRS	OT WAGES	VAC HRS	VAC WAGES	HOL HRS	HOL WAGES	SICK HRS	SICK WAGES	MISC HOUR	MISC PAY	OTHER EARN1	OTHER EARN2	CASH WAGES
****** 000100 KITCHEN															
01/03	80.00	1240.00	2.50	22.50											1262.50
MTD	80.00	1240.00	2.50	22.50											1262.50
****** 000101 WAIT STAFF															
01/03	152.00	756.00	6.75	48.44											804.44
MTD	152.00	756.00	6.75	48.44											804.44
****** ALL DEPARTMENTS															
01/03	232.00	1996.00	9.25	70.94											2066.94
MTD	232.00	1996.00	9.25	70.94											2066.94

EMPLOYEE WITHHOLDING TAXES SUMMARY

CHECK DATE	SOC SEC W/H	MED W/H	FED W/H	STATE NAME	STATE W/H	LOCAL NAME	LOCAL W/H	LOCAL NAME	LOCAL W/H	LOCAL NAME	LOCAL W/H	OTHER NAME	OTHER W/H	TOTAL W/H TAX
01/03	144.65	33.84	227.57	OR	145.36									551.42
MTD	144.65	33.84	227.57	OR	145.36									551.42
QTD 1	144.65	33.84	227.57	STATE	145.36									551.42
YTD	144.65	33.84	227.57	STATE	145.36									551.42

EMPLOYEE VOLUNTARY DEDUCTIONS AND ADJUSTMENTS SUMMARY

CHECK DATE	WORK COMP 1	WORK HOURS 2	TIPS 3	MEALS 4	DRAMS 5				NET PAY
01/03	2.65	241.25	266.13	29.25	250.00				1233.62
MTD	2.65	241.25	266.13	29.25	250.00				1233.62
QTD 1	2.65	241.25	266.13	29.25	250.00				1233.62
YTD	2.65	241.25	266.13	29.25	250.00				1233.62

EMPLOYER TAX EXPENSES SUMMARY

CHECK DATE	SOC SEC EXP	MED EXP	FUTA EXP	STATE NAME	SUI PERCENT	SUI EXP	OTHER NAME	OTHER EXP	EMPLOYER TAX EXP
01/03	144.65	33.84	18.67	ORSUI	2.4000	56.00			253.16
MTD	144.65	33.84	18.67	ORSUI	2.4000	56.00			253.16
QTD 1	144.65	33.84	18.67			56.00			253.16
YTD	144.65	33.84	18.67			56.00			253.16

MISCELLANEOUS INFORMATION

CHECK DATE	FED TAX LIABILITY	TOTAL COMPENSATION
01/03	584.55	2333.07
MTD	584.55	2333.07
QTD 1	584.55	2333.07
YTD	584.55	2333.07

0090-1461 JOES SAMPLE CAFE   PERIOD END DATE   CHECK DATE   RUN DATE

FIGURE 13-4
Department Summary   *Courtesy of PAYCHEX.*

40004 (R-6) PAYROLLS BY PAYCHEX

PAYROLL JOURNAL

0090- 1461 JOES SAMPLE CAFE PAGE 1

EMP NBR	EMPLOYEE NAME	TYPE	HOURS RATE	HOURS REG	HOURS OT	EARNINGS REGULAR	EARNINGS OT	1 OE I / 2 OE II	WAGES	SOC SEC / MED.	WITHHOLDING TAXES FEDERAL	STATE	LOCAL DBL/SUI	1 WORK COMP	2 WORK HOURS INFO	3 TIPS COMP	4 MEALS	5 DRAWS	NET PAY	CHK NBR
****	000100 KITCHEN																			
0001	JOHNSON, TIM A		6000	4000	250	24000	2250		26250	1674 392	2550	1620 OR		47	4250	750	1075		18892	7
0002	TURNER, GARY			4000		100000			100000	6200 1450	12031	7250 OR		44	4000			25000	48025	8
****	000101 WAIT STAFF																			
0005	DYER, LINDA		4850	4000	225	19400	1637		21037	1619 379	3154	1659 OR		46	4225	5083	600		13580	9
0003	FRANKLIN, SHERRY		5500	4000		22000			22000	1834 429	2937	1817 OR		44	4000	7580	750		14189	10
0006	PILOTTE, JOYCE		4750	3200		15200			15200	1203 281		627 OR		35	3200	4200			13054	11
0004	WENTZEL, DEBBY		4750	4000	450	19000	3207		22207	1935 453	2085	1563 OR		49	4450	9000	500		15622	12

TOTALS

PAY TYPE		HOURS	EARNINGS	OTHER EARNINGS		WAGES	FICA	FEDERAL	STATE	LOCAL DBL/SUI	WORK COMP	WORK HOURS	TIPS	MEALS	DRAWS	NBR ENTRIES
REGULAR		23200	199600	OE I		206694	SOC SEC	22757	14536		265	24125	26613	2925	25000	6
OVERTIME		925	7094		00		14465									
VACATION	VA	00	00													
HOLIDAY	HO	00	00	OE II			MEDICARE						TOTAL WAGES			206694
QUAL SICK	QS	00	00		00		3384						NET PAY			123362
NONQUAL SICK	NS	00	00										VOUCHER NET			
MISCELLANEOUS	MI	00	00										TOTAL NET			123362

0090- 1461 JOES SAMPLE CAFE PERIOD END DATE CHECK DATE RUN DATE

FIGURE 13-5
Payroll Journal *Courtesy of PAYCHEX.*

ther controls and documents the employee's time. The actual time worked is computed and totaled for each day (see Figures 13-3 and 13-4). The regular and overtime hours are recorded along with wage rates and totals for the period. Finally, upon receiving a paycheck, the employee should double-check the days, hours, and positions worked (if more than one), and sign the bottom of the time card acknowledging receipt of pay and verifying the time recorded as being correct.

Overtime

Overtime occurs when an employer is required to pay an employee more than the normal wage. Usually employees are paid in increments of 1.5, 2.0, 2.5, or 3.0 times their normal hourly rate of pay. Avoiding overtime helps to keep payroll costs down. The primary causes of overtime include:

Overtime
Time worked over 40 hours per week by employees covered by the Fair Labor Standards Act.

- Poor scheduling so that employees are required to work longer hours to meet customer needs (a result of not having an adequate number of employees scheduled to work).

- Unexpected increases in the number of customers.

- Circumstances caused by sudden changes in the weather.

- Medical or other emergencies that require an employee to leave work early, therefore requiring other employees to work longer hours than originally scheduled.

Overtime can usually be averted with sufficient planning. In some operations, overtime requires management approval. Also, many time and attendance machines are programmed so that employees cannot work overtime unless approved to do so.

Overtime pay is mandated by law. Employees who work more than 40 hours during one week must be paid overtime, with limited exceptions.

PAYROLL COST REPORT

The payroll cost report in Table 13-6 begins with the *total gross wages*. Total gross wages are all wages, including indirect costs. This amount is taken from the payroll cost sheet or Payroll Journal (Figure 13-5) and prepared by the foodservice operation's accountant, bookkeeper, or payroll service. Some operations include both salaries and hourly wages in calculating controllable payroll expenses, while others use only hourly wages. In addition to wages, the cost of employee meals, if provided, should be added. Employee meals are a form of compensation and are therefore a part of the payroll costs.

In most cases the meal credit is assigned a value per given shift. Perhaps $3.00 per eight-hour shift is the dollar amount representing the actual cost of the food, not the retail selling price. This dollar amount at cost could represent as much as $8.00 for the retail menu price, thus allowing the employee to eat up to that amount. The cost of employee meals is typically deducted from the employee's pay. If an employee decides not to eat the meal, obviously there is no deduction.

The total payroll cost is divided by the total gross sales and multiplied by 100 to generate the payroll cost percentage. The total gross sales figure is obtained by adding the daily sales totals for the period. The sales per person-

Table 13-6   Payroll Cost Report

Period Ending __1/17/XX__

Total gross wages $10,054.75

Total employee meals   +_____789.00_____

Total payroll cost $10,843.75

TOTAL PAYROLL COST
__$10,843.75__

(divide) ÷   =

PAYROLL COST PERCENTAGE
__.288__ × __100__ = __28.8%__

TOTAL GROSS SALES
__$37,650.25__

TOTAL GROSS SALES
__$37,650.25__

(divide) ÷   =

SALES PER PERSON-HOUR
__$41.13__

TOTAL HOURS WORKED
__915.5__

Prepared by _____Clerical_____   Date ____1/20/XX____

hour, which measures productivity, is obtained by dividing the total gross sales by the total hours worked. The total hours worked are taken from a payroll cost sheet or payroll journal.

Payroll cost, like food cost, will vary by the type of operation. So it is difficult to compare the payroll cost of a fine-dining restaurant to that of a fast-food restaurant.

In hotels, resorts, schools, health care, and large foodservice operations, payroll may be determined by department. In a hospital, there may be a cafeteria, coffee shop, dining room, and executive dining room. Each of these dining facilities may have its own kitchen and its own cooks and waitstaff. That

■ ■ ■ ■ ■

Table 13-7   Typical Yearly Foodservice Employee Turnover Rates

SEGMENT	SALARIED EMPLOYEES	HOURLY EMPLOYEES	COMBINED
Family Restaurant	20%	107%	100%
Fine Dining	15%	102%	95%
Fast Food (Quick Serve)	25%	122%	120%
Cafeteria	15%	107%	98%
Buffet	15%	107%	98%

being the case, each would have its own sales and cost centers, and each would determine its own payroll cost percentage.

Management Quality and Employee Turnover

One measure of management quality is directly tied to payroll cost control. Payroll cost control results from competent management, which involves selecting and using the correct equipment, efficiently utilizing space and work flow, exercising good hiring and training practices, properly training employees, and reducing **employee turnover.** Ineffective management can result in costly errors, high employee turnover, and a poor work environment. History has repeatedly shown that effective management improves both profit and work conditions.

Among the most challenging tasks of management is to hire and manage a quality workforce. If a foodservice manager hires competent and skilled individuals but fails to train them properly, the outcome will be poor work quality. The vital ingredient of any foodservice operation is the quality of the workforce and how well that workforce is managed and motivated. High employee turnover is a sign of ineffective management or a poor working environment created by the owners and/or managers.

The reasons most often given by employees who have left their jobs in the foodservice industry are ranked as follows:

1. Poor management supervision.
2. Long hours, odd days off, split shifts, and frequent work schedule changes.
3. Frustrating working conditions.
4. Dead-end jobs with little opportunity for advancement.
5. Noncompetitive wages.

Employee turnover
The number of times that the total number of positions are filled with employees during an accounting period. Turnover is often expressed as a percentage of the average number of employees needed to operate a foodservice operation.

COST OF EMPLOYEE TURNOVER

Employee turnover is expensive. Direct costs of employee turnover include:

■ Recruiting costs—newspaper classified ads, employment agencies, and so on.

■ Training costs—cost of time to train and orient to the job function.

Some hidden costs are often overlooked because it is difficult to assign them a direct value. Hidden costs include:

- New employee training time.
- New employee learning mistakes.
- Management time used to interview potential employees.
- Customer loss as a result of mistakes or poor service.
- Accounting and reporting costs (payroll expenses related to employee turnover).
- Loss of productivity by departing employees prior to leaving the job.

Determining the actual cost of employee turnover is extremely difficult, though foodservice managers should be aware of and track these costs as much as possible. At the end of the year, the total amount should be calculated and the information used to identify employee turnover costs.

CALCULATING EMPLOYEE TURNOVER RATE AND COST

Table 13-8 shows employee turnover for a fine-dining restaurant that employs 65 people on average. The accountant prepared 212 W-2s at the end of the year to be sent out to current and past employees. In the example, there are 65 current employees; thus there are 147 past employees (212 W-2 forms − 65 = 147 past employees). The 147 past employees divided by the 65 average number of employees equals 2.26. This number converted to a percentage (2.26 × 100) equals a turnover rate of 226 percent.

The cost of employee turnover is difficult to calculate. As shown in Table 13-8, during the year the restaurant spent $7,350 to advertise for and train new employees with additionally scheduled work hours. This cost still does not reflect some of the hidden costs that cannot be specifically identified. This amount divided by 147 (the number of past employees) equals $50 per past employee.

Compare the employee turnover rate in Table 13-8 with the typical fine-dining turnover rate in Table 13-7. The employee turnover rate in the example is 226 percent. The typical average for this type of restaurant is 95 percent. The employee turnover rate in the example is over twice the typical average. What is the cost of this difference? The cost of employee turnover in the example is $7,350. The cost of employee turnover using the typical employee turnover rate should be about $2,850. The difference is $4,500. The conclusion is that the foodservice operation in the example spent about $4,500 more than it should have. This amount of money could have gone directly into profits if management had quickly recognized and reduced the high turnover rate.

Some foodservice operations claim as much as a 300 or 400 percent annual employee turnover rate. This means that if the foodservice operation needs 100 employees to operate, 400 employees were hired during the year. The direct and hidden costs associated with such a high employee turnover are tremendous. Remember from a discussion earlier in this chapter that the primary reason former foodservice employees give for leaving a job is poor management supervision. Competent management is the best resource for reducing employee turnover.

■ ■ ■ ■ ■

Table 13-8 Employee Turnover Rate and Cost Chart

Period Ending 12/31/XX

Employee Turnover Rate

Number of W-2's Completed		Current Number of Employees		Number of Past Employees
1. 212	–	65	=	147

Number of Past Employees		Average Number of Employees Employed		Employee Turnover Rate
2. 147	÷	65	=	2.26 × 100 = 226%

Cost of Employee Turnover

Number of Past Employees		Cost to Hire Each		Cost of Employee Turnover
3. 147	×	$ 50.00	=	$7,350.00

Factors in Reducing or Controlling Payroll Cost

The goal of every successful foodservice manager should be to recruit, motivate, guide, direct, and lead employees in achieving optimal performance. This results in high overall efficiency. To further support this goal, a productive and conducive workplace needs to exist, which includes the following:

1. Labor-saving equipment, such as a power chopper, as opposed to hand chopping when several recipes require chopped food products.

2. Well-arranged floor plans in order to save time and steps. When the work flow is smooth, employees feel that they are able to accomplish more with less stress. This improves productivity and increases profits.

3. Improved efficiency of employees through a strong, ongoing training program.

4. Using prepared foods where applicable, such as purchasing prepared vegetables and salads and refrigerated and frozen soups, entrées, and desserts instead of making these items from scratch.

5. Lower employee turnover through competent supervision, competitive wages and benefits, good working conditions, and a positive work environment to which employees can remain loyal.

Remember that good management needs to do the following: hire the right people, train them to do the job, provide the necessary resources to do the job, and then get out of their way and let them do their job (while monitoring results and being available when needed).

Hiring the Right People

Job description
A document that describes the job objectives, the work to be performed, job responsibilities, skills needed, working conditions, and the relationship of the job to other jobs.

Hiring the right people is the first step to controlling payroll costs. This starts with knowing what is required to do the job. Thus, the **job description** is critical for operational success. At the minimum, the job description should clearly define job qualifications, responsibilities, and functions.

The job description should include the following components:

1. Required skills and competencies.

2. A complete explanation of the work to be performed and the schedule of days and shifts to be worked.

3. A concise list of specific duties, tasks, responsibilities, and performance standards.

4. Who (what position) is the person's immediate supervisor.

5. Prerequisites needed by a person interested in applying for the job.

6. (Optional) Wage range and review dates.

7. (Optional) Name and telephone number of immediate supervisor.

Keeping these seven components in mind, examine the job description example in Table 13-9. This job description was adapted from *Model Position Descriptions for the Hospitality and Tourism Industry,* which was compiled by the International Council on Hotel, Restaurant and Institutional Education. These descriptions were developed with a grant from the U.S. Department of Labor.

Compare how closely the example in Table 13-9 meets the five required and two optional components of a job description. The required skills and competencies are stated and there is a complete explanation of the work. There is a concise list of specific duties, tasks, and responsibilities. In addition, the performance standards are referenced. Finally, the job description indicates the position that the person would report to as well as the necessary prerequisites. Work hours and days are not listed because individual operations will make these decisions.

HIRING TO THE JOB DESCRIPTION

After establishing a clear job description, management can evaluate possible candidates for the job to see if they possess the qualities needed to do the job.

Without the job description, the hiring process is hit-and-miss. There is no way to compare the attributes of possible employees to needed job requirements, and the process of selection becomes less focused on the actual labor to be performed.

The process of hiring involves selecting a group of people to be interviewed, conducting interviews, and hiring the most qualified person. There are a variety of theories on how to accomplish this. Basically, the process comes down to comparing the possible candidates according to needed competencies and prerequisites. The best way to do this is to use a **selection sheet,** as illustrated in Figure 13-6.

Selection sheet
Used to compare the prerequisites and competencies of employment applicants.

It is permissible to use pre-employment tests if they are related to the job. Such tests are used to prove that the person is capable of performing job tasks. In this example, the person should be able to multiply decimals and whole numbers, do simple accounting that would be related to completing cash register deposits, and write simple reports about what occurs during the day. The potential employee should also be able to complete a work schedule that meets payroll goals.

The interview process begins with selecting the applicants that come closest to meeting the requirements. All applicants should be asked the same questions and the job description should have been given to all the applicants prior to their completion of the application. The interview questions should be based upon job-related issues and the job description. Therefore, the job description is the primary document that should be used to select employees.

Training

Once the employee is selected, it is the manager's responsibility to ensure that the employee be trained to perform the tasks listed in the job description. Again, the job description is used as the primary source document to train employees to perform so that they meet the expectations of management. How the training should take place is beyond the scope of this book. However, the training must take place, especially if performance standards are based upon the job description. Finally, using control procedures to hire employees is just as critical as using a payroll cost report to ensure the success of the foodservice operation.

Setting Employee Performance Standards

Performance standards are generally based on the tasks listed in the job description. The actual transformation of a task written in the job description into a performance standard is unique to the requirements of each foodservice operation. For example, task 2 in Table 13-9 states, "Monitors daily performance of staff and ensures compliance with established timetables." This task may be transformed into a standard in the following ways:

Performance standard
The statement of a job task in terms of activity requirements.

- "Preparation for meal periods is completed no less than 15 minutes before a meal period."

Table 13-9   Job Description

POSITION DESCRIPTION

POSITION TITLE:	COUNTER SUPERVISOR
Reports to:	Manager
Position Summary:	The Counter Supervisor directly supervises the daily operation of a specified unit and ensures that daily activity schedules and established quality standards are maintained. This includes the coordination of individual and collective efforts of assigned staff.

Tasks and Competencies:

TASKS	COMPETENCIES
1. Demonstrates complete understanding of departmental requirements and interprets their intent accurately to staff members.	1. Resources 2. Interpersonal 3. Technology 4. Information
2. Monitors daily performance of staff and ensures compliance with established timetables.	1. Resources 2. Interpersonal 3. Technology 4. Information
3. Monitors quality of products and services produced by staff and ensures compliance with established standards.	1. Resources 2. Interpersonal 3. Technology
4. Monitors sanitation and food-handling practices of assigned unit and ensures staff compliance with established standards.	1. Resources 2. Interpersonal 3. Technology
5. Routinely inspects areas of assigned responsibility and reports all substandard safety, security, or equipment conditions to manager.	1. Resources 2. Interpersonal 3. Technology
6. Consistently monitors standards and makes recommendations for change as observed by manager.	1. Resources 2. Information
7. Supervises staff in a consistently fair and firm manner. Maintains steady productivity through close observation. Provides direction when necessary.	1. Resources 2. Interpersonal 3. Systems
8. Schedules staff to assigned unit within daily F.T.E. allocation and projected workload.	1. Resources 2. Systems
9. Adjusts daily schedule and shifts personnel to complete essential duties when the need arises.	1. Resources 2. Systems 3. Interpersonal
10. Coordinates work of staff to promote efficiency of operations.	1. Resources 2. Interpersonal 3. Systems
11. Consistently recommends actions necessary for staff discipline, terminations, promotions, and so on.	1. Resources 2. Interpersonal 3. Information
12. Trains staff, as assigned, and assists with orientation of new employees in a timely and efficient manner.	1. Resources 2. Interpersonal 3. Systems 4. Information

13. Schedules employee time off so as not to interfere with heavy workload periods.	1. Resources 2. Interpersonal
14. Monitors employee attendance and notices all absence patterns and brings to the attention of management all relevant findings.	1. Resources 2. Interpersonal
15. Monitors customer traffic and makes appropriate adjustments to decrease waiting time.	1. Resources 2. Information 3. Systems
16. Monitors customer buying trends and makes relevant recommendations for product additions and deletions.	1. Resources 2. Information 3. Systems
17. Accurately inventories supplies daily and requisitions items needed to meet par levels.	1. Resources 2. Information
18. Ensures that supplies are utilized properly and cost-effectively as per standards.	1. Resources 2. Information
19. Reports changes in menus or item substitutions to managers.	1. Resources 2. Interpersonal
20. Ensures that all food and supplies are stored and/or maintained under proper conditions as per standards.	1. Resources 2. Systems
21. Monitors food and supply quality and makes relevant recommendations for product utilization.	1. Resources 2. Systems
22. Inspects all unit storage facilities each day so that proper temperatures and conditions are maintained and food is covered, labeled, and dated.	1. Information 2. Systems
23. Completes counter supervisor reports in an accurate and timely manner.	1. Information 2. Systems
24. Completes employee appraisals in a timely fashion.	1. Interpersonal 2. Information 3. Systems
25. Keeps immediate supervisor informed of all relevant information and encourages suggestions for service and/or quality improvements.	1. Resources 2. Interpersonal
26. Meets routinely with assigned staff to relay relevant information and encourages suggestions for service and/or quality improvements.	1. Resources 2. Interpersonal
27. Works effectively and efficiently with other department supervisors and consistently demonstrates the ability to solve problems at this level.	1. Interpersonal 2. Systems
28. Analyzes relevant data to make informed decisions compatible with department philosophy.	1. Information 2. Systems
29. Treats staff with courtesy, respect, and empathy and displays good listening skills.	1. Resources 2. Interpersonal
30. Displays team-building skills and always handles all assignments with a positive and enthusiastic attitude.	1. Resources 2. Interpersonal
31. Maintains professional appearance as per standards.	1. Interpersonal

PREREQUISITES:

Education: High school diploma or equivalent.

Experience: A minimum of two years as a counter server or equivalent position.

Physical: Position requires walking and giving direction most of the working day. May be required to push heavy food carts. May be required to lift trays of food or food items weighing up to 30 pounds.

ATTRIBUTES	JOHN	MARY	DAN	SUE	LES	NANCY
PREREQUISITES						
High school diploma	Yes	No	GED	Yes	Yes	Yes
Two years as counter server or equivalent position	No Exp.	5 yrs	2 yrs	1 yr	3 yrs	No Exp.
Can lift 30-lb trays	Yes	Yes	Yes	Yes	Yes	Yes
Can push heavy food carts	Yes	Yes	Yes	Yes	Yes	No
CRITICAL COMPETENCIES						
Passed math test	No	Yes	Yes	Yes	No	No
Passed written test	Yes	Yes	No	Yes	Yes	Yes
Passed payroll cost test	No	No	No	Yes	Yes	No
Passed work schedule test	No	No	Yes	Yes	Yes	No

FIGURE 13-6
Selection Sheet

■ "95% of all banquets are served on time according to the event planner of the banquet."

Task 13 states, "Schedules employee time off so as not to interfere with heavy workload periods." The standard could be: "An adequate number of employees are present to do the work required for the shift."

Another example could be task 17, "Accurately inventories supplies daily and requisitions items needed to meet par levels." The standard is established by the supervisor to ensure that there are no **outs.** This means that all the products needed to prepare the meal period items are present. To do this, par amounts need to be maintained. Table 13-10 shows a partial conversion of the job description in Table 13-9 to a list of performance standards to be used to evaluate a person's job performance.

Outs
Occur when a menu item cannot be provided to a customer because there are not enough raw ingredients to prepare the item.

Performance standards should be known by all those who work in the foodservice establishment. Good management means that both managers and employees have a mutually clear understanding of the job tasks and performance standards. All employees know what they need to do and against what standards their performance will be measured. In this type of work environment, employees have the freedom to improve and employee turnover will decrease as job frustration is eliminated or reduced to a minimum.

SUMMARY

1. Payroll cost is the total cost of employee labor and will vary according to the sales volume of the foodservice operation.

2. Payroll cost (sometimes referred to as labor cost) is expressed as a percentage of sales.

Table 13-10 Performance Standards (Partial List)

POSITION DESCRIPTION

POSITION TITLE: COUNTER SUPERVISOR

Reports to: Manager

Position Summary: The Counter Supervisor directly supervises the daily operation of a specified unit and ensures that daily activity schedules and established quality standards are maintained. This includes the coordination of individual and collective efforts of assigned staff.

Tasks and Standards:

TASKS	STANDARDS
1. Demonstrates complete understanding of departmental requirements and interprets their intent accurately to staff members.	When asked the department requirements, is able to list them with 90% accuracy.
2. Monitors daily performance of staff and ensures compliance with established timetables.	Prep for food periods is completed 15 minutes before the food period.
3. Monitors quality of products and services produced by staff and ensures compliance with established standards.	Randomly checks three entrée items during the meal period to ensure that they are prepared according to specifications.
4. Monitors sanitation and food-handling practices of assigned unit and ensures staff compliance with established standards.	Follows sanitation procedure manual.
5. Routinely inspects areas of assigned responsibility and reports all substandard safety, security, or equipment conditions to manager.	Completes safety check every day and uses maintenance request form to inform management of needed changes or improvements.

---

3. Payroll cost may be controlled by establishing budgets, using work schedules, and monitoring actual costs by using a payroll cost sheet. Each of these control processes may be accomplished manually or electronically.

4. Payroll cost is calculated by tracking the time an employee works on a time card, multiplying the total number of hours worked during the accounting period by the rate of pay, adding the cost of taxes and benefits, and totaling these calculations for all the employees in the foodservice operation. The total cost is described in a payroll cost report.

5. One of the major contributing factors to high payroll cost is excessive employee turnover.

6. Turnover is caused by a number of contributing factors: poor staff selection, poor supervision, long hours, odd days off, split shifts, frequent work schedule changes, frustrating working conditions, dead-end jobs with little opportunity for advancement, and non-competitive wages.

7. The solution for reducing turnover is to use job descriptions as control documents to properly hire, train, and evaluate employees.

8. By using proper control processes, better management of employees can be accomplished for the financial health of the foodservice operation.

KEY CONCEPTS

Controllable expenses
Employee turnover
Income statement
Indirect payroll costs
Job description
Outs
Overtime
Payroll cost budgets
Payroll cost control

Payroll cost report
Payroll cost sheet
Performance standard
Salaries
Selection sheet
Time cards
Wages
Work schedule

DISCUSSION QUESTIONS AND EXERCISES

1. Define the following terms: payroll cost, payroll cost control, controllable expenses, income statement, indirect payroll costs, social security tax, Medicare tax, payroll cost budget, work schedule.

2. How often should payroll cost be determined?

3. Why is payroll cost control a process?

4. Explain the manual method of calculating payroll costs.

5. Explain how payroll cost is calculated electronically.

6. Create a fictitious income statement that demonstrates that you understand the basic income statement formula.

7. Explain the purpose of using a payroll cost report.

8. Assume that you have just completed a payroll cost sheet. The payroll cost for hourly and salaried employees is $600 for the day. The indirect cost rate is 12 percent. What is the total payroll cost for the day?

9. Why is it important to include the indirect costs when calculating payroll cost for the day?

10. Why is it important to use time cards? Explain what justification there might be for not using time cards.

11. Explain the relationship between sales and costs.

12. Explain how electronic systems can be used to reduce payroll costs.

13. If sales were $100,000 for the month, calculate the percentage of sales for the following items: food cost, $30,000; controllable costs, $50,000; occupation costs, $7,500; depreciation and interest costs, $5,500.

14. Using a blank payroll cost report form from Appendix A, calculate the payroll cost percentage and sales per person-hour. Use the following information: total sales, $150,000; total employee meals, $900; total gross wages, $42,800; and total hours worked, 1,800.

15. What are payroll budgets and what are they used for?

16. What must be taken into consideration when developing a work schedule?

17. Explain how a work schedule and a payroll budget estimate can be used to help control payroll costs.

18. Given the following information, determine if the foodservice operation will meet its weekly target payroll budget of 22 percent: expected sales for week, $15,000; food preparation staff hours scheduled, 145; waitstaff hours scheduled, 290; average wage for food preparation staff, $8.00; average wage for waitstaff, $5.50; and indirect payroll costs (social security tax, Medicare, state and federal unemployment tax, workers' compensation, and other benefits, 20 percent.

19. Why is it important to calculate the employee turnover rate?

20. How is the employee turnover rate calculated?

21. Given the following information, calculate the employee turnover rate for a fast-food restaurant and the turnover cost for the past year: number of W-2s used during the year, 242; normal number of employees, 100; current number of employees, 121; and estimated cost of turnover per employee, $60.

22. In Question 21, is the employee turnover rate higher or lower than the typical average?

23. List at least five ways of reducing payroll costs.

24. What are the leading reasons that people quit their jobs in the foodservice industry?

25. What are generally considered the direct costs of employee turnover?

26. What are the hidden costs of employee turnover?

27. What kind of foodservice operation has the lowest employee turnover rate?

28. What is a job description?

29. How can job descriptions be used to hire new employees?

30. Describe the process of hiring a new employee by using a job description throughout.

31. Why is it important to develop job descriptions as a method of reducing employee turnover?

32. Describe the five required and two optional components of a job description. Why is it important to include all of these components in a job description?

33. Make up a job description for a dishwasher that includes the five required components of a job description.

34. What is a performance standard?

35. Write three performance standards based upon the job description you developed for a dishwasher.

14

Measuring Staff Performance and Productivity

■   ■   ■   ■   ■   ■   ■   ■   ■   ■   ■   ■   ■   ■   ■

Learning Objectives

After reading this chapter and completing the discussion questions and exercises, you should be able to:

1. Create a process for gathering information on sales per hour, covers per hour, and number of production people employed per hour.

2. Use a shift productivity chart to measure current levels of productivity.

3. Use a monthly productivity chart and an annual productivity chart to measure long-term productivity.

4. Set goals to improve productivity and use tools to measure productivity.

5. Recognize that the waitstaff are the primary sales personnel of a foodservice establishment.

6. Understand that waitstaff production can be divided into three parts: amount of sales, number of people served, and quality of service.

7. Use a waitstaff production chart for evaluating sales and volume of work accomplished by the waitstaff.

8. Describe the relationship between the foodservice system, job descriptions, and performance evaluations of service personnel.

9. Develop a service system chart.

About Measuring Staff Performance and Productivity

Performance and productivity measurements indicate the amount of work produced in a given period of time, or amount of sales produced by a specified number of employees. Performance and productivity can be measured by several different methods and compared to various standards that are either common to the foodservice industry or unique to a certain foodservice operation.

The goal of management is to maintain the desired level of performance and productivity within the managed foodservice operation. Management continually seeks production methods and procedures that can improve upon existing employee performance. This may be accomplished in the kitchen through the use of new and improved food products that can be purchased completely or partially prepared. Also, through advanced technology, new cooking systems speed up and simplify cooking procedures.

Kitchen staff and waitstaff performance and productivity continue to be a focus of management's attention, as increasing demand for fast and efficient customer service prevails. Technology with new and improved computer applications has become commonplace, facilitating communication between waitstaff and kitchen staff. This results in faster, more efficient service. Consequently, many foodservice operations are improving their food production and service systems in order to remain competitive.

A key factor in creating a highly efficient foodservice operation with high standards is the proper recruiting, training, and evaluating of a professional staff.

Productivity

Productivity
A measurement of how well employees are meeting or exceeding performance standards.

Productivity is a term used to describe how well hourly employees (also known as *variable cost employees*) are performing their work. High productivity indicates that they are meeting or exceeding performance standards (expected employee performance). Low productivity reflects that the employees are not producing at established performance standards. The factors considered to be part of a performance standard are:

1. Quantity—how much work is performed in a measurable period of time.

2. Efficiency—how much work is completed in relation to sales generated.

3. Quality—how many mishaps are avoided.

4. Dependability and responsibility—how much supervision management must provide for the employee to accomplish his or her work.

Measuring Kitchen Staff Productivity and Performance

This section deals with measuring the productivity of those who produce the meals and beverages served to customers—the back-of-the-house personnel. The principles of measuring productivity are not very different between front-of-the-house (customer service personnel) and back-of-the-house personnel.

Basically, management is interested in knowing if value is being obtained from employees. Some typical questions that management may ask are as follows:

- Was the employee performing his or her duties the entire time he or she was at work?
- Did the employee perform according to established standards and the standards required by the needs of the day's business?
- Was the employee self-directed in accomplishing the work?

The manner in which these questions will be answered is unique to each foodservice operational situation. As a way to understand at least one method of answering these questions, productivity can be analyzed on a shift, monthly, and annual basis. A manual or electronic system may be employed.

PREPARING A SHIFT PRODUCTIVITY CHART

The **shift productivity chart** examines productivity per shift. The chart, or a similar tool, is used to collect information and organize it into a meaningful manner for use by management. Inputs of information must be gathered and organized by using a shift productivity chart.

Shift productivity chart
A form used to measure the productivity of food preparation personnel.

The **inputs** of productivity are distinctive to each foodservice operation. Inputs generally include the type of equipment, layout, physical structure, customers, employee availability, culture, location of the facility, and financial strength of the foodservice operation. The amount of training and the technical expertise of the employees also influence productivity. Finally, the volume of business has a direct effect upon productivity.

Inputs
Items that are put into a system or process to accomplish a designated purpose.

Generally, the major input used to measure food production productivity is the amount of labor time required in relation to sales and the number of people that may be served for a specific period of time. The problem is that sales and the number of people served are usually unknown until the moment the food is served. By tracking sales, a foodservice manager can estimate fairly accurately what is going to happen. Over time, the unexpected is averaged out. The foodservice manager then can make decisions based upon long-term averages. See Table 14-1 and read the following explanation to better understand how to prepare a shift productivity chart.

Hours of Operation is the first column. Every foodservice operation has certain hours of operation that comprise the shift or shifts. In Table 14-1 the breakfast shift goes from 6:00 A.M. to 10:00 A.M. Hours of operation are established to attract customers and fulfill their foodservice needs. The hours should remain the same if the productivity figures are to be used to compare what occurred from one period to another.

Most foodservice operations that have computer application software or point-of-sale computer systems are able to collect hourly information. Even if a computer is not used, the cashier can easily be trained to obtain the three necessary pieces of data required to complete the form.

The three necessary pieces of information required are:

1. The amount of sales that occurred during an hour of operation (easily taken from the point of sale terminal/cash register).

2. The number of people working in food preparation for each hour (taken from the time cards or work schedule).

Table 14-1   Shift Productivity Chart

Department	Bagel Shop Kitchen Staff	Page	1 of 1
Shift	Breakfast	Prepared by	Bagel Shop Manager
Date	January 17, XXXX		

HOURS OF OPERATION	(1) SALES PER HOUR	(2) COVERS PER HOUR	(3) PERSON-HOURS	(4) SALES PER PERSON-HOUR (1 ÷ 3)	(5) COVERS PER PERSON-HOUR (2 ÷ 3)	(6) MISHAPS PER HOUR	(7) MISHAP PERCENTAGE (6 ÷ 2)
6:00–7:00 A.M.	$ 75.00	13	1	$ 75.00	13.00	1	7.7%
7:00–8:00 A.M.	335.00	59	3	111.67	19.67	5	8.5
8:0–9:00 A.M.	380.00	63	4	95.00	15.75	6	9.5
9:00–10:00 A.M.	175.00	29	4	43.75	7.25	1	3.4
Shift Average	$241.25	41	3	$80.41	13.67	3.25	7.93%

3. The number of people consuming and paying for food and beverages during each hour (taken from the guest checks).

From these three inputs, necessary productivity data can be calculated. Sales per hour (1) is the amount of sales that occurred during an hour of operation. Covers per hour (2) is the number of people eating and paying for meals during the hour. Person-hours (3) is the total of all the hours worked by all persons who worked. So if one person works, one person-hour has transpired. If three people worked, then three person-hours have transpired. Obviously, the more people working, the more person-hours have taken place.

The sales per person-hour (4) measures efficiency. It informs management of the amount of sales generated per preparation person. The idea is that each person produces a certain amount of product per hour. The higher the sales per hour, the greater the productivity of the producer. Preparation personnel who constantly try to improve their productivity are worth more to the foodservice operation.

The covers per person-hour (5) measures quantity and, to some degree, capacity. The higher the number, the greater the output per input. Capacity is the maximum number of people for whom a preparation staff can prepare. Since most of the time food preparation personnel work in teams, covers per person-hour is an average of how many covers are prepared by each member of the team.

The mishaps per hour (6) is a measurement of quality. This number is how many mistakes (such as items dropped on the floor, overcooked or undercooked food, and food returned to the kitchen for a variety of reasons) occur on average per hour. Whether the food was served at its peak of flavor, hot food hot and cold food cold, will be considered later. The focus of mishaps per hour is to keep track of the ability of the preparation staff to prepare food without making too many mistakes.

The mishap percentage (7) is also part of measuring quality. The mishap percentage is the ratio of mishaps to total covers served. It is calculated by dividing mishaps per hour (6) by covers per hour (2).

At the bottom of the shift productivity chart, the shift average figures are calculated. In Table 14-1, the sales per hour is $241.25. This is determined by adding the sales per hour for each hour and then dividing by the number of hours in the shift ($75.00 + $335.00 + $380.00 + $175.00 = $965.00 ÷ 4 = $241.25). This process is performed for each of the columns.

Sales per person-hour is determined by dividing the sales per hour by the person-hours. In Table 14-1, the sales from 7:00 A.M. to 8:00 A.M. were $335.00. Dividing $335.00 by 3 person-hours gives $111.67. This dollar amount represents the sales per person-hour ($335.00 ÷ 3 = $111.67).

Covers per person-hour are similar to sales per person-hour. The covers per person-hour are determined by dividing the covers per hour by the number of person-hours. The covers from 7:00 A.M. to 8:00 A.M. total 59; therefore, 59 covers per hour divided by 3 person-hours gives 19.67 covers per person-hour (59 ÷ 3 = 19.67).

Mishaps per hour is the number of mishaps that occur during an hour. The only mishaps counted are those directly attributed to the preparation staff. The total number of mishaps per hour from 7:00 A.M. to 8:00 A.M. was 5. This number divided by the covers per hour equals the mishap percentage of 8.47 percent (5 ÷ 59 = .08474 × 100 = 8.47%). Whether this percentage is too

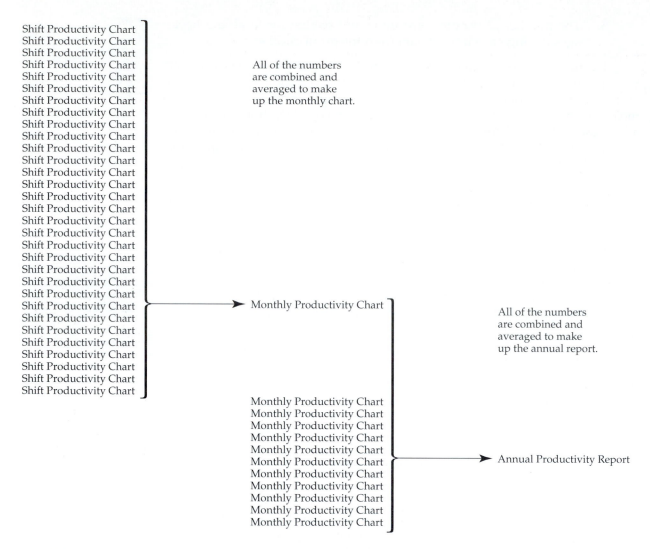

FIGURE **14-1**
Integration of Productivity Charts

high will depend upon management's interpretation of allowable mistakes. Generally, a foodservice operation should not experience a mishap-per-hour rate higher than 1 percent of total transactions. That is, if 100 entrees are served, no more than one should be wasted through mishaps.

THE MONTHLY AND ANNUAL PRODUCTIVITY CHARTS

The second step is to determine the long-term productivity measures. This is accomplished by completing the **monthly productivity chart** and the **annual productivity report.** Each of these reports builds upon the other. To visualize how these reports work together, refer to Figure 14-1.

The monthly productivity chart (Table 14-2) lists the shift averages by each day of the month. For example, the lunch shift average sales per hour (1) are listed as they were calculated on the shift productivity report. Then the column for average sales per hour is totaled. The total is divided by the number of days in the month. The final number is the monthly average sales per hour.

Monthly productivity chart A chart that summarizes the information reported on the shift productivity chart.

Annual productivity report A report that summarizes the information reported on the monthly productivity chart.

• • • • •

Table 14-2   Monthly Productivity Chart

Department Bagel Shop Kitchen Staff   Page 1 of 1

Month January   Prepared by Bagel Shop Manager

Year XXXX

DATE/DAY	SHIFT	(1) AVERAGE SALES PER HOUR	(2) AVERAGE COVERS PER HOUR	(3) AVERAGE PERSON-HOURS	(4) AVERAGE SALES PER PERSON-HOUR (1 ÷ 3)	(5) AVERAGE COVERS PER PERSON-HOUR (2 ÷ 3)	(6) AVERAGE NUMBER OF MISHAPS PER HOUR	(7) AVERAGE MISHAP PERCENTAGE (6 ÷ 2)
1/10/XX	Breakfast	$240.92	44	3	$ 80.31	14.67	1.00	2.27%
Friday	Lunch	380.63	59	4	95.16	14.75	6.00	10.20
	Dinner	165.68	21	3	55.23	7.00	.31	1.15
1/11/XX	Breakfast	190.13	32	3	63.38	10.67	1.17	3.65
Saturday	Lunch	165.22	25	2	82.61	12.50	.29	1.18
	Dinner	320.19	36	4	80.05	9.00	.63	1.75
1/12/XX	Breakfast	290.19	48	3	96.73	16.00	.60	1.25
Sunday	Lunch	310.65	34	4	77.66	8.50	1.39	4.1
	Dinner	125.41	16	2	62.71	8.00	.44	2.75
1/13/XX	Breakfast	241.75	41	3	80.58	13.67	.53	1.3
Monday	Lunch	300.03	46	3	100.01	15.34	1.56	3.4
	Dinner	125.11	16	2	62.56	8.00	.42	2.63

■ ■ ■ ■ ■

Table 14-3   Annual Productivity Report

| Department | Bagel Shop Kitchen Staff | Page | 1 of 1 |
| Prepared by | Bagel Shop Manager | Year | XXXX |

MONTH/YEAR	SHIFT	(1) AVERAGE SALES PER HOUR	(2) AVERAGE COVERS PER HOUR	(3) AVERAGE PERSON– HOURS	(4) AVERAGE SALES PER PERSON–HOUR (1 ÷ 3)	(5) AVERAGE COVERS PER PERSON–HOUR (2 ÷ 3)	(6) AVERAGE NUMBER OF MISHAPS PER HOUR	(7) AVERAGE MISHAP PERCENTAGE (6 ÷ 2)
January XXXX	Breakfast	$220.45	37	3	$ 73.48	12.33	2.13	5.76%
	Lunch	343.27	51	4	85.82	12.75	1.79	3.5
	Dinner	180.61	21	3	60.20	7.00	.35	1.67

This same process is used to calculate the monthly average covers per hour (2), the average person-hours (3), and the average number of mishaps per hour (6). These monthly averages are then used to calculate the average sales per person-hour (4), average covers per person-hour (5), and average mishap percentage (7). The process is repeated for the annual productivity report (Table 14-3) using the monthly productivity charts as sources.

USING PRODUCTIVITY INFORMATION

Productivity measures do not dramatically change over time. The information collected reflects the long-run productivity of a foodservice operation. Shift reports may be compared to data from a previous day, a previous month, or a previous year. By correctly utilizing this information, the foodservice manager can set goals to improve upon previous productivity records.

For example, if the monthly productivity chart indicates that the dinner shift average sales per person-hour for the month is $45 and the annual productivity chart indicates that the average sales per person-hour is $65, the manager knows that corrective action needs to be taken. If the lunch covers per person-hour are 14.22 and the annual productivity chart indicates 12.12, the manager might want to know why things are going so well. Covers per person-hour is a fundamental tool for trying to improve quantity of production.

The mishap percentage is a method for measuring efficiency and quality. The percentage, like the other tools, should be used to help set goals and monitor how well employees are performing their jobs.

easuring Waitstaff Productivity and Performance

The waitstaff comprises the sales force of the foodservice operation. By definition, waitstaff are people who take orders from customers, deliver the orders to the kitchen, and serve the food to the customers. How this is done constitutes service to the guest. Three parts of the waitstaff job are sales, number of people served, and quality of work performed.

A waitstaff production chart (Table 14-4) is the primary tool for measuring waitstaff production. The chart measures sales, the number of people served, sales per customer, and other sales objectives. The chart should be prepared at least once per week, or more often if management deems it necessary. Figure 14-2 shows similar information generated by a point-of-sale system.

PREPARING A WAITSTAFF PRODUCTION CHART

The waitstaff production chart (Table 14-4) measures the productivity of each waitperson. The chart has 8 components:

1. *Waitstaff name.* The name of each waitperson on the given day, date, and scheduled shift.

2. *Station number.* The station number indicates a designated work area. It should be recognized that certain stations may be more active than others. A station that includes counter service or is close

Table 14-4 Waitstaff Production Chart

Department Bagel Shop
Day Friday   Date 1/17/XX
Shift 11:00 A.M. – 7:00 P.M.

(1) WAITSTAFF NAME	(2) STATION NUMBER	(3) NUMBER OF HOURS WORKED	(4) TOTAL SALES	(5) SALES PER PERSON-HOUR (4 ÷ 3)	(6) TOTAL NUMBER OF CUSTOMERS	(7) AVERAGE CUSTOMER SALE (4 ÷ 6)	(8) SALES SALADS *10%	(8) SALES SOUPS 25%	(8) SALES GRANITAS 2%
Ann Server	1	7	$576.25	$82.32	96	$6.00	*8 (–2)	16 (–8)	4 (+2)
Mary Server	3	6	538.65	89.78	81	6.65	9 (+1)	26 (+6)	11 (+9)
Jack Server	4	7	651.90	93.13	121	5.39	6 (–6)	16 (–14)	13 (+11)
Sue Server	2	7	547.60	78.23	107	5.18	11 (0)	8 (–19)	1 (–1)

*Note: The numbers are calculated by multiplying column 6 by the sales goal percentage in each category. The number in parentheses will be plus or minus from the sales goal.

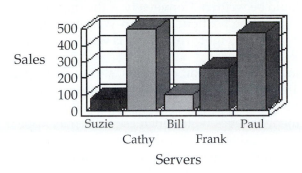

Server Sales Lunch

FIGURE **14-2**
Waitstaff Sales Performance The figure demonstrates real-time graphical reporting viewed at the point-of-sale terminal. *Courtesy of Micros.*

to the entrance of the restaurant may be busier than other stations in the restaurant.

3. *Number of hours worked.* This is the total number of hours worked on the floor. It does not include lunch and shift breaks.

4. *Total sales.* This is the total sales for each waitperson.

5. *Sales per person-hour.* This is the sales per person per hour. It is calculated by dividing the total sales for each waitperson by the number of hours worked. For Ann Waitress, sales per person-hour is calculated by dividing her total sales of $576.25 by the number of hours she worked on the floor, 7. Her sales per person-hour is $82.32 ($576.25 ÷ 7 = $82.32).

6. *Total number of customers.* The total number of customers is taken directly from the customer guest checks. The waitperson should write how many people were served on each guest check, or the information should be entered into a computer terminal at the time the order is placed.

7. *Average customer sale.* This is obtained by dividing total sales by the total number of customers. For Ann Waitress, the average customer sale is calculated by dividing $576.25, total sales, by 96, total number of customers. Her average sale is $6.00 ($576.25 ÷ 96 = $6.00).

8. *Sales.* This is a special section of the production chart. It deals with sales of items that management wants to track. In this case, the sales of salads, soups, and granitas are totaled from the guest checks or from data provided by computer application software.

The waitstaff production chart table shows sales goal percentages underneath the type of sale goal. The sales goal for salads is 10 percent. The sales goal for soups is 25 percent. The sales goal for granitas is 2 percent. The percentages are taken from the total number of customers.

If the sales goal for 96 customers is 10 percent, then 10 customers should buy the item. Ann Waitress should have sold 10 salads out of a potential of 96 salad sales that she could have made. The chart is used to record the actual number of salads sold; for Ann, this was eight salads. Next to the listed number of items sold, in parentheses, the number that represents the difference between the goal and the actual number sold is written. If the number sold is greater than the goal, a plus would be written. Conversely, if the number sold is less than the goal, a minus would be written. For Ann Waitress, the goal was ten and the actual number sold was eight. Thus, a − 2 is written in parentheses. She sold two salads short of the goal.

Sales goals are set by management. Instead of salads, soups, and granitas, the sales goals may have been for appetizers, specialty coffees, and *add-ons* (items in addition to the standard item, such as shrimp added to a lunch salad). Any item that management believes would increase sales may appear in the Sales columns. An additional advantage for the waitperson to seek to reach sales goals is the potential for a larger tip. Overall, the waitstaff production chart allows management to analytically review the performance of every waitperson, recognizing that the waitstaff is the sales force for the foodservice operation.

SERVICE STANDARDS AND THE SERVICE SYSTEM

The concept of a standardized method can be used in serving the customer. Every foodservice operation should carefully consider how customers will be served from the time they come in until they leave the foodservice environment. Each detail of service must be carefully examined. The details are the **service standards** (see Table 14-5). Service standards are the individual actions taken by service personnel that collectively create the service experience provided to the customer as defined by management. The example of service standards shown in Table 14-5 is only one possibility among many as to the best way a service standard should be developed. Each foodservice operation should develop its own standards.

The standardized method for providing service is a **service system chart** (also known as a *cycle of service* or *service cycle*; see Table 14-5). The chart lists the tasks, service standards, and who is responsible for accomplishing each task. It also formalizes the way the foodservice manager believes the customer should be served, and can be used for training, evaluation, and marketing.

The service system chart can be used as a way to transfer information from the service standard to the job description, which is then used as a guide for training the employee. The following list shows how the transfer of information should occur:

1. The service standard in the service system chart states that the waitperson should clear the dishes after each course is served.

2. The job description should state that the waitperson should clear the dishes after each course is served.

3. The newly hired waitperson should be trained to clear the dishes after each course is served.

If the foodservice manager trains according to the service system chart, all employees who serve customers will know what they need to do. The service system chart can also be used as a source document for training. The service system chart lists the service standards that employees should be trained to do. Training is focused upon doing the operational processes required to

Service standards The service tasks assigned by management that define the service experience to be offered to customers.

Service system chart A form used to list the service tasks, service standards, and who is responsible for accomplishing each service task.

Table 14-5   Service System Chart

Manager General Manager	Page 1 of 2

TASK	SERVICE STANDARD	PERSON RESPONSIBLE
Answer Phone	Within 3 rings.	Host/Hostess
Take Reservations	100% accuracy: name, phone number, number in party, time, special requests, table assignment.	Host/Hostess
Greeting the Customer	Within 1 minute of entering restaurant, use an approved greeting format, check for customer reservation.	Host/Hostess
Seating the Customer	Personally escort customers to preassigned table, seat women first, distribute menus, mention the evening special and the name of the person who will be their server.	Host/Hostess
Water Service	Ask if the customers want water.	Busperson
Waitstaff Greeting the Customer	Stand at a table corner if a four-top, or at the center end of the table if a booth, and introduce yourself. Mention the evening special; request any orders from the bar and ask if they want appetizers. If the customers order, take the orders. If they don't, invite the customers to look at the menu.	Waitstaff
Taking Meal Order	Return to table within 3 minutes. Ask for dinner order. Ask customers for add-ons (shrimp in salad, etc.).	Waitstaff
Processing Meal Order	Take meal order to waitstaff station and input into computer. Order-in should be completed in 2 minutes.	Waitstaff
Order Preparation	From printout, prepare menu item using standardized recipes. All the meals for a specific table should be prepared within 15 minutes.	Cook Staff
Salad Service or Appetizers	After order-in has taken place, take a basket of rolls and butter to the table. If any of the orders require salads or appetizers, prepare in the waitstaff station and take to the table. Deliver any beverages ordered.	Waitstaff
Water Service	While customers are waiting, check to see if they need water glasses refilled.	Busperson
Dinner Ready	When dinners are ready for the table, notify the waitperson using the silent pager.	Cook
Deliver Dinner	Order is picked up within 1 minute of notification and delivered to table. Ask for beverage orders or refills.	Waitstaff
Check Backs	After the order is placed before the customer, check back within 2 minutes and see if the customers are enjoying the meal. Ask for additional beverage orders or refills.	Waitstaff
Clearing the Table	When the customers have finished each course, ask for permission to take plates. Using clearing procedure, clear table.	Waitstaff
Dessert Order	When the last customer has finished eating and the table is cleared, take the dessert tray out to the customers and ask if they would like to select a dessert item.	Waitstaff
Final Coffee/ Beverage	Offer coffee or other beverages. This should be done whether the customers order dessert or not. If they order dessert, bring the beverage with the dessert.	Waitstaff
Bill Preparation	Go to waitstation and print out the bill.	Waitstaff
Bill Delivery	While customers are eating dessert and/or drinking coffee, present them with the bill, thank them, and instruct customers to pay the bill at the cashier's station.	Waitstaff
Final Payment	When the customers reach the cashier's station, ask if they enjoyed their dinner and invite them to return. If a customer is not happy, follow unhappy customer procedure. Thank customers for coming.	Host/Hostess

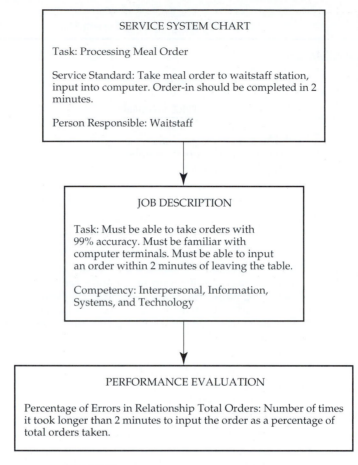

FIGURE 14-3
From Service System Chart to Performance Evaluation

serve the customer correctly. The outcome should be that all employees recognize that they are members of a team, and that each person's work is dependent on how well others do their work.

The tasks and standards in the service system chart can be used to evaluate staff performance. An employee either does or does not perform the task according to the standard described. The service system chart may be used by management and employees to develop a job-based **personal performance review** (see Figure 14-3). The service system chart provides the basis for evaluating individual employee performance of his or her job. Probably the greatest strength of a service system chart is that all the employees know the standards. When everyone knows the standards, there is the possibility that the employees will encourage and reinforce the performance standards with each other. If this happens, the manager can concentrate on increasing business rather than on getting employees to do their jobs.

The foodservice operation may use the service system chart as a marketing document in two or more ways. One way is to use the service standards in the service system chart as part of an advertising claim (see Figure 14-4). For example, if a service standard is speed in processing the meal order, the advertising claim could be "The quicker the kitchen gets your order, the quicker you get your food." (See Figure 14-4.) Another way is to use the ser-

Personal performance review A formal evaluation of an employee's on-the-job performance.

```
┌─────────────────────────────────────────┐
│         SERVICE SYSTEM CHART             │
│                                          │
│  Task: Processing Meal Order             │
│                                          │
│  Service Standard: Take meal order to    │
│  waitstaff station, input into computer. │
│  Order-in should be completed in 2       │
│  minutes.                                │
│                                          │
│  Person Responsible: Waitstaff           │
└─────────────────────────────────────────┘
                    │
                    ▼
┌─────────────────────────────────────────┐
│        NEWSPAPER ADVERTISEMENT           │
│                                          │
│   The Quicker the Kitchen Gets Your      │
│              Order,                      │
│   The Quicker You Get Your Food          │
│                                          │
│            At Hilsands                   │
│         we just started using            │
│   the latest point-of-sale system        │
│            available.                    │
│   Your order travels to the kitchen      │
│           faster so                      │
│  you'll be able to enjoy our ribs,       │
│      steaks, and tortes                  │
│      just a few minutes faster.          │
│    Waiting for a taste of heaven         │
│    just got shorter at Hilsands.         │
│                                          │
│              HILSANDS                    │
│     20889 S.E. VIRGINIA STREET           │
│       BALTIMORE, MD 10021                │
│              880-8080                    │
└─────────────────────────────────────────┘
```

FIGURE 14-4
From Service System Chart to Newspaper Advertisement

vice standard as part in the development of customer comment cards. It forms the basis for having customers evaluate how well the entire foodservice operation is performing. For example, if a foodservice operation has a standard that the customer is to be greeted within one minute of entering the restaurant, the customer comment card should ask if they were greeted within one minute.

The measurement and control tools presented in this chapter are designed to improve production, efficiency, and quality: the shift productivity chart, monthly productivity chart, annual productivity report, and a waitstaff production chart. The primary tool, the service system chart, can be used to set the standards for service, show how the job description can be put into action, and as a tool for training is the service system chart. Carefully used, these tools will help reduce employee turnover and enhance the foodservice manager's ability to deliver service promises communicated to customers.

SUMMARY

1. The focus of this chapter has been to discuss control techniques that can be used to accomplish the production and service goals of any foodservice establishment.

2. Production is measured by examining quantity, efficiency, quality, dependability, and responsibility of employees.

3. Food production can be measured by examining what occurs during a specific time period of operation, revenues per time period, number of people working during the time period, and the number of mishaps per time period. From this information, productivity data can be generated.

4. Food productivity data are sales per hour, covers per hour, person-hours, sales per person-hour, covers per person-hour, mishaps per hour, and mishap percentage. These data may be compiled by using a shift productivity chart.

5. To measure long-term kitchen staff food production performance, shift productivity charts should be summarized monthly and yearly into monthly productivity charts and annual productivity reports.

6. Service production may be examined in two ways. First, data can be analyzed for each worker according to total sales, sales per hour, number of customers served, average sales per customer, and whether sales goals have been achieved. Second, performance may be measured to ensure that service standards are being met.

7. Productivity charts and service system charts can be used to develop promotional materials, job descriptions, and performance evaluations.

KEY CONCEPTS

Annual productivity report	Productivity
Inputs	Service standards
Monthly productivity chart	Service system chart
Personal performance review	Shift productivity chart

DISCUSSION QUESTIONS AND EXERCISES

1. Teach the principles of measuring kitchen staff performance and productivity to someone else.

2. How should kitchen staff performance and productivity be evaluated?

3. How do you prepare a shift productivity chart for food production?

4. Why should productivity information be compiled monthly and annually?

5. How should productivity information be used?

6. What does the monthly productivity chart tell management about the operation and how can this chart be used?

7. Describe a service standard and how it can be used as a control device for better operating a foodservice operation.

8. Write a service standard for washing your hands.

9. Describe how a service standard may be used to develop a job description.

10. Describe how a service standard may be used to do a performance evaluation or personal performance review.

11. Describe the purpose of developing a service system chart and what information is incorporated in such a chart.

12. Go to a local restaurant, dine there, and then write up a service system chart for that business.

13. Discuss how a manager can effectively measure waitstaff performance.

14. Why should managers set sales goals for items or categories of items on the menu?

15. Finish the following waitstaff production chart, given the information already presented. After the chart is finished, evaluate the performance of the waitstaff. Should any of the waitstaff be retrained or reassigned?

Waitstaff Production Chart

Department Bagel Shop

Day Friday   Date 1/17/XX

Shift 11:00 A.M. – 7:00 P.M.

Prepared by Bagel Shop Manager

Approved by Owner/Manager

(1) WAITSTAFF NAME	(2) STATION NUMBER	(3) NUMBER OF HOURS WORKED	(4) TOTAL SALES	(5) SALES PER PERSON-HOUR (4 ÷ 3)	(6) TOTAL NUMBER OF CUSTOMERS	(7) AVERAGE CUSTOMER SALE (4 ÷ 6)	(8) SALES		
							SOUPS 5%	DESSERTS 15%	ADD-ONS 20%
Ann Server	1	5	$576.35		89		5 ( )	5 ( )	16 (−2)
Mary Server	4	6	568.45		80		9 ( )	17 ( )	10 (−6)
Jack Server	3	7	657.90		109		2 ( )	2 ( )	5 (−17)
Sue Server	2	7	707.60		115		1 ( )	5 ( )	5 (−18)

15

Control Practices Applied to Human Resources Issues, Gratuities, Wage Laws, and Working Conditions

■ ■ ■ ■ ■ ■ ■ ■ ■ ■ ■ ■ □ □ □

Learning Objectives

After reading this chapter and completing the discussion questions and exercises, you should be able to:

1. Recognize that ignorance of labor laws does not excuse management from complying with these laws.

2. Prevent sexual harassment in the workplace by setting the proper example, training staff, and posting and complying with sexual harassment policies.

3. Understand what reasonable accommodations, as specified by law, should be made for those with disabilities.

4. Make provisions for those on family or medical leave.

5. Recognize how to avoid discriminating against anyone, especially those in protected groups.

6. Properly document citizenship of a new employee and complete an I-9 form.

7. Understand how to comply with proper record-keeping requirements of OSHA (Occupational Safety and Health Act).

8. Understand the requirements and processes needed to ensure that the foodservice operation is in compliance with OSHA regulations.

9. Understand how to comply with the requirements of the Tax Equity and Fiscal Responsibility Act of 1982.

10. Manage how tips are to be allocated.

11. Describe the regulations pertaining to federal and state wage laws.

12. Understand the laws regulating working conditions, especially those related to minors.

13. Understand that in a litigious society, employers should have workers' compensation insurance.

About Human Resources Issues, Gratuities, Wage Laws, and Working Conditions

Today's business environment requires foodservice owners and managers to be thoroughly aware of employees' rights and privileges under the law, as well as management's responsibilities for complying with federal and state regulations. Violation of an employee's rights through ignorance, carelessness, or deliberate action can result in large penalty fines and civil judgments against owners and managers of foodservice operations. In certain situations when health and safety are at risk, the foodservice operation may actually be closed down. Therefore, thorough knowledge, understanding, and application ability are requirements for sound management and are directly associated with the control of financial liability.

To prevent financial loss due to litigation and to be socially responsible, foodservice operations should periodically conduct a human resources audit. To understand how to do a human resources audit requires that managers understand federal and state laws dealing with sexual harassment, disabilities, equal employment, and equal treatment of employees; regulations dealing with illegal aliens; and occupational safety laws.

Reporting tip income so that the operation complies with the Tax Equity and Fiscal Responsibility Act (TEFRA) is another responsibility of the foodservice manager. It is very important to understand the calculation procedures applicable to the specific types of operations as set forth by the requirements. Correct tax reporting fulfills the foodservice operation's legal responsibility to the government and its employees, and enables managers to take advantage of the most beneficial tax rules. Keep in mind that countless numbers of foodservice operations have been financially ruined because they did not correctly pay their tax obligations.

Working conditions, especially those that involve minors, have been the focus of much attention by the media and the federal government. Foodservice operations have historically employed minors. Often, the first job a person has is in the foodservice industry. Managers must understand the work condition laws that affect minors, adults, those who work for an hourly wage, and those who work for a salary.

Human Resources Issues

All foodservice operations must comply with federal and state regulations. The best way to comply is to avoid behaviors that would invite complaints.

This chapter will review the legal issues covering civil rights and discriminatory practices.

The human resources audit (Table 15-1), which is discussed later in the chapter, is presented as a control tool that may be used by foodservice managers and applied to all types of foodservice operations. The form provides a type of self-audit that helps foodservice managers determine whether they are in compliance with a variety of federal laws. Nearly all sources on human resource management suggest that businesses develop a human resources audit to help them comply with the laws and to serve as a reminder of how to treat employees. The form suggested in this chapter would need to be adjusted to meet the needs of specific foodservice operations.

To understand the form and what it does, the foodservice manager should be familiar with issues and laws that deal with discrimination, illegal aliens, and safety regulations. Discussions of sexual harassment, the requirements of the Americans with Disabilities Act, equal employment opportunity issues, the Family and Medical Leave Act, laws related to illegal aliens, and laws related to occupational safety are presented in this chapter. The discussions are based upon the current laws; keep in mind that laws and enforcement rules often change.

AVOIDING SEXUAL HARASSMENT LITIGATION

Sexual harassment is defined as any unwelcome sexual advances, requests for sexual favors, or any other unwelcome verbal or physical conduct of a sexual nature. This behavior can be between an employee and supervisor, between employees, or from customers. In fact, if an owner or manager condones sexual harassment by customers directed toward employees, the owner or manager is considered to be practicing sexual harassment.

> **Sexual harassment**
> Any unwelcome sexual advances, requests for sexual favors, or any other verbal or physical conduct of a sexual nature.

Sexual harassment may also be interpreted as involving behaviors other than those generally considered to be offensive or abusive sexual contact. It can take many forms, including the following:

- Repeated and unwelcome flirtations, advances, or propositions.
- Continued or repeated verbal abuse of a sexual nature.
- Degrading comments about an individual or about his or her appearance.
- Display of suggestive objects or pictures.
- A customer grabbing or touching waitstaff.
- Physically rubbing up against an employee by forcing the person against a wall or piece of equipment.
- Making comments about a person's physical shape.

All of these actions could be considered sexual harassment.

To minimize the risk of sexual harassment charges, foodservice operators should do the following:

1. Have a written policy prohibiting sexual harassment. Topics that should be covered in an effective sexual harassment policy are shown in Figure 15-1.
2. Clearly explain the sexual harassment policy to all employees.

Sexual harassment and discrimination claims are an enormous, generally uninsured drain on a foodservice company's resources. Adoption of a policy against sexual harassment and discrimination serves two purposes: it reduces the likelihood of a claim by preventing harassment and providing a prompt, effective means for addressing it when it occurs, and it provides the employer with a legal defense to a hostile work environment claim.

An effective anti-sexual harassment policy:

■ Defines and prohibits sexual harassment.

■ Encourages prompt reporting of all complaints to an independent representative of the employer.

■ Includes a procedure for bypassing one's supervisor in cases where the supervisor is the offender.

■ Ensures expeditious, thorough, and impartial investigation and resolution of all complaints.

■ Provides for immediate and appropriate remedial action, up to and including termination for violations of the employer's policy.

■ Provides for progressive discipline if the harassment reoccurs.

■ Applies to all employees, including managers and supervisors.

■ Prohibits retaliation against employees.

■ Does not conflict with contractual, civil service, or other rights of the employees. If such conflicts exist, the conflicting requirements should be modified to accommodate the need for an effective anti-sexual harassment policy.

Employee training enhances the value of the antiharassment policy. The training should be based upon the employer's antiharassment policy, and it should illustrate that policy through examples, role playing, hypotheticals, quizzes, and discussion in a way that enhances every employee's, supervisor's, and manager's understanding of appropriate workplace behavior, the claims reporting and investigation process, discipline, and nonretaliation for making a claim.

This information is not a complete discourse on the law in this area. It is not intended, and should not be used, as legal advice.

Karen Sutherland is the chair of Ogden Murphy Wallace, P.L.L.C.'s Employment Law Practice Group in Seattle, Washington. Her employment law experience includes (among other things) investigating harassment and discrimination claims and sexual harassment training.

FIGURE 15-1
Policies against Sexual Harassment and Discrimination by Karen Sutherland

3. Train all employees and managers how to report, respond, investigate, and handle sexual harassment charges.

4. Institute a procedure for investigating reported sexual harassment charges.

5. Investigate all sexual harassment charges immediately.

6. Take disciplinary action against those doing the harassing.

7. Follow up to ensure that the situation does not occur again.

How to Respond to a Sexual Harassment Complaint

When an employee makes a complaint of sexual harassment, the employer should conduct a prompt and thorough investigation. First, a determination must be made of whether a sexual harassment situation occurred. Second, if one did occur, the employer should take a detailed statement from the person making the complaint. The employer should also take statements from the alleged harasser and any witnesses. The employer should determine if the allegations are supported by the investigative report. A consultation with an attorney during this process further supports the investigative process.

Employers are liable for sexual harassment by the supervisors and managers they employ. The employer may be liable not only for the conduct of supervisors and managers, but also for that of co-workers and even nonemployees. Employers who take immediate and appropriate corrective action can avoid liability for harassment between co-workers.

Employers must take sexual harassment issues seriously. An employer may lose tens of thousands of dollars by not adhering to the law. In fact, the willful disregard of sexual harassment laws may cause a business to fail because of the financial burden adjudged against it by the courts.

COMPLYING WITH THE AMERICANS WITH DISABILITIES ACT (ADA)

The **Americans with Disabilities Act** is concerned with equal employment opportunities for those with disabilities. Specifically, the act prohibits discrimination in the hiring process, requires equal accessibility to all services provided by governments, and outlaws discrimination in public accommodations and services operated by a wide range of businesses serving the public. The following focuses upon the impact of the legislation as it pertains to hiring and managing those with disabilities.

Americans with Disabilities Act A federal law that prohibits discrimination toward those with disabilities.

The term **disability** has different implications for everyone. The ADA's definition is broad, providing civil rights protection for people who fall into one of the following three categories:

Disability
A term used to describe the state of a person who has or is recovering from a physical or mental impairment or who is perceived to have a physical or mental impairment.

1. People who have a physical or mental impairment that substantially limits one or more major life activities. This means that the person's impairment significantly restricts him or her in the performance of an activity that an average person can perform with little or no difficulty—for example, activities such as walking, seeing, hearing, speaking, learning, and working.

2. People who have a record of an impairment that substantially limits major life activities, but who have recovered or are recovering from such impairment. Examples include people with a history of mental or emotional illness, heart disease, or cancer, and recovering alcoholics and drug addicts.

3. People who do not have an impairment that substantially limits major life activities but who are regarded by others as having such an impairment. Examples include victims of severe burns and people who wear hearing aids.

ADA and Employment

An employer may not discriminate against any qualified person with a disability who, with or without reasonable accommodation, can perform the essential functions of a job. Discrimination applies to hiring, firing, pay, promotions, and other terms and conditions of employment.

A person is not qualified for a job unless he or she can perform the essential job functions. However, a reasonable accommodation should be made so that the person can perform the job. *Essential functions* are job tasks that are fundamental and not marginal to job performance. In determining essential job functions, the **Equal Employment Opportunity Commission** (EEOC) or a court will consider the employer's judgment as to what functions are essential. The EEOC or a court will also consider whether an employer has prepared a written job description before advertising or interviewing applicants for the job. In other words, the employer must decide what an essential job requirement is before beginning the hiring process.

Specific requirements of the ADA include:

- Employers must reasonably accommodate the disabilities of qualified applicants or employees, unless doing so would result in undue hardship upon the employer.

- Employers may not discriminate against a qualified individual with a disability simply because a reasonable accommodation is not desirable.

- Employers may not use employment tests or other selection criteria that tend to screen out people with disabilities, unless it can be shown that the tests or criteria are job related and consistent with business necessity.

- Pre-employment inquiries concerning medical conditions must be strictly job related. Generally, it is safer not to make any medical inquiries until a conditional offer of employment is made. And even then, employers should keep the medical inquiries strictly related to the job in question and its essential functions.

- Employers may not require a pre-employment medical exam. However, employers may make a conditional offer of employment pending the results of a confidential medical exam. This can be done only if an employer requires all new employees to take such an exam. Employers may not reject any applicant because of information revealed on a medical exam, unless the reasons for the rejection are job related and consistent with business necessity.

- Employers may not discriminate against a qualified individual because he or she has a relationship or association with an individual with a disability.

- Employers may counter discrimination charges by proving that the alleged discrimination standards are job related and consistent with business necessity—in other words, that the person could not have done the job even with reasonable accommodation.

- Employers have the right to reject applicants or fire employees who pose a significant risk to the health or safety of other individuals in the workplace. Generally, a person with HIV/AIDS is not considered a significant

Equal Employment Opportunity Commission
A federal agency that has the responsibility to enforce the various federal laws that pertain to equal treatment of all employees or potential employees.

risk for a foodservice operation, while a person with hepatitis A is considered to be a risk.

■ The ADA does not prohibit employers from using traditional risk assessment considerations when designing health benefit plans. However, employers may not maintain discriminatory restrictions in health insurance plans as a way to evade the purpose of the ADA.

Who Must Comply?

As of July 26, 1994, all employers with fifteen or more employees are required to comply with this law. Some states may have enacted laws that require all employers or employers with fewer than fifteen employees to comply as well.

Who Enforces the ADA?

Complaints are first filed with the EEOC. Remedies may include reinstatement, back pay, and attorneys' fees. Under the 1991 Civil Rights Act, individuals can sue for compensatory and punitive damages as well.

COMPLYING WITH THE EQUAL EMPLOYMENT OPPORTUNITY ACT

The basic provisions of several federal laws and subsequent presidential executive orders are to prevent discriminatory acts committed against the aged, minorities, women, and the disabled. This section is a summary of regulations that all foodservice operators should follow.

No foodservice employer may discriminate based upon gender, religion, national origin, color, or ethnicity. Implications of this regulation are:

■ A foodservice manager cannot hire just one gender unless a bona fide occupational requirement exists, such as a requirement for a male to work in a men's locker room.

■ A foodservice manager cannot discriminate when hiring. This means that an employer cannot ask questions such as: Do you have a car? Are you pregnant? Do you have children? How old are you? Have you been arrested? These questions violate protected rights.

■ A foodservice manager cannot exclude any protected group from dining.

■ Both genders must be paid comparably for doing comparable work.

■ Foodservice contractors that do business with the government must comply with all EEOC regulations and executive orders.

■ Women who are pregnant are to be treated like anyone else with a disability.

Employment Tests

Drug tests are considered legal if everyone is subjected to taking them in the same way. If one person is required to take a drug test for employment, then every applicant must be tested. Testing employees for drug use must be universally required or truly random. An employer may have to prove that such tests are administered in a random fashion.

Any pre-employment test must be job related. If the job requires lifting heavy sacks of flour, then it is appropriate to ask the prospective employee to lift a typical heavy sack of flour. If a cook needs to know how to bake, it is appropriate to have the cook bake as part of the application process. A secretary may have to demonstrate typing skills of 60 words per minute.

The Civil Rights Act of 1991 prohibits discrimination on the basis of race and prohibits racial harassment on the job. It places the burden of proof that discrimination did not occur on the employer. The law reinforces the illegality of hiring, firing, or promoting decisions on the basis of race, ethnicity, gender, or religion. It permits those who feel they have been treated unfairly to seek punitive damages in intentional discriminatory claims.

COMPLYING WITH THE FAMILY AND MEDICAL LEAVE ACT

Family and Medical Leave Act A federal law that allows employees to take up to twelve weeks of unpaid leave, with their job or similar position being held for them while they manage a pregnancy or prolonged family illness.

The main provisions of the **Family and Medical Leave Act** of 1993 are the following:

- An employee may take up to twelve weeks of unpaid leave in any twelve-month period for the birth of a child or an adoption. The act also allows employees to take leave to care for themselves or a child, spouse, or parent with a serious health condition.

- The employee must be restored to his or her original position or its equivalent with equivalent pay, benefits, and other employment terms upon returning to work.

- An employer must keep providing health care benefits during the leave, as though the employee were still employed. All benefits accrued prior to taking leave must remain intact.

- Employers are not required to pay employees who are on leave.

- An employee cannot collect unemployment or other government compensation while on leave.

- The act covers employees who have been employed for at least twelve months and have worked at least 1,250 hours for a company with 50 or more employees who live within 20 miles of the work site.

Probably the biggest impact of the Family and Medical Leave Act upon employers is that it restricts their ability to maintain a workforce at an optimum productive level. Since employers are required to keep the person's old job available or its equivalent, it is difficult to hire and maintain a temporary person in the position. The foodservice industry has a high rate of employee turnover, so keeping positions open yet having a temporary person work in the position is difficult. Using temporary employees has not been viable in the foodservice industry.

COMPLYING WITH THE IMMIGRATION REFORM AND CONTROL ACT

Hiring employees without complying with the employment eligibility verification requirements is a violation of the employer sanctions provisions of the Immigration Reform and Control Act of 1986. Employees hired after November 6, 1986, must present documentation that establishes identity and employment eligibility. Employers must record this information on Form I-9 for each employee. Employers may not discriminate against employees on the basis of national origin or citizenship status. A copy of Form I-9 is shown in Figure 15-2.

A simple, step-by-step explanation of what employers must do to meet their responsibilities under the law is available in the *Handbook for Employers*, which is published by the Immigration and Naturalization Service (INS). The handbook answers questions about the following:

- Completing and returning Form I-9.
- Avoiding discrimination.
- Employees hired before November 6, 1986.
- Federal income tax obligations.

This handbook is available from the Employment Relations Office of the INS. For a local office, check the white pages in your telephone directory. Copies of Form I-9 may be ordered in bulk from the Superintendent of Documents, U.S. Government Printing Office, Washington, DC 20402.

COMPLYING WITH THE OCCUPATIONAL SAFETY AND HEALTH ACT (OSHA)

The **Occupational Safety and Health Act** (OSHA) is designed to protect employees while at work. It outlines comprehensive safety and health standards that employers and employees must follow. The impact of OSHA regulations has not been as dramatic in the foodservice industry as in other industries. Primary injuries that occur in the foodservice industry are falls, burns, cuts, and strains.

Occupational Safety and Health Act A federal law that requires employers to provide a safe work environment for their employees.

All employers must comply with regulations specific to their businesses. There are three ways to obtain information that will help the foodservice manager comply with OSHA regulations. The first is to obtain information from the state restaurant association, which in most states is associated with the National Restaurant Association. This represents one of the best sources for obtaining information.

The other two suggestions require contacting the area Occupational Safety and Health Administration (OSHA) office. Each office has information on compliance requirements that they will mail to any employer at no cost. An employer may also request an inspection from an OSHA office. OSHA basically has two thrusts—being an educator and being a police force. If any violations are discovered during a requested visitation, the company will not be fined. However, the company will have to fix the problems. During the inspection, the foodservice manager will become aware of what needs to be corrected.

Information and copies of the act, specific OSHA safety and health standards, and other applicable regulations may be obtained from the nearest regional OSHA office. OSHA administration may be conducted by state agencies. Twenty-four states have their own versions of OSHA, referred to as *state plans*. In some states, such as Washington, the regulations may be stiffer than the federal law. The state regulations must be at least as stringent as the federal law.

U.S. Department of Justice
Immigration and Naturalization Service

OMB No. 1115-0136
Employment Eligibility Verification

Please read instructions carefully before completing this form. The instructions must be available during completion of this form. **ANTI-DISCRIMINATION NOTICE.** It is illegal to discriminate against work eligible individuals. Employers CANNOT specify which document(s) they will accept from an employee. The refusal to hire an individual because of a future expiration date may also constitute illegal discrimination.

Section 1. Employee Information and Verification. To be completed and signed by employee at the time employment begins

Print Name: Last	First	Middle Initial	Maiden Name

Address (Street Name and Number)	Apt. #	Date of Birth (month/day/year)

City	State	Zip Code	Social Security #

I am aware that federal law provides for imprisonment and/or fines for false statements or use of false documents in connection with the completion of this form.

I attest, under penalty of perjury, that I am (check one of the following):
- ☐ A citizen or national of the United States
- ☐ A Lawful Permanent Resident (Alien # A_____)
- ☐ An alien authorized to work until_____/_____/_____
  (Alien # or Admission #_____)

Employee's Signature	Date (month/day/year)

Preparer and/or Translator Certification. *(To be completed and signed if Section 1 is prepared by a person other than the employee.) I attest, under penalty of perjury, that I have assisted in the completion of this form and that to the best of my knowledge the information is true and correct.*

Preparer's/Translator's Signature	Print Name

Address (Street Name and Number, City, State, Zip Code)	Date (month/day/year)

Section 2. Employer Review and Verification. To be completed and signed by employer. Examine one document from List A OR examine one document from List B **and** one from List C as listed on the reverse of this form and record the title, number and expiration date, if any, of the document(s).

List A	OR	List B	AND	List C
Document title: _____		_____		_____
Issuing authority: _____		_____		_____
Document #: _____		_____		_____
Expiration Date (if any): ___/___/___		___/___/___		___/___/___
Document #: _____				
Expiration Date (if any): ___/___/___				

CERTIFICATION - I attest, under penalty of perjury, that I have examined the document(s) presented by the above-named employee, that the above-listed document(s) appear to be genuine and to relate to the employee named, that the employee began employment on (month/day/year) ___/___/___ and that to the best of my knowledge the employee is eligible to work in the United States. (State employment agencies may omit the date the employee began employment).

Signature of Employer or Authorized Representative	Print Name	Title

Business or Organization Name	Address (Street Name and Number, City, State, Zip Code)	Date (month/day/year)

Section 3. Updating and Reverification. To be completed and signed by employer

A. New Name (if applicable)	B. Date of rehire (month/day/year) (if applicable)

C. If employee's previous grant of work authorization has expired, provide the information below for the document that establishes current employment eligibility.

Document Title:_____ Document #:_____ Expiration Date (if any):___/___/___

I attest, under penalty of perjury, that to the best of my knowledge, this employee is eligible to work in the United States, and if the employee presented document(s), the document(s) I have examined appear to be genuine and to relate to the individual.

Signature of Employer or Authorized Representative	Date (month/day/year)

Form I-9 (Rev. 11-21-91) N

FIGURE 15-2
Form I-9

OSHA standards are enforced based upon standards associated with five situations. In descending order of seriousness, the five situations are: imminent danger, serious accidents, employee complaints, inspections of targeted industries, and random inspections.

Imminent danger means that an employee is in a situation where an accident is about to occur. This is considered the top priority of OSHA. In some cases, businesses may be closed down if the imminent danger is prevalent.

The second level is *serious accidents*. A serious accident occurs when an employee must be hospitalized and will lose several days of work. All serious accidents must be reported to the nearest OSHA field office within 48 hours. This gives OSHA investigators a chance to inspect the site and determine the cause of the accident.

The third level is *employee complaints*. Employees who believe they are working in unsafe conditions have the right to call OSHA for an investigation. The worker may refuse to work on the item in question until OSHA has investigated the complaint.

The fourth level is *inspections of targeted industries*, which are conducted to discover whether the operation is violating OSHA regulations. Generally, the foodservice industry is not a targeted industry. However, in some states it may be a targeted industry if there have been several accidents. The foodservice operation must have a representative accompany the OSHA inspector (a manager is preferred) when an inspection is performed. Random inspections are performed with all industries, especially when a new regulation, directive, or noncompliance is suspected. Random means just that: businesses are selected at random to be inspected.

If a foodservice operation violates OSHA regulations, it may be fined up to $5,000 for each serious violation and $300 for each other safety violation. Penalties of up to $7,000 per day may be imposed for failure to correct violations within the proposed time period and for each day the violation continues beyond the abatement date. Fines are higher if the employer willfully violates the law repeatedly. In some cases, the employer may be charged with criminal penalties and be fined up to $70,000.

While regulations vary between the 24 state plans and the 26 states administered by OSHA, a foodservice operation will be in compliance if it posts the Instructions for how to fill out the "Log and Summary of Occupational Injuries and Illnesses" (available on request from OSHA). Businesses with ten or fewer employees do not need to post these items.

Safety education and committees have become a priority with OSHA. Safety committees meet to identify safety problems, suggest solutions, and educate employees regarding safety issues. All foodservice operations that have eleven or more employees (fewer for some occupations) must have safety committees. If a company has more than one unit, the total number of employees must be counted toward this requirement.

Material Safety Data Sheets (MSDSs) are required to identify hazardous chemicals. All chemicals used for cleaning are generally considered hazardous. See Figure 15-3 for an example. Suppliers should be able to provide these sheets to operators. If a foodservice manager chooses to buy chemicals in bulk and then use them in smaller quantities by putting the chemicals in smaller containers, each container must be labeled so that the person using the container knows what is inside. Standard warning labels are available.

Material Safety Data Sheets Often referred to as MSDSs; forms used to record information about hazardous chemicals used in a foodservice operation.

Prepared by Department of
Consumer & Business Services
**Oregon Occupational
Safety & Health Division**

PRODUCT DESIGNATION

Trade name (as labeled): Clear Out
Synonyms: Clout
Chemical name: O, O-Dimethyl phosphorodithioate of diethyl mercapotosuccinate
Common name: Malathion

SECTION I - HAZARDOUS INGREDIENTS

Chemical names:
O, O-Dimethyl phosphorodithioate of diethyl mercapotosuccinate CAS: 121—75-5
Percent*: 57.0
Aromatic Petroleum Derivative Solvent CAS: 64742-95-6
Percent: 31.0
(C_8 - C_{10} aromatic hydrocarbons)

SECTION II - PHYSICAL & CHEMICAL DATA

Appearance & odor: Clear, amber-colored liquid, aromatic solvent, and mercaptan odor
Boiling point (°F): Greater than 300°F
Vapor Density (Air = 1): <0.1
Evaporation rate (Butyl Acetate = 1): Slower than Butyl Acetate Specific Gravity: 1.06
Vapor pressure: 28.4 mm at 100°F
Solubility in (water): Emulsifies in water

SECTION III - FIRE, REACTIVITY & EXPLOSION DATA

Flash-point: 109°F (Pensky Martin TCC)
Flammability classification: Class II
Flammable limits in air, volume %: No applicable information found
Extinguishing media: Foam, CO_2, dry chemical, water spray
Unusual fire & explosion hazards:
Vapors and fumes from fire are hazardous. Evacuate people downwind from fire.
Special fire fighting procedures:
Fight fire upwind. Avoid heavy hose streams. Fire fighters should wear self-contained breathing apparatus and rubber clothing. After fire, firemen should shower and change clothing. Decontaminate used clothing with liquid chlorine bleach. If water is used as extinguishing media, dike to keep contaminated water out of all water sources.
Stability: Stable
Incompatibility: Strong alkalies and strong oxidizers
Hazardous decomposition products:
Storage at high temperature (above 120°F) leads to non-hazardous decomposition
Hazardous polymerization: Will not occur
Conditions to avoid: Temperatures above 120°F

SECTION IV - HEALTH HAZARD DATA

Effects of overexposures:
Immediate: Weakness, headache, tightness of chest, blurred vision, non-reactive pinpoint pupils, excessive salivation, excessive sweating, nausea, vomiting, diarrhea and abdominal cramps.
Long-term: No applicable information found

SECTION V - PRIMARY ROUTES OF ENTRY

May be fatal if swallowed or absorbed through skin. Avoid breathing spray mist, eye and skin contact.

SECTION VI - PERMISSIBLE EXPOSURE LIMITS

Malathion: 10 mg/m^3, 8 hr TWA (skin). Source: ACGIH - TLVs R. Aromatic Petroleum Derivative Solvent: 435 mg/m^3, 8 hr TWA (skin). Source: Supplier MSDS.

* Not required. Space provided for optional use.

Note: All categories should be addressed. If any item is not applicable, or if no information is available, the space must be marked "No Applicable Information Found."

FIGURE 15-3
Completed MSDS Form (front)

SECTION VII - CANCER HAZARD

NO: <u>X</u> This product's ingredients are not found in the lists below.
YES: ___ Federal OSHA ___ NTP ___ IARC ___ OR-OSHA

SECTION VIII - PRECAUTIONS, SPILLS

DOT storage category: RQ Malathion Solution ORM-A NA2783

Precautions for handling and storing: Do not use, pour, spill, or store near heat or open flame. Keep container closed. Use with adequate ventilation. Do not reuse empty container. Do not store at temperatures below 0°F.

Other precautions: Wash thoroughly if on skin and after handling. Avoid contamination of feed and foodstuffs. Do not use on household pets or humans. Do not permit children or pets to go onto sprayed grass until the spray has completely dried. Do not use in the home. Do not contaminate fish ponds or water; toxic to fish. Highly toxic to bees exposed to direct contact or residues on crops.

Action if released or spilled: Eliminate ignition sources. Wear appropriate protective equipment and clothing. Absorb in clay or soda ash. Sweep up and place in a waste disposal container. Treat contaminated area with full-strength liquid household chlorine bleach. Let stand for 15 minutes and repeat procedure. Flush area with water. Do not allow flush water to contaminate water sources.

Waste disposal method: Metal containers — triple rinse (or equivalent), then offer for recycling or reconditioning, or puncture and dispose of in a sanitary landfill. Plastic — follow instructions for metal containers, or incinerate. If state and local regulations allow, burn, but stay out of smoke. Note: Dispose of all wastes in accordance with federal, state, and local regulations.

SECTION IX - CONTROLS, PROTECTION

Precautions during use: Do not breathe fumes
Ventilation & engineering controls: Work in well-ventilated area
Respiratory protection: Not required for normal handling
Protective gloves & clothing: Wear rubber gloves when handling
Eye & face protection: Splash-proof goggles
Special protective measures for maintenance work: Eye wash facilities. Use clothing and equipment consistent with good pesticide handling and application procedures

SECTION X - FIRST AID & EMERGENCY PROCEDURES

Eye contact: Flush with plenty of water for at least 15 minutes and get medical attention

Skin contact: Wash contaminated skin with soap and water
Inhaled: Move to clear atmosphere. If symptoms occur get medical attention
Swallowed: Call physician or Poison Control Center immediately. Drink 1-2 glasses of water and induce vomiting by touching the back of throat with finger. Repeat until vomit fluid is clear. Do not induce vomiting or give anything by mouth to an unconscious person.
Medical conditions aggravated by exposure and notes to physician: This product may cause cholinesterase inhibition. Atropine is antidotal. 2-PAM may be effective as an adjunct to atropine.

SECTION XI - MSDS PREPARATION DATES

Date Prepared: 5-5-87   Preparer: John Q. Jones

SECTION XII - CONTACT PARTY

Manufacturer's Name & Address: LOCATION   Emergency Telephone No.: 111-111-1111
                                                 Information Telephone No.: 333-333-3333

FIGURE 15-3
Completed MSDS Form (back)

Tax Equity and Fiscal Responsibility Act

The **Tax Equity and Fiscal Responsibility Act** of 1982 (TEFRA) was designed to produce additional revenue through federal spending cuts, tax increases, and federal tax code reform measures. Tip reporting by employees in food and beverage operations was one area targeted. All tips received by employees are required by law to be reported to the federal government. This has always been the law, though only 16 percent of tip income was being reported by restaurant and bar employees until 1982, according to the Internal Revenue Service. With TEFRA, government efforts to collect taxes on unreported tip income by these employees have intensified.

Since 1982, the IRS has instituted various initiatives to strengthen its ability to enforce tip reporting requirements. One of the most recent was the creation of the Tip Reporting Alternative Commitment (TRAC). This pro forma agreement, worked out by representatives of the foodservice industry and the Internal Revenue Service, provides both employers and the IRS an important tool in the tasks of compliance and enforcement.

Through TEFRA, requirements have been established to encourage better reporting of tip income. These requirements do not replace existing tip reporting rules for the employee.

DETERMINING WHETHER A FOODSERVICE OPERATION MUST COMPLY

Only large food and beverage establishments must comply with the TEFRA reporting requirements. An establishment is considered large if it meets all of the following conditions:

- Food and/or beverages are served to customers on the premises. Fast-food operations are excluded.

- Tipping is customary in the establishment.

- More than ten people were employed on a typical business day during the preceding calendar year. All employees of the operation are included in this count, not just tipped employees.

To determine whether ten people were employed on a typical business day, the IRS uses the following four-step procedure:

Step One Using the month with the greatest amount of gross receipts from the previous year, divide the total hours worked by all employees during that month by the number of days the establishment was open for business. This step calculates the average number of hours worked per business day.

Step Two Repeat the first step, using the month with the least amount of gross receipts.

Step Three Add the results from Steps One and Two.

Step Four Divide the total from Step Three by 2 to calculate the average number of employee hours worked on a typical business day. If this average is more than 80 hours, you must comply with the TEFRA tip reporting requirements. The determining factor is 80 hours. If a restaurant has fewer than ten employees but averages more than 80 hours, it must comply.

A new foodservice operation must begin to comply when two consecutive months average more than 80 hours. At this point, the operation is considered to have more than ten employees on a typical day. The operation must comply with TEFRA reporting requirements beginning with the first payroll period after the first two months in which the average hours worked exceeded 80 hours.

FILING FORM 8027

Foodservice operators comply with TEFRA requirements by filing an Employer's Annual Information Return of Tip Income and Allocated Tips (Form 8027; see Figure 15-4). This form reports:

- *Gross receipts* from food and/or food and beverage operations.
- Total *charged receipts* on which there were charged tips.
- Total *charged tips* (tips included as part of a credit transaction).
- Total *service charges* of less than 10 percent paid as wages to employees (this applies to employees in states where a tip credit against minimum wage is allowed).
- Total tips reported by indirectly tipped employees.
- Total tips reported by employees who are part of a *tip pool*.
- Total tips reported by *directly tipped employees*.
- Total *allocated tips* to employees, if the total amount of reported tips is less than 8 percent (or a lower rate) of gross receipts.

This form must be filed even if there were no tip allocations to report. Form 8027 is due on or before the last day of February of the year following the report period. The reportable items are described in the following paragraphs.

Gross receipts include cash sales, charge receipts, and charges to hotel rooms. Gross receipts should not include carryout sales, sales with an added service charge of 10 percent or more, and state or local taxes.

Charged receipts are sales that are charged on credit cards or billed directly. Only those charges in which tips were reported must be included.

Charged tips are recorded on vouchers. Several credit card companies track charged tips and report them to foodservice operators. The more astute credit card companies inform foodservice operators of the discount fees on charged tips on a daily basis. Operators then subtract the discount before reimbursing the tipped employee. Foodservice operators who do not do this are subsidizing the waitstaff by paying the credit card fee on the tip left by the customer. Some operations have saved thousands of dollars a year by taking the discount on charged tips. Paying the discount for the employee is unreportable income to the employee, it is a cost that should be borne by the employee.

Service charges are frequently assessed on customer meals by foodservice establishments for banquets or large parties. Such service fees are paid direct-

Form **8027** Department of the Treasury Internal Revenue Service	**Employer's Annual Information Return of Tip Income and Allocated Tips**	OMB No. 1545-0714 **1995**

Use IRS label.
Make any
necessary
changes.
Otherwise,
please type or
print.

Name of establishment

Number and street (See instructions.)   Employer identification number

City or town, state, and ZIP code

Type of establishment (check
only one box)

☐ **1**   Evening meals only

☐ **2**   Evening and other
     meals

☐ **3**   Meals other than
     evening meals

☐ **4**   Alcoholic beverages

Employer's name

Establishment number
(See instructions.)

Number and street (P.O. box, if applicable.)   Apt. or suite no.

City, town or post office, state, and ZIP code (if a foreign address, enter city, province or state, postal code, and country.)

Check the box if applicable: Final Return ☐   Amended Return ☐

1	Total charged tips for 1995	**1**
2	Total charged receipts (other than nonallocable receipts) showing charged tips	**2**
3	Total amount of service charges of less than 10% paid as wages to employees	**3**
4a	Total tips reported by indirectly tipped employees	**4a**
b	Total tips reported by directly tipped employees	**4b**
c	Total tips reported (Add lines 4a and 4b.)	**4c**
5	Gross receipts from food or beverage operations (other than nonallocable receipts) . . .	**5**
6	Multiply line 5 by 8% (.08) or the lower rate shown here ▶ _____ granted by the district director. Attach a copy of the district director's determination letter to this return .	**6**

Note: *If you have allocated tips using other than the calendar year (semimonthly, biweekly, quarterly, etc.), put an* **X** *on line 6 and enter the amount of allocated tips from your records on line 7.*

7   Allocation of tips. If line 6 is more than line 4c, enter the excess here **7**

This amount must be allocated as tips to tipped employees working in this establishment. Check the box below that shows the method used for the allocation. (Show the portion, if any, attributable to each employee in box 8 of the employee's Form W-2.)

a   Allocation based on hours-worked method (See instructions for restriction.) . . . ☐
     Note: *If you checked line 7a, enter the average number of employee hours worked per business day during the payroll period. (See instructions.)* _____

b   Allocation based on gross receipts method . . . . ☐

c   Allocation based on good-faith agreement (Attach copy of agreement.) . . . . . ☐

8   Enter the total number of directly tipped employees at this establishment during 1995 ▶

Under penalties of perjury, I declare that I have examined this return, including accompanying schedules and statements, and to the best of my knowledge and belief, it is true, correct, and complete.

Signature ▶   Title ▶   Date ▶

For Paperwork Reduction Act Notice, see the separate instructions.   Cat. No. 49989U   Form **8027** (1995)

11–29–95

69

FIGURE 15-4
Form 8027

ly to employees as part of their wages. The service charges may be split among several people so that the effective rate is actually less than 10 percent of the meal amount. The tip amount, even if it is less than 10 percent per person, must be reported.

An **indirectly tipped employee** is a participant in a **tip pool**. A tip pool is a depository of all tips earned during a shift or other period of time. The money in the tip pool may be split among bussers, service bartenders, and cooks. It is important to note that not all foodservice operations allow tip pools. Some waitstaff share their tips with bussers and food preparation personnel because of the goodwill it creates.

A **directly tipped employee** receives tips directly from the customers. This includes employees who, after receiving tips, turn all the tips over to a tip pool. Examples of directly tipped employees are waitstaff and bartenders. A *tip allocation* is a tip amount which is allotted to employees to make up the difference between the total tips reported and 8 percent of the establishment's gross receipts.

LOWERING THE PERCENTAGE RATE

Employees or an employer may request that the percentage of gross receipts be reduced from 8 percent but not below 2 percent. A written request must be submitted to the IRS district director. The request must be substantiated with the following information:

- Type of establishment.
- Location of the establishment.
- Charged tip rate that currently exists.
- Menu prices.
- Amount of self-service.

Until the establishment is notified in writing of a reduced rate by the district director, the employer must continue to use 8 percent of gross receipts when allocating tips.

METHODS FOR ALLOCATING TIPS

Foodservice establishments must **allocate tips** among employees who receive tips only if the total tips reported during any reporting period are less than 8 percent of the gross receipts for that period. Allocations can be figured annually or on a more frequent basis during the calendar year. For example, the foodservice operation may choose to allocate tips each pay period or quarterly. However, the reporting period selected must remain in effect for the entire calendar year. An employer must allocate tips using one of these methods:

- A good-faith agreement.
- An IRS formula based on the employee's individual gross receipts.
- An IRS formula based on the employee's directly tipped hours. This method is restricted to establishments that employ fewer than the equivalent of 25 full-time employees during a payroll period. An employer qualifies if the average number of employee hours worked per business day during a payroll period is less than 200 hours.

Indirectly tipped employee An employee who participates in a tip pool.

Tip pool A depository of all tips earned during a shift or other period of time by all tipped employees.

Directly tipped employee An employee who receives tips directly from the customers.

Allocating tips A method of dividing the required tip reporting amounts to tipped employees to comply with TEFRA.

Once one of these methods has been selected, the method must be used for the entire calendar year (January through December). A different method may be used the following calendar year.

Using a Good-Faith Agreement

A **good-faith agreement** is an agreement between management and employees. It specifies how the employer should allocate tips when the reported tips do not reach 8 percent of the gross receipts. To be binding, the agreement must:

- Be written.

- Be consented to by the employer and at least two-thirds of the employees in each tipped category.

- Specify a method of allocating tips that reflects a good-faith approximation of the actual distribution of tip income among tipped employees.

- Begin with a reporting period that starts within 30 days of adoption and is renewed annually.

- Be attached annually when filing Form 8027.

A good-faith agreement may be revoked by a written agreement adopted by at least two-thirds of the tipped employees.

How the IRS Allocates Tips

The IRS formula includes the following steps to calculate the 8 percent share of gross receipts, the total share related to directly tipped employees, each employee's share of gross receipts, employee shortfall, and employee allocation. The IRS formula for calculating the allocation of tips is as follows:

Step One Multiply the establishment's gross receipts by 8 percent (or a lower rate).

Step Two Subtract the tips reported by indirectly tipped employees from the 8 percent of gross receipts. This determines the directly tipped employees' share of 8 percent of the gross receipts.

Step Three For each directly tipped employee, multiply the amount calculated in Step 2 by one of the fractions based on your allocation method:

1. The employee's gross receipts for the period over the establishment's gross receipts.

2. The directly tipped hours worked by the employee over the total number of directly tipped hours worked by all directly tipped employees.

This step calculates the employee's share of gross receipts.

Step Four Subtract the tips reported by each employee from the employee's share of 8 percent of gross receipts as calculated in Step Three. This step calculates the employee's shortfall. If tips reported are more than the employee's share of 8 percent of gross receipts, the employee does not have a short-fall and, therefore, no tip allocation is made.

Step Five Subtract the total tips reported by all employees (including indirect tips) from the amount calculated in Step One. This step calculates the total amount of tip allocation necessary.

Step Six For each directly tipped employee with a shortfall, multiply the total allocation amount, as calculated in Step Five, by a fraction consisting of the employee's shortfall over the total amount of all shortfalls for all directly tipped employees. The result is the employee's tip allocation amount for the period covered.

Examples of the gross receipts and hours methods are shown in Figure 15-5 and 15-6, respectively.

Employers must report tip allocations made to employees on W-2 forms. The total amount of tip allocations made to employees must also be reported on Form 8027. Employers who fail to report tip allocation amounts for employees will probably be audited and may be subject to civil penalties.

Employees must also report tips allocated to them on their W-2 form. It is the employee's responsibility to include the amount as taxable income when filing his or her personal income tax return.

If an employee does not agree with the allocation amount, he or she has the right to report a lesser allocation amount on his or her personal income tax return as gross income. However, the employee must be able to prove the lesser amount with adequate records.

OTHER TIP REPORTING RESPONSIBILITIES OF EMPLOYEES

All tipped employees have tip reporting responsibilities, not just tipped employees who are employed by qualifying TEFRA establishments. These requirements are:

1. *Reporting all tips received as income.* Every employee who receives more than $20.00 in tips during a calendar month is required by law to report all tips received as income. Tips must be reported to the employer on or before the tenth day of the following month. Employers should ask employees to report tips weekly, biweekly, or semimonthly, depending on their payroll schedule. Employees must observe the dates established by their employer.

   Note: This tip reporting law is enforced not only for employees employed by qualifying TEFRA establishments, but for all tipped employees. With TEFRA, any tip amount not reported can make the difference between the foodservice operation allocating and not allocating tips.

2. *Providing the employer with a tip statement.* All tipped employees must provide their employer with a written and signed statement reporting the total tips received during the covered period (see Figure 15-7).

3. *Maintaining adequate records.* All tipped employees are required to maintain an accurate accounting of tips received and reported to their employer for their personal records (see Figure 15-8).

	Gross receipts for the reporting period	$34,000.00
	Total tips reported by employees for the period	$2,400.00
	Directly tipped employees reported	$2,140.00
	Indirectly tipped employees reported	$260.00

DIRECTLY TIPPED EMPLOYEES	GROSS RECEIPTS FOR REPORTING PERIOD	TIPS REPORTED
A	$10,200.00	$ 600.00
B	8,000.00	650.00
C	6,750.00	420.00
D	9,050.00	470.00
	$34.000.00	$2,140.00

The Allocation Computations Would Be:

1. $34,000.00 × .08 (or lower rate) = $ 2,720.00

2. $2,720.00 – $260.00 = $2,460.00

3.

DIRECTLY TIPPED EMPLOYEES	DIRECTLY TIPPED SHARE OF 8% GROSS		GROSS RECEIPTS RATIO		EMPLOYEE SHARE OF 8% GROSS
A	$2,460.00	×	$10,200.00/34,000.00	=	$ 738.00
B	$2,460.00	×	8,000.00/34,000.00	=	578.82
C	$2,460.00	×	6,750.00/34,000.00	=	488.38
D	$2,460.00	×	9,050.00/34,000.00	=	654.80
					$2,460.00

4.

DIRECTLY TIPPED EMPLOYEES	EMPLOYEE SHARE OF 8% GROSS		TIPS REPORTED		EMPLOYEE SHORTFALL
A	$738.00	–	$600.00	=	$138.00
B	578.82	–	650.00	=	
C	488.38	–	420.00	=	68.38
D	654.80	–	470.00	=	184.80
					$391.18

Since employee B has no shortfall, an allocation is not made.

5. $2,720.00 – $2,400.00 = $320.00 (total allocable amount to shortfall employees)

6.

DIRECTLY TIPPED EMPLOYEES	TOTAL ALLOCATION		SHORTFALL RATIO		EMPLOYEE ALLOCATION*
A	$320.00	×	$138.00/391.18	=	$112.89
C	320.00	×	68.38/391.18	=	55.94
D	320.00	×	184.80/391.18	=	151.17
					$320.00

FIGURE 15-5
Gross Receipts Method

*May be off cents due to rounding.
Note: The total allocation amount may be less than the total employee shortfall. Tips reported in excess of the allocation percent are applied to the total allocation amount, therefore it is reduced.

	Gross receipts for the reporting period	$43,270.00
	Total tips reported by employees for the period	$3,247.50
	Directly tipped employees reported	$3,026.00
	Indirectly tipped employees reported	$221.50

DIRECTLY TIPPED EMPLOYEES	HOURS WORKED FOR REPORTING PERIOD	TIPS REPORTED
A	36.00	$462.00
B	21.00	390.00
C	32.00	540.00
D	42.00	581.00
E	34.75	580.00
F	28.50	473.00
	194.25	$3,026.00

Tip Allocation Computations Would Be:

1. $43,270.00 × .08 (or lower rate) = $3,461.60

2. $3,461.60 − $221.50 = $3,240.10

3.

DIRECTLY TIPPED EMPLOYEES	DIRECTLY TIPPED SHARE OF 8% GROSS		HOURS WORKED RATIO		EMPLOYEE SHARE OF 8% GROSS
A	$3,240.10	×	36.00/194.25	=	$600.48
B	3,240.10	×	21.00/194.25	=	350.28
C	3,240.10	×	32.00/194.25	=	533.77
D	3,240.10	×	42.00/194.25	=	700.56
E	3,240.10	×	34.75/194.25	=	579.63
F	3,240.10	×	28.50/194.25	=	475.38
					$3,240.10

4.

DIRECTLY TIPPED EMPLOYEES	EMPLOYEE SHARE OF 8% GROSS		TIPS REPORTED		EMPLOYEE SHORTFALL
A	$600.48	−	$462.00	=	$138.48
B	350.28	−	390.00	=	0
C	533.77	−	540.00	=	0
D	700.56	−	581.00	=	119.56
E	579.63	−	580.00	=	0
F	475.38	−	473.00	=	2.38
					$260.42

Since employee B, C, and E have no shortfall, allocations are not made.

5. $3,461.60 − $3,247.50 = $214.10 (total allocable amount to shortfall employees)

6.

DIRECTLY TIPPED EMPLOYEES	TOTAL ALLOCATION		SHORTFALL RATIO		EMPLOYEE ALLOCATION*
A	$214.10	×	$138.48/260.42	=	$113.85
D	214.10	×	119.56/260.42	=	98.29
F	214.10	×	2.38/260.42	=	1.96
					$214.10

FIGURE 15-6
Hours Method

*May be off cents due to rounding.
Note: The total allocation amount may be less than the total employee shortfall. Tips reported in excess of the allocation percent are applied to the total allocation amount, therefore it is reduced.

Form **4070**
(Rev. July 1996)
Department of the Treasury
Internal Revenue Service

**Employee's Report
of Tips to Employer**
▶ For Paperwork Reduction Act Notice, see back of form.

OMB No. 1545-0065

Employee's name and address

Social security number

Employer's name and address (include establishment name, if different)

1 Cash tips received

2 Credit card tips received

3 Tips paid out

Month or shorter period in which tips were received
from _____ , 19 _____ , to _____ , 19 _____

4 Net tips (lines **1 + 2 - 3**)

Signature

Date

FIGURE 15-7
Employee's Report of Tips to Employer

EMPLOYERS CAN HELP EMPLOYEES MEET TEFRA REQUIREMENTS

Employers should review and discuss tip reporting requirements with employees, especially TEFRA and its rules and reporting requirements. Employers should also provide employees with a tip statement report for submitting tip information. Form 4070A can be obtained from an IRS district office. Figure 15-8 shows an example of this form.

THE TIP REPORTING ALTERNATIVE COMMITMENT

The IRS introduced the Tip Reporting Alternative Commitment (TRAC) in June 1995. The word *alternative* is important, for a TRAC provides an option to two common initiatives that will continue to be used by the IRS—the Tip Rate Determination Agreement (TRDA) and the tip examination.

A *tip examination* (also known as a tip audit) is a comprehensive look at an operation's tip rates and compliance. The IRS has the authority to conduct audits on liability for reported and unreported payroll taxes on tips.

The IRS can offer a TRDA in lieu of a tip audit. A TRDA is an agreement in which an operation agrees to determine the average rate of tipping. The manager must get a majority of workers to report tips at that rate or higher.

The TRAC program was developed by the IRS in cooperation with representatives of the foodservice industry as an alternative to the TRDA. While somewhat similar to a TRDA, a TRAC shifts a great deal of emphasis to educating employees about the responsibilities and benefits of proper tip reporting, establishing tip reporting procedures, and proper tax filing and payments. For conscientious efforts in these areas, business owners are exempted from "employer first" and "employer only" audits.

Employers participating in the TRAC program must provide three things, and these are spelled out in Section III of the TRAC agreement. They are the following:

Form **4070A**
(Rev. July 1996)
Department of the Treasury
Internal Revenue Service

Employee's Daily Record of Tips

This is a voluntary form provided for your convenience.
See instructions for records you must keep.

OMB No. 1545-0065

Employee's name and address	Employer's name	Month and year
	Establishment name (if different)	

Date tips rec'd.	Date of entry	a. Tips received directly from customers and other employees	b. Credit card tips received	c. Tips paid out to other employees	d. Names of employees to whom you paid tips
1					
2					
3					
4					
5					
Subtotals					

For Paperwork Reduction Act Notice, see Instructions on the back of Form 4070.　　　　　　Page 1

Date tips rec'd.	Date of entry	a. Tips received directly from customers and other employees	b. Credit card tips received	c. Tips paid out to other employees	d. Names of employees to whom you paid tips
6					
7					
8					
9					
10					
11					
12					
13					
14					
15					
Subtotals					

Page 2

FIGURE 15-8
Employee's Daily Record of Tips (Pages 1 and 2)

1. *Educational programs.* Food and beverage operations must start, and maintain for each calendar quarter, an educational program that explains reporting obligations to employees.

2. *Returns, taxes, and records.* Food and beverage operations must meet the requirements for filing Form 941 (Employer's Quarterly Federal Tax Return), Form 8027 (Annual Information Return of Tip Income and Allocated Tips) if required, and Forms W-2. An employer also agrees to comply with requirements for paying and depositing taxes

131:1832 FEDERAL TAX FORMS No. 170

Date tips rec'd.	Date of entry	**a.** Tips received directly from customers and other employees	**b.** Credit card tips received	**c.** Tips paid out to other employees	**d.** Names of employees to whom you paid tips
16					
17					
18					
19					
20					
21					
22					
23					
24					
25					
Subtotals					

Page 3

No. 170 FORM 4070-A 131:1833

Date tips rec'd.	Date of entry	**a.** Tips received directly from customers and other employees	**b.** Credit card tips received	**c.** Tips paid out to other employees	**d.** Names of employees to whom you paid tips
26					
27					
28					
29					
30					
31					
Subtotals from pages 1, 2, and 3					
Totals					

1. Report total cash tips (col. **a**) on Form 4070, line **1.**

2. Report total credit card tips (col. **b**) on Form 4070, line **2.**

3. Report total tips paid out (col. **c**) on Form 4070, line **3.**

Page 4

FIGURE 15-8
Employee's Daily Record of Tips (Pages 3 and 4)

due, to maintain certain records, and to make quarterly totals available to the IRS upon request.

3. *Tip reporting procedure.* Food and beverage operations agree to set up a tip reporting procedure for directly and indirectly tipped employees. This includes cash and charged tips.

An agreement can be revoked for failure to "substantially comply" with any of the three parts. However, the IRS has indicated that if an employer is willing to work with them to correct the reasons for the proposed revocation, the agreement may stay in effect. To participate, food and beverage operations must apply to their district IRS office.

Minimum Wage Laws

All employers must comply with federal and state laws regulating the payment of minimum wage, overtime, and general working conditions. State laws supersede federal laws in this area if they are more rigorous.

General Working Conditions

Regulations regarding work conditions vary from state to state. Foodservice operators should make an ongoing effort to ensure that they are in compliance. State restaurant associations are good sources of information; managers may also directly contact state agencies. Most states have an agency referred to as the Department of Labor. As a general guideline, operators should:

1. Establish and maintain a regular scheduled payday. A pay period should not exceed 35 days.

2. Provide meal periods of 30 minutes or more if the workday is six hours or longer. The employee should be relieved of all duty during this time. If the employee cannot be relieved, the meal period must be paid. A paid meal period can be as short as 20 minutes if the employer can identify an industry practice or custom. The scheduling of meal periods is flexible and depends upon the length of the work day.

3. Provide paid rest periods of at least ten minutes during each four-hour work period.

EMPLOYMENT OF MINORS

Federal regulations set minimum standards for the employment of **minors**. Unless employed as part of an agricultural operation, minors cannot be employed under the age of 14. There are specific regulations that apply to 14- and 15-year-old minors. State laws generally cover work conditions for those 16 and 17 years of age.

Minor
A person under the age of eighteen.

Regulations regarding employment certificates (work permits) vary from state to state. Generally, one must be filled out for each minor employed. Certificates must be filed with a state agency or designee. Many states require that a certificate be applied for within 48 hours of employing a minor. Certificates or work permits are normally required for all working minors, ages 14 through 17. The federal government accepts state certificates for record-keeping purposes. Generally, employers are required to check whether a minor has a certificate before hiring him or her.

Working-hours restrictions apply to minors. The following are the federal restrictions by age.

For 14- and 15-year-olds when school is in session:

3 hours per day

8 hours on nonschool days

Maximum of 18 hours per week

Only between the hours of 7:00 A.M. and 7 P.M.

Working is not allowed during school hours

For 14- and 15-year-olds when school is not in session:

8 hours per day

Maximum of 40 hours per week from June 1 through Labor Day

Only between the hours of 7 A.M. and 9:00 P.M.

For 16- and 17-year-olds:

Any hours

Maximum hours per week varies by state

Work condition requirements for all age groups may vary according to state. The following are general recommendations.

1. Meal periods of at least 30 minutes should be provided no later than five hours and one minute after the minor reports to work.

2. During the meal period, 14- and 15-year-olds should be fully relieved of work duties. Sixteen- and 17-year-old employees may work during a meal period, but should be paid for their time.

3. Rest periods of at least fifteen minutes should be provided during each four hours of work time.

4. Minors must not be employed in dangerous occupations, according to federal law. Fourteen- and 15-year-olds may not operate any dangerous power-driven machinery such as meat slicers and grinders, food choppers and cutters, and bakery-type mixers. They may not do cooking except at soda fountains, lunch counters, snack bars, or cafeteria serving counters. Other state laws may apply. There are exceptions if the person is in a bona fide training program or work-education program.

5. Adequate work should be provided if the employer requires the minor to report to work. Adequate work means enough work (or compensation in lieu of work) to earn at least half of the scheduled day's earnings.

WORKERS' COMPENSATION INSURANCE

Workers' compensation insurance protects the employer from financial burdens caused by employees who are injured on the job. The insurance also protects the employee from catastrophic medical bills and temporary loss of income from injuries sustained on the job. This type of compensation insurance is primarily for employee protection and is carried by the employer for medical bills and vocational rehabilitation in some states.

How much a company pays for workers' compensation insurance depends upon the risk factors of the job and the performance history of the company. Fortunately, foodservice jobs are not considered high risk. Most injuries are falls, cuts, and burns. Very rarely do employees suffer debilitating injuries in the foodservice industry.

Occasionally employees hurt themselves to the point of needing hospitalization and rehabilitation. This can be very expensive for an employer. To keep insurance rates low and to maintain control of other related costs, employers should observe the following practices:

- Have an OSHA inspection to ensure that the work environment complies with regulations. OSHA cannot fine an operator who requests an inspection. However, OSHA can require that deficiencies be corrected. If deficiencies are not corrected, the operation risks being fined.

- Design an early-return-to-work program for injured employees who are able to do light work.

- Offer incentives for employees to observe safety practices. For example, a cash bonus may be given if so many days go by without an accident.

It is important that employees follow OSHA regulations and complete the necessary forms when there is an accident. Also, when an accident occurs, employers should have employees seek immediate medical attention.

Conducting a Human Resources Audit

The **human resources audit** is a good self-check to ensure that the foodservice operation is in compliance with a variety of laws (see Table 15-1). The audit should be customized to the regulations faced by each foodservice operation, depending upon its state of residence.

Human resources audit
A form used to evaluate whether the foodservice operation is compliant with federal, state, and local laws.

The audit should be done by a variety of people. Managers tend to have one view of compliance and employees may have another. The point is to create a positive and safe working environment. Employees doing the audit may observe things that managers might miss. The reverse is also true. The audit should be done at least twice a year. If management wants to use it as a learning tool, it can be done more frequently.

The audit form is divided into four columns. The Issue column describes what is being examined. This is the column that should be customized, especially the OSHA category.

The next two columns indicate the auditor's opinion of whether the foodservice operation is in compliance or not in compliance. A simple check in the column will indicate the auditor's opinion. A check in the In Compliance column means that as far as the auditor is concerned, the issue being examined seems to comply with the letter and intent of the law. Obviously, a check in the Not in Compliance column indicates that the auditor does not believe that the foodservice operation is in compliance with the letter and intent of the law.

The auditor should use the fourth column, the Comments column, to indicate why the operation is not in compliance or any thoughts regarding any of the issues examined. The auditor should suggest what should be done to correct violations so that the business would be in compliance.

Table 15-1   Human Resources Audit

Auditor Manager	Date June 30, XXXX		Page 1 of 3
ISSUE	**IN COMPLIANCE**	**NOT IN COMPLIANCE**	**COMMENTS**
SEXUAL HARASSMENT			
Number of claims made during the past year.	✓		No claims.
Written policy posted.	✓		
Procedure established for reporting sexual harassment claims.	✓		
All employees are aware of what constitutes sexual harassment.		✓	Not all new employees have been trained. A consistent program will begin by July 15, XXXX.
All employees have been trained how to make, respond to, investigate, and handle sexual harassment charges.		✓	This will begin by July 15, XXXX.
If any sexual harassment claims were made, were they investigated immediately?	✓		No claims.
If any sexual harassment claims were made, was disciplinary action taken?	✓		No claims.
ADA COMPLIANCE			
Job descriptions have been adjusted to ensure that reasonable accommodation has been reviewed.	✓		
Physical facilities have been examined by local specialists to ensure that the facilities comply with ADA regulations.	✓		Association for Employing the Disabled inspected the facility on January 8, XXXX.
Any employment tests being used have been checked to ensure that they are not discriminatory against the disabled.	✓		
Are qualified potential employees with disabilities not being hired due to health insurance considerations?	✓		No insurance limitations.
EEOC CONSIDERATIONS			
Pre-employment tests are directly related to the job.	✓		
Interviews do not use forbidden questions.	✓		
Employees hired are of both genders.	✓		
Both genders are paid equally for comparable work.	✓		

Continued

ISSUE	IN COMPLIANCE	NOT IN COMPLIANCE	COMMENTS
Promotions are based upon quantifiable performance data.	✓		
FAMILY AND MEDICAL LEAVE ACT			
Employee qualification to take leave—has worked for 12 months and at least 1,200 hours.	✓		No one took it.
Have any employees taken up to 12 weeks of unpaid leave in any 12-month period?	✓		Not applicable.
Employees are placed in previous or equivalent positions upon returning to work.	✓		No employees fell into this category.
Health care benefits are continued during leave.	✓		No employees fell into this category.
IMMIGRATION REFORM ACT			
Employer has I-9 forms.	✓		
Employer does not discriminate against a person who is not a citizen of the United States.	✓		
Employer obtains verification of citizenship to complete I-9 forms.	✓		
OSHA			
OSHA information poster is posted.	✓		
Form 200 or its replacement is posted.	✓		
MSDS forms are available for all chemicals used in the business.	✓		
All chemical containers are labeled correctly.	✓		
Have any situations that could be classified as imminent danger been identified?	✓		
If the number of employees exceeds 11, does the business have a functioning safety committee?	✓		Safety committee consists of 3 people.
Have there been any serious injuries that required employees to miss days of work?	✓		No serious injuries during the past year.
The premises meet OSHA standards for safety.	✓		

Continued

ISSUE	IN COMPLIANCE	NOT IN COMPLIANCE	COMMENTS
TIP REPORTING REQUIREMENTS			
Is Form 8027 used for tip allocation?	✓		
Is a good-faith agreement being used? (Answer: Yes of No)	No		
If one is being used, are the five conditions present to make the agreement binding?			
Are employees trained concerning tip reporting requirements?	✓		
Are employees using Form 4070A?	✓		
MINIMUM WAGE LAW & WORKING CONDITIONS			
Is the federal/state minimum wage law being honored?	✓		
Are proper payroll deductions being made (social security, Medicare, federal and state income taxes, etc.)?	✓		
Is there a scheduled payday?	✓		
Are meal periods of 30 minutes provided if employee is working 6 hours or longer?	✓		
Have employees been able to take 10-minute work breaks for each 4-hour work period?		✓	Need to be more consistent.
Have terminated employees been paid in a timely manner?	✓		
Are 14- and 15-year-olds working more than 3 hours per school day or 8 hours on a nonschool day?	✓		
Are 14- and 15-year-olds working only between 7 A.M. and 9 P.M.?	✓		
Are 14- 17-year-olds working with prohibited equipment, for instance, a meat slicer?	✓		
Are working conditions for minors regarding breaks and meal periods being met?	✓		

SUMMARY

1. Foodservice managers should know the numerous laws that regulate human resources issues.

2. A foodservice operation can avoid sexual harassment occurrences by formulating and instituting a sexual harassment policy. Foodservice operators should clearly explain the sexual harassment policy to all employees; train employees and managers how to report, respond to, investigate and handle sexual harassment charges; and use disciplinary actions when appropriate.

3. Foodservice operations can comply with ADA regulations by making reasonable accommodations that allow people with disabilities to work. Hiring practices and work conditions may need to be modified to accommodate the disabled.

4. Foodservice operations must comply with EEOC laws. No employer may discriminate based upon gender, religion, national origin, color, or ethnicity. This means that foodservice operations may not discriminate when hiring, promoting, scheduling, or disciplining any employee. Also, any rules, pre-employment tests, or tests required of employees must be applied to all equally.

5. Foodservice operations must comply with the Family and Medical Leave Act, which allows any employee to take leave for a pregnancy, to care for a child, spouse, or parent with a serious health condition, or to care for a personal health condition. The employee's job or a similar position must be held for the employee during his or her time of absence.

6. Foodservice operations must comply with the Immigration Reform and Control Act. All employees must provide information regarding their citizenship and this information must be recorded on Form I-9.

7. Foodservice operators must comply with OSHA regulations to protect employees, maintain proper documentation of accidents, and maintain MSDS forms.

8. If foodservice operations meet certain federal guidelines, they must report 8 percent of gross revenues allocated to tipped employees. Tipped employees should keep track of their tips and must report their tip income to their employer. Foodservice operations must report tip income to the IRS.

9. Foodservice operators that employ minors must comply with federal regulations that set minimum standards for working conditions and hours that minors may be scheduled.

10. To keep workers' compensation insurance rates low, foodservice operations should provide a safe work environment, design an early-return-to-work program, and offer incentives for employees to observe safety practices.

11. The human resources audit is a control tool that managers can use to ensure that the foodservice operation is complying with the broad range of laws that affect every part of their operation.

KEY CONCEPTS

Allocating tips

Americans with Disabilities Act

Directly tipped employee

Disability

Equal Employment Opportunity
  Commission

Family and Medical Leave Act

Good-faith agreement

Human resources audit

Indirectly tipped employee

Material Safety Data Sheets

Minor

Occupational Safety and Health
  Act

Sexual harassment

Tax Equity and Fiscal
  Responsibility Act

Tip pool

DISCUSSION QUESTIONS AND EXERCISES

1. Describe what constitutes sexual harassment.

2. Describe how a foodservice operation can avoid sexual harassment complaints.

3. What does "reasonable accommodation of the disabled" mean?

4. What are some of the implications of complying with the Equal Employment Opportunity Act?

5. How are foodservice operations affected by the Family and Medical Leave Act?

6. Make a list of questions that should not be asked in a job interview.

7. Describe what foodservice managers must do to be in compliance with the Immigration Reform and Control Act.

8. What five levels of seriousness does OSHA deal with concerning on-the-job safety issues?

9. If an employee files a complaint with OSHA, does the employer have the right to fire the employee?

10. What types of fines may be assessed by OSHA against an employer and for what reasons?

11. What are MSDS forms and what are they used for?

12. What are the tip reporting requirements of tipped employees?

13. What is the purpose of Form 8027?

14. What is the federal minimum wage? What is the minimum wage in your state?

15. After how many hours of work during a work week is an employer required to pay overtime?

16. What are the regulations for employees who are minors with regard to the number of hours they can work during school and during breaks from school.

17. Are there any restrictions on what minors can do?

18. What are the recommended work conditions for minors?

16

Monitoring the Sales Process

■   ■   ■   ■   ■   ■   ■   ■   ■   ■   ■   ■   ■   ■

Learning Objectives

After reading this chapter and completing the discussion questions and exercises, you should be able to:

1. Balance the total of the guest checks with the cash register reading and the actual cash and credit taken in.
2. Practice effective cash, check, and credit collection procedures.
3. Properly complete a cashier's report.
4. Understand the value of documenting cash and charge information so that it can be compared with a daily sales report.
5. Understand why waitstaff should always use a guest check to take an order from a guest.
6. Understand why the guest check must be filled out accurately and systematically.
7. Understand the process of using guest checks and presenting the bill to the guest.
8. Understand that all guest checks must be accounted for with the same accuracy as a bank check.

About Monitoring the Sales Process

The foodservice business is like every other business when it comes to recording sales, correctly handling cash and credit card charges taken in, and maintaining control of the process that documents customer orders (guest checks).

Selling the products, recording the sales, and ensuring that all the money goes to the right place are specific functions. These functions can all be accomplished through a few quick and easy steps that should be performed as a simple business routine. An established procedure will also provide a comfort level of accountability for the employees handling money. Once the employees are trained to the level of management's expectations, they can perform their tasks with a certainty of correctness.

A foodservice operation may range from a small beverage cart to a multi-unit operation. Whatever the size, cash handling should not be left to chance. Procedures and accountability will eliminate errors and temptation that may lead to theft.

Introduction to Sales, Cash, and Credit Control

Sales are the dollar amount of food and beverage items sold in a given period of time. Cash and credit card transactions must be tightly controlled and documented through the use of appropriate control procedures. A cashier's report can be used to control the cash and credit card charges by balancing the total of the guest checks with the cash register reading and the actual cash and credit card charges taken in. The daily sales report recaps the entire day's sales activity by each department and shift, with the accompanying totals.

Thorough training for cashiers is essential. Cashiers should be trained in proper cash, check, and credit card handling procedures. Along with being trained for accuracy, they should also be trained to be personable and congenial, for the cashier is often the last person to make contact with the customer. The cashier is in a position to foster goodwill and become aware of any customer dissatisfaction.

Cashier Control

Cashier's report
A form used to account for the total revenue collected during a specific period of time, such as a shift.

Cash turn-in report
A form used to account for cash collected during a specific period of time, such as a shift.

At the end of each shift, prior to completing a **cashier's report** (Table 16-2), the cashier should complete a **cash turn-in report** (Table 16-1). Typically, this report is printed on the side of a cash deposit envelope. The purpose of the form is to assist the cashier in counting the cash drawer at the end of a shift. It is very similar to preparing a deposit slip for a bank deposit. The total cash turn-in report is used to complete the cashier's report (Table 16-2).

A cashier's report should be prepared at the end of every shift. If more than one cash register is used during a shift, a cashier's report should be completed for each cash register. The following paragraphs detail the procedure that should be followed if the foodservice operation is using a traditional cash register system. The procedure may vary according to the type of computerized point-of-sale terminal in use.

The cashier should separate the receipts into two categories: guest checks that were paid by cash or check, and guest checks paid by credit or debit card. After each group is totaled, the amounts should be written in lines 1 and 2 on the cashier's report (Table 16-2). Both categories are added together on line 3 to ascertain total receipts for the shift. Lines 4 and 5 compare the total of the guest checks paid by cash or check to the total of the cash and checks turned in. If there is a difference it must be adequately explained (see lines 6 and 7).

Table 16-1   Cash Turn-In Report

Date	1/11/XX		Department	Hamburger Hut
Day	Saturday		Cashier	Marie Sample
Shift	6:00 A.M. – 2:00 P.M.		Checked by	Manager

ITEM	NUMBER	AMOUNT
Beginning Bank		$ 250.00
Currency		
$ 100	0	0
$ 50	4	200.00
$ 20	19	380.00
$ 10	15	150.00
$ 5	18	90.00
$ 2	0	0
$ 1	7	7.00
Coin		
$ .25	10	2.50
$ .10	45	4.50
$ .05	21	1.05
$ .01	35	.35
Total Currency and Coin		$1,085.40
Checks	12	212.74
Subtotal		$1,298.14
Less Bank		250.00
Total Turn-In		$1,048.14

The second part of the process is to compare the cash collected with what the cash register or point-of-sale computer terminal reports should be present. The ending register reading is taken by a manager at the end of every shift and recorded on line 8. The register tape is removed from the cash register and immediately taken to the office. In the office, it is used for preparing the cashier's report. Next, the register reading must be determined. To calculate the register reading, the manager first takes the beginning reading, which was the previous shift's ending reading, and records it on line 9. This amount is subtracted from the current ending reading. The difference is the register reading, as shown on line 10. The register reading (line 11) is compared to the total receipts (line 12). Any difference (line 13) is explained on line 14.

Table 16-2   Cashier's Report

Date	1/11/XX	Department	Hamburger Hut
Day	Saturday	Cashier	Marie Sample
Shift	6:00 A.M. – 2:00 P.M.	Prepared by	Manager

(1)	Total Cash Guest Checks		$1,048.19
(2)	Total Charged Guest Checks		+ 231.53
(3)	Total Receipts		$1,279.72
(4)	Total Cash Guest Checks		1,048.19
(5)	Total Cash Turned In		1,048.14
(6)	Difference		$ (– .05) (plus/minus)
(7)	Reason for difference	Error in making change	

Register Reading

(8)	Ending Reading	002115418
(9)	Beginning Reading	– 001987424
(10)	Difference	1,279.94

Register Reading to be Taken by Department Manager Only

(11)	Register Reading	$1,279.94
(12)	Total Receipts	1,279.72
(13)	Difference	$ (– .22) (plus/minus)
(14)	Reason for difference Overring	

The cashier's report checks the accuracy of the cashier. It not only analyzes shift receipts, but also detects mistakes made by the cashier. The difference amounts should be small and always followed by an acceptable reason. If the reason is not acceptable, management should take immediate corrective action.

RECOMMENDED CASH HANDLING PROCEDURE

The following cash handling procedure is a recommended standard for every cashier:

1. Take the guest check from the customer. Sincerely inquire as to the quality of the food and service.

2. Look at the guest check and tell the customer the total amount. For example, a guest check with a balance of $13.95 should be verbalized, "Thirteen dollars and ninety-five cents."

3. Repeat the amount that the customer tenders. If the customer gives the cashier a $20.00 bill, the cashier should state, "Thirteen ninety-five out of twenty dollars."

4. Put the amount given on the cash register ledge.

5. Ring the sale by first entering the amounts of each food and beverage item if using a traditional cash register system. A point-of-sale system may require only pushing a single button for a menu item to be recorded.

6. Make change by counting upward from the total of the check. The cashier would say, "Thirteen ninety-five, fourteen, fifteen, twenty." As the cashier states these amounts, he or she hands back a nickel, a one-dollar bill, and a five-dollar bill.

7. Put the amount given (the $20.00 bill) into the cash register drawer after giving the guest the change, remembering to always keep the cash register drawer closed between customers.

When a customer believes that the correct change was not given, either the manager or cashier must assess the need to correctly collect what is owed to the foodservice operation against risking the loss of a valuable customer. Often, if the discrepancy is five dollars or less, the policy is to take the customer's word for it and give the person the change he or she requested, considering any losses as good public relations. If the amount in dispute is larger, the cashier should take the customer's name, complete address, and telephone number. Then the cashier should explain to the customer that the office will check the cash balances and cash register readings at the end of the day and will immediately be in contact.

During any rush time, human error is apt to occur in terms of an **overring** or **underring** on the cash register. Should this occur, the recommended procedure is to re-ring the guest check correctly. On a separate sheet of paper, the error should be listed and recorded with the guest check number as well as the signatures of the cashier and manager.

PREVENTING THE ACCEPTANCE OF BAD CHECKS

Every foodservice operation should establish a check-cashing policy that protects the business and is friendly to the customer. Customer relations are important and nothing is more humiliating and irritating to a customer than to have his or her check rejected. The following is a sample policy that could be adjusted to fit just about any local situation:

1. A sign should be posted in a conspicuous place that states the check-cashing policy. The sign is a public notice that informs everyone of the rules and protects the operation from discrimination lawsuits.

2. Only local checks should be accepted. Each foodservice operation will have to define what is considered local. For some it may be just the city, for others the county, and still others the state.

3. Required forms of identification should be stated, such as a driver's license, check guarantee card, and so on.

4. Checks should be accepted for the amount of purchase only, plus tip.

Overring
Describes when a cashier rings a higher amount than the sale on a cash register or point-of-sale terminal.

Underring
Describes when a cashier rings a lower amount than the sale on a cash register or point-of-sale terminal.

5. Collection fees should be indicated, such as $25.00 or whatever is required.

6. Two-party or endorsed checks should not be accepted.

Besides the items mentioned in the check-cashing policy, some things cashiers should look out for when accepting a check are the following:

- That the date written on the check is the same as the day the check is written. Do not accept post-dated checks.

- That the "Pay to the Order Of" line has the name of the foodservice operation written or stamped on it. (If a large number of checks are accepted, a stamp with the foodservice operation's name should be near the cash register for easy use by the cashier.)

- That the amount written in the dollar area is the same as the amount written on the dollars line.

- That the check is signed.

When accepting a check, look at it to verify that:

- It has at least one perforated edge.

- It is numbered.

- It is printed using magnetic ink, which appears dull.

Features of an acceptable check are demonstrated in Figure 16-1. If the foodservice operation processes a substantial number of checks, a convenient way to add further safety is to use a check verification machine. The cashier simply runs the check through the machine, enters the amount of the check, and the check service will send a signal with a code number indicating whether the check is acceptable or not acceptable.

ACCEPTING TRAVELER'S CHECKS

Traveler's checks
A type of check that can be used by the person who buys them from a financial institution such as a bank.

Traveler's checks represent another form of payment. People often use them when traveling because they are insured against loss or being stolen. Using traveler's checks is a protection for those who buy them. When the check is purchased, it is signed by the person purchasing the check. When the check is redeemed or used to purchase goods and services, the check is signed again. The double signature is a control or protection that the check is original and that the person cashing it is the owner.

The cashier should check the signatures and make certain they are the same. The traveler's check should be signed in the presence of the cashier. If the check is already signed, the cashier should ask the guest to sign a piece of paper and then compare all of the signatures to verify that they are the same. In addition, the cashier may want to check some other form of identification.

PROPER CREDIT AND DEBIT CARD PROCEDURES

Credit card discount
A fee paid by foodservice operations to financial institutions for processing credit and debit card transactions.

Credit cards are the predominant method of payment in many foodservice operations. Accepting credit cards involves understanding the costs of accepting cards and credit card processing procedures. Financial institutions that support the use of credit cards earn their money by charging the foodservice operation a fee. The amount of the fee, called a **discount**, depends upon the

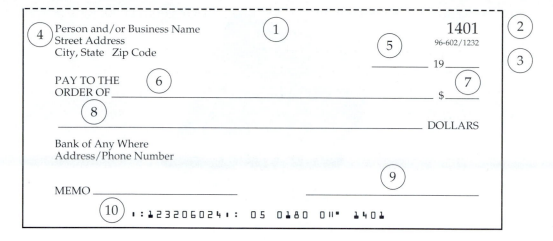

1. All checks should have at least one perforated edge.

2. Checks should be individually numbered.

3. Bank routing numbers should correspond with the bank identification number located on the bottom left corner of the check.

4. The name of the person or business should be printed on the check. Preferably, a street address and phone number should be present. Only local checks should be accepted.

5. The date of purchase should be written on the check; no post-dated checks should be accepted.

6. Checks should be made out to the foodservice operation. Do not accept checks made out to someone or another company. No two-party checks should be accepted.

7. Checks should be made out only for the amount of purchase plus tip.

8. The amount written in words should be the same as the amount written in numbers.

9. Checks should be signed and the signature should be compared to another source of identification as protection for both the person who is writing the check and the foodservice operation.

10. The ink that is to be used to print the bank numbers at the bottom of the check is typically dull.

FIGURE 16-1
Features of an Acceptable Check

negotiated arrangement that the foodservice operation has with the bank and the credit card company. State restaurant associations often offer negotiated discount fees to their members, although most independent foodservice operations are subject to the standard fee schedule being offered at any given time.

In today's high-tech world, credit card authorization terminals (also known as *merchant machines*) are used by nearly all foodservice operations (see Figure 16-2). These terminals offer the opportunity to complete the credit transaction electronically. These machines check the credit card to ensure that it is not stolen, verify that the credit card holder is authorized to charge the amount being tendered, and electronically deposit the amount of the transaction, less the discount fee, into the merchant's checking account.

Typically the transaction occurs as follows: The cashier takes the guest's credit card and passes it through the slot. The magnetic code on the card identifies the credit card number. The cashier enters the amount of the guest check

FIGURE 16-2
Credit Card Authorization Terminal The Express 3200 is a versatile terminal for restaurants, retailers, travel agencies, and cruise lines. It provides quick authorization and submission of charges made on all major credit cards. An easy-to-read two-line lighted display provides helpful prompts that guide personnel through the entire transaction process.

into the terminal. The terminal identifies the merchant's account number. Once the transaction is approved, the terminal is automatically signaled to print the charge receipt. The customer simply signs the receipt, which also doubles as a voucher. The receipt/voucher is placed in the cash drawer and is treated with the same security precautions as cash. The customer will also be given a copy of the receipt.

Credit card voucher
A paper receipt that is used to record a sale made to a customer using a credit card.

Employees should be taught that **credit card vouchers** (also known as *tickets*) are as important as cash. They are the only record of the transaction, and there is always the possibility that the financial institution may not credit the foodservice operation's account properly. Most important, the vouchers are counted along with the checks and cash to compare against the totals report on the cash register or point-of-sale terminal.

If the operation does not use a credit card authorization machine, a voucher must be filled out by hand. The credit card must be checked to see if it is stolen. This usually requires that the foodservice operator call a designated number to receive verbal approval and an authorization number that must be entered on the voucher. Once approval has been received, the voucher is run though a hand-operated or electromechanical device. The voucher is filled out and signed.

Debit card
A card that looks exactly like a credit card; charges made using a debit card are subtracted from the cardholder's checking account at the end of the day's business.

Debit cards are treated the same as credit cards. A **debit card** allows the guest to pay for the meal as if writing a check, except that a card is used. Processing debit cards is the same as processing credit cards. Foodservice operators are charged a fee for accepting debit cards just as with credit cards.

To avoid problems with accepting stolen cards, the cashier could ask guests to write their phone number on the voucher and check the signature on the voucher against another form of identification. If there is a dispute or problem later, the number allows a manager to contact the guest quickly and resolve the problem.

As with checks, cashiers should ask to see another form of identification that has a signature. Compare the signature on the identification with that on the credit voucher and on the back of the credit card. Also, always check to see whether the credit card has expired. All credit cards have the expiration dates imprinted on them.

Credit card fraud is a serious problem. To ensure that the foodservice operation is not victimized, cashiers should be trained to check credit cards that are tendered for the following symptoms of being bogus:

- blurred holograms
- glue on the edges
- numbers changed, such as 3 to 8 or 5 to 6
- misaligned numbers

All of these are indications of possible credit card tampering.

THE COST OF CREDIT CARDS

Foodservice operations are charged a discount fee for every credit card transaction processed. The fee for some cards may be fixed, such as a flat 3 percent of the total amount of every voucher processed. Thus, a foodservice operation with a 3 percent discount would pay a $.60 fee to the credit card company for a $20.00 transaction ($20.00 X .03 = $.60). Others have a sliding scale based upon the dollar amount of an individual transaction.

Another option used is the average dollar amount per foodservice transaction. If the average transaction is $50.00, a rate of 3 percent might be used; if the average is $30.00, a rate of 4 percent might be used; and so on. Discounts typically do not go below 1.65 percent.

Not all banks and credit card companies are the same. Rates and costs should always be compared. Foodservice operators may find the best deal available through a professional association, such as a state restaurant association that contracts with a bank for a large volume of business.

Daily Sales Control

The **daily sales report** is a daily sales record used for review and analysis. It also can be used as a permanent accounting record. The daily sales report (Table 16-3) begins with the department name (for larger foodservice operations having more than one unit within the operation). This is followed by the shift number and cash register readings. The register readings are taken from the cashier's report along with the total receipts including cash and charges. The over and short amounts are also listed. Finally, the sales breakdown includes the total sales, food sales, and bar sales (where liquor is served). The totals are taken for each department, as well as the final totals for the entire foodservice operation. It is important to recognize that many cash registers that include computerized functions can generate a very extensive detailed analysis of sales.

The daily sales report shown reports the activity for three shifts in two departments that occurred in one day. Two different cash registers were used.

Daily sales report
A daily sales record used for review and analysis.

Table 16-3 Daily Sales Report

Date 1/11/XX
Day Saturday
Weather Rain

Page 1 of 1
Prepared by Clerical
Approved by Owner/Manager

DEPARTMENT	SHIFT	REGISTER READINGS			TOTAL RECEIPTS			OVER OR OR SHORT	SALES BREAKDOWN		
		ENDING READING	BEGINNING READING	DIFFERENCE	CASH	CHARGE	TOTAL		TOTAL SALES	FOOD SALES	BAR SALES
Hambrgr Hut	1	2115418	1987424	1,279.94	1,048.14	231.53	1,279.67	(.27)	1,279.94	1,179.44	100.50
	2	2213465	2115418	980.47	784.38	196.09	980.47	—	980.47	900.47	80.00
Dept. Total			2,260.41		1,832.52	427.62	2,260.14	(.27)	2,260.41	2,079.91	180.50
Terrace D.R.	1	3738651	3535221	2,034.30	406.80	1,617.27	2,024.07	(10.23)	2,034.30	1,925.25	109.05
TOTALS				4,294.71	2,239.32	2,044.89	4,284.21	(10.50)	4,294.71	4,005.16	289.55

The Hamburger Hut department has two shifts and the Terrace Dining Room department has one shift. Once the day's business has ended, the daily sales report is completed and the manager is assured that cash, charges, and accountability for overs or shorts have been finalized. An example of a computer-generated daily sales report is shown in Figure 16-3.

Introduction to Guest Service Accounting

The cycle of guest service accounting begins when the guest places an order and ends when the manager or bookkeeper reconciles the cash register amounts with the guest checks. The distinguishing difference between commercial foodservice operations (restaurants) and noncommercial foodservice operations (institutional foodservice operations) is the timing and method of ordering meals and paying for those meals. Restaurants normally collect payment for food and service at the time they are rendered. Institutional foodservice operations (schools, health care facilities, and so on) commonly collect for food and service after they are rendered or during a specific billing period. Institutional foodservice operations typically do not collect for food and service at the time of the meal.

Guest checks are used in restaurants to record information on what the guests order. In most institutional foodservice operations, there are no guest checks, as food selections are usually based upon a limited offering of food items. Given the differences between commercial and noncommercial foodservice operations, the focus here will be upon commercial accounting of guest checks.

The cycle of guest accounting in restaurants is illustrated in Figure 16-4. The cycle usually involves the following steps:

1. The waitperson is issued guest checks if a manual system is used, or is granted access to a computer terminal or point-of-sale terminal to order food from the kitchen.

2. The order is taken from the customer.

3. The order is delivered to the kitchen either manually or electronically.

4. The guest check is delivered to the guest; with electronic systems it is in the form of a printout.

5. The guest pays the total amount on the guest check.

There are many variations of this cycle, depending upon the type of restaurant concept. For instance, the guest may make a selection using a **menu board**, which is common in fast-food restaurants. The order may be entered into a computer terminal (point-of-sale terminal) while being taken by the waitperson/cashier. The kitchen receives a printout of the order as soon as the cashier presses the Enter button on the terminal, and the guest pays for the order at the time the order is placed. The order is then assembled and delivered by the waitperson, who calls out the order number until the

Guest check
A form used to record guest food orders and prices, total sales to guests, and request food from the kitchen.

Menu board
A sign that may be made of several different types of materials on which the menu is recorded.

Daily System Sales Detail
Mike Rose Cafe - Beltsville, MD

NEAL MAHAFFEY

Printed on Monday, December 09, XXXX - 11:57 AM

Friday   09/27/ XXXX

Net Sales	18,895.07	Returns	0	0.00
+Service Charge	1,705.03	Voids	84	-296.01
+Tax Collected	947.22	Credit Total		-23.10
=Total Revenue	21,547.32	Change Grand Ttl		22,180.51
		Rounding Total		0.00
Item Discount	0.00	Grand Total		22,180.51
+Subtotal Discount	-314.08	Training Total		0.00
=Total Discounts	-314.08	Mgr Voids	0	0.00
		Error Corrects	285	1,018.85
		Cancel	134	289.26

Gross Receipts	19,168.82		
Charged Receipts	3,038.20		
		Carried Over	0	0.00
Service Charges	935.46	+Checks Begun	1,117	21,547.32
+Charged Tips	762.27	-Checks Paid	1,116	21,475.93
+Tips Declared	0.00	=Outstanding	1	71.39
=Total Tips 8.86%	1,697.73		
Tips Paid	1,697.73		
Tips Due	0.00		

Order Type	Net Sales	% of Ttl	Checks	% of Ttl	Avg/Chk	Guests	% of Ttl	Avg/Guest
1 - Dine In	18,588.52	98.38%	1,094	97.94%	16.99	1,217	97.67%	15.27
2 - To Go	306.55	1.62%	23	2.06%	13.33	29	2.33%	10.57
Total	18,895.07		1,117		16.92	1,246		15.16

Tables	% of Ttl	Avg/Tbl	Turn Time
46	93.88%	404.10	0.62
3	6.12%	102.18	1.64
49		385.61	

1 - System Tracking

	Count	Value
Food	4,220	12,066.90
Less To Go	0	306.55
Total Food	0	0.00
Liquor	1,640	4,809.88
Beer	458	1,197.62
Wine	188	725.48
Soft Beverage	595	409.27
Total Liquor	0	0.00
Gift Certificates	0	0.00
Novelties	0	0.00
Liquor Issue	0	0.00
+ To Go	0	306.55
	0	0.00
Food Tax	0	611.89
Subtotal	7,101	20,434.14

	Count	Value
Beverage Tax	0	335.33
	0	0.00
Charged Tip	95	762.27
15% Gratuity	124	942.76
Non Rev Svc Chg	0	0.00
	0	0.00
Less Discounts	54	-314.08
	0	0.00
100% Discount	7	-57.35
60% Employee Meal	12	-45.78
40% Employee Meal	1	-2.46
40% Employee Comp	0	0.00
20% Coupon	0	0.00
Dead Food	23	-157.54
Subtotal	316	1,463.15

	Count	Value
Dead Liquor	11	-50.95
20% Teacher	0	0.00
Barter	0	0.00
House 10	0	0.00
House 11	0	0.00
House 12	0	0.00
House 13	0	0.00
House 14	0	0.00
House 15	0	0.00
House 16	0	0.00
House 17	0	0.00
Cash	995	15,404.93
Less Tips	218	1,697.73
Cash Due	0	0.00
Subtotal	1,224	17,051.71

FIGURE 16-3
Computer-Generated Point-of-Sale Printout   *Courtesy of Micros.*

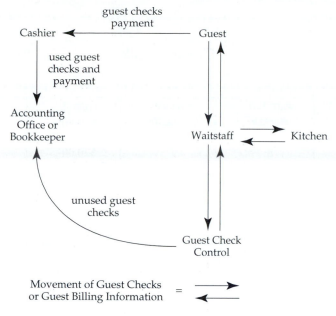

FIGURE 16-4
Cycle of Guest Accounting

guest identifies himself or herself as having placed the order. The accounting cycle will be explained in more detail as follows.

Taking the Guest Order in a Restaurant with Waitstaff

Waitstaff or counterpersons are the sales force of any restaurant. How the order should be taken by the waitstaff is itemized by the service system chart presented in Chapter 14. Waitstaff should use sales techniques such as suggestive selling to enhance the guest's experience and increase sales. Sales are recorded on customer guest checks by the waitperson. The order must be taken accurately and communicated clearly to the kitchen staff. The guest check represents the customer's order and bill.

Guest checks may take many different forms. Traditionally, they are thought of as a form similar to the one in Figure 16-5. Another typical format is a form with a preprinted menu on it. Yet another method is a point-of-sale terminal with a keyboard coded with the menu or a hand-held computer terminal. There are many possibilities.

HOW TO USE CUSTOMER GUEST CHECKS

Even though the manual use of customer guest checks is on the decline, reviewing a manual system makes the process of billing the guest for menu items easier to understand. The customer guest check is also the itemized food and beverage bill that is presented to the customer for payment. Therefore, it must be presented in a clear, concise, and correct manner. The guest check, manual or electronic, is typically divided into sections that include the following (see Figure 16-5):

```
************************************************************

                    Guest Check

************************************************************
```

TABLE NUMBER	WAITSTAFF NUMBER	NUMBER OF GUESTS	CHANGE AMOUNT	CHECK 37201
21	8	2	$20.00	
1	Cheeseburger Deluxe			5.25
1	Chef's Salad			5.95
2	Lg. Coke			1.98
1	Apple Pie			2.50
1	Cherry Pie			2.50
			Total	18.18
			Tax	1.09
			Total Amount	19.27

Guest Check

TABLE NUMBER	WAITSTAFF NUMBER	NUMBER OF GUESTS	TOTAL AMOUNT	CHECK 37201
21	8	2	$19.27	

FIGURE 16-5
Guest Check

1. The *table number* helps the waitstaff associate the order with the given restaurant tables. Some food delivery systems require that the first available waitperson pick up the order and deliver it to the guest. The only way the waitperson would know to what table to deliver the food is if a table number is indicated on the guest check.

2. The *waitstaff number* identifies the waitperson who wrote the information on the guest check. This helps to track sales by individual waitstaff members. It also allows the manager to measure performance.

3. The *number of guests* helps the waitperson in taking the customer orders. It helps the manager keep track of total customer counts (often referred to as covers). This data is essential for determining productivity of both the kitchen staff and the waitstaff. The information is also used for tracking promotional efforts and as a general barometer of how well the restaurant is doing.

4. The *change amount* being recorded will help reduce the risk of making improper change. In Figure 16-5, the customer paid the check with a $20.00 bill; that amount is written in the change amount box. The customer is less likely to receive incorrect change. Restaurants can easily lose money if cashiers and waitstaff are not careful in how they make change. The type of guest check depicted is especially useful to foodservice operations where waitstaff also carry a bank and act as their own cashier.

5. The *check number* is used to control the issuance of guest checks. Each guest check is sequentially numbered. Each waitperson is responsible for every assigned check. At the end of every shift, the checks are put into sequential order and individually accounted for.

6. The middle section of the guest check is for recording the quantity, item description, and price. How the order is written helps the waitperson to deliver the food in the proper manner and to ensure that guests receive what they order. Trained and experienced waitstaff write the order in such a manner that they can easily identify each guest in a party's specific order. If every waitperson in the restaurant uses the same system, all waitstaff are interchangeable with regard to picking up the order and serving the guest.

7. The bottom part of the guest check, the *stub*, will usually be torn along the perforated edge as the guest's copy of the check. Most of the information that appears on the heading of the check is also recorded on the customers' receipt.

The procedural use and control of customer guest checks will vary according to the policy of management, but the following should be accomplished:

- All guest checks should be tightly controlled. All checks should be accounted for and kept in a secured and locked area. The only people who should have access to guest checks are the manager, head waitperson, or cashier. These individuals have full responsibility for issuing guest checks to the waitstaff.

- The waitstaff should be instructed to write in ink, which will make any erasure difficult. Should a mistake occur in writing the customer's order, a single line should be drawn through the mistake, and the manager or head waitperson should initial the error.

Several systems can be used in placing the orders with the kitchen. One method is through the use of a **dupe** (duplicate) **pad**. A dupe pad is a pad of order checks that are sequentially numbered and issued to the waitstaff. The waitperson writes the initial order on the dupe pad, submits it to the kitchen for preparation, and recopies it onto the guest check for the customer.

Both the dupe check and the guest check are compared for accuracy at the end of every shift. This system is typically used in large restaurants when there is more than one cook's station. An example would be as follows: If a customer orders a prime rib dinner along with a shrimp cocktail appetizer, one dupe check goes to the appetizer/salad prep cook; then as the customer is served the appetizer, a second dupe check goes to the hot-food cook, allowing smooth and timely service (see Figure 16-6).

Dupe pad
A pad of order checks that are numbered in sequence and used in submitting orders to the kitchen.

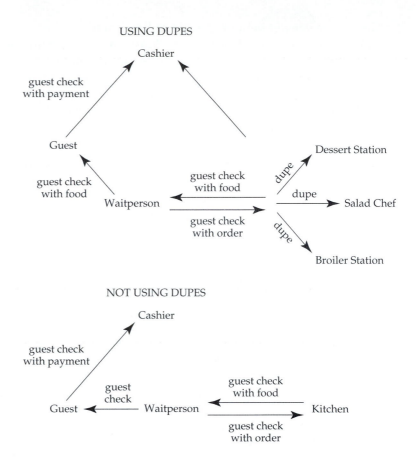

USING DUPES

Cashier

guest check
with payment

Guest

guest check
with food

Waitperson

guest check
with food

guest check
with order

dupe

dupe

dupe

Dessert Station

Salad Chef

Broiler Station

NOT USING DUPES

Cashier

guest check
with payment

Guest

guest
check

Waitperson

guest check
with food

guest check
with order

Kitchen

FIGURE 16-6
Two Guest Check Systems   Because of their importance, the dupes should be monitored using a guest check control process.

Another method would be through the use of a two-copy order, with the original going to the customer and the copy remaining with the cook. This is conveniently done with NCR (no carbon required) paper. The traditional one-copy method is most often used, serving both the kitchen (for the order) and the customer (for the bill).

Finally, many excellent computer-generated ordering and guest check writing systems are available for all types of foodservice operations. These systems are most effective. Figure 16-9 shows an example of that type of system. One of the key differences between a manual system and a computerized system is that in the latter, the computer application software generates guest check numbers only when an order is input using a keyboard; thus the need for tracking guest check numbers is eliminated.

CONTROLLING CUSTOMER GUEST CHECKS

Guest check daily record
A form used to track the use of customer guest checks by the waitstaff.

The **guest check daily record**, as shown in Table 16-4, serves to control the issue and use of customer guest checks. The waitstaff names are recorded along with an assigned waitstaff number. The use of the number system allows speed in writing for the waitperson and ease in identifying a waitperson with a customer guest check.

The beginning check number is the very first number in the book of guest checks, which will be either a new book or one that has previously been

Table 16-4 Guest Check Daily Record

Department Hamburger Hut			Page 1 of 1			
Day Monday			Prepared by Manager			
Date 1/13/XX						

WAITSTAFF NAME	WAITSTAFF NUMBER	BEGINNING CHECK NUMBER	ENDING CHECK NUMBER	NUMBER OF CHECKS USED	NUMBER BY ACTUAL COUNT	NUMBER OF MISSING CHECKS	WAITSTAFF SIGNATURE
Ann Waitress	4	0147	0199	52	52	0	Ann Waitress
Mary Waitress	2	0233	0276	43	43	0	Mary Waitress
Jack Waiter	1	0519	0591	72	71	1 walk out	Jack Waiter
Sue Waitress	7	0315	0373	58	58	0	Sue Waitress

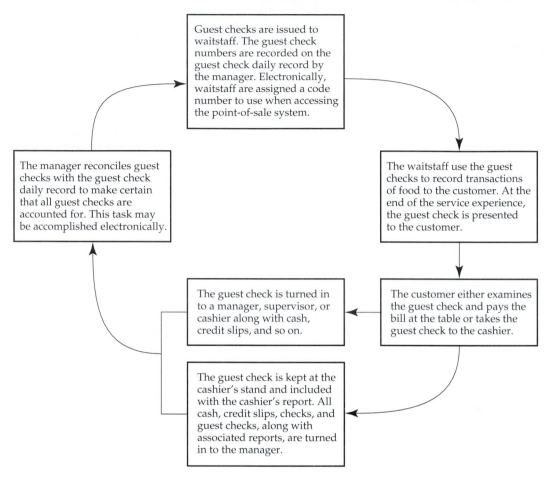

FIGURE 16-7
Guest Check Control System

in use but has remaining blank checks. The beginning check number is the number of the last check that is returned by the waitperson at the end of the preceding scheduled shift. That number is recorded, and then the beginning check number will be subtracted from that ending number to determine the number of checks used.

The number by actual count is then compared to the number of checks used to identify any missing checks, as in the case of the customer walkout shown in Table 16-4.

Finally, the waitperson signature indicates that he or she has taken the responsibility for the guest checks issued. The guest check daily record is usually kept by the manager, a head waitperson, or a cashier who is responsible for guest check control. The process is illustrated in Figure 16-7.

This entire process becomes unnecessary when a foodservice operation uses computers. The application software in the computer tracks guest checks by using a guest check or transaction number. What was known as a guest check number may also become a transaction number in a computer. Security is provided through proper access to the computer. Only those with passwords or codes are allowed access to the computer. An example of a computer-generated guest check daily record is shown in Figure 16-8.

```
                              Employee Open Guest Checks                              Bruno The Manager
                              MICROS Systems - Bar & Grille
                                                             Printed on May 13, XXXX - 8:23 PM

Check      Table/Group   Guests   Check ID   Open Date & Time    Subtotal   Tax Total   Svc Total   Payment Total

1 Phoebe
  975          1/1         4                 05/13 - 8:20pm          8.75       0.44        0.00         0.00
  976          4/1         4                 05/13 - 8:20pm        192.85       9.16        0.00         0.00
  977          1/2         4                 05/13 - 8:21pm         35.40       1.77        0.00         0.00
         Employee Total   12                          3           237.00      11.37        0.00         0.00

2 Chandler
  978          1/3         4                 05/13 - 8:22pm         40.25       0.20        0.00         0.00
         Employee Total    4                          1            40.25       0.20        0.00         0.00

3 Rachel
  979         78/1         4                 05/13 - 8:22pm          6.25       0.31        0.00         0.00
         Employee Total    4                          1             6.25       0.31        0.00         0.00

5 Ross
  980         47/1         4                 05/13 - 8:22pm         26.85       1.34        0.00         0.00
         Employee Total    4                          1            26.85       1.34        0.00         0.00

6 Monica
  981         44/1         4                 05/13 - 8:22pm         91.05       4.56        0.00         0.00
         Employee Total    4                          1            91.05       4.56        0.00         0.00

11 Joey
   314                     0                 05/13 - 1:32pm          0.00       0.00        0.00         0.00
         Employee Total    0                          1             0.00       0.00        0.00         0.00

         Grand Total      28                          8           401.40      17.78        0.00         0.00
```

FIGURE 16-8
Computer Generated Guest Check Daily Record   *Courtesy of Micros.*

BALANCING AND THE CYCLE OF GUEST SERVICE ACCOUNTING

Guest check control, either manually or electronically, offers three major benefits. First, it assists in the balancing of food ordered by the guest and food produced by the kitchen. It assists in the necessary accounting for every bit of food produced by the kitchen. The food ordered by the waitstaff should be the food delivered to the guest. Sometimes, waitstaff and kitchen staff want to give away food to guests or friends. The amount of food given away needs to be accounted for regardless of whether it is for guests or friends. The process of using guest checks helps to prevent food from being given away.

Second, an effective guest check control system prevents theft by guests and employees. Without guest checks, orders would be called in and delivered to a guest without accountability. Lack of accountability enables the waitperson to serve food to a guest and keep the money paid by the guest. The waitperson would be able to give away food as an inducement for a larger tip. Also, without the use of guest checks, employees would be able to eat whatever they wanted with no accountability.

Source document
A document used to initiate an accounting process.

Third, an effective guest check control system helps to track the flow of all food and beverages. The guest check is a **source document** used in the accounting process to track total sales, individual sales, and productivity. The guest check also is used to help track inventory and waste. As a source document, it is essential for keeping a set of accounts.

Special Controls for Beverage Service

There are many ways to lose control of a beverage operation. Controlling how the beverage order is processed is essential for lounges and bars if they are to be successful.

At a minimum, guest checks should be used for beverage service, and all beverages prepared by a bartender should have a guest check. All beverages should be paid for when they are served, and a **tab** should be granted only if a guest has a credit card imprinted or pays in advance.

Tab
A form of credit whereby a waitperson does not collect payment for alcoholic beverages until the person is through being served.

SUMMARY

1. Proper recording of sales, cash, and credit, as well as guest check control, is vital to the success of any foodservice operation.

2. Sales are monitored using traditional cash registers, electronic registers, or a point-of-sale computer system.

3. Cash from the register is monitored by using a cash turn-in report. To ensure that cash handling is done properly, a seven-step procedure is recommended. Cashiers should be trained to avoid accepting bad checks, bad traveler's checks, or stolen credit or debit cards.

4. Credit card sales are monitored 90 percent of the time by special credit card authorization terminals that authorize the purchase and credit the user's account. The dollar amount is automatically deposited into the foodservice operation's account, minus the discount, at the end of each business day. If the foodservice operation is not using a credit card authorization terminal (merchant

FIGURE 16-9
Point-of-Sale System Terminal The system combines point-of-sale capabilities, such as order transfer to kitchen and tracking sales data, with information that can monitor sales, employee scheduling, manage production, control costs, and so on. *Courtesy of Micros.*

machine), the credit card voucher is treated the same as a check for depositing into the foodservice operation's account. Debit cards are treated in the same manner as credit cards.

5. Sales are monitored using a daily sales report. A daily sales report lists the information from cash register readings to ascertain sales, which have been categorized into cash and charge sales. Also, sales are monitored according to whether they are food or beverage sales.

6. Sales made to guests are monitored by using guest checks, which list the items purchased by guests. Checks are electronically or manually created. Manual guest checks are managed using a guest check daily record. The guest check daily record monitors waitstaff use of guest checks. Guest checks are important for performing accurate service accounting, preventing theft, measuring productivity, tracking sales, controlling inventory, and preventing waste.

KEY CONCEPTS

Cashier's report	Guest check daily record
Cash turn-in report	Menu board
Credit card discount	Overring
Credit card voucher	Source document
Daily sales report	Tab
Debit card	Traveler's checks
Dupe pad	Underring
Guest check	

DISCUSSION QUESTIONS AND EXERCISES

1. On Monday, 1/13/XX, the following information was taken from the cash register:

   a. Ending register reading for Monday, shift 1, was 8870844.

   b. Ending register reading for Monday, shift 2, was 8974863.

   c. Total cash guest checks were $430.02.

   d. Total charge guest checks were $610.19.

   e. Total cash in the register, less the opening bank amount, was $429.02.

   Complete a cashier's report for the second shift, 2:00 P.M. to 10:00 P.M. (See Appendix A for a blank form.) After completing the cashier's report, explain how you did your work.

2. List what some of the probable causes of overages and shortages could be.

3. Role-play the following scenario: The customer has just brought a guest check for $34.72 to the cashier. The customer tenders a $50.00 bill as he or she approaches the cashier stand. How would you complete the transaction?

   Three people need to participate: an observer, a customer, and a cashier. The role of the observer is to make notes regarding the role-playing situation. After the role-play, the observer should comment on what he or she saw and make comments on whether the situation represented a valid way of handling the customer. The criteria for success are outlined in the text in the section that discusses the recommended cash handling procedure.

4. Teach a fellow student what to look out for so that he or she will not be victimized by credit card fraud.

5. Explain the value of using a daily sales report.

6. Teach another person the principles of guest service accounting.

7. Why should the waitperson always use a guest check to take an order from a guest?

8. How would you train a waitperson to complete a guest check?

9. Describe what a typical cycle of guest accounting may be like in a full-service, fine-dining restaurant.

10. Describe at least two different kinds of guest check systems that may be used.

11. How can technology help foodservice operations be more efficient in taking food orders from guests?

12. How does an operation control the issuance and use of guest checks?

13. How does a manager balance the use of checks to ensure their proper use?

14. What special considerations should be thought of regarding the serving of alcoholic beverages?

17

Pricing and Sales Forecasts

Learning Objectives

After reading this chapter and completing the discussion questions and exercises, you should able to:

1. Identify what the competition offers their customers.
2. Use market prices to establish menu prices.
3. Use the food (or beverage) cost percentage and contribution methods of pricing.
4. Treat special pricing situations separately from pricing the balance of the menu.
5. Understand the consequences of pricing the menu on future sales.

About Pricing and Sales Forecasts

Successful foodservice managers consistently monitor menu pricing as a part of competing for customers. Along with quality food and good customer service, a foodservice operation must always be competitively priced.

A fair price/value perception needs to exist for customers to remain loyal as well as to attract new customers. This is particularly true within the fast-food segment of the foodservice industry, which strongly competes for customers.

Many communities have a large number of fast-food restaurants, family restaurants, and buffets all competing for the same customer base, and each wanting to increase their market share. This means increasing their number of customers in relation to all potential customers that go to foodservice establishments in the market segment. Therefore, when menu items are similar in quality and in service presentation, price can become the dominant factor that affects the number of menu items sold. A pioneer in value pricing has been Taco Bell, as reflected in their rapid expansion and sales growth in recent years.

Foodservice operations are structured to do a specific dollar volume in sales per period of time—day, week, month, and so on—in order to remain profitable. When that volume can be increased, profits will usually increase accordingly. In the competitive environments in which most foodservice operations exist, effective pricing and sales forecasting are critical functions to remaining in business.

Considerations in Pricing a Menu

Pricing a menu
The process of establishing the prices to be charged for the food and beverage items listed on the menu.

Some of the toughest decisions a foodservice manager must make are made when **pricing a menu**. The term refers to the act of setting prices for items to be listed on a menu or changing the prices that are currently listed on the menu.

To properly price a menu, the following questions should be addressed:

- Who are the primary customers?
- What is the type of foodservice facility?
- Where is the foodservice facility located?
- Who are the competitors and how many are there?
- What method should be used for calculating a menu price?
- Are there any special pricing situations that should be considered?
- What are the projected consequences of pricing changes (that is, will sales increase or decrease and by what amounts)?
- What are the customers willing to pay for in relation to the type of food and service being offered?
- What other types of foodservice facilities are available in the area that offer a similar menu?

WHO ARE THE CUSTOMERS?

Foodservice establishments typically appeal to certain types of customers. For example, fast-food restaurants generally appeal to young families and those interested in a quick meal at an affordable price; buffets and cafeterias are attractive to senior citizens; a small ethnic restaurant may appeal to the residents of a certain neighborhood; a deli in an office building focuses on the needs of those who occupy the building; and health care foodservice caters to a variety of customers—doctors, allied health professionals, administrators, and patients.

To establish menu prices effectively, the specific needs of current and potential customers must be recognized. The deli in the office building may need to offer foods that appeal to the health-conscious office staff, along with large hefty sandwiches for the less health conscious, and all food must be available quickly for those with 30-minute lunch breaks. This type of planning is needed for all types of foodservice establishments, from the neighborhood family restaurant to the special-event, fine-dining restaurant to the contract foodservice operator in a manufacturing plant.

Foodservice managers must know their customers. This can be accomplished by answering the following questions:

- What kind of work do the customers do? The type of work that potential customers do implies that they have a certain income level. It also identifies the general attitude customers may have concerning eating out and the nature of their lifestyle.

- How much time do customers have to eat? Even fine-dining restaurants need to understand how long a customer has to eat. The longer the time available, the more cook-to-order food can be offered to customers who are willing to pay a higher price.

- How price sensitive are customers? Every location has a price threshold for meals. In one location it may be $5.00 for lunch and $10.00 for dinner. In another, the price threshold may be as high as $12.00 for lunch and $36.00 for dinner.

- How strong is the "take a lunch to work" attitude? Some communities have more people who brown-bag their lunches than do others. In these communities, a foodservice manager will need to assess whether a comfortable facility offering a dining experience will work, or whether to be "fast and limited" with takeout service offering very low prices.

- How far do customers have to travel to eat? If the selection of foodservice facilities is limited, the foodservice operation may be in the enviable position of being able to charge higher prices because other foodservice facilities are not conveniently located. The distance that people are willing to travel to eat depends upon how much time they have to eat, the purpose of the meal, and the price threshold of the location.

- Why do customers choose a particular place to eat? Most foodservice managers assume that they know why people eat in their establishments, but in fact those assumptions may not be correct. A type of foodservice establishment may be chosen because it provides a place to get out of the weather, or because it has clean restrooms. Various perceived values may affect the reasons people have for choosing a place to eat—reasons that are not known to the foodservice manager.

By answering these questions, foodservice managers can develop a business instinct for recognizing how much customers are willing to spend on food at their establishments. After understanding who the customers are and the factors that influence where the customers eat, the local competitive environment should be examined.

WHAT IS THE COMPETITION DOING?

A successful foodservice manager sets menu prices after examining what the competition is doing. To better understand the competition, the foodservice operator should conduct a **competitive analysis** that answers the following questions:

- What is the total demand for eating out in the competitive geographic area? The *competitive geographic area* is the area defined as that from which most customers originate. In small communities, this question is fairly easy to answer. In larger communities, it becomes more difficult

Competitive analysis
The process of determining the number of competitors and analyzing their strengths and weaknesses to discover opportunities.

Table 17-1   Customer Source Analysis

Location: Hyde Park	Tillamuck Village	14th to 16th between Congress & State	17th to 20th between Congress & State
⊠ ⊠ ⸱	⊠ ☐	⌐⸱	
Location: Out-of-town (in state)	Out-of-town (other state)		
Location:			
Location:			

Use the tally system illustrated in Figure 9-2 for tracking. Each dot and line represents one person. The dots are made into a square. A line is drawn between dots. A cross is made in the square. The ending symbol is ⊠ . This represents 10 people. In this example, the tallies in the first column represent 22 people. The second column represents 18 people. The third represents 6 people.

and requires an investment into doing some research. A relatively easy way to find out is to ask customers diplomatically where they live or work when they pay the guest check. The information gathered should then be categorized. An example of this is shown in Table 17-1. Obviously, institutional and contract foodservice operators usually have an easier time determining the source of their customers by using employment or enrollment data. Some foodservice operators have installed computer terminals for easy customer use that request the customer's name, address, telephone and/or fax number, birth date, anniversary date, and so on. The incentive for the customer to enter the information is to receive complimentary meals on personal holidays, and the like.

■ How many competitors exist? Once the trading area is determined, travel the area and identify the competitors. Most foodservice managers know who the competition is just by driving to work and consciously taking note.

■ What are competitors' **customer counts**? The only way to determine this information is to actually count the number of guests in a competitor's establishment. A reasonably accurate guess is acceptable. This can be accomplished by counting tables and booths and determining seating capacity, by actually eating at the competition and taking a physical cus-

Customer count
The number of customers that eat during a designated period of time, such as a meal period, day, week, month, or year.

tomer count during peak periods, and by checking the number of cars in the parking lot.

- What do competitors charge for similar items? This is probably the easiest information to obtain. All the foodservice manager needs to do is obtain a copy of a competitor's menu and compare prices by visiting the competitor as a customer and taking notes.

- What are the **signature items** of competitors? Signature items are menu items that distinguish competitors from each other. A McDonald's Big Mac is an example. Some foodservice establishments have desserts that distinguish their operation, some have appetizers, and still others may have a drink or service style. These items establish the uniqueness of a foodservice operation. Institutional foodservice operations also have signature items. For example, a hospital may serve steak dinners to couples with newborn infants. The price of a signature item provides a basis for understanding the pricing of high-demand menu items, because it will identify the price customers are willing to pay for the items.

Signature item
A menu item that is unique to a specific foodservice operation.

A tool that can help a foodservice manager is to complete a competitive analysis form (Table 17-2). This form is designed to give an overview of the competition. Read over the table before continuing. Assume that the Shamrock Inn's customers have requested meat loaf similar to that offered at the Toll House and at Murphy's. All management has to do is create a similar dish and offer it at a competitive price between $6.50 and $7.50. If the manager of Shamrock Inn wants to compete on a price basis to bring in more customers, he or she could offer it at less than $6.50. If management creates a signature item of meat loaf so that customers rave and go out of their way to eat the Shamrock Inn's famous meat loaf, the price may be established at $7.95. People will pay a premium for an item if they feel a value received.

If a new restaurant were to open in the same area as the Shamrock Inn, the Toll House, and Murphy's, the management of the new restaurant should recognize that pricing fettuccine at $12.00 is probably not going to work unless the restaurant is unique in design and location, perhaps with a spectacular view. Watching competitors' menus provides the information necessary to price a menu. If prices are in line with the amount of food being offered, customers generally will believe they are receiving a good value.

A good **value** is normally viewed as a relationship between the amount and quality of food and the price charged. Presenting a menu that will be perceived as having good values is subjective in nature and is often determined by what other successful foodservice operations are offering. Management should constantly monitor customer responses to the price/value perception by calculating the sales activity for each menu item, as discussed in Chapter 9.

Value
The relationship between the amount and quality of food received and the price paid.

How to Set a Menu Price

The menu price often determines how profitable a foodservice operation has the potential of becoming. There are essentially two methods that can be used to determine a menu price for a particular menu item. The first is the food (or beverage) cost percentage method and the second is the contribution method.

■ ■ ■ ■ ■
Table 17-2   Competitive Analysis Form

Prepared by   Manager _____   Date 1/13/XX _____

| | COMPETITOR | | |
ITEM	SHAMROCK INN	TOLL HOUSE	MURPHY'S
Chicken & Dumplings	$6.95	$7.50	$7.50
Poached Salmon Fillet	9.99	11.00	
Country Fried Steak	8.95	8.95	9.50
Meat Loaf		6.50	7.50
Yankee Pot Roast	8.95	9.95	7.95
Ravioli	7.95	7.25	7.25
Spaghetti	6.95	6.95	6.95
Fettuccine	8.50	9.00	9.00
Hamburgers	5.50	5.25	5.00
French Dip	6.25	6.00	6.00
Chicken Breast Sandwich	6.25	6.00	6.35
Roast Beef Sandwich	6.95	7.25	7.45
Hamburger Platter	5.00	5.25	5.50

FOOD (OR BEVERAGE) COST PERCENTAGE METHOD

The **food** (or beverage) **cost percentage method,** also known as the *cost as a percentage of sales method*, is based upon the presumption that costs should be maintained as a fixed percentage of sales. Simply stated, the relation between the amount of money spent on purchasing raw products and the sales revenues generated by converting raw products into final menu products should always be the same. If the food cost has been determined to be 25 percent and sales are expected to be $400, then the food cost should be $100 ($400 × .25 = $100). Regardless of the amount of sales, food costs should be 25 percent. If sales are $1,600, the expected food cost would be $400 ($1,600 × .25 = $400).

The food cost percentage is determined by the foodservice owner or manager. To price a menu using the food cost percentage method, the cost is divided by the established percentage. The price must be determined on each individual menu item. The cost is determined by completing a recipe cost chart (Table 7-2) and/or a plate cost chart (Table 7-7). By using these charts, the foodservice manager has a clear understanding of production costs and is able to quickly determine prices.

For example, if the plate cost chart indicates that the cost of a hamburger platter is $1.65, this amount should be divided by the desired food cost percentage. (See Table 17-3.) If 30 percent is the desired food cost percentage, the price of the hamburger platter should be $5.50 ($1.65 ÷ .30 = $5.50). This price is within the range of competitors (see Table 17-2), as competitors are offering this menu item from $5.00 to $5.50.

Likewise, if a foodservice operation sells hash browns as a side dish, the recipe cost chart would indicate the serving cost. The serving cost then would be divided by the desired food cost percentage. For example, if the recipe cost chart indicates that the serving cost for hash browns is $ .20 and the desired food cost percentage is 25 percent, then the menu price should be about $.95 ($.20 ÷ .25 = $.80, rounded up to $.95).

Foodservice operation owners or managers select a food cost percentage based upon two major factors. These factors are:

- *Market situation.* This is determined by answering the questions listed earlier in this chapter.

- *Overall costs of the foodservice operation.* The selected food cost percentage cannot be too high. If it is, there simply will not be enough funds to operate profitably. For example, if a food cost percentage of 45 percent is cho-

> **Food cost percentage method** The process of setting a menu price by dividing the food cost by the desired food cost percentage.

■ ■ ■ ■ ■
Table 17-3   Food Cost Percentage Method

COST	÷	DESIRED PERCENTAGE	=	PRICE (NOT ROUNDED)
.50	÷	.25	=	$2.00
.50	÷	.30	=	1.67
.50	÷	.35	=	1.43
.50	÷	.40	=	1.25
.50	÷	.45	=	1.11

Table 17-4   Income Statement

Period Ending __1/31/XX__

Sales				
Food sales		$40,000		80.0%
Beverage sales	+	10,000		20.0%
Total sales	=		$50,000	100.0%
Cost of sales				
Cost of food sold		$12,800		32.0%
Cost of beverages sold	+	2,200		22.0%
Total cost of sales	=		$15,000	30.0%
Controllable expenses				
Salaries and wages		$14,000		28.0%
Employee benefits	+	1,500		3.0%
Direct operating expenses	+	1,750		3.5%
Marketing	+	1,000		1.5%
Energy and utility service	+	2,250		4.5%
Administrative expenses	+	1,000		2.0%
Repairs and maintenance	+	1,500		3.0%
Total controllable expenses	=	+ 23,000		46.0%
Total cost of sales and controllable expenses		=	− 38,000	76.0%
Income before occupation costs, depreciation and interest			= $12,000	24.0%
Occupation costs				
Rent and other occupation costs			− 3,750	7.5%
Income before depreciation and interest			= $8,250	16.5%
Depreciation		$ 1,750		
Interest	+	1,000		
Total depreciation and interest	=		− 2,750	5.5%
Net income before taxes			= $5,500	11.0%
Income taxes			− 1,485	3.0%
Net income			= $4,015	8.0%

sen, and controllable and occupation costs are 60 percent, the foodservice operation is going to lose five cents on every dollar of revenue. If a food cost percentage of 15 percent is chosen, the cost of running the operation may appear to be very favorable, but the cost of the menu items might be so high that customers probably would not patronize the foodservice establishment.

Table 17-4 is an example of how a food cost percentage of 32 percent would appear on an income statement. Assume that the foodservice operation is a fast-food establishment and that the market situation may best be served by portion sizes that can be priced at 32 percent of sales. The foodservice owner or manager must decide whether the operation will be profitable at a 32 percent food cost percentage. The actual selection of a 32 percent food cost percentage may be described as follows:

- The National Restaurant Association is consulted. The association provides information on food cost percentages. Managers may assume that these national statistics can be used to help determine whether the decisions being made regarding food cost percentage are sound. Typical food cost percentages are shown in Table 2-1.

- After a percentage is selected, then the manager needs to estimate what the overall costs are going to be. In Table 17-4, a fast-food foodservice operation offers a limited menu and no table service. Accordingly, industry guidelines indicate that the food cost percentage should be between 30 and 39 percent. After examining the expected controllable expenses and occupation costs, the manager may decide that 32 percent is a reasonable food cost percentage goal. Therefore, all menu items will be priced at 32 percent or less.

- This food cost percentage goal of 32 percent will work only if the customer is receiving a perceived good value. The foodservice manager must price menu items and then inquire from customers whether they got enough to eat for the price paid and whether the food was to the customers' liking.

Chapter 18 presents tools that can be used to ascertain whether the customer is receiving a good value for the dollars spent. Also, as previously stated, the foodservice manager must determine whether the price of the menu item is competitive with others in the geographic location.

Setting Beverage Prices

The pricing process is the same for pricing alcoholic or nonalcoholic beverages. The cost of the drink is determined using a pour cost chart (Table 12-1). The pour cost example in Chapter 12 for a Pink Lady is $.662. If the beverage cost percentage goal is 20 percent, then the price of the Pink Lady should be $3.45 ($.662 ÷ .20 = $3.31, price rounded to $3.45).

Price Rounding Rules

A common rounding rule is that all prices should be just under half and whole dollars. Research has shown that people generally do not perceive much of a difference in the price between $4.25 and $4.45. In the Pink Lady example, the price could either be $3.31 or $3.45. The price difference is not enough to cause the buyer resistance to the price. The price selected will depend upon competition and the nature of the operation. If the choice is to round down, it should be kept in mind that there should be other menu items that have an opportunity to be rounded up. This decision is often based upon competitive market prices.

CONTRIBUTION METHOD

The term **contribution method** refers to the contribution that the sale of each menu item should make toward covering the production costs and profit.

Contribution method
The process of setting a menu price by adding the cost and profit associated with each customer to each menu item, except for single food items such as desserts or appetizers.

Table 17-5 Calculating Contribution

ITEM	DOLLAR AMOUNT
Gross food sales	$8,000.00
Cost of food sold	– 2,400.00
Gross profit (total contribution margin)	$5,600.00
Number of customers	÷ 2,000.00
Contribution cost	$ 2.80

How contribution as calculated is shown in Table 17-5. Basically, the foodservice manager must calculate how much each menu item should contribute to a predetermined profitability level of the operation. The contribution method is valuable for those who believe that profit should be treated as an expense to be covered by sales and not as the money left over after expenses.

The determination of menu prices can be explained by applying the contribution cost determined in Table 17-5 to the hamburger platter example. If the plate cost of a hamburger platter is $1.65, the menu price should be $4.45 ($1.65 + $2.80 = $4.45). This cost seems to be less than with the food cost percentage method. This is offset by understanding that all menu items have the contribution cost added to them. The food cost percentage method may indicate that the price of a piece of pie should be $2.17 (recipe cost of $.65 ÷ .30 = $2.17). Using the contribution method, the price would be $3.45. The idea is that everything sold should contribute equally to the cost of production and profit.

The contribution method is particularly useful to those who operate seasonal foodservice establishments. It may also discourage customers from buying less expensive items because of a poor perceived value. For some items, using the contribution method may not be advisable, such as for pricing a side order of fries or other typically low-priced items.

The method of choice should be the method that generates the highest profit for each specific foodservice operation. The food cost percentage method may best be used in operations that have marginal profits or low prices and consistently steady business. The contribution method would best be used in less price-sensitive operations that have medium to high prices or are seasonal.

pecial Pricing Situations

Food bar
A generic term for a salad bar or buffet display of food where customers pay one price and then serve themselves.

Food Bars Food bars are unique. They appeal to customers who are value conscious—who seek a large amount of food for a relatively small amount of money. The challenge is to price the food so that a reasonable profit can be made.

Either the food cost percentage method or the contribution method may be used. Determining the cost was discussed in Chapter 7, Table 7-5. This figure is restated in Table 17-6. The challenge is tracking the customer count—that is, the number of people who purchase a salad bar or food bar menu

■ ■ ■ ■ ■
Table 17-6   Calculating the Cost of a Salad Bar

ITEM	COST
5 heads of lettuce, iceberg with salad mix	$ 5.35
5 lb four-bean salad	8.46
1 pint cottage cheese	1.65
5 lb elbow macaroni salad	5.40
5 lb potato salad	6.25
1 pint french dressing	2.17
1 pint blue cheese dressing	3.65
1 pint ranch dressing	3.04
1 pint Italian dressing	2.70
1 lb Town House crackers	3.50
1 lb croutons	2.03
TOTAL COST	$44.20
Number of people who ate (this number is taken from the guest checks)	85
Cost per person ($44.20 ÷ 85 = .52)	$ .52 per person

choice. Once the cost is established, it can either be divided by the desired food cost percentage or have the contribution cost added to the food cost. For the salad bar listed in Table 17-6, the cost of $.52 is divided by .30 for a price of $1.95 ($.52 ÷ .30 = $1.73, rounded to $1.95). If we use the contribution method with the costs in Table 17-6, the cost of $.52 is added to the contribution cost of $2.80 for a price of $3.32. If competitors charge $3.00 for a similar item, the final pricing of the salad bar is a matter of judgment, based upon market conditions. Also, it should be recognized that the price of produce will fluctuate with seasonal changes. It probably would be wise to price this item using the highest expected prices to be paid for the preparation ingredients.

Beer and Wine Pricing beer and wine can be a bit confusing because of the variety of ways that these products are purchased and served. Both beer and wine may be purchased in bulk or in bottles. Bulk beer is purchased in kegs; bulk wine is purchased by the liter in plastic bags that are contained in boxes. Bulk-purchased beverages are poured directly into the glass when served. The cost of purchasing in bulk is considerably lower than by the bottle. Yet serving sizes of poured products may vary according to glass size. In both cases, beer and wine may be priced using the beverage cost percentage method or the contribution method.

Beer purchased by the bottle is nearly always sold by the bottle. The bottle size is fixed and the cost is fixed. Wine purchased by the bottle is usually sold by the bottle, although many operations offer wine by the glass. Pricing bottled beverages by using the beverage cost percentage method usually results in a very high price. If the price is too high, the alternatives are recalculating with a higher beverage cost percentage or using the contribution method.

Sales Forecasts

Sales forecast
An estimate of the food-service operation's sales based upon the number of expected customers and the average amount each customer will spend.

The **sales forecast** is directly related to pricing. A forecast depends upon two factors. One is the count or number of people purchasing items prepared by the foodservice operation. The other is the menu price of the items sold. There are two methods of doing a sales forecast. One is an overall forecast of sales. The other is a projection of menu item sales. The latter is particularly important if a food or beverage cost percentage is used to determine price.

A sales forecast is the count multiplied by the average check per person. During a month, if 10,000 customers are expected to eat lunch and the expected check average is $5.50, then the calculation would be as follows: $10,000 \times \$5.50 = \$55,000$. Simply put, the foodservice operation is expected to have sales of $55,000. If a food cost percentage is used, the percentage multiplied by the estimated sales equals the food cost ($.30 \times \$55,000 = \$16,500$). It would be difficult to estimate the food cost using the contribution method. To use the Contribution Method, a foodservice manager would have to do a sales forecast by menu item.

A sales forecast by menu item would be similar to a food sales recap report or a menu analysis (see Chapter 9). The difference is that the food sales recap report and the menu analysis are based upon an actual sales history, while a forecast is an estimate of what is expected to happen. Table 17-7 shows a menu item sales forecast. Using a menu item sales forecast is the best method for projecting sales and food costs if the contribution method is used for pricing.

A sales forecast is necessary to see the consequences of setting menu prices. There are many reasons for changing menu prices after the initial menu has been developed. For example, after doing a menu analysis, one conclusion may be to raise the price of an item. If the menu is changed, new prices will be determined. New specials always need to be priced. Whatever the reason, the menu should be analyzed to make certain that the prices will do what is intended.

A sales forecast sets an estimate that managers may also use as a sales goal. At the end of an accounting period, a menu analysis will show what actually occurred. At that point, management will learn if they estimated correctly. If they didn't, hopefully they will gain an understanding of why the forecast was not met.

Another valuable reason for calculating food cost percentage is to establish budgets. If the food cost goal is 35 percent, or if the labor cost goal is 25 percent, a sales forecast provides a dollar estimate for establishing a budget. For example, if sales are estimated to be $10,000 for the upcoming week, the food cost budget would be $3,500 ($10,000 \times .35 = \$3,500$) and the labor cost budget would be $2,500 ($10,000 \times .25 = \$2,500$). The foodservice manager would use these figures when buying food so that the dollar amount is not exceeded. The manager would also use the labor cost budget to schedule employees so that the budget is not exceeded.

■ ■ ■ ■ ■
Table 17-7   Menu Item Sales Forecast

Department Deli Shop				Page 1 of 12			
Prepared by Clerical				Week of 1/13/XX			
Category Sandwiches							

MENU ITEM	SALES ESTIMATE	PERCENT OF SALES	MENU PRICE	PLATE COST	CONTRIBUTION	SALES	FOOD COST
BLT	100	4.2%	$3.00	1.00	2.00	$300.00	$ 100.00
Hamburger	800	33.3	3.00	1.00	2.00	2,400.00	800.00
Cheeseburger	900	37.5	3.31	1.31	2.00	2,979.00	1,179.00
Chicken Sal San	100	4.2	2.80	.80	2.00	280.00	80.00
Meat Loaf Spec	200	8.3	4.05	2.05	2.00	810.00	410.00
Chili Dog	300	12.5	2.65	.65	2.00	795.00	195.00
Total	2,400	100.00%				$7,564.00	$2.764.00

SUMMARY

1. Proper pricing requires judgment often developed over several years of being a foodservice manager.

2. Identifying competing foodservice operations and their prices provides a guide as to how a foodservice manager should price similar items.

3. There are two basic methods of pricing: the food (or beverage) cost percentage method and the contribution method.

4. The food cost percentage method of pricing involves calculating the food cost of a menu item and dividing the cost by the desired food cost percentage. For instance, if a hamburger costs $1.00 and the desired food cost percentage is 25 percent, the menu price would be $4.00 ($1.00 ÷ .25 = $4.00). The food cost percentage method is desirable in foodservice operations that are not seasonal and whose volume of sales remains constant.

5. The contribution method is more complicated to calculate than the food cost percentage method. The premise is that the costs, including profit for operating a foodservice operation, should be covered by each of the estimated number of customers that will patronize the operation. All nonfood costs, plus a reasonable profit, are divided by the expected number of customers. For example, if a foodservice operation expects costs for the period to be $100,000 and the number of customers to be 100,000, then the contribution is $1.00 per customer. This dollar amount is added to the food cost to determine the item's menu price. For example, if a hamburger has a food cost of $1.00 and the expected contribution is $1.00, then the menu price should be $2.00 ($1.00 + $1.00 = $2.00).

6. There are special pricing situations for food bars and beer and wine items.

7. Determining a sales forecast is necessary for projecting sales and food costs. Sales forecasts can also be used to help budget labor costs. That is, if the sales forecast is $10,000 and the budgeted labor cost is 22 percent, $2,200 should be the dollar amount budgeted for labor ($10,000 × .22 = $2,200). A sales forecast may also be used for determining the profitability of a particular menu mix.

8. A sales forecast is determined by multiplying the expected number of customers by the average check for a specific period of time.

KEY CONCEPTS

Competitive analysis	Pricing a menu
Contribution method	Sales forecast
Customer count	Signature item
Food bar	Value
Food cost percentage method	

DISCUSSION QUESTIONS AND EXERCISES

1. List five questions that may be used to discover who are the customers of a foodservice establishment.

2. Why is it important to know who the customers are when pricing a menu?

3. What is a competitive analysis and how do you do one?

4. Using a blank competitive analysis form from Appendix A, go to three foodservice establishments that appear to be similar and complete the form. Compare similar menu items, decor, type of customer, and prices.

5. How many restaurants are in the trade area where you live?

6. Estimate the customer count of a foodservice operation in your geographical area.

7. If the plate cost for a menu item is $2.00 and the desired food cost percentage is 25 percent, what would be the price? If the desired food cost percentage is 35 percent, what would be the price?

8. If total food sales were $600,000 for the year, the food cost was $200,000, and 100,000 customers were served during the year, calculate the contribution cost for each customer.

9. What should the price be if the plate cost is $2.00 and the contribution cost is $2.50? Calculate the price if the plate cost is $3.00 and the contribution cost is $2.50.

10. What factors should be taken into consideration when deciding whether to use the food cost percentage method or the contribution method for pricing menu items?

11. Why should there be special pricing considerations for food bars and beer or wine?

12. What is the connection between pricing and doing a sales forecast?

13. Describe the purpose of doing a menu item sales forecast.

14. During the year, the expected average check is $6.50 and the expected customer count is 250,000. What is the sales forecast for the year? If the count is revised down to 200,000, what is the revised sales forecast? If the average check is $6.00 and the count is 225,000, what is the sales forecast? How would you describe the relationship between average check and customer count?

18

Select Topics: Self-Inspections, Customer Feedback, Nonfood Inventories, and Espresso Drinks

■ ■ ■ ■ ■ ■ ■ ■ ■ ■ ■ ■ ■

Learning Objectives

After reading this chapter and completing the discussion questions and exercises, you should be able to:

1. Understand the importance of continually inspecting an operation to ensure that food and service standards are met.

2. Recognize that part of inspecting a foodservice operation is collecting verbal and written information about operational performance from guests by a variety of methods.

3. Explain how information about customer perceptions can be obtained by customer comment reports, shopper reports, and surveys.

4. Understand that foodservice operations involve a considerable investment in nonfood and nonbeverage items that require accounting and other controls that are as exacting as those for food and beverage products.

5. Describe the three basic types of espresso drinks and be able to define the ingredients and preparation procedures for each.

6. Calculate the cost and profit of preparing espresso drinks.

About Miscellaneous Controls

As a final measure of the successful management of any type of foodservice operation, it is the attention given to the miscellaneous details and controls that often makes a significant difference to the financial performance of the operation.

Customer expectations regarding food quality, selection, price, and service must be consistently fulfilled. Various methods can assure that these expectations are known and met through constantly monitoring the details of preparation and service.

Attention to the nonfood and nonbeverage expense items that support the foodservice operation is equally important. These items include such things as paper goods (where applicable: napkins, cups, plastic spoons, and so on), china, and flatware. All of these items need to be monitored to prevent shrinkage due to breakage and theft. Finally, equipment that services the entire foodservice operation, from the kitchen and service sections to the customer dining areas, needs to be accounted for and managed.

Monitoring the Details with a Focus on Quality

Foodservice managers who constantly look at the details are more likely to have successful operations. This chapter discusses several operational areas that are important and should be controlled, but do not constitute a large enough body of knowledge to have separate chapter treatment in and of themselves. Thus, this chapter will examine a variety of concerns, including continuous overall inspection, customer feedback, and controlling and accounting for all foodservice equipment, both large and small.

The first area addresses the problem of how a foodservice manager can systematically examine the operation to ensure that quality service and food presentation are taking place. In previous chapters, each of these areas has been analyzed in detail regarding the inventory and production of food and the control of service, but little attention has been given to quality customer experiences.

To find out if customers are having a quality experience, foodservice managers need to examine the entire dining experience. A variety of methods can be used to measure quality. Most involve some type of internal and/or external evaluation.

An internal evaluation may be accomplished by doing one or all of the following:

- *Walk-through audit.* The manager walks through the operation, examining the appearance, service, and food quality being presented.

- *Listening to guest comments.* Employees can gather information by listening to guest comments while dining. Other comments made via customer requests also provide valuable information. Formalization of what is heard may be accomplished by using a **customer contact report**, discussed later.

- *Customer comment report.* This information is gathered via **customer comment cards** and can provide information after the dining experience has ended.

- *Exit interviews.* In this method, which is similar to using customer comment cards, customers may be interviewed by the manager or designee. An **exit interview** may be conducted to gather in-depth information about the dining experience.

Customer contact report
A form used to document customer comments regarding their dining experience.

Customer comment cards
Cards used to ask customer opinions regarding their dining experience.

Exit interviews
Interviews conducted to gather in-depth information from customers as they leave the foodservice establishment.

External evaluations may be conducted by using the following:

- *Shopper reports.* The foodservice manager may hire a firm or select people in the community to do **shopper reports.** Similar to a customer comment report, a shopper report typically provides a structured printed form for the guest to fill out after the dining experience has been completed.

- *Customer surveys.* Customer surveys may be developed by the foodservice manager or a consulting firm that specializes in gathering and analyzing customer surveys. A customer survey may be completed by mail or telephone. Surveys may be of those who have recently dined at the foodservice facility or potential customers. Insights concerning the foodservice operation's image, as held by experienced or potential customers of a particular foodservice operation, could provide important data that will guide the development of the menu and service strategy.

- *Focus groups.* **Focus groups** may consist of past customers or potential customers. Focus groups are often used to test new menu items. The focus group may be put together by the manager or by a consulting firm. Focus groups are sometimes used to test customer surveys prior to their being mailed.

Shopper reports
Structured printed forms that evaluate a dining experience.

Focus groups
A group of people, usually past or potential customers, who meet and express their opinions about a common experience, or to test new items.

WALK-THROUGH AUDIT

The walk-through audit, as the name implies, occurs when the foodservice manager walks though the operation. As the manager walks through, he or she evaluates what is observed (see Table 18-1).

A walk-through audit examines the quality of appearance, service, and food. The audit should be based upon the food and service standards set forth by management. In Table 18-1, the first part of the walk-through audit provides an opportunity for the foodservice manager to examine the service system thoroughly. The service system is described in Chapter 14. (The tasks and service standards were initially developed and presented in Table 14-5.) The Task column in Table 18-1 lists the tasks that constitute the service. The Service Standard column explains the standard for comparison. The Responsible column lists who is responsible for the standard to be met. The Standard Met? column is an evaluation of whether or not the person responsible met the standard. The Comments column provides a place for the evaluator to make comments about his or her observations.

The second part of the walk-through audit is an evaluation of the products being served. The questions evaluate all of the food for a variety of quality characteristics such as color, texture, temperature, flavor, and aroma. Each area of the menu needs to be evaluated. Obviously, if management finds a standard unmet, the situation requiring improvement is immediately pinpointed for corrective action.

COLLECTING INFORMATION FROM CUSTOMER CONTACT

One of the most valuable sources of information comes directly from customers. Part of the service cycle is to check back with the table and ask, "How was your shrimp scampi?" This open-ended question provides an opportunity for customers to respond to service, quality of food, or whatever strikes their interest.

■ ■ ■ ■ ■

Table 18-1 Walk-Through Audit—Service

Name Manager _____   Date 1/13/XX _____

TASK	SERVICE STANDARD	PERSON RESPONSIBLE	STANDARD MET?	COMMENTS
Answer Phone	Within 3 rings.	Host/Hostess	Yes	None
Take Reservations	100% accuracy: name, phone number, number in party, time, special requests, table assignment.	Host/Hostess	No	Sharon didn't ask how many in party.
Greeting the Customer	Within 1 minute of entering restaurant, use an approved greeting format, check for customer reservation.	Host/Hostess	Yes	None
Seating the Customer	Personally escort customers to preassigned table, seat women first, distribute menus, mention the evening special and name of the person who will be their server.	Host/Hostess	Yes	None
Water Service	Ask if the customers want water.	Busperson	Yes	None
Waitstaff Greeting the Customer	Stand at a table corner if a four-top, or at the center end of the table if a booth, and introduce yourself. Mention the evening special; request any orders from the bar and ask if they want appetizers. If the customers order, take the orders. If they don't, invite the customers to look at the menu.	Waitstaff	No	Joyce did not mention specials until guest asked.
Taking Meal Order	Return to table within 3 minutes. Ask for dinner order. Ask customers for add-ons (shrimp in salad, etc.).	Waitstaff	No	Joyce did not ask for add-ons.
Processing Meal Order	Take meal order to waitstaff station and input into computer. Order-in should be completed within 2 minutes.	Waitstaff	Yes	None
Order Preparation	From printout, prepare menu item using standardized recipes. All the meals for a specific table should be prepared within 15 minutes.	Cook Staff	Yes	None
Salad Service or Appetizers	After order-in has taken place, take a basket of rolls and butter to the table. If any of the orders require salads or appetizers, prepare in the waitstaff station and take to the table. Deliver any beverages ordered.	Waitstaff	Yes	None

Table 18-1   Walk-Through Audit—Service

Name Manager _____

Date 1/13/XX

TASK	SERVICE STANDARD	PERSON RESPONSIBLE	STANDARD MET?	COMMENTS
Water Service	While customers are waiting, check to see if they need water glasses refilled.	Busperson	No	Ted missed table 10.
Dinner Ready	When dinners are ready for the table, notify the waitperson using the silent pager.	Cook	Yes	Hard to tell when this doesn't happen.
Deliver Dinner	Order is picked up within 1 minute of notification and delivered to table. Ask for beverage orders or refills.	Waitstaff	Yes	None
Check Backs	After the order is placed before the customer, check back within 2 minutes and see if the customers are enjoying the meal. Ask for additional beverage orders or refills.	Waitstaff	Yes	None
Clearing the Table	When the customers have finished each course, ask for permission to take plates. Using clearing procedure, clear table.	Waitstaff	Yes	None
Dessert Order	When the last customer has finished eating and the table is cleared, take the dessert tray out to the customers and ask if they would like to select a dessert item.	Waitstaff	Yes	None
Final Coffee / Beverage	Offer coffee or other beverages. This should be done whether the customers order dessert or not. If they order dessert, bring the beverage with the dessert.	Waitstaff	Yes	None
Bill Preparation	Go to waitstation and printout the bill.	Waitstaff	Yes	None
Bill Delivery	While customers are eating dessert and/or drinking coffee, present them with the bill, thank them, and instruct customers to pay the bill at the cashier's station.	Waitstaff	No	Joyce did not thank guest.
Final Payment	When the customers reach the cashier's station, ask if they enjoyed their dinner and invite them to return. If a customer is not happy, follow unhappy customer procedure. Thank customers for coming.	Host/Hostess	Yes	None

Table 18-1 Walk-Through Audit—Food

Name Manager   Date 1/13/XX

Appetizers:
1. Hot appetizers served hot — ☑ Yes ☐ No
2. Cold appetizers served cold — ☑ Yes ☐ No
3. Rate the flavor — ☑ Exceptional ☐ Good ☐ Average ☐ Needs Improvement ☐ Poor
4. Rate overall quality — ☐ Exceptional ☑ Good ☐ Average ☐ Needs Improvement ☐ Poor

Comments *Rotisserie chicken not crisp enough*

Salads:
1. Cold salads served on cold plates — ☑ Yes ☐ No
2. Cold salads, lettuce is crisp — ☑ Yes ☐ No
3. Rate the flavor — ☐ Exceptional ☑ Good ☐ Average ☐ Needs Improvement ☐ Poor
4. Rate overall quality — ☑ Exceptional ☐ Good ☐ Average ☐ Needs Improvement ☐ Poor

Comments *Shrimp soft*

Entrées:
1. Cold entrées served on cold plates — ☑ Yes ☐ No
2. Cold entrées served cold — ☑ Yes ☐ No
3. Hot entrées served on hot plates — ☑ Yes ☐ No
4. Hot entrées served hot — ☑ Yes ☐ No
5. Rate the flavor — ☑ Exceptional ☐ Good ☐ Average ☐ Needs Improvement ☐ Poor
6. Rate overall quality — ☑ Exceptional ☐ Good ☐ Average ☐ Needs Improvement ☐ Poor

Comments *Ate chicken with cheese sauce. Excellent!*

Desserts:
1. Cold desserts served on cold plates — ☑ Yes ☐ No
2. Cold desserts served cold — ☑ Yes ☐ No
3. Hot desserts served on hot plates — ☐ Yes ☑ No
4. Hot desserts served hot — ☑ Yes ☐ No
5. Rate the flavor — ☑ Exceptional ☐ Good ☐ Average ☐ Needs Improvement ☐ Poor
6. Rate overall quality — ☑ Exceptional ☐ Good ☐ Average ☐ Needs Improvement ☐ Poor

Comments *Key lime pie was perfect*

Beverages:
1. Cold drinks served cold — ☑ Yes ☐ No
2. Hot drinks served hot — ☑ Yes ☐ No
3. Rate the flavor — ☑ Exceptional ☐ Good ☐ Average ☐ Needs Improvement ☐ Poor
4. Rate overall quality — ☐ Exceptional ☑ Good ☐ Average ☐ Needs Improvement ☐ Poor

Comments *Nonalcoholic strawberry sunrise needs more flavor*

Side Orders (SO):
1. Cold SO served on cold plates — ☑ Yes ☐ No
2. Cold SO served cold — ☑ Yes ☐ No
3. Hot SO served on hot plates — ☑ Yes ☐ No
4. Hot SO served hot — ☑ Yes ☐ No
5. Rate the flavor — ☑ Exceptional ☐ Good ☐ Average ☐ Needs Improvement ☐ Poor
6. Rate overall quality — ☑ Exceptional ☐ Good ☐ Average ☐ Needs Improvement ☐ Poor

Comments *Didn't check flavor or quality*

■ ■ ■ ■ ■
Table 18-2 Customer Contact Report

Name Ann Waitress	Date 1/13/XX
Position Waitress	Shift 7:00 A.M. to 11:00 A.M.

Comments heard about service:

Table 17 commented that they waited a long time to be seated.

Comments heard about food:

Table 18 commented that the Eggs Benedict were the best he had ever tasted. Table 20 commented that the pancakes were cold. Table 22 commented that we should be offering espresso.

Comments heard about physical facility:

Table 21 mentioned that the women's restroom was very clean.

Management should try to collect information gleaned from customers by waitstaff, hosts and hostesses, and others with front-of-the-house responsibilities. The information should be documented if it is to be useful to management. Table 18-2 is an example of a form that can be used in any type of foodservice operation.

After a period of time, the comments should be summarized into various categories such as food quality, food desirability, new menu ideas, and so on. There is no value in collecting the comments if they are not summarized and examined.

CUSTOMER COMMENT CARDS

Customer comment cards ask those who just dined how they felt about their experience. Customer comment cards are distributed to guests in a variety of ways. Some foodservice operations put a customer comment box in a conspicuous place for customers to respond; others place the forms on the tables; still others have waitstaff personally bring the card to the table at the conclusion of the dining experience.

Regardless of how the card is distributed, the idea is to get a response as the customer leaves. Experience has shown that an opportunity to respond immediately following a meal provides the most accurate information. The card shown in Table 18-3 is only an example. Several items could be added or deleted from the card. If the foodservice operation wants to evaluate the wait time of guests who come in, such a question can be added to the items being evaluated. Each customer comment card should be customized to the specific type of foodservice operation.

Table 18-3 Customer Comment Card

Appetizers:	**Desserts:**

Appetizers:

What did you order? _____

1. Hot appetizers served hot ☐ Yes ☐ No
2. Cold appetizers served cold ☐ Yes ☐ No
3. Rate the flavor:
   ☐ Exceptional ☐ Good ☐ Average ☐ Needs Help ☐ Poor
4. Rate overall quality:
   ☐ Exceptional ☐ Good ☐ Average ☐ Needs Help ☐ Poor

Comments: _____

Desserts:

What did you order? _____

1. Cold desserts served on cold plates ☐ Yes ☐ No
2. Cold desserts served cold ☐ Yes ☐ No
3. Hot desserts served on hot plates ☐ Yes ☐ No
4. Hot desserts served hot ☐ Yes ☐ No
5. Rate the flavor:
   ☐ Exceptional ☐ Good ☐ Average ☐ Needs Help ☐ Poor
6. Rate overall quality:
   ☐ Exceptional ☐ Good ☐ Average ☐ Needs Help ☐ Poor

Comments: _____

Salads:

What did you order? _____

1. Hot salads served hot ☐ Yes ☐ No
2. Cold salads served cold ☐ Yes ☐ No
3. Rate the flavor:
   ☐ Exceptional ☐ Good ☐ Average ☐ Needs Help ☐ Poor
4. Rate overall quality:
   ☐ Exceptional ☐ Good ☐ Average ☐ Needs Help ☐ Poor

Comments: _____

Beverages:

What did you order? _____

1. Cold drinks served cold ☐ Yes ☐ No
2. Hot drinks served hot ☐ Yes ☐ No
3. Rate the flavor:
   ☐ Exceptional ☐ Good ☐ Average ☐ Needs Help ☐ Poor
4. Rate overall quality:
   ☐ Exceptional ☐ Good ☐ Average ☐ Needs Help ☐ Poor

Comments: _____

Entrées:

What did you order? _____

1. Cold entrées served on cold plates ☐ Yes ☐ No
2. Cold entrées served cold ☐ Yes ☐ No
3. Hot entrées served on hot plates ☐ Yes ☐ No
4. Hot entrées served hot ☐ Yes ☐ No
5. Rate the flavor:
   ☐ Exceptional ☐ Good ☐ Average ☐ Needs Help ☐ Poor
6. Rate overall quality:
   ☐ Exceptional ☐ Good ☐ Average ☐ Needs Help ☐ Poor

Comments: _____

Side Orders (SO):

What did you order? _____

1. Cold SO served on cold plates ☐ Yes ☐ No
2. Cold SO served cold ☐ Yes ☐ No
3. Hot SO served on hot plates ☐ Yes ☐ No
4. Hot SO served hot ☐ Yes ☐ No
5. Rate the flavor:
   ☐ Exceptional ☐ Good ☐ Average ☐ Needs Help ☐ Poor
6. Rate overall quality:
   ☐ Exceptional ☐ Good ☐ Average ☐ Needs Help ☐ Poor

Comments: _____

Service:

1. Did you wait too long to be greeted when you came into the restaurant? ☐ Yes ☐ No
2. Were you made to feel welcome? ☐ Yes ☐ No
3. Did you feel you had to wait too long to be seated? ☐ Yes ☐ No
4. How would you rate the overall service provided by the waitperson who served you?
   ☐ Exceptional ☐ Good ☐ Average ☐ Needs Help ☐ Poor
5. How would you rate the friendliness of all the staff?
   ☐ Exceptional ☐ Good ☐ Average ☐ Needs Help ☐ Poor
6. Did the pace of service seem just right? ☐ Yes ☐ No

Comments: _____

Physical Facilities:

1. How would you rate the cleanliness of the dining area?
   ☐ Exceptional ☐ Good ☐ Average ☐ Needs Help ☐ Poor
2. How would you rate the cleanliness of the restrooms, if used?
   ☐ Exceptional ☐ Good ☐ Average ☐ Needs Help ☐ Poor
3. Was the lighting comfortable? ☐ Yes ☐ No
4. Was the temperature comfortable? ☐ Yes ☐ No

Comments: _____

One Last Question:

1. Would you recommend this restaurant to your friends?
   ☐ Yes ☐ No

EXIT INTERVIEWS

Exit interviews are difficult to do. The idea is the same as for customer comment cards. As guests leave, they are personally interviewed. The disadvantage to doing an exit interview is that people would like to leave and go about their business. They often will not take time to be interviewed. The primary advantage is that the one-on-one conversations allow the interviewer to ask in-depth questions. If a guest says that he or she was not served in a friendly manner, the person doing the interview can find out what happened. Such information is very valuable for making improvements to the foodservice operation.

The form for doing an exit interview really depends upon what the manager wants to know. An expanded version of a customer comment card could be used as a basis for doing exit interviews. The person doing the exit interview should be familiar with the following interview techniques:

- Ask all the questions in the same way, using the same body language (and facial expressions).
- If the customer comment card is used, ask why the customer chose the indicated response to each question.
- Write all the comments that are made. Do not try to abbreviate or use shorthand.
- Talk using a professional demeanor.

Some questions that are common for exit interviews are:

- If you owned this restaurant (or if you managed this foodservice establishment), what would you do differently?
- What did you like best about your dining experience?
- What did you like least about your dining experience?
- Was there anyone in this restaurant that you feel should be recognized because of his or her outstanding job performance?

SHOPPER REPORTS AND CUSTOMER SURVEYS

Many foodservice operations have found that a shopper report helps to obtain a candid view of what is happening in the foodservice operation. A shopper report generally functions as follows:

- Shoppers are selected. A shopper is a person who has agreed to come into the foodservice operation and do an evaluation of the food and service. Usually a shopper will participate for a free meal plus a small stipend for travel expenses.
- The shopper is given a shopper report to fill out. This form is usually mailed to the shopper with instructions regarding how to fill out the form.
- The shopper eats at the establishment and fills out the report.
- The report is mailed to the foodservice manager.
- Management reviews the responses.
- Management makes changes based upon the findings.

Place check in
the box

Yes   No

HOSPITALITY—HOST/GREETER POSITION

14. Did the host/greeter ask for requirements and/or special requests?

15. If there was a wait, did the host/greeter volunteer directions to a waiting area? (NA if no wait)

TABLE SERVICE

20. Was the server neat in appearance? (clean uniform, well-groomed, etc.)

21. Did the server wear a name badge? (NA if no one in the restaurant wore a name badge)

OVERALL/STAFF

54. Were staff members friendly? (polite, cordial, focused yet not rushed)

55. Were staff members professional? (tended to business, mature in actions, not silly)

VALUE PERCEPTION

61. Would you recommend this restaurant to your friends?

62. Was overall staff performance better than other restaurants under similar circumstances?

FIGURE 18-1
Partial Shopper Report   This abbreviated sample shopper report is taken from *Customer Service Evaluation—Hospitality Industry*, a shopper instrument developed by Vickie L. Henry, CEO, FEED-BACK Plus, Inc., Dallas, Texas. Used with permission.

The form used by shoppers is usually more complete than the customer comment card. Shopper reports will be specifically tailored to the foodservice operation being evaluated. An example of a partial shopper report is shown in Figure 18-1.

FOCUS GROUPS

A focus group is a small group of around 5 to 21 people. Focus groups may be used to:

■ Obtain opinions about the quality of food and service.

■ Test new menu items by having members of the group eat a small portion of the item and then express an opinion regarding taste and quality.

■ Help develop a customer comment card.

■ Express opinions about products and services that they would like to see the foodservice operation offer.

■ Test a newly developed shopper report to see if it measures what management wants measured.

The purposes of using a focus group may involve other reasons than those listed.

Members of a focus group may be repeat customers, randomly selected people who are shopping nearby the foodservice operation, or randomly selected people whose names were taken from the local phone book. *Random* means that there is an equal chance that anyone who is shopping or whose name is in the telephone book may be selected. Generally, a cross section of people is needed to obtain opinions that better reflect the community or typical customer. Sometimes, a focus group may be composed of a specific group of people, such as college-age women or members of a specific business group, if the foodservice operator wants to understand the opinions of members of such a group.

Preparation is the key to successfully obtaining information from a focus group. To avoid interruptions from employees or others, the focus group should either come to the foodservice operation when it is closed or meet away from the foodservice facility.

The meeting should have a specific agenda. If opinions are being sought, open-ended questions should be asked. If possible, a professional facilitator should be retained to help with seeking information from a focus group. If this is not possible, the person working with the focus group should be inquisitive and ask questions. Using a tape recorder can ensure accuracy in documenting comments made by group members. Being sincerely curious and asking questions based upon that curiosity is the best way to obtain information from a focus group if the foodservice manager is not an experienced researcher. If menu items are being tested, make certain that all focus group members eat the same item served at the same temperature and in a similar fashion.

Focus groups are an excellent way to obtain information from those external to the organization. However, collecting information in this manner requires considerable time, effort, and sincere curiosity.

onfood Inventory Control

The last section of this chapter deals with nonfood inventory control and comprises three categories—paper goods, china and flatware, and equipment. Each of these areas may dramatically affect the profitability of a foodservice operation, for example, paper goods lost or given out in an excessive manner; flatware thrown out rather than taken to the dishwasher area; and lost or misplaced equipment. The control techniques given are adequate to ensure that all nonfood items are accounted for.

PAPER GOODS INVENTORY

Paper goods inventory
This inventory represents the total financial value of paper goods and accounts for usage.

In limited-menu, limited-service foodservice operations, paper goods are generally used to deliver food and beverage items to customers. Accounting for the use of paper goods is similar to the methods used for food and beverage items. Many foodservice managers choose to include paper goods as part of their food and beverage or dry-goods inventory. Table 18-4 shows an inventory form used to track paper goods. Accounting for paper goods is done as follows:

Table 18-4 Paper Goods Inventory

Date	1/17/XX		Page	1 of 12
Time	10:00 A.M.		Department	Storeroom
Taken by	Storeroom Manager		Location	Shelves
(and)	Assistant		Priced by	Storeroom Manager
Approved by	Owner/Manager		Extended by	Clerical

ITEM DESCRIPTION	UNIT	QUANTITY	PRICE		EXTENSION	
Napkin 15 × 17 2 Ply White	3000 ct	3	30	24	90	72
Napkin 17 × 17 Linen Soft White	2000 ct	1	68	38	68	38
Napkin 15 × 17 2 Ply Lilac	1000 ct	1	46	20	46	20
Tray Cover 13 × 18 White	1000 ct	5	38	62	193	10
Cover Toilet Seat	250 ct	4	2	69	10	76
Tissue Toilet 2 Ply	1 ct	50		475	23	75
Towel Multifold Bleached	4000 ct	1.5	32	94	49	41
Cutlery Spoon Med Wht Plystyne	1000 ct	5	20	77	103	85
Cutlery Fork Med Wht Plystyne	1000 ct	4	20	77	83	08
Cutlery Knife Med Wht Plystyne	1000 ct	4	20	77	83	08
Platter 7.5 × 10 Oval Wht	500 ct	2	50	99	101	98
Bowl 8 oz Wht Paper	1000 ct	1	54	36	54	36
Bag Paper Wht #6 6 × 3.6 × 11	500 ct	4	10	26	41	04
Cup Cold 12 oz Coke	2500 ct	2	76	12	152	24
Lid for 12/14 oz	1000 ct	5	13	51	67	55
Film 12″ × 2000′	Roll	3	11	19	33	57
PAGE TOTAL					$ 1,203	07

1. A physical inventory, taken at the end of the scheduled period, becomes the beginning inventory for the following period. The easiest way to take inventory is to use a preprinted form with similar items grouped together, such as napkins, plastic forks, plastic spoons, and so on, when fixed items are in constant use.

2. Paper goods are purchased throughout the period. The amounts added to inventory are taken from the invoices supplied by the vendors.

3. Another physical inventory is taken at the end of the period.

4. Paper cost for the period is calculated by adding the beginning inventory and purchases together and subtracting the ending inventory. For example, if the beginning inventory was $400, the purchases of paper goods during the month were $800, and the ending inventory was $600, the paper cost for the period would be $600.

As another example, suppose inventory on April 30, XX is $895; thus, the beginning inventory on May 1, XX is $895. During the first week of May, the operation purchases $1,200 in paper goods. The amount of paper goods in inventory and purchased during the week equals $2,095 ($895 + $1,200 = $2,095). On May 7, XX, inventory is $600. The paper cost for the period is $1,495 ($2,095 − $600 = $1,495).

If the paper costs are significantly higher than those planned, it is advisable to track the usage of individual paper items such as napkins, which could be used inappropriately by overportioning with takeout orders.

CHINA AND FLATWARE INVENTORY

China and flatware represent a significant investment for the foodservice operation. In fine-dining facilities, the china and flatware investment may be hundreds of dollars per place setting. The same careful attention to food and beverage inventory must be extended to china and flatware inventory. The principles of managing food and beverage inventory are transferable to china and flatware inventory.

The term *china* often includes plates, cups, and glassware. Flatware usually refers to metal eating utensils. China and flatware inventory is typically taken on a quarterly basis. If there is excessive breakage or theft, then inventory should be taken more often.

The china and flatware inventory form (Table 18-5) is an excellent way to track the shrinkage of china and flatware. Shrinkage refers to the loss of china and flatware as part of the function of doing business. The form is also designed to track inventory and compare the inventory with what is supposed to be on hand.

The china and flatware inventory form functions as follows:

Item Description The Item Description column lists each item and includes all specific data regarding the item. The items listed in the first column are bread baskets, plates, coffee cups, glasses, and teaspoons.

Par The par amount is an amount established that will be able to adequately handle the business during peak periods. Par amounts are determined based on the experience of the operation. The par amount for 9¼-inch plates is 450.

China and flatware inventory Represents the total value of all plates, cups, glassware, and flatware (eating utensils) used in a foodservice establishment.

Table 18-5 China and Flatware Inventory

Date	1/15/XX	Page	1 of 5
Taken by	Deli Shop Manager	Department	Deli Shop
(and)	Assistant	Approved by	Owner/Manager

ITEM DESCRIPTION	PAR	INVENTORY					TOTAL	+ OR −\nBALANCE
		A	B	C	D	E		
Bread Baskets	72	68	4	1			73	+1
Plates 9¼″	450	301	90	28			419	-31
Coffee Cups	360	151	161				312	-48
Glasses 8 oz	480	120	160	20	112		412	-68
Teaspoons	480	122	168	201	30	44	565	+85

Inventory China and flatware are not kept all in one place. Some may be kept in the dishwashing area, some in waitstaff stations, and some in other storage areas. The inventory is listed according to the storage area in which it is stored. The form uses A, B, C, D, and E to represent individual counts in different storage areas, reflecting that the merchandise is not all in one place. In the example, plates are kept in three locations.

Total Columns A through E are added together to derive the amount listed in the Total column. Adding columns A, B, and C for 9¼-inch plates totals 419.

Plus or Minus Balance The difference between the total and the par is listed in this column. Par is subtracted from the total. There is either a plus, minus, or zero balance. A plus balance would be the result of someone overreacting to a shortage by purchasing and putting more in use than is actually needed. As a general rule, there will be a minus balance, chiefly due to shrinkage. Calculating the plus or minus balance for 9¼-inch plates is done as follows: the total of 419 subtracted from the par of 450 equals –31 (419 – 450 = –31).

Occasionally, the foodservice manager should go through the trash container in the dishwashing area and other areas, looking for china and flatware. This way employees will know that management is concerned about china and flatware being thrown away. China and flatware represent a considerable expense to any operation and should be tightly controlled.

EQUIPMENT INVENTORY

One small piece of equipment may cost hundreds of dollars; larger portable pieces of equipment may cost thousands of dollars. For example, a small tabletop mixer may cost $350 with attachments; a large steam table on wheels used as part of a food bar may be worth $3,500; refrigeration units may cost over $10,000; and a combi-oven (combination convection-steam oven) may cost as much as $20,000 or more.

Foodservice managers need to be accountable for the equipment used for preparing and serving food. If a conscious effort is not expended to track this inventory, it simply may disappear as a result of theft or careless use. An example of careless use would be leaving equipment at a catering site or losing equipment if it is moved from one kitchen area to another.

An equipment inventory should be prepared at least once a year, or more often as deemed necessary. This inventory represents a total of all foodservice equipment used by each food preparation area. Single, stand-alone operations should have an inventory only for that specific facility. If multiple operations exist within one building, such as a large office building or a hotel, then multiple inventories by department or kitchen should be prepared.

Tracking equipment inventory is simple if an equipment inventory report is used (see Table 18-6). The form is organized into five parts and functions:

Equipment Description The equipment description should list type of equipment, brand name, and serial number. The equipment should be listed on the form in an order that coincides with the placement of the equipment in the foodservice operation.

Equipment Inventory
Represents the total value of all equipment for the foodservice operation.

■ ■ ■ ■ ■

Table 18-6   Equipment Inventory

Date 1/15/XX		Page 1 of 1
Taken by Deli Shop Manager		Department Deli Shop
(and) Assistant		Approved by Owner/Manager

EQUIPMENT DESCRIPTION (NAME, SERIAL NUMBER)	UNIT COUNT	OFFICE COUNT	DIFFERENCE	EXPLANATION
Refrigerated Display Case for Pies #3789471	1	1		
Malt Mixer - Hamilton Beach (3 mixer arms) #19960	1	1		
Steam Table Pans (12x10x2)	8	10	–2	Transfer to main kitchen
Toasters - Toastmaster #246788, #32568	2	2		

Unit Count The unit count represents the actual physical count or number of units.

Office Count The office count is the count as it appears on previous records. This is the number of pieces of equipment that should be present.

Difference The difference is the comparison of the unit count with the office count. The difference is calculated by subtracting the office count from the unit count. The unit count for steam table pans was 8 and the office count was 10. The difference, 8 minus 10, equals –2.

Explanation If a difference exists, the reason should be listed in the Explanation column. The only explanation needed is for steam table pans. Two of them were transferred to the main kitchen. The form shown in Table 18-6 is presented as a teaching tool. As mentioned before, foodservice operations may create their own custom forms for tracking equipment inventory.

E spresso Drinks

Espresso drinks continue to grow in popularity ranging from **caffe lattes** (approximately 10% espresso, 80% steamed milk, and 10% milk foam), **cappuccinos** (approximately 10% espresso, 45% steamed milk, and 45% foam), and **mochas** (approximately 10% espresso, 8% chocolate syrup, and 82% steamed milk). These percentages will vary according to the size of the drink and according to various drink mix combinations. Such as, by adding Italian syrups, whereby a wide variety of flavored drinks can be created.

True espresso coffee is a process in which a specialty blended and roasted coffee, finely ground, is brewed rapidly (20 to 25 seconds) under pressure, through a fine mesh screen filter. Espresso coffee is traditionally served in a demitasse (small) cup.

Espresso machines consist of a pump to create pressure, steam boiler tank with element to produce hot water and steam, a continuous *flow cycle through heat exchange to produce freshly extracted espresso* coffee, a hot water valve and a steam valve with a steaming wand to steam milk. Some espresso machines are fully (super) automatic and some provide a small refrigeration unit and container for milk. This is integrated with the machine as shown in Figure 18-2. The automatic machines are time saving and ensure quality and consistency. The machines allow the press of a single button to start the entire process which begins with grinding the coffee beans. The touch pad allows for several different one-touch product buttons for quick, precise drinks.

ESPRESSO

One shot of espresso is typically made from 7 grams of finely ground coffee as per espresso machine setting and will produce an average 1.5 ounces of espresso. This will yield approximately 60 shots of espresso per pound of espresso coffee beans with an average waste factor of 5 to 7 percent. This is calculated as follows:

Caffe Latte
An approximate mixture of 10% espresso, 80% steamed milk, and 10% milk foam.

Cappuccino
An approximate mixture of 10% espresso, 45% steamed milk, and 45% foam.

Mocha
An approximate mixture of 10% espresso, 8% chocolate syrup, and 82% steamed milk.

FIGURE 18-2
Automatic Espresso Machine   *Courtesy of Espresso Specialists, Inc.*

- 1 pound = 453.6 grams
- 453.6 g × .07 = 31.75g waste factor
- 453.6g – (minus) 31.75 = 421.9 g net yield
- 421.9 g / (divided by) 7 g per shot = 60 shots

Espresso coffee beans will have an average cost of $7.50 per pound. Therefore, $7.50 / (divided by) 60 shots per pound = 12.5 cents per shot.

The typical serving sizes are 8, 12, 16, and 20 ounces. An 8 or 12 ounce drink usually contains a single shot while the 16 and 20 ounce drinks contain double shots. Occasionally customers order additional shots, which would be charged as "added shots," usually ranging from 35 to 60 cents per shot. Management should establish a standard shot quantity per serving size along with the selling price to be shown on a beverage menu.

MILK

Milk is poured into a stainless steel pitcher and placed under the steam wand nozzle to be heated and steamed (unless an automatic machine is used). When steamed, milk will foam up and expand. The expansion will typically range from 20 to 50 percent, depending upon its intended use (latte, mocha, or cappuccino). It is also important to calculate an average waste factor of 10 percent for the remaining amount of milk that remains unused in the pitcher. When calculating a 10 percent waste factor, the net yield for espresso drinks should be as follows:

- *Lattes and mochas* the volume increases 10 percent.
- *Cappuccinos* the volume increases 40 percent (half steamed milk half foam).

Milk will have an average cost of $2.60 per gallon. Therefore,

$2.60 / (divided by) 128 ounces per gallon = 2 cents per ounce.

Customers may prefer nonfat (skim milk), 2%, or half-and-half. When half-and-half is requested, there is usually an additional charge ranging from 35 to 60 cents per serving. Whipped cream topping is also a favorite choice for many customers and is sometimes included with the price of the drink, although the customer is typically charged an additional 25 or 30 cents per serving when whipped cream is requested. Some operators top off the whipped cream topping with choices of spices, such as cinnamon, nutmeg, vanilla powder, ground sweet chocolate, or hazelnut, along with various other garnishes that are often available for customers at a self service counter.

CHOCOLATE SYRUP

Mochas are typically prepared with chocolate syrup that is either added to the cup or steamed with the milk. An average cost for chocolate syrup is $5.75 per 96 ounce can. Therefore, $5.75 / (divided by) 96 ounces = 6 cents per ounce.

The typical serving size is 1 ounce of chocolate syrup for an 8 or 12 ounce mocha, 1.5 ounces for a 16 ounce mocha, and 2 ounces for a 20 ounce mocha.

ITALIAN SYRUPS

Espresso drinks can be enhanced with a number of different Italian syrups that are available in a variety of flavors. An example of a popular Italian syrup is shown in Figure 18-3. It is important to recognize that different syrup brands will have different flavor intensities. Therefore, a typical one ounce syrup serving may need to be increased or decreased in serving size to achieve the desired taste standard.

Italian syrups will have an average cost of $4.60 per 946 mL (32 ounce) bottle. Therefore, $4.60 / (divided by) 32 ounces = 14.4 cents per ounce.

The typical serving size for a 12 ounce espresso is one ounce of syrup, and the additional charge usually ranges from 35 to 50 cents per flavor serving. For 16 and 20 ounce drinks, customers may request double or triple servings of syrup flavor and would therefore be charged accordingly for each additional syrup serving.

DISPOSABLE PAPER COSTS

The majority of espresso drinks that are sold in coffee houses, espresso carts as shown in Figure 18-4, and drive-thrus are prepared in disposable cups. When using disposable paper, the following costs must be identified: cups, lids, stir sticks, insulated cup covers (if used), and napkins.

FIGURE **18-3**
Italia D'Oro Italian Syrup *Courtesy of Boyd Coffee Company*

FIGURE **18-4**
Techni-Brew Signature Series Mini-Grandé Cart *Courtesy of Boyd Coffee Company*

Includes:

- Cart / 54″ Carts of Gold beverage cart; 220 V; w/2.7 cu. ft. refrigerator
- Double Sink with hot and cold running water
- Shelf / 18″ foldout
- Grinder shelf for maximum working space
- Shelf / Front convenience (8″ × 54″)
- Deluxe trim package 54″

ESPRESSO DRINK COST ANALYSIS

The example shown in Table 18-7, Espresso Drink Cost Analysis, represents a standard that may be set forth by management in establishing drink sizes, identifying ingredient costs, a competitive selling price (based upon market conditions), and a cost percentage in relationship to selling price. It is important to recognize that a vast number of combinations exist within each category of lattes, cappuccinos, and mochas, as customers will customize their own drinks by adding extra shots of espresso and adding selections from a wide variety of Italian syrup flavors. Therefore, each drink can result in a different selling price based upon the customer's choice of ingredient combinations.

SUMMARY

1. Measuring the dining experience is accomplished by evaluations from three different sources: management, customers, and focus groups.

2. The management evaluation is accomplished by a walk-through audit performed by the foodservice manager. This audit uses a form listing required tasks, the standards for completing each task, the person responsible for completing each task, whether the standards are completed, and any comments about how the standards are met by employees. The audit examines customer service and the quality of food and beverages served.

3. Gathering of evaluations by customers may range from casual comments overheard and captured by employees, completed customer contact reports, structured customer comment cards to be completed by the customers after dining, open-ended exit interviews of customers by managers or their designees, or shopper reports completed by preselected customers recruited by management to dine and then complete structured evaluations.

4. Another method of collecting information about the guest experience or desired experience is the use of focus groups. A focus group may be a group of past customers or people the foodservice operation would like as customers.

5. Nonfood inventories include paper goods, china and flatware, and equipment.

6. The process of controlling paper goods in inventory is the same as for food and beverage items.

7. Controlling china and flatware is focused upon counting the number of units on hand and comparing it to the number that should be on hand (a set par).

8. Controlling equipment inventory is similar to china and flatware with one exception: it is usually completed annually.

9. Espresso drinks such as caffe lattes, cappuccinos, and mochas will continue to grow in popularity. The drinks are usually made from one to three shots of espresso, depending upon the size of the cup being served, steamed milk, chocolate syrup (used for mochas), and a variety of Italian syrups that customers may request.

Table 18-7 Espresso Drink Cost Analysis

TYPE OF DRINK	SIZE					
LATTES	**12** OUNCES		**16** OUNCES		**20** OUNCES	
Espresso (1.5 oz per shot)	1 shot =	$0.125	2 shots =	$0.25	2 shots =	$0.25
Steamed Milk	10 oz =	$0.20	12 oz =	$0.24	16 oz =	$0.32
	Total =	$0.325	Total =	$0.49	Total =	$0.57
Selling Price		$2.15		$2.70		$2.95
Cost Percentage	.325 / 2.15 = 15%		.49 / 2.70 = 18%		.57 / 2.95 = 19%	
CAPPUCCINOS						
Espresso (1.5 oz per shot)	1 shot =	$0.125	2 shots =	$0.25	2 shots =	$0.25
Steamed Milk	7.5 oz =	$0.15	9.5 oz =	$0.19	12.5 oz =	$0.25
Foam (no cost)		.00		.00		.00
	Total =	$0.275	Total =	$0.44	Total =	$0.50
Selling Price		$2.15		$2.70		$2.95
Cost Percentage	.275 / 2.15 = 13%		.44 / 2.70 = 16%		.50 / 2.95 = 17%	
MOCHAS						
Espresso (1.5 oz per shot)	1 shot =	$0.125	2 shots =	$0.25	2 shots =	$0.25
Chocolate Syrup	1 oz =	$0.06	1.5 oz =	$0.09	2 oz =	$0.12
Steamed Milk	8.5 oz =	$0.17	10.5 oz =	$0.21	14 oz =	$0.28
	Total =	$0.355	Total =	$0.55	Total =	$0.65
Selling Price		$2.40		$2.95		$3.20
Cost Percentage	.355 / 2.40 = 15%		.55 / 2.95 = 19%		.65 / 3.20 = 20%	

COST PER UNIT	
Espresso (1.5 oz)	$.125 per shot
Milk	$.02 per ounce
Chocolate Syrup	$.06 per ounce
Italian Syrup	$.144 per ounce
Half & Half	$.04 per ounce
Whipped Cream Topping	$.04 per ounce

SELLING PRICE	
Extra Shot	$.55 per shot
Italian Syrup	$.35 per flavor
Half & Half	$.55 per serving
Whipped Cream Topping	$.25 per serving

10. The potential profit margins for espresso drinks are high, as beverage cost percentages typically range from 13 to 20 percent.

KEY CONCEPTS

China and flatware inventory
Customer comment cards
Customer contact report
Equipment inventory

Exit interviews
Focus groups
Paper goods inventory
Shopper reports

DISCUSSION QUESTIONS AND EXERCISES

1. Why is it a good idea to use more than one kind of method for examining food quality and service?

2. Teach another person the principles presented in this chapter.

3. Develop a walk-through audit for a local restaurant and present it to the manager to review its completeness and usefulness. (Request permission from the manager before doing this assignment.)

4. What kinds of reports would you use to try to understand what customers think about a foodservice operation that you might manage?

5. Describe how to control paper goods inventory.

6. Describe how to control china and flatware inventory.

7. Describe how to control equipment inventory.

8. Discuss potential problems of completing each of the miscellaneous controls in Questions 5, 6, and 7.

The next two questions are based upon the following information.

■ ■ ■ ■ ■
China and Flatware Inventory

Date 1/15/XX   Page 1 of 1

Taken by Deli Shop Manager   Department Deli Shop

(and) Assistant   Approved by Owner/Manager

ITEM DESCRIPTION	PAR	INVENTORY					TOTAL	+ OR − BALANCE
		A	B	C	D	E		
Bread Baskets	60	50	4	1			55	
Plates 9¼"	450	300	90	28			418	
Coffee Cups	300	125	150				275	
Glasses 8 oz	450	120	160	20	112		412	
Teaspoons	420	122	168	101	30	44	465	

9. What is the balance for coffee cups?

10. What is the balance for teaspoons?

11. Using Table 18-7, determine the selling price of a 16 ounce latte with an extra shot of espresso and two shots of Italian syrup.

12. Explain the mixture percentages in the following espresso drinks: latte, cappuccino, and mocha.

APPENDIX *A*
Blank Forms

This appendix is a compilation of all the forms used in the text. They are to be photocopied and used to complete chapter exercises, or they are to be used in operating a foodservice operation. Further, nearly all of the forms have been reproduced using Microsoft Excel and are available by request from Tim Hill at thill@cocc.edu.

Period Ending _____

DEBITS

Opening Inventory   _____

Total Food Purchases   _____

Debit Total   _____   (A)

CREDITS

Closing Inventory   _____

Employee Meal Credit   _____

Promotional/Free Meals   _____

Steward Sales   _____

Credit Total   _____   (B)

COST OF FOOD SOLD . . . . _____   (C)
(a − b = c)

TOTAL FOOD SALES . . . . _____

COST OF FOOD SOLD

(divide) ÷   =

FOOD COST PERCENTAGE
____ × _100_ = ____

TOTAL FOOD SALES

Prepared by _____   Date _____

Debit is an accounting term used to indicate an inflow into an account. In this example, opening inventory and total food purchases are inflows into the food cost.
Credits are outflows from the food cost account. In this example, closing inventory, employee meal credit, promotional/free meals, and steward sales are outflow food costs.

Department _____   Period Ending _____

DEBITS

Opening Inventory   _____

Total Food Requisitions:

    Storeroom   _____

    Production Kitchen   _____

    Transfers In   _____

Debit Total _____ (A)

CREDITS

Closing Inventory   _____

Employee Meal Credit   _____

Promotional/Free Meals   _____

Transfers Out   _____

Credit Total _____ (B)

COST OF FOOD SOLD . . . . _____ (C)
(a − b = c)

TOTAL FOOD SALES . . . . _____

COST OF FOOD SOLD

(divide) ÷   =

FOOD COST PERCENTAGE
_____ × 100 = _____

TOTAL FOOD SALES

Prepared by _____   Date _____

■ ■ ■ ■ ■
Table 3-1 Inventory Sheet

Date		Page	of
Time		Department	
Taken by		Location	
(and)		Priced by	
Approved by		Extended by	

ITEM DESCRIPTION	UNIT	QUANTITY	PRICE		EXTENSION	
PAGE TOTAL				$		

■ ■ ■ ■ ■
Table 3-2   Spoilage Report

Spoilage Report		
Department _____		Date _____
		Prepared by _____

QUANTITY/ITEM DESCRIPTION	PRICE	EXPLANATION
TOTAL		

■ ■ ■ ■ ■

Table 3-3   Perpetual Inventory Chart

Location:						
Item:					Unit:	

DATE	BEGINNING	ADDITIONS	DELETIONS	ENDING	UNIT PRICE	EXTENSION	INITIAL

■ ■ ■ ■ ■
Table 4-1　Par Amount Requisition

Date		Requisition Number	
Time		Department	
Prepared by		Priced by	
Delivered by		Extended by	
Received by		Approved by	

ITEM DESCRIPTION	PAR	ON HAND	ORDER	PRICE		EXTENSION	
TOTAL					$		

Original Copy: To remain in the storeroom.
Duplicate Copy: To be returned to the issuing department.

■ ■ ■ ■ ■

Table 4-2   Blank Requisition

Date	_____	Requisition Number	_____
Time	_____	Department	_____
Prepared by	_____	Priced by	_____
Delivered by	_____	Extended by	_____
Received by	_____	Approved by	_____

ITEM DESCRIPTION	UNIT	QUANTITY	PRICE		EXTENSION	
TOTAL				$		

Original Copy: To remain in the storeroom.
Duplicate Copy: To be returned to the issuing department.

■ ■ ■ ■ ■
Table 4-3   Transfer

| Transfer from _____ to _____ |

Date _____	Transfer Number _____
Time _____	Priced by _____
Prepared by _____	Extended by _____
Delivered by _____	Approved by _____
Received by _____	

ITEM DESCRIPTION	UNIT	QUANTITY	PRICE		EXTENSION	
TOTAL				$		

Original Copy: To remain with the issuing department.
Duplicate Copy: To be sent to the receiving department.

■ ■ ■ ■ ■
Table 5-1   Order Sheet

Supplier _____   Date _____

Item Description	Unit	Mon	Order	Tue	Order	Wed	Order	Thu	Order	Fri	Order	Sat	Order	Sun	Order

■ ■ ■ ■ ■
Table 5-2 Bid Sheet

ITEM DESCRIPTION	QUANTITY UNIT	METRO SUPPLY	SUPPLIER'S NAME ALL STAR SERVICE	TRI-STATE WHOLESALE
Total				

Date _____

■ ■ ■ ■ ■
Table 5-3 Purchase Order

Name _____

Address _____

_____

PURCHASE ORDER NUMBER

Tel _____ Fax _____ Authorized by_____ Date Issued _____
                                                    Signature

SUPPLIER

_____
Company Name

_____
Street Address

_____
City, State, Zip Code

Telephone   *Fax*

_____

Contact Name

Required Deliver Date _____

Terms _____

_____

Freight Charges ☐ Collect (Amount) $ _____
☐ FOB   ☐ Pre-paid

Special Instructions _____

_____

QUANTITY	UNIT	ITEM DESCRIPTION	UNIT COST	EXTENSION
			TOTAL $	

Copies to: Purchasing, Receiving, Accounts Payable

■ ■ ■ ■ ■
Table 6-1 Invoice Payment Schedule

Period Ending _____   Page _____ of _____

Prepared by _____   Invoices Certified Correct by

Date _____   _____

DATE	INVOICE NO.	SUPPLIER	AMOUNT		TOTAL AMOUNT	

PAGE TOTAL . . . . $

■ ■ ■ ■ ■

Table 7-1   Standardized Recipe

RECIPE NAME:		
RECIPE NO.		
QUANTITY	INGREDIENTS	PROCEDURE

■ ■ ■ ■ ■
Table 7-2 Recipe Cost Chart

Recipe Number		Page _____ of _____
Recipe for _____		Date Priced _____
Total Yield _____		Number of Servings _____
Usage _____		Portion Size _____

AMOUNT/UNIT	INGREDIENTS	UNIT PRICE	EXTENSION
		TOTAL COST	$
		PORTION COST	$

■ ■ ■ ■ ■

Table 7-3 Cooking Yield Chart

Prepared by	Date _____

ITEM DESCRIPTION:

Gross weight or volume	
Cooking or preparation loss	–
Yield after cooking	
ALLOWANCE FOR SERVICE LOSS:	
Trimming, slicing, and tasting	–
Net yield	

PREPARATION PROCEDURE

■ ■ ■ ■ ■
Table 7-7   Plate Cost Chart

Menu Item _____

Date Cost Calculated _____

AMOUNT/UNIT	INGREDIENTS	UNIT PRICE	EXTENSION
		TOTAL COST	$

■ ■ ■ ■ ■
Table 8-1   Food Sales Recap Report

Department _____   Page _____

Prepared by _____   Week of _____

MENU ITEMS	DATE: MONDAY	TUESDAY	WEDNESDAY	THURSDAY	FRIDAY	SATURDAY	SUNDAY	TOTALS
Weather								
Other conditions								

■ ■ ■ ■ ■
Table 8-2   Food Production Chart

Department _____				Page _____ of _____				
Prepared by _____				Week _____				

ITEM DESCRIPTION	Recipe Number	MONDAY	TUESDAY	WEDNESDAY	THURSDAY	FRIDAY	SATURDAY	SUNDAY

■ ■ ■ ■ ■

Table 8-3 Portion Control Chart

Department _____ Page _____ of _____
Day _____ Final Amounts Recorded by _____
Date _____ Amounts Sold/Differences by _____
Time _____ Approved by _____

ITEM DESCRIPTION	RECIPE NUMBER	QUANTITY PREPARED	PORTION SIZE	POSSIBLE NUMBER	AMOUNT SOLD	DIFFERENCE	AMOUNT LEFT	+ OR – DIFFERENCE
		____/						
		____/						
		____/						
		____/						
		____/						
		____/						
		____/						
		____/						
		____/						
		____/						
		____/						
		____/						

■ ■ ■ ■ ■
Table 8-4   Food Mishap Report

Department _____				Week of _____	
DAY	**DATE**	**TIME**	**ITEM DESCRIPTION**	**MISHAP**	**NAME**

Report: To be sent to the office at the end of the week.

■ ■ ■ ■ ■
Table 9-1   Food Sales Recap Report

| Department | | | | Page | | of | | |
| Prepared by | | | | Week of | | | | |

MENU ITEMS	MONDAY DATE:	TUESDAY	WEDNESDAY	THURSDAY	FRIDAY	SATURDAY	SUNDAY	TOTALS

■ ■ ■ ■ ■

Table 9-2   Menu Analysis Chart

Department				Page _____ of _____		
Prepared by				Week of _____		
Category						

MENU ITEM	NUMBER SOLD	PERCENT SOLD	MENU PRICE	PLATE COST	GROSS PROFIT ($)	TOTAL GROSS PROFIT	PROFIT PERCENT
Total							

■ ■ ■ ■ ■
Table 10-1   Beverage Cost Report

DATE	DAY		SALES
	Sunday	(1st shift)	
		(2nd shift)	
	Monday	(1st shift)	
		(2nd shift)	
	Tuesday	(1st shift)	
		(2nd shift)	
	Wednesday	(1st shift)	
		(2nd shift)	
	Thursday	(1st shift)	
		(2nd shift)	
	Friday	(1st shift)	
		(2nd shift)	
	Saturday	(1st shift)	
		(2nd shift)	
	TOTAL		$

$$\frac{\text{Cost of goods sold (\$\qquad)}}{\text{Total beverage sales (\$\qquad)}} = \text{Beverage cost percentage (}\qquad \times 100 = \qquad \%)$$

Prepared by _____

DATE _____

Bar Location _____

Period Ending _____

■ ■ ■ ■ ■
Table 10-2   Beverage Cost Report

Bar Location _____   Period Ending _____

ITEM	SUNDAY ___	MONDAY ___	TUESDAY ___	WEDNESDAY ___	THURSDAY ___	FRIDAY ___	SATURDAY ___	WEEK TOTAL
1ST SHIFT SALES								
Liquor								
Wine								
Beer								
Shift Total								
2ND SHIFT SALES								
Liquor								
Wine								
Beer								
Shift Total								
DAILY TOTAL								

PERIOD BEVERAGE COST BREAKDOWN   SALES MANAGEMENT ANALYSIS

ITEM	COST OF GOODS SOLD	SALES (SHIFT TOTALS)		BEVERAGE COST %		SALES	RETAIL VALUE	OVER (SHORT)
Liquor								
Wine								
Beer								
TOTAL								

Prepared by _____   Date _____

Table 11-2   Liquor Storeroom Inventory Report

Date _____   Time . _____   Page _____ of _____

Period Ending _____   Taken by _____

Prepared by _____   Approved by _____

ITEM DESCRIPTION	UNIT	OPENING INVENTORY	PURCHASES	TOTALS (A)	REQUISITIONS BY DAY OF PERIOD MONTH:									TOTALS (B)	BALANCE A LESS B	CLOSING INVENTORY	+ OR −	PRICE	EXTENSION

Page Total

Table 11-3   Bar and Inventory Control Report
Period Ending _____

Date _____
Time _____
Taken by _____
(and) _____

Bar Location _____
Page _____ of _____
Prepared by _____
Approved by _____

ITEM NO. 1 ITEM DESCRIPTION	2 UNIT	3 OPENING INVENTORY	4 REQUISITIONS BY DAY OF PERIOD MONTH:							5 TOTAL (3 + 4)	6 CLOSING INVENTORY	7 AMOUNT SOLD (5 − 6)	8 PRICE	9 COST OF GOODS SOLD (7 × 8)	10 NO. OF DRINKS SOLD	11 SALES PRICE	12 TOTAL RETAIL VALUE (10 × 11)	13 LIQUOR COST % (9 ÷ 12)
Total																		

■ ■ ■ ■ ■

Table 12-1   Pour Cost Chart

Name of Drink _____

Priced by _____   Date _____

UNIT	ITEM DESCRIPTION	PRICE/OZ	TOTAL
Subtotal			
Loss	5% spirits/12% tap products		
Total			

■ ■ ■ ■ ■
Table 12-2   Daily Incident Log

Day _____   Date _____   Shift _____

Who Prepared Log _____   Manager on Duty _____

INCIDENT (DESCRIBE, PATRON'S NAME, ADDRESS, PHONE #)	TIME IT OCCURRED	NAME/PHONE # OF EMPLOYEE INVOLVED	WITNESS NAMES/ PHONE NUMBERS

To the best of my knowledge, the above incidents occurred as described.

Shift Servers: Witnesses:

_____   _____

_____   _____

_____   _____

■ ■ ■ ■ ■

Table 12-3   Alcoholic Service Training

Server Name _____

Date Employed _____   Evaluated by _____

OUTCOME	DATE DEMONSTRATED	NEEDS IMPROVEMENT
1. Can describe visible signs of intoxication.		
2. Knows the general drink limits.		
3. Demonstrates how to track the number of drinks that customers have consumed.		
4. Knows not to serve more than one drink per person at a time.		
5. Knows the house policies on serving drinks.		
6. Knows how to slow service if a customer is nearing intoxication.		
7. Knows how to cut off service.		
8. Knows the procedures for dealing with difficult customers.		
9. Knows to encourage customers to order food and nonalcoholic drinks.		

■ ■ ■ ■ ■
Table 13-3 Work Schedule

Week of _____   Department _____

Date Prepared _____   Prepared by_____

POSITION	NAME	MONDAY	TUESDAY	WEDNESDAY	THURSDAY	FRIDAY	SATURDAY	SUNDAY
	(Scheduled Lunch Break) —→							
	(Scheduled Lunch Break) —→							
	(Scheduled Lunch Break) —→							
	(Scheduled Lunch Break) —→							
	(Scheduled Lunch Break) —→							
	(Scheduled Lunch Break) —→							
	(Scheduled Lunch Break) —→							
	(Scheduled Lunch Break) —→							
	(Scheduled Lunch Break) —→							

■ ■ ■ ■ ■
Table 13-4   Payroll Budget Estimate

Week of _____   Department _____

Date Prepared _____   Prepared by _____

NAME	POSITION	RATE OF PAY	SCHEDULED HOURS	SCHEDULED OVERTIME	TOTAL EARNED
HOURLY EMPLOYEES					
Total					

Allowance for Social Security, Medicare, Federal & State Unemployment Taxes:

Total Hourly Wages _____ × Rate _____ =

EMPLOYEE MEALS
Note: Could be added to or subtracted from the payroll according to management's policy.

	ESTIMATED NUMBER OF MEALS	*COST*	
Total			

TOTAL (Wages & Meals)		
Estimated Sales for Week		
Estimated Payroll Cost Percentage for Week		
Payroll Cost Percentage Goal		

■ ■ ■ ■ ■
Table 13-5   Payroll Cost Sheet

Prepared by _____   Day _____   Date _____

NAME	POSITION	RATE OF PAY	HOURS WORKED	OVERTIME WORKED	TOTAL EARNED
HOURLY EMPLOYEES					
Total					

Allowance for Social Security, Medicare, Federal & State Unemployment Taxes:

Total Hourly Wages _____ × Rate ____ =

NAME	POSITION	RATE OF PAY	HOURS WORKED	OVERTIME WORKED	TOTAL EARNED
SALARIED EMPLOYEES					
Total					

Allowance for Social Security, Medicare, Federal & State Unemployment Taxes: Total Salaries _____ × Rate ____ =

TOTAL (Hourly + Salaried)

■ ■ ■ ■ ■
Table 13-6 Payroll Cost Report

Period Ending _____

Total gross wages $ _____

Total employee meals   +   _____

Total payroll cost $ _____

TOTAL PAYROLL COST
$

(divide) ÷   =

PAYROLL COST
____ × _100_ = ____ %

TOTAL GROSS SALES
$

TOTAL GROSS SALES
$

(divide) ÷   =

SALES PER PERSON-HOUR
$

TOTAL HOURS WORKED

Prepared by _____   Date _____

■ ■ ■ ■ ■

Table 13-8   Employee Turnover Rate and Cost Chart

Period Ending _____

Employee Turnover Rate

Number of W-2's Completed	Current Number of Employees	Number of Past Employees
1.	−	=

Number of Past Employees	Average Number of Employees Employed	Employee Turnover Rate
2.	÷ =	× 100 = %

Cost of Employee Turnover

Number of Past Employees	Cost to Hire Each	Cost of Employee Turnover
3.	× $	= $

Table 14-1   Shift Productivity Chart

		Department _____		Page _____ of _____			
		Shift _____		Prepared by _____			
		Date _____					

HOURS OF OPERATION	(1) SALES PER HOUR	(2) COVERS PER HOUR	(3) PERSON– HOURS	(4) SALES PER PERSON–HOUR (1 ÷ 3)	(5) COVERS PER PERSON–HOUR (2 ÷ 3)	(6) MISHAPS PER HOUR	(7) MISHAP PERCENTAGE (6 ÷ 2)
Shift Average							

■ ■ ■ ■ ■

Table 14-2 Monthly Productivity Chart (Food Production)

Department _____   Page _____ of _____

Month _____   Prepared by _____

Year _____

DATE/DAY	SHIFT	(1) AVERAGE SALES PER HOUR	(2) AVERAGE COVERS PER HOUR	(3) AVERAGE PERSON-HOURS	(4) AVERAGE SALES PER PERSON-HOUR (1 ÷ 3)	(5) AVERAGE COVERS PER PERSON-HOUR (2 ÷ 3)	(6) AVERAGE NUMBER OF MISHAPS PER HOUR	(7) AVERAGE MISHAP PERCENTAGE (6 ÷ 2)

■ ■ ■ ■ ■

Table 14-3   Annual Productivity Report (Food Production)

Department _____   Page _____ of _____

Prepared by _____   Year _____

MONTH/YEAR	SHIFT	(1) AVERAGE SALES PER HOUR	(2) AVERAGE COVERS PER HOUR	(3) AVERAGE PERSON-HOURS	(4) AVERAGE SALES PER PERSON-HOUR (1 ÷ 3)	(5) AVERAGE COVERS PER PERSON-HOUR (2 ÷ 3)	(6) AVERAGE NUMBER OF MISHAPS PER HOUR	(7) AVERAGE MISHAP PERCENTAGE (6 ÷ 2)

Table 14-4 Waitstaff Production Chart

Department _____

Day _____ Date _____

Shift _____

Page _____ of _____

Prepared by _____

Approved by _____

(1) WAITSTAFF NAME	(2) STATION NUMBER	(3) NUMBER OF HOURS WORKED	(4) TOTAL SALES	(5) SALES PER PERSON-HOUR (4 ÷ 3)	(6) TOTAL NUMBER OF CUSTOMERS	(7) AVERAGE CUSTOMER SALE (4 ÷ 6)	(8) SALES		
							ITEM %	ITEM %	ITEM %

■ ■ ■ ■ ■
Table 14-5   Service System Chart

| Manager _____ | Page _____ of _____ |

TASK	SERVICE STANDARD	PERSON RESPONSIBLE

■ ■ ■ ■ ■

Table 15-1 Human Resources Audit

Auditor _____		Date _____	Page ____ of _____

ISSUE	IN COMPLIANCE	NOT IN COMPLIANCE	COMMENTS
SEXUAL HARASSMENT			
Number of claims made during the past year:			
Written policy posted.			
Procedure established for reporting sexual harassment claims.			
All employees are aware of what constitutes sexual harassment.		.	
All employees have been trained how to make, respond to, investigate, and handle sexual harassment charges.			
If any sexual harassment claims were made, were they investigated immediately?			
If any sexual harassment claims were made, was disciplinary action taken?			
ADA COMPLIANCE			
Job descriptions have been adjusted to ensure that reasonable accommodation has been reviewed.			
Physical facilities have been examined by local specialists to ensure that the facilities comply with ADA regulations.			
Any employment tests being used have been checked to ensure that they are not discriminatory against the disabled.		.	
Are qualified potential employees with disabilities not being hired due to health insurance considerations?			
EEOC CONSIDERATIONS			
Pre-employment tests are directly related to the job.			
Interviews do not use forbidden questions.			
Employees hired are of both genders.			
Both genders are paid equally for comparable work.			

Continued

| Auditor _____ | Date _____ | Page ____ of ____ | | |

ISSUE	IN COMPLIANCE	NOT IN COMPLIANCE	COMMENTS
Promotions are based upon quantifiable performance data.			

FAMILY AND MEDICAL LEAVE ACT

ISSUE	IN COMPLIANCE	NOT IN COMPLIANCE	COMMENTS
Employee qualification to take leave—has worked for 12 months and at least 1,200 hours.			
Have any employees taken up to 12 weeks of unpaid leave in any 12-month period?			
Employees are placed in previous or equivalent positions upon returning to work.			
Health care benefits are continued during leave.			

IMMIGRATION REFORM ACT

ISSUE	IN COMPLIANCE	NOT IN COMPLIANCE	COMMENTS
Employer has I-9 forms.			
Employer does not discriminate against a person who is not a citizen of the United States.			
Employer obtains verification of citizenship to complete I-9 forms.			

OSHA

ISSUE	IN COMPLIANCE	NOT IN COMPLIANCE	COMMENTS
OSHA information poster is posted.			
Form 200 or its replacement is posted.			
MSDS forms are available for all chemicals used in the business.			
All chemical containers are labeled correctly.			
Have any situations that could be classified as imminent danger been identified?			
If the number of employees exceeds 11, does the business have a functioning safety committee?			
Have there been any serious injuries that required employees to miss days of work?			
The premises meet OSHA standards for safety.			

Continued

Auditor _____	Date _____		Page ____ of _____
ISSUE	**IN COMPLIANCE**	**NOT IN COMPLIANCE**	**COMMENTS**
TIP REPORTING REQUIREMENTS			
Is Form 8027 used for tip allocation?			
Is a good-faith agreement being used?			
If one is being used, are the five conditions present to make the agreement binding?			
Are employees trained concerning tip reporting requirements?			
Are employees using Form 4070A?			
MINIMUM WAGE LAW & WORKING CONDITIONS			
Is the federal/state minimum wage law being honored?			
Are proper payroll deductions being made (social security, Medicare, federal and state income taxes, etc.)?			
Is there a scheduled payday?			
Are meal periods of 30 minutes provided if employee is working 6 hours or longer?			
Have employees been able to take 10-minute work breaks for each 4-hour work period?			
Have terminated employees been paid in a timely manner?			
Are 14- and 15-year-olds working more than 3 hours per school day or 8 hours on a nonschool day?			
Are 14- and 15-year-olds working only between 7 A.M. and 9 P.M.?			
Are 14- and 17-year-olds working with prohibited equipment, for instance, a meat slicer?			
Are working conditions for minors regarding breaks and meal periods being met?			

Table 16-1 Cash Turn-In Report

Date		Department	
Day		Cashier	
Shift		Checked by	

ITEM	NUMBER	AMOUNT
Beginning Bank		
Currency		
$ 100		
$ 50		
$ 20		
$ 10		
$ 5		
$ 2		
$ 1		
Coin		
$ .25		
$ .10		
$ .05		
$ .01		
Total Currency and Coin		
Checks		
Subtotal		
Less Bank		
Total Turn-In		

. . . . .

Table 16-2   Cashier's Report

Date _____	Department _____
Day _____	Cashier _____
Shift _____	Checked by _____

(1)	Total Cash Guest Checks	_____	
(2)	Total Charged Guest Checks	+ _____	
(3)	Total Receipts	_____	
(4)	Total Cash Guest Checks	_____	
(5)	Total Cash Turned In	_____	
(6)	Difference	_____	(plus/minus)
(7)	Reason for difference	_____	

Register Reading

(8)	Ending Reading	_____	
(9)	Beginning Reading	– _____	
(10)	Difference	_____	

Register Reading to be Taken by Department Manager Only

(11)	Register Reading	_____	
(12)	Total Receipts	_____	
(13)	Difference	_____	(plus/minus)
(14)	Reason for difference	_____	

Table 16-3   Daily Sales Report

Date _____
Day _____
Weather _____

Page _____ of _____
Prepared by _____
Approved by _____

| DEPARTMENT | SHIFT | REGISTER READINGS | | | TOTAL RECEIPTS | | | OVER OR (SHORT) | SALES BREAKDOWN | | |
		ENDING READING	BEGINNING READING	DIFFERENCE	CASH	CHARGE	TOTAL		TOTAL SALES	FOOD SALES	BAR SALES
TOTALS											

■ ■ ■ ■ ■
Table 16-4 Guest Check Daily Record

Department _____   Page _____ of _____

Day _____   Prepared by _____

Date _____

WAITSTAFF NAME	WAITSTAFF NUMBER	BEGINNING CHECK NUMBER	ENDING CHECK NUMBER	NUMBER OF CHECKS USED	NUMBER BY ACTUAL COUNT	NUMBER OF MISSING CHECKS	WAITSTAFF SIGNATURE

■ ■ ■ ■ ■

Table 17-1   Customer Source Analysis

Location:			
Location:			
Location:			
Location:			

Use the dot-line method for tracking. Each dot and line represents one person. The dots are made into a square. A line is drawn between dots. A cross is made in the square. The ending symbol is ⊠ . This represents 10 people.

Table 17-2   Competitive Analysis Form

ITEM	COMPETITOR		
Prepared by _____ Date _____			

Table 17-7   Menu Item Sales Forcast

Department _____				Page _____ of _____			
Prepared by _____				Week of _____			
Category _____							

MENU ITEM	SALES ESTIMATE	PERCENT OF SALES	MENU PRICE	PLATE COST	CONTRIBUTION	SALES	FOOD COST
Total							

■
■ ■ ■ ■ ■

Table 18-1　Walk-Through Audit—Service

Name _____　　Date _____　　Page _____ of _____

TASK	SERVICE STANDARD	PERSON RESPONSIBLE	STANDARD MET?	COMMENTS

Table 18-1 (Continued)   Walk-Through Audit—Food

Name _____   Date _____   Page _____ of _____

Appetizers:

1. Hot appetizers served hot   ☐ Yes   ☐ No
2. Cold appetizers served cold   ☐ Yes   ☐ No
3. Rate the flavor
    ☐ Exceptional   ☐ Good   ☐ Average   ☐ Needs Improvement   ☐ Poor
4. Rate overall quality
    ☐ Exceptional   ☐ Good   ☐ Average   ☐ Needs Improvement   ☐ Poor

Comments _____

Salads:

1. Cold salads served on cold plates   ☐ Yes   ☐ No
2. Cold salads, lettuce is crisp   ☐ Yes   ☐ No
3. Rate the flavor
    ☐ Exceptional   ☐ Good   ☐ Average   ☐ Needs Improvement   ☐ Poor
4. Rate overall quality
    ☐ Exceptional   ☐ Good   ☐ Average   ☐ Needs Improvement   ☐ Poor

Comments _____

Entrées:

1. Cold entrées served on cold plates   ☐ Yes   ☐ No
2. Cold entrées served cold   ☐ Yes   ☐ No
3. Hot entrées served on hot plates   ☐ Yes   ☐ No
4. Hot entrées served hot   ☐ Yes   ☐ No
5. Rate the flavor
    ☐ Exceptional   ☐ Good   ☐ Average   ☐ Needs Improvement   ☐ Poor
6. Rate overall quality
    ☐ Exceptional   ☐ Good   ☐ Average   ☐ Needs Improvement   ☐ Poor

Comments _____

Desserts:

1. Cold desserts served on cold plates   ☐ Yes   ☐ No
2. Cold desserts served cold   ☐ Yes   ☐ No
3. Hot desserts served on hot plates   ☐ Yes   ☐ No
4. Hot desserts served hot   ☐ Yes   ☐ No
5. Rate the flavor
    ☐ Exceptional   ☐ Good   ☐ Average   ☐ Needs Improvement   ☐ Poor
6. Rate overall quality
    ☐ Exceptional   ☐ Good   ☐ Average   ☐ Needs Improvement   ☐ Poor

Comments _____

Beverages:

1. Cold drinks served cold   ☐ Yes   ☐ No
2. Hot drinks served hot   ☐ Yes   ☐ No
3. Rate the flavor
    ☐ Exceptional   ☐ Good   ☐ Average   ☐ Needs Improvement   ☐ Poor
4. Rate overall quality
    ☐ Exceptional   ☐ Good   ☐ Average   ☐ Needs Improvement   ☐ Poor

Comments _____

Side Orders (SO):

1. Cold SO served on cold plates   ☐ Yes   ☐ No
2. Cold SO served cold   ☐ Yes   ☐ No
3. Hot SO served on hot plates   ☐ Yes   ☐ No
4. Hot SO served hot   ☐ Yes   ☐ No
5. Rate the flavor
    ☐ Exceptional   ☐ Good   ☐ Average   ☐ Needs Improvement   ☐ Poor
6. Rate overall quality
    ☐ Exceptional   ☐ Good   ☐ Average   ☐ Needs Improvement   ☐ Poor

Comments _____

■ ■ ■ ■ ■
Table 18-2   Customer Contact Report

Name _____	Date _____
Position _____	Shift _____

Comments heard about service:

Comments heard about food:

Comments heard about physical facility:

Table 18-3   Customer Comment Card

Appetizers:

What did you order? _____

1. Hot appetizers served hot ☐ Yes ☐ No
2. Cold appetizers served cold ☐ Yes ☐ No
3. Rate the flavor:
   ☐ Exceptional ☐ Good ☐ Average ☐ Needs Help ☐ Poor
4. Rate overall quality:
   ☐ Exceptional ☐ Good ☐ Average ☐ Needs Help ☐ Poor

Comments: _____

Desserts:

What did you order? _____

1. Cold desserts served on cold plates ☐ Yes ☐ No
2. Cold desserts served cold ☐ Yes ☐ No
3. Hot desserts served on hot plates ☐ Yes ☐ No
4. Hot desserts served hot ☐ Yes ☐ No
5. Rate the flavor:
   ☐ Exceptional ☐ Good ☐ Average ☐ Needs Help ☐ Poor
6. Rate overall quality:
   ☐ Exceptional ☐ Good ☐ Average ☐ Needs Help ☐ Poor

Comments: _____

Salads:

What did you order? _____

1. Hot salads served hot ☐ Yes ☐ No
2. Cold salads served cold ☐ Yes ☐ No
3. Rate the flavor:
   ☐ Exceptional ☐ Good ☐ Average ☐ Needs Help ☐ Poor
4. Rate overall quality:
   ☐ Exceptional ☐ Good ☐ Average ☐ Needs Help ☐ Poor

Comments: _____

Beverages:

What did you order? _____

1. Cold drinks served cold ☐ Yes ☐ No
2. Hot drinks served hot ☐ Yes ☐ No
3. Rate the flavor:
   ☐ Exceptional ☐ Good ☐ Average ☐ Needs Help ☐ Poor
4. Rate overall quality:
   ☐ Exceptional ☐ Good ☐ Average ☐ Needs Help ☐ Poor

Comments: _____

Entrées:

What did you order? _____

1. Cold entrées served on cold plates ☐ Yes ☐ No
2. Cold entrées served cold ☐ Yes ☐ No
3. Hot entrées served on hot plates ☐ Yes ☐ No
4. Hot entrées served hot ☐ Yes ☐ No
5. Rate the flavor:
   ☐ Exceptional ☐ Good ☐ Average ☐ Needs Help ☐ Poor
6. Rate overall quality:
   ☐ Exceptional ☐ Good ☐ Average ☐ Needs Help ☐ Poor

Comments: _____

Side Orders (SO):

What did you order? _____

1. Cold SO served on cold plates ☐ Yes ☐ No
2. Cold SO served cold ☐ Yes ☐ No
3. Hot SO served on hot plates ☐ Yes ☐ No
4. Hot SO served hot ☐ Yes ☐ No
5. Rate the flavor:
   ☐ Exceptional ☐ Good ☐ Average ☐ Needs Help ☐ Poor
6. Rate overall quality:
   ☐ Exceptional ☐ Good ☐ Average ☐ Needs Help ☐ Poor

Comments: _____

Service:

1. Did you wait too long to be greeted when you came into the restaurant? ☐ Yes ☐ No
2. Were you made to feel welcome? ☐ Yes ☐ No
3. Did you feel you had to wait too long to be seated? ☐ Yes ☐ No
4. How would you rate the overall service provided by the waitperson who served you?
   ☐ Exceptional ☐ Good ☐ Average ☐ Needs Help ☐ Poor
5. How would you rate the friendliness of all the staff?
   ☐ Exceptional ☐ Good ☐ Average ☐ Needs Help ☐ Poor
6. Did the pace of service seem just right? ☐ Yes ☐ No

Comments: _____

Physical Facilities:

1. How would you rate the cleanliness of the dining area?
   ☐ Exceptional ☐ Good ☐ Average ☐ Needs Help ☐ Poor
2. How would you rate the cleanliness of the restrooms, if used?
   ☐ Exceptional ☐ Good ☐ Average ☐ Needs Help ☐ Poor
3. Was the lighting comfortable? ☐ Yes ☐ No
4. Was the temperature comfortable? ☐ Yes ☐ No

Comments: _____

One Last Question:

1. Would you recommend this restaurant to your friends?
   ☐ Yes ☐ No

■ ■ ■ ■ ■
Table 18-4   Paper Goods Inventory

Date		Page	of	
Time		Department		
Taken by		Location		
(and)		Priced by		
Approved by		Extended by		

ITEM DESCRIPTION	UNIT	QUANTITY	PRICE	EXTENSION
PAGE TOTAL			$	

Table 18-5 China and Flatware Inventory

Date		Page		of	
Taken by		Department			
(and)		Approved by			

ITEM DESCRIPTION	PAR	INVENTORY					TOTAL	+ OR − BALANCE
		A	B	C	D	E		

■ ■ ■ ■ ■
Table 18-6   Equipment Inventory

Date _____   Page _____ of _____

Taken by _____   Department _____

(and) _____   Approved by _____

EQUIPMENT DESCRIPTION (NAME, SERIAL NUMBER)	UNIT COUNT	OFFICE COUNT	DIFFERENCE	EXPLANATION

APPENDIX B

Computer Applications

■ ■ ■ ■ ■ ■ ■ ■ ■ ■ ■ ■ ■

Introduction

In today's operating environment, foodservice management professionals must be able to use desktop computers, sophisticated point-of-sale terminals, and application software if they are going to be successful. Appendix B is designed to introduce you to some of the features typically available in application software. This Appendix is organized as follows:

Introduction

Learning Objectives

About ChefTec Application Software

Getting the Program Installed

Getting Started

Exercises

Learning Objectives

After learning about ChefTec software, you should be able to:

1. Understand how proprietary software can be used to provide valuable information to foodservice management professionals.

2. Understand how the principles contained in this textbook are used in a different software format from the tables in the chapters.

3. Print recipes and recipe cost sheets.

4. Scale recipes to produce different quantities of portions.

5. Generate a nutrition facts printout about a recipe.

6. Manipulate the selling price, gross margin, and food cost percentage and recognize how these changes impact each other.

7. Add a purchase using the invoice function of ChefTec.

8. Perform an inventory extension after being given a physical inventory work sheet.

9. Generate management reports regarding inventory, purchases, invoices, and recipes.

About ChefTec Application Software

ChefTec is application software designed for the foodservice industry. Specifically, it is designed to be used in restaurants to assist managers, kitchen managers, owners, and operators to control information so that they can make wise choices and track what they are doing. Culinary Software Services developed the ChefTec program, which has been designed to be flexible, friendly, and very easy to use. Throughout ChefTec, the screens, drop-down menus, and icons are all consistent and clear. Compressive online help is also available throughout the program.

The commercial (complete) ChefTec Software package will enable the user to:

- Keep constant records of unlimited recipes and provide convenient printouts at any time.
- Cost recipes, menus, functions, or complete catering events within minutes.
- Instantaneously see the effect of price increases on current costs and margins.
- Enter a price once with the result that every recipe using the item automatically reflects the change.
- Ask "What if" questions to analyze food cost, profit margins, and pricing.
- Rescale recipes at the click of a button.
- Add photographs and diagrams to recipes.
- Write recipes with customizable fonts: type, size, and color.
- Calculate nutritional data instantly, based on USDA guidelines.
- Track supplier bids.
- Interface with suppliers' online ordering systems to instantly download bids and prices.
- Create physical inventory worksheets, based on actual location including shelf-order.
- Generate orders automatically and fax them directly from ChefTec.
- Be informed of the price fluctuations of inventory items.
- Be able to identify the supplier that offers the lowest product cost.

The ChefTec Tutor software program accompanies this book, *Foodservice Profitability: A Control Approach.* This software will allow the reader/ user to understand how to use technology to control costs better, thus increasing profitability and competitiveness. Culinary Software Services is a software developer that has consistently provided the foodservice industry with functional software backed by telephone technical support and training. For more information on the full ChefTec program, call Culinary Software Services in Boulder, Colorado, at 303.447.3334 or 1.800.447.1466 or visit their web site on line at **www.culinarysoftware.com**.

To use the Chef/Tec program, you must meet the following system requirements:

IBM PC or compatible

Windows 98, Windows 95, Windows NT 4.0, or later

486 processor

16mb RAM

18mb hard disk space

800 by 600 VGA

Recommended, Pentium Processor

G etting ChefTec Installed

First, you need to install the program onto your computer. Install ChefTec using the following steps:

1. Insert CD-ROM into the CD-ROM drive.

2. a) After approximately one minute, the program will automatically load and provide instruction prompts, OR

   b) Click on the Start Button, Select Run…Type D:\SETUP (were D: refers to CD-ROM drive) and press <Enter>.

3. Follow the instructions in the tutorial.

Having had experience with computers and with Windows is a definite advantage to operating the ChefTec program.

G etting Started

Once you have begun Windows, you should be able to see the **ChefTec** icon displayed on the desktop. Double click on the **ChefTec** icon to begin the program. You will see an array of buttons and headings. (See Figure B-1) Take time to become familiar with the screen. Click on **Help** and a drop down menu will appear. Click on the **ChefTec** icon with the multiple question marks next to it. A directory will appear with simple to follow instructions on how to use the program. For the more adventurous student, you may keep clicking on the various buttons until you have figured out how to make the program work. To become competent in using this software, you should obtain hands-on experience by completing the exercises that comprise most of Appendix B.

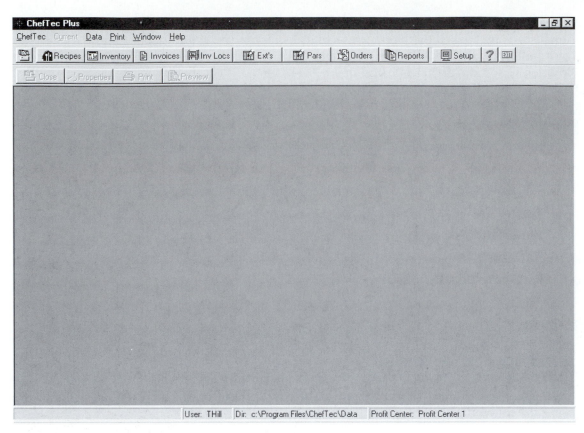

FIGURE B-1
ChefTec Screen

Exercises

INTRODUCTION

The following exercises are designed to help you better understand the features of application software. Each exercise illustrates different capabilities and uses of information needed to successfully operate a foodservice facility. Each exercise outcome is stated, followed by a description of how to achieve it, which is followed by an illustration of what it should look like. The exercises follow on the next several pages.

EXERCISE ONE—PRINTING RECIPES

Basic to understanding this software is understanding its features. Particularly, you should be able to find information and print it off. One of the strengths of ChefTec is how recipe information is presented and displayed.

This exercise requires that you print the following parts:

A. a list of all recipe names included with the software tutorial.

B. the recipe, recipe cost, and nutritional facts for Béchamel Sauce—Thick.

C. the recipe and recipe cost for Chili Sauce.

D. the recipe and recipe cost for Shrimp Bisque.

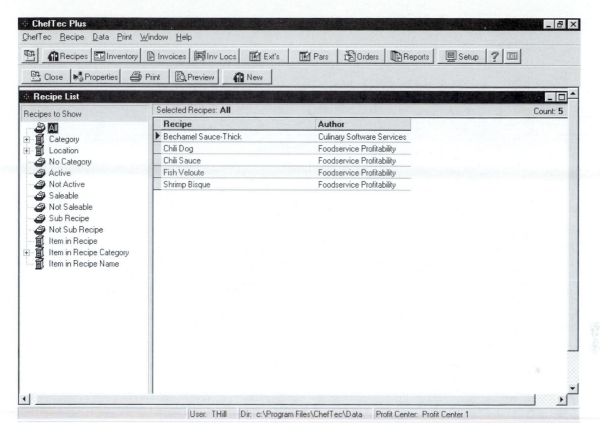

FIGURE B-2
Recipe List

Follow the directions below to complete exercise one.

Exercise One, Part A, is to print a list of all recipe names included with the software tutorial. To successfully complete this exercise you should do the following, after you have clicked the **ChefTec** icon on the desktop and the program is up on your screen. (See Figure B-1)

1. Click on the **Recipes** button. This button is toward the upper left portion of the screen. You may also click on **ChefTec**, then click on **Open**, then follow the drop down menu until you see recipe. Click on **Recipes**.

2. At this point you should see a new screen appear below the rows of buttons. The title of the screen is written in white with a dark blue bar across the top. It should state "Recipe List."

3. The screen "Recipe List" should be divided into two parts. The part on the left says "Recipes to Show". Underneath, the word "All" should be highlighted. You may want to click on the different icons just to get acquainted with the program, but the only icon you need to be concerned with is the file box with the highlighted "All". (See Figure B-2)

4. In the part of the screen to the right are listed the recipes that come with the tutorial. This is the recipe list that you need to print.

5. Click on the **Preview** button and the list will appear, as it will when printed.

6. To print you may click on the **Print** button.

The recipe list is shown below.

ChefTec Software

Recipe List

Foodservice Profitability

Recipes: All

Sorted by: Recipe

Recipe

Bechamel Sauce-Thick
Chili Dog
Chili Sauce
Fish Veloute
Shrimp Bisque

Exercise One, Part B, is to print the recipe, recipe cost, and nutritional facts for Béchamel Sauce—Thick. Click on the **Recipes** button. This button is toward the upper left portion of the screen. You may also click on **ChefTec**, then click on **Open**, and then follow the drop down menu until you see Recipes. Click on **Recipes**.

1. At this point you should see a new screen appear below the rows of buttons. The title of the screen is written in white with a dark blue bar across the top. It should state "Recipe List."

2. The screen "Recipe List" should be divided into two parts. The part on the left says "Recipes to Show". Underneath, the word "All" should be highlighted.

3. In the part of the screen to the right are listed the recipes that come with the tutorial. This is the recipe list that you printed in Part A.

4. Move the cursor to just left of Béchamel Sauce—Thick. A dark triangle ▶ will appear just to the left of the recipe name that becomes shaded.

5. Double click on the triangle.

6. The recipe should appear. Take a few minutes to carefully read the screen. The screen is divided into three areas stacked upon each other. Move the scroll bars so that you can see the entire recipe ingredients and instructions for preparation. (See Figure B-3)

7. Above the recipe ingredients you should see what appears to be file tabs labeled Recipe, Costs, Nutrition, Photo, and Video. Click on each of these tabs and the lower part of the screen will change showing you different types of information.

8. Click on the <Recipe> tab.

9. Click on the **Preview** button and the recipe appears, as it will when it is printed.

10. Click on the **Print** button.

11. To print the "Cost" and "Nutrition" information repeat steps eight through ten.

The recipe, recipe cost, and nutrition facts should look like pages 393–395.

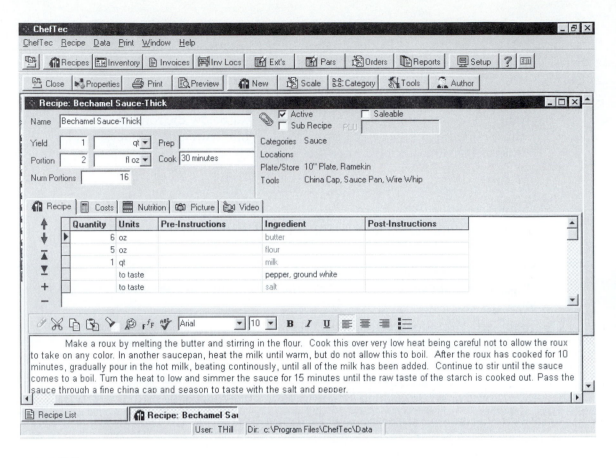

FIGURE B-3
Recipe

Exercise One, Part C, is to print the recipe and recipe cost for Chili Sauce.
Click on the **Recipes** button. This button is toward the upper left portion of
the screen. You may also click on **ChefTec**, then click on **Open**, and then follow the drop down menu until you see Recipes. Click on **Recipes**.

1. Move the arrow to just left of Chili Sauce. A dark triangle ▶ will
    appear and the recipe name will become shaded.

2. Double click on the triangle ▶ .

3. The recipe should appear. Take a few minutes to carefully read the
    screen. The screen is divided into three areas stacked upon each
    other. Move the scroll bars so that you can see the entire recipe
    ingredients and instructions for preparation.

4. Above the recipe ingredients you should see what appears to be file
    tabs labeled Recipe, Costs, Nutrition, Photo, and Video.

5. Click on the <Recipe> tab.

6. Click on the **Preview Button** and the recipe appears, as it will when
    it is printed.

ChefTec Software

Bechamel Sauce-Thick

Foodservice Profitability

Categories Sauce
Tools   China Cap, Sauce Pan, Wire Whip
Locations
Plate/Store 10" Plate, Ramekin

			Prep	
Yield	1	qt	**Cook**	30 minutes
Portion	2	fl oz		
Num Portions	16			

Ingredients

6	oz	butter
5	oz	flour
1	qt	milk
	to taste	ground white pepper
	to taste	salt

Make a roux by melting the butter and stirring in the flour. Cook this over very low heat being careful not to allow the roux to take on any color. In another saucepan, heat the milk until warm, but do not allow this to boil. After the roux has cooked for 10 minutes, gradually pour in the hot milk, beating continously, until all of the milk has been added. Continue to stir until the sauce comes to a boil. Turn the heat to low and simmer the sauce for 15 minutes until the raw taste of the starch is cooked out. Pass the sauce through a fine china cap and season to taste with the salt and pepper.

ChefTec Software

Bechamel Sauce-Thick

Foodservice Profitability

Categories Sauce

Tools   China Cap, Sauce Pan, Wire Whip

Locations

Plate/Store 10" Plate, Ramekin

			Prep
Yield	1	qt	**Cook** 30 minutes
Portion	2	fl oz	
Num Portions	16		

Ingredients			Cost	% of Total
6	oz	butter	$0.48	36.8%
5	oz	flour	$0.05	3.7%
1	qt	milk	$0.78	59.5%
	to taste	ground white pepper	$0.00	
	to taste	salt	$0.00	
			$1.30	

	Single Portion	Entire Recipe
Cost	$0.08	$1.30
Price	$0.00	$0.00
% Cost	0.0%	0.0%
Margin	($0.08)	($1.30)

ChefTec Software
Bechamel Sauce-Thick
Foodservice Profitability

Author	Culinary Software Services
Categories	Sauce
Tools	China Cap, Sauce Pan, Wire Whip
Locations	
Plating	10" Plate, Ramekin

Prep

Yield 1 qt   **Cook** 30 minutes

Portion 2 fl oz

Num Portions 16

Nutrition Facts

Serving Size 2 fl oz

Servings Per Container 16

Amount Per Serving

Calories 143 Calories From Fat 95

	% Daily Value
Total Fat 11g	16%
Saturated Fat 7g	30%
Cholesterol 31mg	10%
Sodium 116mg	5%
Total Carbohydrates 9g	3%
Dietary Fiber 0g	1%
Protein 3g	

Vitamin A	8%	Vitamin C	1%
Calcium	7%	Iron	3%

* Percent Daily Values are based on a 2000 calorie diet.

Nutrition Descriptors

Low Sodium

The following items are not included in the label data

Ingredient	**Reason**
pepper, ground white	No quantity specified
salt	No quantity specified

7. Click on the **Print** button. After the recipe is printed, click on the cost tab and then the print button.

The recipe and recipe cost should look like this and the next page.

ChefTec Software
Chili Sauce
Foodservice Profitability

Categories Sauce
Tools
Locations
Plate/Store

Prep
Yield   5   gal   **Cook** 3 hours medium heat
Portion 2   fl oz
Num Portions 320

Ingredients

5	lb	ground 90% lean beef
10	lb	chopped onion
20	oz	chili powder
6	oz	paprika
1	oz	red pepper
1	oz	garlic salt
1	oz	ground black pepper
1 1/2	oz	salt
3	46 oz can	tomato soup
3	46 oz can	tomato juice
3	46 oz can	water
4	oz	sugar

1. Thoroughly cook ground beef, then slowly add chopped onions and completely mix. 2. Drain, then add chili powder, paprika, red pepper, garlic salt, black pepper, and salt, completely mixing with ground beef and onions. 3. Using a 5 gallon pot, add to the mix tomato soup, tomato juice, water and sugar, thoroughly stirring. 4. Bring to boil and continually stir to allow for thorough cooking. Simmer and serve.

Chili Sauce

Foodservice Profitability

Categories Sauce

Tools

Locations

Plate/Store

Prep

Yield   5   gal   **Cook** 3 hours medium heat

Portion 2   fl oz

Num Portions 320

Ingredients			Cost	% of Total
5	lb	ground 90% lean beef	$12.25	37.6%
10	lb	onion	$5.90	18.1%
20	oz	chili powder	$4.40	13.5%
6	oz	paprika	$1.38	4.2%
1	oz	red pepper	$0.33	1.0%
1	oz	garlic salt	$0.10	0.3%
1	oz	ground black pepper	$0.31	1.0%
1 1/2	oz	salt	$0.03	0.1%
3	46 oz can	tomato soup	$4.86	14.9%
3	46 oz can	tomato juice	$2.88	8.8%
3	46 oz can	water	$0.00	
4	oz	sugar	$0.12	0.4%

$32.56

	Single Portion	Entire Recipe
Cost	$0.10	$32.56
Price	$0.00	$0.00
% Cost	0.0%	0.0%
Margin	($0.10)	($32.56)

Exercise One, Part D, is to print the recipe and recipe cost for Shrimp Bisque. Directions for obtaining and printing the requested information have been presented three times. This time, do it on your own for printing the recipe and recipe cost for Shrimp Bisque.

The recipe and recipe cost should look like this and the next page.

◆◆◆ *ChefTec Software*
Shrimp Bisque
Foodservice Profitability

Categories Soup/Stock
Tools
Locations
Plate/Store

Prep .75 hours

Yield 5 gal   **Cook**
Portion 12 oz
Num Portions 21

Ingredients

1	lb	shrimp shells
1	lb	onion, minced
1	lb	carrot, minced
1	lb	celery, minced
4	oz	butter
2	clove	garlic
1	bunch	thyme
1	fl oz	paprika
8	oz	tomato sauce
1	cup	brandy
1 1/2	gal	Fish Veloute
1	qt	heavy cream
1 1/2	lb	shrimp, peeled and deveined
6	fl oz	sherry
	to taste	salt
	to taste	tabasco sauce
	to taste	worcestershire

1. Saute shrimp shells and onions, carrots and celery in butter. 2. Add the garlic and thyme and cook for about 5 minutes. 3. Add the paprika and tomato sauce and cook until mixture is lightly browned. 4. Add the brandy and deglaze. 5. Add the fish veloute. Simmer for 45 minutes and strain. 6. Add the heavy cream. 7. Dice the shrimp, saute, and add to the soup. 8. Add the sherry. 9. Season to taste with a dash of salt, Tabasco, and Worcestershire sauce.

ChefTec Software
Shrimp Bisque
Foodservice Profitability

Categories Soup/Stock
Tools
Locations
Plate/Store

Prep .75 hours
Cook

Yield 5 gal
Portion 12 oz
Num Portions 21

Ingredients			Cost	% of Total
1	lb	shrimp shells	$4.29	12.4%
1	lb	onion	$0.59	1.7%
1	lb	carrot	$0.49	1.4%
1	lb	celery	$0.29	0.8%
4	oz	butter	$0.32	0.9%
2	clove	garlic	$0.23	0.7%
1	bunch	thyme	$0.69	2.0%
1	fl oz	paprika	$0.22	0.6%
8	oz	tomato sauce	$0.11	0.3%
1	cup	brandy	$1.22	3.5%
1 1/2	gal	Fish Veloute	$16.88	48.6%
1	qt	heavy cream	$2.75	7.9%
1 1/2	lb	shrimp	$5.80	16.7%
6	fl oz	sherry	$0.82	2.4%
	to taste	salt	$0.00	
	to taste	tabasco sauce	$0.00	
	to taste	worcestershire	$0.00	

$34.70

	Single Portion	Entire Recipe
Cost	$1.65	$34.70
Price	$5.25	$110.25
% Cost	31.5%	31.5%
Margin	$3.60	$75.55

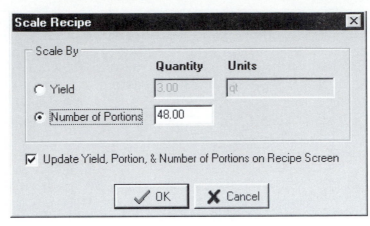

FIGURE **B-4**
Pop-up Menu for Scaling

EXERCISE TWO—SCALING, PRICE, FOOD COST, AND MARGIN ADJUSTMENTS

This exercise focuses upon manipulating information that is part of the recipe. This feature allows cooks to rescale recipes based upon the anticipated number of portions that need to be prepared and it also adjusts for changes in prices and costs.

This exercise requires you to:

A. Use the scaling feature. Specifically, what would be the preparation amounts needed to prepare Béchamel Sauce—Thick if it were prepared for 48 portions?

B. Change the price of Shrimp Bisque to $6.29. What is the new food cost percentage?

C. Change the food cost percentage of Shrimp Bisque to 30%. What is the new price?

D. Change the gross margin of Shrimp Bisque to $3.00. What is the new price? What is the new food cost percentage?

Follow the directions below to complete Exercise Two.

Exercise Two, Part A, is to use the scaling feature. Specifically, what would be the preparation amounts needed to prepare Béchamel Sauce—Thick if it were prepared for 48 portions. The answer is a printed recipe.

At this point, it is assumed that you know how to obtain a recipe and display it on the screen. To complete Part A, you need to:

1. Click the **Rescale** button toward the top of the screen and slightly to the right.

2. A pop up screen will appear. (See Figure B-4) You can scale by yield or number of portions.

3. For this exercise you are to scale by number of portions. Enter the number of portions that you need to scale to, in this case, 48.

4. Click on **Print** to print the recipe.

The amounts needed to prepare 48 portions are listed in the recipe. The following is a printout of the rescaled Béchamel Sauce-Thick.

◆▓◆ *ChefTec Software*

Bechamel Sauce-Thick

Foodservice Profitability

Categories Sauce

Tools China Cap, Sauce Pan, Wire Whip

Locations

Plate/Store 10" Plate, Ramekin

Prep

Yield 3 qt   **Cook** 30 minutes

Portion 2 fl oz

Num Portions 48

Ingredients

1 1/8	lb	butter
15	oz	flour
3	qt	milk
	to taste	ground white pepper
	to taste	salt

Make a roux by melting the butter and stirring in the flour. Cook this over very low heat being careful not to allow the roux to take on any color. In another saucepan, heat the milk until warm, but do not allow this to boil. After the roux has cooked for 10 minutes, gradually pour in the hot milk, beating continously, until all of the milk has been added. Continue to stir until the sauce comes to a boil. Turn the heat to low and simmer the sauce for 15 minutes until the raw taste of the starch is cooked out. Pass the sauce through a fine china cap and season to taste with the salt and pepper.

Exercise Two, Part B, change the price of Shrimp Bisque to $6.29. What is the new food cost percentage?

The answer to this question can be determined by:

1. Pulling up on the screen the "Shrimp Bisque" recipe and clicking on the <Costs> tab.

2. Look for the price window. It is toward the middle left of the screen.

3. Click in the window and enter the new price. You will need to remove the old price by using the delete key or backspacing.

4. Press the <Enter> key. As you press the enter key, notice how all the other recipe cost information changes.

The answer is on the following page that shows a printout of the new price. Write the new food cost percentage here _____.

Exercise Two, Part C, change the food cost percentage of Shrimp Bisque to 30%. What is the new price?

Use the same process that you did for Part B to get the answer. See the new price on pages 403 and 404. Write the new price here_____.

Exercise Two, Part D, change the gross margin of Shrimp Bisque to $3.00. What is the new price? What is the new food cost percentage?

Use the same process that you did for Part B to get the answer. See the new price on one of the following pages. Write the new price here _____. Write the new food cost percentage _____. The printout is on the page 405.

ChefTec Software

Shrimp Bisque

Foodservice Profitability

Categories Soup/Stock

Tools

Locations

Plate/Store

Prep .75 hours

Yield 5 gal   **Cook**

Portion 12 oz

Num Portions 21

Ingredients			Cost	% of Total
1	lb	shrimp shells	$4.29	12.4%
1	lb	onion	$0.59	1.7%
1	lb	carrot	$0.49	1.4%
1	lb	celery	$0.29	0.8%
4	oz	butter	$0.32	0.9%
2	clove	garlic	$0.23	0.7%
1	bunch	thyme	$0.69	2.0%
1	fl oz	paprika	$0.22	0.6%
8	oz	tomato sauce	$0.11	0.3%
1	cup	brandy	$1.22	3.5%
1 1/2	gal	Fish Veloute	$16.88	48.6%
1	qt	heavy cream	$2.75	7.9%
1 1/2	lb	shrimp	$5.80	16.7%
6	fl oz	sherry	$0.82	2.4%
	to taste	salt	$0.00	
	to taste	tabasco sauce	$0.00	
	to taste	worcestershire	$0.00	

$34.70

	Single Portion	Entire Recipe
Cost	$1.65	$34.70
Price	$6.29	$132.09
% Cost	26.3%	26.3%
Margin	$4.64	$97.39

ChefTec Software
Shrimp Bisque
Foodservice Profitability

Categories Soup/Stock
Tools
Locations
Plate/Store

Prep .75 hours
Cook

Yield 5 gal
Portion 12 oz
Num Portions 21

Ingredients			Cost	% of Total
1	lb	shrimp shells	$4.29	12.4%
1	lb	onion	$0.59	1.7%
1	lb	carrot	$0.49	1.4%
1	lb	celery	$0.29	0.8%
4	oz	butter	$0.32	0.9%
2	clove	garlic	$0.23	0.7%
1	bunch	thyme	$0.69	2.0%
1	fl oz	paprika	$0.22	0.6%
8	oz	tomato sauce	$0.11	0.3%
1	cup	brandy	$1.22	3.5%
1 1/2	gal	Fish Veloute	$16.88	48.6%
1	qt	heavy cream	$2.75	7.9%
1 1/2	lb	shrimp	$5.80	16.7%
6	fl oz	sherry	$0.82	2.4%
	to taste	salt	$0.00	
	to taste	tabasco sauce	$0.00	
	to taste	worcestershire	$0.00	
			$34.70	

	Single Portion	Entire Recipe
Cost	$1.65	$34.70
Price	$5.51	$115.65
% Cost	30.0%	30.0%
Margin	$3.86	$80.96

ChefTec Software

Shrimp Bisque

Foodservice Profitability

Categories Soup/Stock
Tools
Locations
Plate/Store

Prep .75 hours
Cook

Yield 5 gal
Portion 12 oz
Num Portions 21

Ingredients

			Cost	% of Total
1	lb	shrimp shells	$4.29	12.4%
1	lb	onion	$0.59	1.7%
1	lb	carrot	$0.49	1.4%
1	lb	celery	$0.29	0.8%
4	oz	butter	$0.32	0.9%
2	clove	garlic	$0.23	0.7%
1	bunch	thyme	$0.69	2.0%
1	fl oz	paprika	$0.22	0.6%
8	oz	tomato sauce	$0.11	0.3%
1	cup	brandy	$1.22	3.5%
1 1/2	gal	Fish Veloute	$16.88	48.6%
1	qt	heavy cream	$2.75	7.9%
1 1/2	lb	shrimp	$5.80	16.7%
6	fl oz	sherry	$0.82	2.4%
	to taste	salt	$0.00	
	to taste	tabasco sauce	$0.00	
	to taste	worcestershire	$0.00	
			$34.70	

	Single Portion	Entire Recipe
Cost	$1.65	$34.70
Price	$4.65	$97.70
% Cost	35.5%	35.5%
Margin	$3.00	$63.00

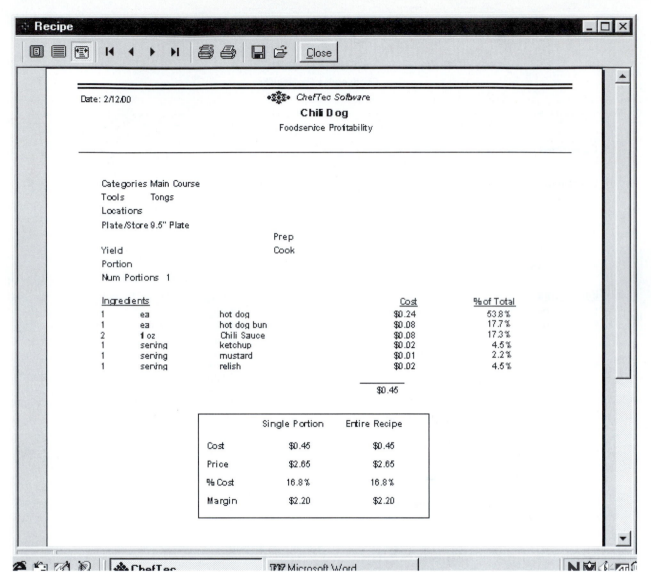

FIGURE B-5
Chili Dog Plate Cost

EXERCISE THREE——PLATE COST

A feature common to many software programs are their ability to determine plate cost. A simple Chili Dog meal has been entered into the ChefTec Tutorial. Find the plate cost for the chili dog meal and print it. If you have competed Exercises One and Two, you should be able to do this without any directions. The plate cost is exhibited in Figure B-5

EXERCISE FOUR——INPUTTING NEW INVOICE

The following is an invoice from a vendor that has just arrived at the restaurant that you manage. You must now use ChefTec to enter the information into the computer.

Old Town Bakery

June 30, 2000

Sold To: Any Restaurant
Invoice # 3176

ITEM	QUANTITY	PRICE/UNIT	COST
Hamburger Buns 8 buns per package	15	$1.39 ea	$20.80

This item has not been used in the operation. However, the item name already exists in the inventory that accompanied the software. Therefore, you need to enter the invoice information. After you have entered the above, print the invoice.

To complete this exercise, you will need to do the following steps. These directions work best if you are working with the program at the same time you read the instructions.

1. Click on **ChefTec** in the upper left-hand corner of the program screen.

2. Click on **New**.

3. Click on **Invoice**.

4. A pop up menu will appear asking you to enter vendor, invoice number, date of invoice, number of items, total amount. (See Figure B-6) All this information is provided on the hard copy invoice listed above. Click in the appropriate boxes and make the changes. Use your mouse to go between the boxes. If you inadvertently press <Enter> another screen will appear. Click on the appropriate area of the screen to complete the information. When you are finished click ✔ **OK** button or press the <Enter> key.

5. The screen will change showing an invoice. The "Item" box should be highlighted. Click in the box and start to write hamburger bun. A pop menu will appear. In the pop up menu, hamburger bun will appear. Scroll to find and click on it.

6. Click on the <Quantity> box. Type 15 in it and then press the enter key. The "Units" box should be highlighted.

7. Click on the box and a triangle ▼ should appear. Click on it and scroll to the word "package" and click on it.

8. Press on the <Enter> key and you will be in the "Cost" box. Type $20.80 and press <Enter>. The cursor will move to another row. Since there is only one item, move the cursor next to hamburger and click. A triangle ▶ should appear.

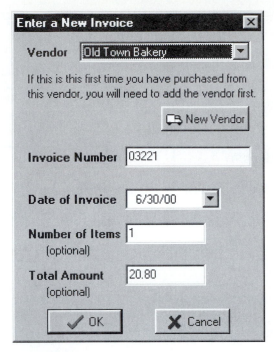

FIGURE **B-6**
Pop-up Menu to Enter a New Invoice

9. Right click on the triangle ▶. A pop menu will appear, click on "Edit Current Item".

10. Another pop up menu will appear listing unit conversions. Across the top of the screen you will see Vendor, Quantity, Units = Quantity, Units. An example of how this equation works is toward the bottom of the screen. Below the example are a series of tabs. (See Figure B-7)

11. First, click in the "Vendor" box, the background should turn blue and a triangle ▼ should appear. Click on triangle ▼ and a drop down menu appears. Click on "Old Town Bakery".

12. Click in the <Quantity> box furthest to the left. Type 1 in the box.

13. Click in the <Unit> box furthest to the left. Click on the triangle ▼ and scroll until you see the word package, click on it.

14. Click on the <Quantity> box that is furthest to the right. The invoice tells us that there are 8 buns in a package, therefore, type 8 in the box.

15. Click on the <Unit> box furthest to the right. Click on the triangle ▼ and scroll until you see "ea.", click on it. Ea. = each an appropriate designation.

16. At the bottom of the screen click on the <Item> tab, a pop up screen will appear. Click on the box next to bakery. This action classifies the category of the item.

17. Click on the <Inv Units> tab. Click on <package>. This tells the program the way in which you want the inventory to be tracked.

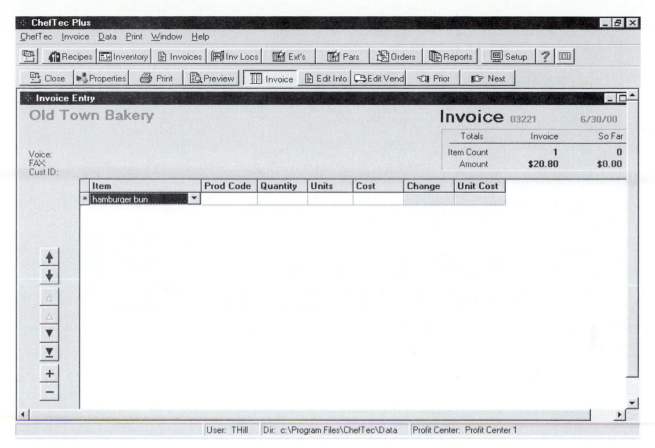

FIGURE B-7
Invoice Entry

18. When you are done with entering the information that you think is important, click on the ✔ **OK** button and the item is added to inventory.

To prove that you have entered the invoice into the system and edited the item correctly, print the invoice. A correct invoice is presented on the following page.

EXERCISE FIVE—EDIT INVENTORY ITEM

The purpose of this exercise is to show you how to edit an inventory item. The item that we are going to edit is hamburger buns. You just completed entering hamburger buns via an invoice as described in Exercise Four.

The following steps will guide you to make changes in the inventory item:

1. Click on the **Inventory** button. The inventory screen will appear. Move the cursor to "hamburger buns" and highlight the item with one click.

2. Move the cursor to the top of the screen and click on **Data**. A pop up screen will appear.

3. Click on <Edit Inventory Item>. Another large pop up screen will appear that should look familiar to you. This is the same screen used

ChefTec Software

Invoice

Foodservice Profitability

Vendor	Old Town Bakery		**Invoice Number**	03221
Contact			**Date**	6/30/00
Address			**Item Count**	1
			Total Amount	$20.80
Phone				
Fax				
Cust ID				

Prod Code	Inventory-Item	Quantity	Units	Cost	Cost/Unit	% Change
	hamburger bun	15	package	$20.80	$1.39/package	

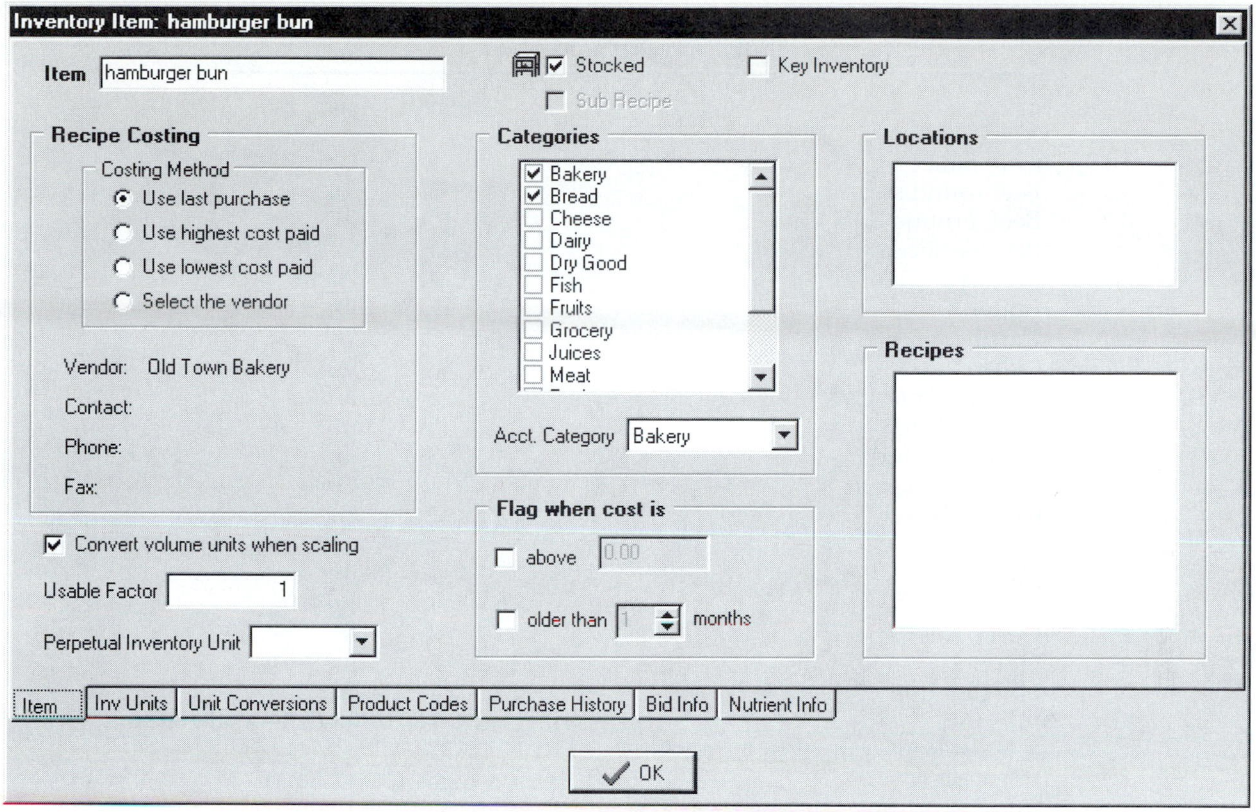

FIGURE B-8
Inventory Item

to enter information about the hamburger bun purchase made when entering an inventory item that has been purchased.

4. At this point, click on the <Item>tab. In the category area, click on bread. As you will notice, you may click more than one category. If needed you could change other information about the inventory item. (See Figure B-8)

When finished, click the ✔ **OK** button and you will return to the inventory screen. To close out of the program, click on the **Close** button.

EXERCISE SIX—INVOICE EXTENSIONS AND ADJUSTMENTS

This exercise will familiarize you with doing inventory extensions. Vital to the financial success of every type of foodservice operation is tracking the use of inventory. To do this properly means that you must count the physical inventory on a regular basis. The information for doing this exercise is listed in a simulated Physical Inventory Worksheet with data collected by doing an actual physical inventory. You are to enter this information using the software. After entering the data, print the extensions.

On the next page is the Physical Inventory Work Sheet, Figure B-9. You will use that information to complete this exercise. To input the physical count and calculate the extensions use the following steps.

■ ■ ■ ■ ■
Physical Inventory Work Sheet

ITEM	AMOUNT	UNIT
Chili Sauce	1	Gal
Beef round steak	5	lb.
Beef, ground 80% lean	10	lb.
Beets— sliced	.833	6/#10 can
Brandy	4	750ml
Butter	12	lb.
Carrot	3	lb.
Celery	5	lb.
Cheese, American	25	lb.
Cheese, brie	3	lb.
Cheese, cheddar	3	lb.
Chili powdered	1	Oz
Cream, heavy	1	Qt
Fish veloute	1	Gal
Flour	1	lb.
Garlic	1	Bulb
Garlic salt	3	lb.
Hot dog	6	lb.
Hot dog bun	2	Package
Juice, V8	1	48/5.5 oz
Juice, Welch's grape	.33	12/46 oz
Juice, apple	.25	12/46 oz
Juice, grapefruit	.83	12/46 oz
Juice, pineapple	.75	12/46 oz
Juice, tomato	1.83	12/46 oz
Juice, tomato 5.5 oz	.479	48/5.5 oz
Ketchup	1	Case
Milk	4	Gal
Mustard	1	Case
Onion	3	lb.
Paprika	2	lb.
Peaches - halves	.833	6/#10
Pears - halves	.33	6/#10
Pepper, ground black	2	lb.
Pepper, red	1	lb.
Relish	1	Case
Salt	3	lb.
Sherry	6	750 ml
Shrimp	5	lb.
Shrimp shells	2	lb.
Sugar	25	lb.
Thyme	5	Bunch
Tomato sauce	1	6/#10
Tomato soup	.167	12/46 oz

Units may be reported in a variety of ways. Most #10 cans are packed 6 to a case, 46 oz cans and boxes are usually packed 12 to a case. 64 oz cans are usually packed 12 to a case. 5.5 oz cans are either paced 24 or 48 to a case. It is important to obtain the most correct information and be consistent in how you list the items in the inventory. Decimals represent partial cases, i.e. .25 6/#10 = 2 cans. The Extension Sheet should look as follows.

FIGURE B-9
Physical Inventory Work Sheet

Extensions

Foodservice Profitability

Extensions Date 6/30/00

All Stocked Items

Item	Cost	Units	Quantity	Extension
chilli sauce	$4.95	gal	1	$4.95
fish veloute	$11.25	gal	1	$11.25
beef round steak	$3.20	lb	5	$16.00
beef, ground 90% lean	$2.45	lb	10	$24.50
beets - shoe string	$18.30	6/#10		$0.00
beets - sliced	$15.76	6/#10	0.833	$13.13
brandy	$3.87	750ml	4	$15.48
butter	$1.28	lb	12	$15.36
carrot	$0.49	lb	3	$1.47
celery	$0.29	lb	5	$1.45
cheese, American	$2.02	lb	25	$50.59
cheese, brie	$4.36	lb	3	$13.07
cheese, cheddar	$2.06	lb	3	$6.17
chili powder	$0.22	oz	1	$0.22
cream, heavy	$2.75	qt	1	$2.75
fish veloute	$11.25	gal		$0.00
flour	$0.15	lb	1	$0.15
fruit cocktail	$26.46	6/#10		$0.00
garlic	$1.41	bulb	1	$1.41
garlic salt	$1.60	lb	3	$4.80
hamburger bun	$1.39	package		$0.00
hot dog	$1.92	lb	6	$11.52
hot dog bun	$0.63	package	2	$1.27
juice, V8	$0.00	12/64 oz		$0.00
juice, V8	$12.96	48/5.5 oz	1	$12.96
juice, Welches grape	$38.16	12/64 oz	0.33	$12.59
juice, apple	$17.88	12/46 oz	0.25	$4.47
juice, grapefruit	$14.04	12/46 oz	0.83	$11.65
juice, grapefruit pink	$14.64	12/46 oz		$0.00
juice, pineapple	$0.00	48/5.5 oz		$0.00
juice, pineapple	$14.04	12/46 oz	0.75	$10.53
juice, tomato	$11.52	12/46 oz	1.83	$21.08
juice, tomato 5.5 oz	$12.96	48/5.5 oz	0.479	$6.21
ketchup	$20.00	case	1	$20.00
ketchup	$0.02	serving		$0.00
milk	$3.10	gal	4	$12.40
mustard	$12.00	case	1	$12.00
onion	$0.59	lb	3	$1.77
paprika	$3.68	lb	2	$7.36
peaches - halves	$23.88	6/#10	0.833	$19.89
peaches - sliced	$0.00	6/#10		$0.00
pears - halves	$23.22	6/#10	0.33	$7.66
pepper, ground black	$4.96	lb	2	$9.92
pepper, red	$5.28	lb	1	$5.28
relish	$24.00	case	1	$24.00
salt	$0.32	lb	3	$0.96
sherry	$3.45	750ml	6	$20.70
shrimp	$3.87	lb	5	$19.33
shrimp shells	$4.29	lb	2	$8.58
sugar	$0.48	lb	25	$12.00
thyme	$0.69	bunch	5	$3.45
tomato juice	$0.00	12/46 oz		$0.00

All Stocked Items

Item	Cost	Units	Quantity	Extension
tomato paste	$0.00	tbl		$0.00
tomato sauce	$21.06	6/#10	1	$21.06
tomato soup	$9.72	case	0.167	$1.62
			Total Extension	$483.03

1. Select **ChefTec**, click on **Open**, and then click on **Inventory Extensions**. A pop up screen appears asking you to input a date.

2. To remain consistent with the inventory that has been placed in the tutorial, write in 6/30/00. Click on ✔ **OK**.

3. A split screen will appear. The information on the left screen displays the various ways that the inventory may be organized. These features are not going to be discussed here. In the left screen, click on <No—Location all stocked>. When you do this you will see the inventory appear in the right screen.

4. In the "Quantity" column enter the physical count that has been given to you on the Physical Inventory Work Sheet, see Figure B-9. You will notice that some items may be listed more than once if they are part of a sub-recipe. Be careful that you always enter the information consistently.

5. After you have entered the Physical Inventory into the Inventory Extensions of the system, click on the **Preview** button. The finished Extension sheet will appear.

6. Click on the **Print** button to obtain a hard copy.

EXERCISE SEVEN—MANAGEMENT REPORTS

Reports are frequently used to guide management in making decisions on what items should be stocked, what vendors should be kept, and whether invoices have been paid or not. This program generates several reports that can be used to analyze data, such as providing valuable information for calculating food costs for the accounting period. This exercise is designed to teach you how to print out the following reports:

A. All stocked inventory items.

B. Detail Purchases List.

C. Period Food Costs

D. Summary of Invoices

To produce these reports, follow the directions provided below.

Exercise Seven, Part A, is to print out a list of all stocked inventory items. This is similar to printing out an inventory extension. Very simply, this can be done using the following steps.

1. Click on the **Inventory** button. In the left screen at the top it states "Inventory to Show". You might explore the features by clicking on the different icons. Inventory can be shown in a variety of ways by location, category, and vendor.

2. For this exercise, click on <All Stocked>. This icon may have appeared when you first clicked on the **Inventory** button.

3. Click on the **Preview** button to see what the printout will look like.

4. Click on **Print** to produce the hard copy. The printouts for all four parts of Exercise Seven follow this description of how to do the different parts of the exercise.

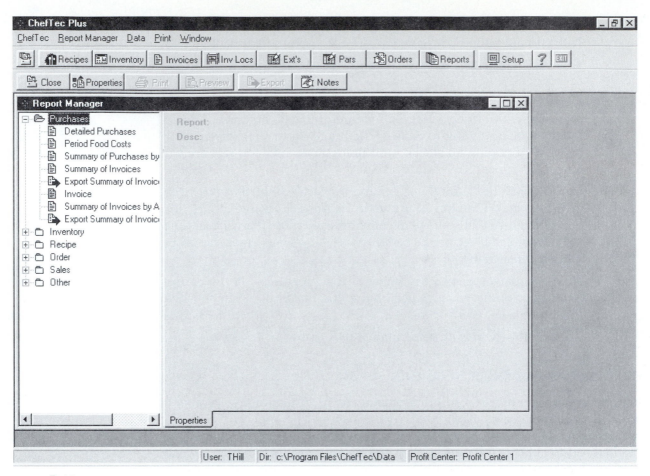

FIGURE **B-10**
Report Manager

Exercise Seven, Part B, is to print a Detail Purchases List. This report tracks the purchases for an established period of time by vendor, category, and other characteristics. Produce this report by doing the following steps.

1. Click on the **Reports** button.

2. For this exercise, click on the box with the cross in it next to "Purchases" in the left screen. When you do this, the screen changes with a list of potential reports appearing such as Detailed Purchases, Period Food Costs, Summary of Purchases by Acct. Category, Summary of Invoices, etc. (See Figure B-10)

3. For this exercise, click < Detailed Purchases>. At this point the right screen will change. You have the opportunity to enter what dates the report will cover. Check the box to the right of the start date. After you check the box, then enter the date 6/1/00. Do the same process for the end date but enter 6/30/00.

4. Click on the **Preview** button to see what the printout will look like.

5. Click on **Print** to produce a hard copy.

Exercise Seven, Part C, is to print a Period Food Costs report. A Period Food Costs report provides information that can be used to determine the food cost and food cost percentage for the accounting period. See Chapter Two, in the text, Food Cost/Food Cost Percentage for more details about this process. The steps are very similar to those used to generate a Detailed Purchases report and are listed as follows:

1. Click on the **Reports** button.

2. Click on the box with the cross in it next to "Purchases" in the left screen. When you do this, the screen changes with a list of potential reports appearing such as Detailed Purchases, Period Food Costs, Summary of Purchases by Acct. Category, Summary of Invoices, etc.

3. For this exercise, click on <Period Food Costs>. At this point the right screen will change. You have the opportunity to enter what dates the report will cover. Check the box to the right of the start date. After you check the box, then enter the date 6/1/00. Do the same process for the end date but enter 6/30/00.

4. Click on the **Preview** button to see what the printout will look like.

5. Click on **Print** to generate a hard copy.

Exercise Seven, Part D, is to print a Summary of Invoices report. As the title suggests, this report summarizes the invoices that have been entered into the system. The summary lists the invoices by vendor and according to the date and number of the invoice. The process is the same as the other three reports and the steps are as follows:

1. Click on the **Reports** button.

2. Click on the box with the cross in it next to "Purchases" in the left screen.

3. For this exercise, click on <Summary of Invoices>. At this point the right screen will change. You have the opportunity to enter what dates the report will cover. Check the box to the right of the start date. After you check the box, then enter the date 6/1/00. Do the same process for the end date but enter 6/30/00.

4. Click on the **Preview** button to see what the printout will look like.

5. Click on **Print** to generate a hard copy.

Inventory List

Foodservice Profitability

All Stocked Items

Inventory Item	Vendor	Quantity	Unit	Cost
chilli sauce	In-house	5.00	gal	$24.76
fish veloute	In-house	1.50	gal	$16.88
ahi, sushi grade				
ale				
alfalfa sprouts				
almonds				
apple				
artichoke, whole				
avocado				
bacon				
baking powder				
banana				
basil, ground				
bay leaf				
beans, fava				
beans, garbanzo				
beef base				
beef bottom round				
beef brisket				
beef round steak	Tri-County Meats	112.00	lb	$358.45
beef, ground 90% lean	Tri-County Meats	5.00	lb	$12.25
beets - shoe string	Metro Supply	1.00	6/#10	$18.30
beets - sliced	Metro Supply	1.00	6/#10	$15.76
brandy	Barney's Foods	1.00	750ml	$3.87
butter	Valley Dairy	5.00	lb	$6.40
carrot	Barney's Foods	5.00	lb	$2.45
celery	Barney's Foods	5.00	lb	$1.45
cereal, Cheerios				
cereal, Raisin Bran Kellogg				
cheese, American	Valley Dairy	40.00	lb	$80.95
cheese, brie	Valley Dairy	10.00	lb	$43.57
cheese, cheddar	Valley Dairy	25.00	lb	$51.40
chili powder	Barney's Foods	20.00	oz	$4.40
cream, heavy	Valley Dairy	1.00	qt	$2.75
fish veloute				
flour	Barney's Foods	50.00	lb	$7.70
flour, all purpose Fisher				
fruit cocktail	Metro Supply	1.00	6/#10	$26.46
fruit punch, Welchade				
garlic	Barney's Foods	1.00	bulb	$1.41
garlic salt	Barney's Foods	1.00	lb	$1.60
gelatin, cherry jello				
ham				
hamburger bun	Old Town Bakery	15.00	packa	$20.80
hot dog	Barney's Foods	1.00	lb	$1.92
hot dog bun	Old Town Bakery	113.00	packa	$71.54
juice, V8	Metro Supply	1.00	48/5.5	$12.96
juice, Welches grape	Metro Supply	1.00	12/64	$38.16
juice, apple	Metro Supply	1.00	12/46	$17.88
juice, grapefruit	Metro Supply	1.00	12/46	$14.04
juice, grapefruit pink	Metro Supply	1.00	12/46	$14.64
juice, pineapple	Metro Supply	1.00	12/46	$14.04

ChefTec Software
Detailed Purchases
Foodservice Profitability

Categories All categories
Start Date 6/1/00
End Date 6/30/00
Select By Stocked, Raw Inventory, No Change, Increases, Decreases

Vendor All Vendors

Item	Date	Vendor	Invoice	Quantity	Units	Cost	Cost/Unit	Flag	% Change
beef round steak	6/13/00	Tri-County Meats	4284	112	lb	$358.45	$3.20/lb		
beef, ground 90% lean	6/1/00	Tri-County Meats	4124	5	lb	$12.25	$2.45/lb		
beets - shoe string	6/19/00	Metro Supply	145687	1	6/#10	$18.30	$18.30/6/#10		
beets - sliced	6/19/00	Metro Supply	145687	1	6/#10	$15.76	$15.76/6/#10		
brandy	6/8/00	Barney's Foods	11325	1	750ml	$3.87	$3.87/750ml		
butter	6/15/00	Valley Dairy	1119	5	lb	$6.40	$1.28/lb		
carrot	6/7/00	Barney's Foods	11312	5	lb	$2.45	$0.49/lb		
celery	6/7/00	Barney's Foods	11312	5	lb	$1.45	$0.29/lb		
cheese, American	6/17/00	Valley Dairy	1258	40	lb	$80.95	$2.02/lb		
cheese, American	6/15/00	Valley Dairy	1119	40	lb	$80.95	$2.02/lb		
cheese, brie	6/17/00	Valley Dairy	1258	10	lb	$43.57	$4.36/lb		-12.9%
cheese, brie	6/13/00	Valley Dairy	1093	10	lb	$50.00	$5.00/lb		
cheese, cheddar	6/13/00	Valley Dairy	1093	25	lb	$51.40	$2.06/lb		
chili powder	6/1/00	Barney's Foods	11211	20	oz	$4.40	$0.22/oz		
cream, heavy	6/1/00	Valley Dairy	822	1	qt	$2.75	$2.75/qt		
fish veloute	6/1/00	Barney's Foods	11211	1	gal	$11.25	$11.25/gal		
flour	6/15/00	Barney's Foods	11427	50	lb	$7.70	$0.15/lb		
fruit cocktail	6/19/00	Metro Supply	145687	1	6/#10	$26.46	$26.46/6/#10		
garlic	6/1/00	Barney's Foods	11211	1	bulb	$1.41	$1.41/bulb		
garlic salt	6/1/00	Barney's Foods	11211	1	lb	$1.60	$1.60/lb		
hamburger bun	6/30/00	Old Town Bakery	03221	15	package	$20.80	$1.39/package		
hot dog	6/1/00	Barney's Foods	11211	1	lb	$1.92	$1.92/lb		
hot dog bun	6/15/00	Old Town Bakery	02842	113	package	$71.54	$0.63/package		4.7%
hot dog bun	6/13/00	Old Town Bakery	02786	160	package	$96.76	$0.60/package		
juice, V8	6/19/00	Metro Supply	145687	1	48/5.5 oz	$12.96	$12.96/48/5.5 oz		
juice, Welches grape	6/19/00	Metro Supply	145687	1	12/64 oz	$38.16	$38.16/12/64 oz		
juice, apple	6/19/00	Metro Supply	145687	1	12/46 oz	$17.88	$17.88/12/46 oz		
juice, grapefruit	6/19/00	Metro Supply	145687	1	12/46 oz	$14.04	$14.04/12/46 oz		
juice, grapefruit pink	6/19/00	Metro Supply	145687	1	12/46 oz	$14.64	$14.64/12/46 oz		
juice, pineapple	6/19/00	Metro Supply	145687	1	12/46 oz	$14.04	$14.04/12/46 oz		
juice, tomato	6/19/00	Metro Supply	145687	1	12/46 oz	$11.52	$11.52/12/46 oz		
juice, tomato 5.5 oz	6/19/00	Metro Supply	145687	1	48/5.5 oz	$12.96	$12.96/48/5.5 oz		
ketchup	6/1/00	Barney's Foods	11211	1	case	$20.00	$20.00/case		
milk	6/15/00	Barney's Foods	11427	1	gal	$3.10	$3.10/gal		

Item	Date	Vendor	Invoice	Quantity	Units	Cost	Cost/Unit	Flag	% Change
mustard	6/1/00	Barney's Foods	11211	1	case	$12.00	$12.00/case		
onion	6/1/00	Barney's Foods	11211	10	lb	$5.90	$0.59/lb		
paprika	6/1/00	Barney's Foods	11211	1	lb	$3.68	$3.68/lb		
peaches - halves	6/19/00	Metro Supply	145687	1	6/#10	$23.88	$23.88/6/#10		
pears - halves	6/19/00	Metro Supply	145687	1	6/#10	$23.22	$23.22/6/#10		
pepper, ground black	6/1/00	Barney's Foods	11211	1	lb	$4.96	$4.96/lb		
pepper, red	6/1/00	Barney's Foods	11211	1	lb	$5.28	$5.28/lb		
relish	6/1/00	Barney's Foods	11211	1	case	$24.00	$24.00/case		
salt	6/1/00	Barney's Foods	11211	10	lb	$3.20	$0.32/lb		
sherry	6/1/00	Barney's Foods	11211	1	750ml	$3.45	$3.45/750ml		
shrimp	6/29/00	Regional Seafood	12118	94	lb	$363.48	$3.87/lb		-3.1%
shrimp	6/11/00	Regional Seafood	11211	2	lb	$7.98	$3.99/lb		
shrimp shells	6/11/00	Regional Seafood	11211	2	lb	$8.58	$4.29/lb		
sugar	6/1/00	Barney's Foods	11211	5	lb	$2.40	$0.48/lb		
thyme	6/7/00	Barney's Foods	11312	1	bunch	$0.69	$0.69/bunch		
thyme	6/7/00	Barney's Foods	11312	1	bunch	$0.69	$0.69/bunch		
tomato sauce	6/7/00	Barney's Foods	11312	1	6/#10	$21.06	$21.06/6/#10		
tomato soup	6/1/00	Barney's Foods	11211	1	case	$9.72	$9.72/case		

Total $1,655.86

Period Food Costs

Foodservice Profitability

Categories All categories

Start Date 6/1/00 **End Date** 6/30/00

Select By Stocked, Raw Inventory

Vendor All Vendors

Inventory Item	Total Purchases	Quantity	Units	Cost
beef round steak	1	112	lb	$358.45
beef, ground 90% lean	1	5	lb	$12.25
beets - shoe string	1	1	6/#10	$18.30
beets - sliced	1	1	6/#10	$15.76
brandy	1	1	750ml	$3.87
butter	1	5	lb	$6.40
carrot	1	5	lb	$2.45
celery	1	5	lb	$1.45
cheese, American	2	80	lb	$161.90
cheese, brie	2	20	lb	$93.57
cheese, cheddar	1	25	lb	$51.40
chili powder	1	20	oz	$4.40
cream, heavy	1	1	qt	$2.75
fish veloute	1	1	gal	$11.25
flour	1	50	lb	$7.70
fruit cocktail	1	1	6/#10	$26.46
garlic	1	1	bulb	$1.41
garlic salt	1	1	lb	$1.60
hamburger bun	1	15	package	$20.80
hot dog	1	1	lb	$1.92
hot dog bun	2	273	package	$168.30
juice, V8	1	1	48/5.5 oz	$12.96
juice, Welches grape	1	1	12/64 oz	$38.16
juice, apple	1	1	12/46 oz	$17.88
juice, grapefruit	1	1	12/46 oz	$14.04
juice, grapefruit pink	1	1	12/46 oz	$14.64
juice, pineapple	1	1	12/46 oz	$14.04
juice, tomato	1	1	12/46 oz	$11.52
juice, tomato 5.5 oz	1	1	48/5.5 oz	$12.96
ketchup	1	1	case	$20.00
milk	1	1	gal	$3.10
mustard	1	1	case	$12.00
onion	1	10	lb	$5.90
paprika	1	1	lb	$3.68
peaches - halves	1	1	6/#10	$23.88
pears - halves	1	1	6/#10	$23.22
pepper, ground black	1	1	lb	$4.96
pepper, red	1	1	lb	$5.28
relish	1	1	case	$24.00
salt	1	10	lb	$3.20
sherry	1	1	750ml	$3.45
shrimp	2	96	lb	$371.46
shrimp shells	1	2	lb	$8.58
sugar	1	5	lb	$2.40
thyme	2	2	bunch	$1.38
tomato sauce	1	1	6/#10	$21.06
tomato soup	1	1	case	$9.72

Inventory Item	Total Purchases	Quantity	Units	Cost
		Total Cost		1,655.86

ChefTec Software

Summary of Invoices

Foodservice Profitability

Start Date 6/1/00
End Date 6/30/00

Barney's Foods

Date	Invoice Number	Number of Items	Total Cost
6/15/00	11427	2	$10.80
6/8/00	11325	1	$3.87
6/7/00	11312	5	$26.34
6/1/00	11211	16	$115.17

Metro Supply

Date	Invoice Number	Number of Items	Total Cost
6/19/00	145687	13	$243.82

Old Town Bakery

Date	Invoice Number	Number of Items	Total Cost
6/30/00	03221	1	$20.80
6/15/00	02842	1	$71.54
6/13/00	02786	1	$96.76

Regional Seafood

Date	Invoice Number	Number of Items	Total Cost
6/29/00	12118	1	$363.48
6/11/00	11211	2	$16.56

Tri-County Meats

Date	Invoice Number	Number of Items	Total Cost
6/13/00	4284	1	$358.45
6/1/00	4124	1	$12.25

Valley Dairy

Date	Invoice Number	Number of Items	Total Cost
6/17/00	1258	2	$124.52
6/15/00	1119	2	$87.35
6/13/00	1093	2	$101.40
6/1/00	822	1	$2.75

Total   1,655.86

Index